AFTER THE DIGITAL TORNADO

Networks powered by algorithms are pervasive. Major contemporary technology trends – Internet of Things, Big Data, Digital Platform Power, Blockchain, and the Algorithmic Society – are manifestations of this phenomenon. The Internet, which once seemed an unambiguous benefit to society, is now the basis for invasions of privacy, massive concentrations of power, and wide-scale manipulation. The algorithmic networked world poses deep questions about power, freedom, fairness, and human agency. The influential 1997 Federal Communications Commission whitepaper *Digital Tornado* hailed the "endless spiral of connectivity" that would transform society, and today, little remains untouched by digital connectivity. Yet fundamental questions remain unresolved, and even more serious challenges have emerged. This important collection, which offers a reckoning and a foretelling, features leading technology scholars who explain the legal, business, ethical, technical, and public policy challenges of building pervasive networks and algorithms for the benefit of humanity. This title is also available as Open Access on Cambridge Core.

Kevin Werbach is Professor of Legal Studies and Business Ethics at the Wharton School, University of Pennsylvania. A world-renowned expert on emerging technology, he examines business and policy implications of developments such as broadband, big data, gamification, and blockchain. Previously, Werbach served on the Obama Administration's Presidential Transition Team, founded the Supernova Group (a technology conference and consulting firm), led Internet policy at the Federal Communications Commission, and created a massive open online course. His books include *For the Win: How Game Thinking Can Revolutionize Your Business* and *The Blockchain and the New Architecture of Trust*.

"An important collection of diverse perspectives on the legal, ethical and social challenges of the information age. Essential reading for anyone interested in the past and future of Internet policy."

Bruce Schneier
Fellow at Harvard Kennedy School and author of Click Here to Kill Everybody

"Kevin Werbach assembles some of the world's best thinkers to analyze the transformations wrought by code, data, and silicon. A masterful meditation on what is next for digital life and how policy might be able to harness technology for good."

Ellen P. Goodman
Professor, Rutgers Law School and Co-Director, Rutgers Institute
for Information Policy & Law

"This book is destined to be as vital to the debate over the future of the Internet as Werbach's ground-breaking white paper *Digital Tornado*. It examines how much the Internet has changed over two decades and looks ahead with concrete recommendations about how to ensure a vibrant and open Internet ecosystem from some of the world's top experts in Internet law and policy."

Gigi Sohn
Distinguished Fellow, Georgetown Law Institute for Technology
Law & Policy, and Benton Senior Fellow

"Some of the sharpest thinkers about technology and society examine where we have come from, what has changed, and what the future may be. Old models, antitrust, new power centers, dehumanized humanity, Blockchain, and more are explored and explained with an eye to what we can and should do next."

Deven Desai
Associate Professor, Georgia Tech Scheller College of Business

After the Digital Tornado

NETWORKS, ALGORITHMS, HUMANITY

Edited by
KEVIN WERBACH
Wharton School, University of Pennsylvania

CAMBRIDGE
UNIVERSITY PRESS

University Printing House, Cambridge CB2 8BS, United Kingdom

One Liberty Plaza, 20th Floor, New York, NY 10006, USA

477 Williamstown Road, Port Melbourne, VIC 3207, Australia

314-321, 3rd Floor, Plot 3, Splendor Forum, Jasola District Centre, New Delhi - 110025, India

103 Penang Road, #05-06/07, Visioncrest Commercial, Singapore 238467

Cambridge University Press is part of the University of Cambridge.

It furthers the University's mission by disseminating knowledge in the pursuit of
education, learning and research at the highest international levels of excellence.

www.cambridge.org
Information on this title: www.cambridge.org/9781108445351
DOI: 10.1017/9781108610018

© Cambridge University Press 2020

This publication is in copyright. Subject to statutory exception
and to the provisions of relevant collective licensing agreements,
no reproduction of any part may take place without the written
permission of Cambridge University Press.

An online version of this work is published at doi.org/10.1017/9781108610018 under a Creative
Commons Open Access license CC-BY-NC-ND 4.0 which permits re-use, distribution and
reproduction in any medium for non-commercial purposes providing appropriate credit to the
original work is given. You may not distribute derivative works without permission. To view a copy
of this license, visit https://creativecommons.org/licenses/by-nc-nd/4.0

All versions of this work may contain content reproduced under license from third parties.

Permission to reproduce this third-party content must be obtained from these third-parties
directly.

When citing this work, please include a reference to the DOI 10.1017/9781108610018

First published 2020
First paperback edition 2022

A catalogue record for this publication is available from the British Library

Library of Congress Cataloging in Publication data
NAMES: Werbach, Kevin, editor.
TITLE: After the digital tornado : networks, algorithms, humanity / edited by Kevin Werbach,
University of Pennsylvania Wharton School of Business.
DESCRIPTION: Cambridge, United Kingdom ; New York, NY : Cambridge
University Press, 2020.
IDENTIFIERS: LCCN 2020009268 (print) | LCCN 2020009269 (ebook) | ISBN 9781108426633 (hardback) |
ISBN 9781108610018 (ebook)
SUBJECTS: LCSH: Internet governance. | Internet – Government policy. | Internet industry.
CLASSIFICATION: LCC TK5105.8854 .A48 2020 (print) | LCC TK5105.8854 (ebook) | DDC
394.3/34–dc23
LC record available at https://lccn.loc.gov/2020009268
LC ebook record available at https://lccn.loc.gov/2020009269

ISBN 978-1-108-42663-3 Hardback
ISBN 978- 1-108-44535-1 Paperback

Cambridge University Press has no responsibility for the persistence or
accuracy of URLs for external or third-party internet websites referred to in
this publication, and does not guarantee that any content on such websites is,
or will remain, accurate or appropriate.

Contents

List of Contributors		*page* vii
	Introduction: An Endless Spiral of Connectivity?	1
	PRELUDE	11
	Digital Tornado: The Internet and Telecommunication Policy (1997) Selected Excerpts Kevin Werbach	13
	PART I NETWORKS	33
1	The Regulated End of Internet Law, and the Return to Computer and Information Law? Christopher T. Marsden	35
2	Networks, Standards, and Network-and-Standard-Based Governance Julie E. Cohen	58
3	Tech Dominance and the Policeman at the Elbow Tim Wu	81
	PART II ALGORITHMS	101
4	Who Do We Blame for the Filter Bubble? On the Roles of Math, Data, and People in Algorithmic Social Systems Kartik Hosanagar and Alex P. Miller	103
5	Regulating the Feedback Effect Viktor Mayer-Schönberger	122

6 Shaping Our Tools: Contestability as a Means to Promote
Responsible Algorithmic Decision Making in the Professions 137
Daniel N. Kluttz, Nitin Kohli, and Deirdre K. Mulligan

PART III: HUMANITY 153

7 Why a Commitment to Pluralism Should Limit How Humanity Is
Re-Engineered 155
Brett Frischmann and Evan Selinger

8 Caveat Usor: Surveillance Capitalism as Epistemic Inequality 174
Shoshana Zuboff

9 The Siren Song: Algorithmic Governance by Blockchain 215
Kevin Werbach

Contributors

Kevin Werbach (editor) is a professor of Legal Studies and Business Ethics at the Wharton School, University of Pennsylvania. His work examines the intersection of business, policy, and emerging technologies. Werbach co-led the review of the Federal Communications Commission for the Obama Administration's Presidential Transition Team. He is the coauthor of *For the Win: How Game Thinking Can Revolutionize Your Business* (Wharton Digital Press, 2012, with Dan Hunter), and author of *The Blockchain and the New Architecture of Trust* (MIT Press, 2018). Nearly 500,000 students have enrolled in his Coursera massive open online course, and he was named Wharton's first-ever "Iron Prof." Previously he served as Editor of *Release 1.0: Esther Dyson's Monthly Report*, and as FCC Counsel for New Technology Policy, where he wrote *Digital Tornado*, the first comprehensive analysis of the Internet's implications for communications policy.

Julie Cohen is the Mark Claster Mamolen Professor of Law and Technology at the Georgetown University Law Center. She teaches and writes about copyright, surveillance, privacy and data protection, and the governance of information and communication networks. She is the author of *Configuring the Networked Self: Law, Code and the Play of Everyday Practice* (Yale University Press, 2012), *Between Truth and Power* (Oxford University Press, 2019), and numerous journal articles and book chapters, and a coauthor of *Copyright in a Global Information Economy* (Aspen Law & Business, 4th ed., 2015). Professor Cohen is a member of the Advisory Board of the Electronic Privacy Information Center.

Brett Frischmann is the Charles Widger Endowed University Professor in Law, Business and Economics at Villanova University. An expert on Internet and intellectual property law, he is an affiliated scholar of the Stanford Center for Internet and Society, and a trustee for the Nexa Center for Internet & Society, Politecnico di Torino. Frischmann's books include *Infrastructure: The Social Value of Shared Resources* (Oxford University Press, 2012); *Governing Knowledge Commons* (Oxford University Press, 2014, with Michael Madison and Katherine Strandburg);

Governing Medical Knowledge Commons (Cambridge University Press, 2017, with Michael Madison and Katherine Strandburg); and *Being Human in the 21st Century: How Social and Technological Tools Are Reshaping Humanity* (Cambridge University Press, 2018, with Evan Selinger).

Kartik Hosanagar is the John C. Hower Professor of Technology and Digital Business and a Professor of Marketing at The Wharton School of the University of Pennsylvania. Kartik's research work focuses on the digital economy, in particular, the impact of analytics and algorithms on consumers and society, Internet media, Internet marketing and e-commerce. He has been recognized as one of the world's top forty business professors under 40, and he is a ten-time recipient of teaching excellence awards at the Wharton School. Hosanagar cofounded Yodle Inc, a venture-backed firm acquired by Web.com. He has been an investor, advisor, or board member to startups including Milo (acquired by eBay) and Monetate.

Chris Marsden is Professor of Internet Law at the University of Sussex. He is author of five monographs on Internet law: *Network Neutrality: From Policy to Law to Regulation* (Manchester University Press, 2017), *Regulating Code* (MIT, 2013, with Ian Brown), *Internet Co-Regulation: European Law, Regulatory Governance and Legitimacy in Cyberspace* (Cambridge University Press, 2011), *Net Neutrality: Towards a Co-Regulatory Solution* (Bloomsbury, 2010), and *Codifying Cyberspace* (Routledge/Cavendish, 2007 with D. Tambini and D. Leonardi). He is also author-editor of two interdisciplinary Internet policy books.

Viktor Mayer-Schönberger is Professor of Internet Governance and Regulation at the Oxford Internet Institute. He is also a faculty affiliate of the Belfer Center of Science and International Affairs at Harvard University. He has published ten books, including the international bestseller *Big Data* (HMH, 2013, with Kenneth Cukier) and the awards-winning *Delete: The Virtue of Forgetting in the Digital Age* (Princeton University Press, 2009). He chaired the Rueschlikon Conference on Information Policy in the New Economy, and in 2014 he received a World Technology Award in the law category. Earlier in his career, he was voted Top-5 Software Entrepreneur in Austria in 1991 and Person of the Year for the State of Salzburg in 2000.

Deirdre Mulligan is an associate professor in the School of Information at UC Berkeley, and a faculty Director of the Berkeley Center for Law & Technology. She is the coauthor of *Privacy on the Ground: Driving Corporate Behavior in the United States and Europe* (MIT, 2015, with Kenneth Bamberger), and in 2016 was corecipient of the International Association of Privacy Professionals Leadership Award. Mulligan is a member of the National Academy of Science Forum on Cyber Resilience, Chair of the Board of Directors of the Center for Democracy and Technology, a founding member of the standing committee for the AI 100 project, and a founding member of the Global Network Initiative.

Tim Wu is a professor at Columbia Law School, and a contributing opinion writer for the *New York Times*. He is author of the books *The Master Switch* (Knopf, 2010), *The Attention Merchants* (Knopf, 2016), and *Who Controls the Internet?* (Oxford University Press, 2008, with Jack Goldsmith), along with *Network Neutrality, Broadband Discrimination*, and other works. In 2013 he was named one of America's 100 Most Influential Lawyers, and in 2017 he was named to the American Academy of Arts and Sciences.

Shoshana Zuboff is the Charles Edward Wilson Professor of Business Administration at the Harvard Business School (emerita). Her career has been devoted to the study of the rise of the digital; its individual, organizational, and social consequences; and its relationship to the history and future of capitalism. Her new work includes *The Age of Surveillance Capitalism: The Fight for a Human Future at the New Frontier of Power*, published in 2019 by Public Affairs in the US and Eichborn in Germany. In 2006, strategy+business named Professor Zuboff among the eleven most original business thinkers in the world. Author of the celebrated classic *In the Age of the Smart Machine: The Future of Work and Power* (Basic Books, 1988), Professor Zuboff has been called "the true prophet of the information age."

Introduction: An Endless Spiral of Connectivity?

In 1997, the US Federal Communications Commission issued my staff working paper, *Digital Tornado: The Internet and Telecommunications Policy*. It was distributed in hard copy and, in a novel twist, digitally through the FCC's website, which I had largely coded on my laptop after work. As the paper relates, only 15 percent of Americans at that time used the Internet, and only 40 percent had personal computers. I didn't think to mention that zero had Internet-capable smartphones, because such devices were still science fiction. Even smaller percentages of other nations were online. China, today the world's largest Internet access market, connected its very first public Internet subscriber the summer before *Digital Tornado* was released.

Two decades later, the paper's optimistic vision of an "endless spiral of connectivity" producing an Internet whose scope "mushroom[s] beyond comprehension"[1] has been realized. The Internet swept tornado-like across the world, scrambling established markets and drawing strength from other technological developments such as cloud computing and artificial intelligence. Yet in the process, it produced many unanticipated effects. We now stand at an opportune moment to assess the implications of the Internet's rise.

A TWENTY-YEAR RETROSPECTIVE OF THE FUTURE

In November 2017, the Wharton School of the University of Pennsylvania hosted a major conference, *After the Digital Tornado: Networks, Algorithms, Humanity*. It assembled an exceptional group of scholars from law, business, information studies, media studies, and related fields to consider the landscape twenty years after the publication of *Digital Tornado*. At the conference, and this edited volume, they evaluated the implications for business and society as the physical and digital worlds merge. Video recordings of all the conference sessions are available at http://digital tornado.net.

---

[1] Kevin Werbach, *Digital Tornado: The Internet and Telecommunications Policy*, FCC Offices of Plans and Policy Working Paper No. 29 (March 1997), at https://transition.fcc.gov/Bureaus/OPP/working_papers/oppwp29.pdf.

2   *Introduction*

Although the *Digital Tornado* paper was not an official FCC statement, it attracted "more than usual interest,"[2] as one of the first examinations by a government agency of the transformative potential of the Internet. The *Washington Post* ran an editorial celebrating that "a government that created the original Internet through public investment nonetheless has sensibly seen that the product of that investment does best on its own."[3] *Wired* lauded *Digital Tornado* as a "seminal" document "designed to help frame future debates on Internet policy in a pro-competitive context."[4] A *New York Times* column called it "eye-popping" and "the best news Net advocates ... have gotten out of Washington"[5] because it suggested that the White House would take a "laissez-faire, market-driven approach to Internet regulation."[6]

Indeed, the Clinton Administration's *Framework for Global Electronic Commerce*,[7] released a few months later, decisively argued that regulators could best realize the benefits of the Internet by getting out of the way. "The private sector should lead" and "Governments should avoid undue restrictions on electronic commerce"[8] were its first two core principles. As fate would have it, I also helped draft those words, as the editor of the document for the interagency working group that produced the report.

The argument was not that regulation was always bad, or that, as some insisted at the time, the Internet was a distinct world that should be exempted from compliance with territorial regulations. Rather, the central claim of *Digital Tornado* was that the FCC could best achieve its regulatory goals, such as promoting competition and unleashing innovation in communications markets, by avoiding unnecessary imposition of legacy rules that poorly fit nascent services. Furthermore, government should take into account the novel technical affordances of Internet-based systems.

In 1997, the United States was home to the vast majority of global Internet users, as well as virtually all the significant commercial Internet service providers and online application platforms. It was the decade between the fall of the Soviet Union and 9/11, a period of US global hegemony unmatched in some ways before or since. America's Internet policy was destined, at least initially, to be the

---

[2] Light Touch on the Net, *Washington Post*, April 7, 1997.

[3] Ibid.

[4] Rebecca Vesely, Scans: Spinning the FCC, *Wired*, August 6, 1997, at www.wired.com/1997/08/scans-spinning-the-fcc/.

[5] Jason Chevrokas and Tom Watson, Administration Set to Assert Role in Cyberspace, *New York Times*, April 25, 1997, at http://movies2.nytimes.com/library/cyber/nation/042597nation.html.

[6] Ibid. The FCC is an independent agency, not subject to the direct authority of the White House. However, as a major technology-focused regulator whose Chair is nominated by the President, its approach is typically consistent with the Administration.

[7] The Framework for Global Electronic Commerce, at https://clintonwhitehouse4.archives.gov/WH/New/Commerce/.

[8] The White House, Framework for Global Electronic Commerce (July 1997), at https://clintonwhitehouse4.archives.gov/WH/New/Commerce/read.html.

Introduction 3

dominant framework globally. The Internet economy as we know it grew up in response to the regulatory approach that *Digital Tornado* represented.

This direction was far from foreordained. Just a year earlier, Congress passed, and President Clinton signed, legislation imposing broadcast-style indecency regulations on the Internet. The Administration was also pushing a plan to mandate government backdoors on strong encryption technology, as media companies pressed for strict online copyright enforcement and telephone carriers urged per-minute fees to prevent dialup Internet usage from overwhelming the phone network. In the end, those arguing that emerging online services should be protected from chilling regulation won the day. The potential benefits for innovation, new competitive entry, and a more open information ecosystem were too great to ignore.

As the Internet grew as a commercial and social force, first in the United States but soon throughout the world, this policy approach, which a later FCC working paper labeled as "unregulation,"[9] was viewed as an unambiguous success. The Internet, and the global web of communities and communications it fostered, was not snuffed out by incumbents. It was not turned into the centrally managed telephone network, or the centrally controlled content pipe of cable television, or a paid service offering of technology titans such as Microsoft. Small startups like Amazon.com and eBay became global commerce powerhouses, while others not yet founded, such as Google, Facebook, Alibaba, and Tencent, became some of the largest and most powerful corporations in the world. Apple, in 1997 a struggling niche vendor of personal computers, rode the smartphone boom to become the first trillion-dollar American company by market capitalization. This sort of revolution was what our small band of Internet policymakers dreamed of in 1997, but we could hardly imagine how dramatic it would be.

Today we find ourselves in a world where little remains untouched by the wave of digital connectivity that *Digital Tornado* anticipated. Yet fundamental questions remain unresolved, and even more serious new questions have emerged.

Networks powered by algorithms are eating everything. Many of the contemporary technology trends with the greatest significance for the economy and for public policy – the Internet of Things, Big Data, Platform Economy, Blockchain, and Algorithmic Society – should be seen as manifestations of this larger phenomenon. Growing tensions around governance, innovation, surveillance, competition, consumer/worker protection, privacy, and discrimination are best understood within a broader frame. The algorithmic networked world poses deep questions about power, freedom, fairness, and human agency.

Ubiquitous networking means the transformation of every form of economic activity, and a large chunk of noneconomic activity, along the same lines as the Internet. Algorithmic control means that increasingly dynamic software will manage

---

[9] Jason Oxman, The FCC and the Unregulation of the Internet, FCC Office of Plans and Policy Working Paper No. 33 (July 1999), at https://transition.fcc.gov/Bureaus/OPP/working_papers/oppwp31.pdf.

not just transactions and communication, but also human systems. Our cultures and institutions are ill-adapted to this new environment. Equally important, systems engineered for a distinct and limited digital world can be ill-suited for the complexities of the "real" world. Already, a number of controversies have arisen, many of which are difficult to address under established legal rules.

Some of the essential questions include: How should organizations appropriately make use of the vast array of data they can now collect, process, and analyze? How can bedrock notions of fairness, justice, trust, and liberty be applied when computers make critical decisions, often based on obscure factors? What new business models will emerge, and how will competitive dynamics evolve? Will there be resistance to a future in which the line between networked people and networked devices becomes increasingly blurred? And can we build new legal structures, and new institutions, to better fit the world we find ourselves in?

The insightful contributions in this volume attack such questions from a range of disciplinary and other perspectives. There is no unitary answer, but taken together, these chapters paint a sophisticated picture of the contemporary digital world, its discontents, and its potential futures.

OUTLINE OF CONTENTS

The initial chapter of this volume reprints key excerpts from the *Digital Tornado* working paper published in 1997. Some portions read as historical artifacts from a time when TCI and Netscape were important players in the digital economy, while Google, Facebook, and Amazon were either tiny or nonexistent. As an FCC document, the paper emphasizes agency-specific question such as whether real-time Internet communications services should be regulated as telephone companies. Yet in some ways, its claims are surprisingly broad and surprisingly fresh:

> The chaotic nature of the Internet may be troubling for governments, which tend to value stability and certainty. However, the uncertainty of the Internet is a strength, not a weakness. With decentralization comes flexibility, and with flexibility comes dynamism. Order may emerge from the complex interactions of many uncoordinated entities, without the need for cumbersome and rigid centralized hierarchies. Because it is not tied to traditional models or regulatory environments, the Internet holds the potential to dramatically change the communications landscape. The Internet creates new forms of competition, valuable services for end users, and benefits to the economy.[10]

The intervening decades have vindicated this strikingly optimistic vision in some ways, while revealing its errors in others. Today, Internet-based platforms count their users in the billions, and are major players in the global economy. Most of the population of the world carries around a smartphone, which is deeply integrated into

---

[10]   *Digital Tornado*, at ii.

Introduction 5

both their business activities and their social lives. Extraordinary amounts of wealth have been created, along with many other benefits. Yet overall, our view of the Internet now is darker, or at least more gray. It has created new concentrations of power that by some measures exceed those before, and it has opened the door to massive violations of privacy, manipulation, discrimination, information warfare, exploitation, and other abuses. Movements toward digital ethics, taking back control of online activities, and new regulations of digital platforms are the prominent features of our current Internet policy debates. The pendulum will doubtless swing again, making it all the more valuable to stop and assess where we are, and where we've come from.

The remainder of the volume is organized along around three pillars, which were also the framework for the conference at Wharton: networks, algorithms, and humanity.

PART I: NETWORKS

The network is the basic organizing structure of our increasingly digital society. *Digital Tornado* urged that "The FCC's goal should not be to foster the development of . . . networks individually, but to maximize the public benefits that flow from the Network that encompasses all of those networks.[11]

Networks are the channels for the collection, aggregation, manipulation, and application of vast quantities of data from every facet of the world. As platforms for economic activity, networks are already shaping global business. As frameworks for the exercise of power, they can be tools for either empowerment or control. The contributions in this section consider how private and governmental actors seek to exploit the networked environment, and what mechanisms could promote the most desirable outcomes for individuals, organizations, and communities.

Chris Marsden frames *Digital Tornado* within a debate between two positions on Internet regulation, where the winner turns out to be a third option. He offers a transatlantic perspective on the past two decades of Internet policy as a corrective to the frequent tendency of American experts to assume they are the only game in town. The United Kingdom and Europe have been far from idle in considering the implications of the "information society," and their policy approaches often vary from the dominant American strain. In particular, they have emphasized the hybrid of governmental and private market oversight known as coregulation. Marsden sees this approach to making regulation more adaptive addressing key dilemmas that fast-moving, slippery technologies pose for the traditional regulator's toolkit. The common thread across the Atlantic that he identifies is that the technocratic consensus for Internet "unregulation" unraveled as it met the cold reality of real-world harms.

---

[11] *Digital Tornado*, at 9.

6 *Introduction*

Julie Cohen offers skepticism that governments can control the operators of cyberspace through force of law. She explains how networks, constituted through standards, have turned into a new transnational and extragovernmental form of regulation. In hindsight, a critical blind spot of the 1990s' vision for the digital economy was the assumption that Internet-based networking would generally lead to the diffusion of power. Astute observers recognized that technical means of regulation might be more restrictive and less democratic than conventional legal forms, but the dominant viewpoint was optimistic. *Digital Tornado* declared that: "The Internet is dynamic precisely because it is not dominated by monopolies or governments."[12] As Cohen demonstrates, the rise of networks has, in many cases, either created new dominant power centers or entrenched old ones. Her key insight is that networks and standards represent a new hybrid legal-institutional form of governance. The rise of networked governance has, in turn, empowered digital platforms to exercise enormous power outside the limitations of regulation or other traditional constraints.

So, what are we to do? While the focus of this collection is not on particular policy responses to specific problems, Tim Wu offers some hope. He does so by, ironically, going back in time to the decades before there was an Internet. His focus is on the IBM antitrust case. Extending from the end of the 1960s to the beginning of the 1980s, when it was finally dropped by the Department of Justice, the IBM case is usually viewed as a cautionary tale of wasteful government overreach into fast-moving technology industries. Wu argues that, far from being a failure, the Justice Department's efforts to rein in IBM led to the creation of independent markets for software and personal computers. IBM's fall from dominance, necessary to open the door for Microsoft, Apple, and the entire Internet industry, was not a foregone consequence of Schumpeterian forces, but the outcome of sustained government action. The vision of unrelenting technological progress embodied in *Digital Tornado's* "endless spiral of connectivity" is not, Wu emphasizes, inherently self-actualizing. While regulators should, as *Digital Tornado* emphasized, consider potential innovation harms of intervention, they should not shy away from bold action to promote innovation in protomarkets that otherwise might never develop.

PART II: ALGORITHMS

The network revolution is moving to a new stage thanks to the development of machine learning, artificial intelligence, and analytics that can automate human decision making. Firms and industries are being reconfigured to capture the benefits of digital platforms and algorithmic systems. And as more and more decisions are automated through systems that substitute correlations for causation and under-standing, foundational notions of legal and ethical responsibility come into

[12] *Digital Tornado*, at 83.

Introduction

question. Algorithms are not neutral; they reflect the preferences and biases of those who design them. The contributions in this section highlight the potential as well as the challenges of an algorithmic world, and suggest responses to the dangers they highlight. In particular, they go beyond the recognition that algorithmic markets and services create policy concerns around data protection, fairness, manipulation, and market competition to offer guidance for firms and governments in developing responses.

Kartik Hosanagar (with Alex Miller) provides a simple framework to understand algorithmic systems in terms of data, algorithmic logic, and human interactions. Abstracting in this way avoids getting caught up in the complexity and variety of data science techniques. It also counterbalances the natural tendency to focus solely on algorithms themselves. Hosanagar and Miller apply their framework to one of the most concerning unanticipated consequences of the Internet: the rise of "filter bubbles," which narrow the scope of users' information environments. While services such as Facebook contribute to filter bubbles by algorithmically recommending content that reinforces existing viewpoints, what users share to begin with and what they click on once surfaced by the algorithm also matter. Through a simulation experiment, Hosanagar and Miller show that filter bubbles emerge or collapse from the interactions of all three factors.

The interaction effects between data and algorithms also have significant business implications, which Viktor Mayer-Schönberger considers in his chapter. As many observers recognize, market concentration is a significant and growing problem in precisely the digital markets where the Internet was supposed to herald an era of healthy competition. Mayer-Schönberger points out that algorithmic systems are subject to a significant new force shifting market competition, which he labels the "feedback effect." More data not only produces better results through traditional scale and scope economies, but also by generating better machine learning models. This means that traditional antitrust remedies, such as those explored by Tim Wu in Chapter 3, are poorly suited to redress competitive imbalances. Instead, Mayer-Schönberger argues, regulators should impose a progressive data-sharing mandate. With this novel mechanism, dominant digital platforms would be required to make data available to competitors, blunting their inherent advantage in algorithm-dominated markets.

Deirdre Mulligan (with Daniel Kluttz and Nitin Kohli) offers another pathway forward. The standard response to concerns about "black box" algorithms is to make those algorithms transparent or explainable. Such approaches, however, involve significant limitations, especially in professional contexts such as medicine, law, or financial advice. Mulligan, Kluttz, and Kohli argue instead for designing systems to be contestable, meaning that those subject to algorithmic decisions can engage with and challenge them. They apply this concept to machine learning in the context of professional expert domains. Both laws and norms can encourage contestability of these automated decisions, but systems designers still must take explicit

8 *Introduction*

steps to promote effective questioning and challenges. The overall message of the chapter, as with the others in this section, is that we cannot take algorithms and their impacts for granted. Just as network platforms sometimes require regulatory oversight, algorithmic systems need conscious evaluation and shaping to blunt their unintended consequences.

PART III: HUMANITY

The final contributors consider the big question: What is the future for humans in an environment increasingly dominated by data-driven algorithms and networked machines? The opportunities in this world to create both new wealth and tighter interpersonal connections are extraordinary. Yet for many, the digital tornado is a destructive force, undermining economic security, creative freedom, or individual agency. What mechanisms of oversight or resistance could counteract these effects? Throughout history, both societies and organizations have innovated in structures of governance to promote social welfare in changing environments. The contributions in this section consider whether, at a time when trust is fraying across the board, there is hope for solutions that expand the pie and promote human flourishing.

Brett Frischmann (with Evan Selinger) argues that networked digital systems are engaged in no less than the reengineering of humanity. While the narrative of artificial intelligence for many decades has been about computers becoming more like people, the reverse is also occurring: People are effectively being turned into machines. Frischmann and Selinger make an impassioned case that promoting human flourishing means allowing for different conceptions of the good life. That means pushing back on the reductionist systems that private companies engineer for their own interests, and respecting the right to turn off. They use Robert Nozick's classic thought experiment of a machine that can simulate any experiences, and a modern-day variant, to test ethical intuitions. What ultimately differentiates humans and machines is that we can and do make choices that diverge from simple optimization functions. The benefits of networking, automation, and new services that digital connectivity provides should not come at the price of our deepest values.

Striking a similar chord, Shoshana Zuboff explains how the combination of pervasive networking, algorithmic decision making, and advertising-based platform business models gave rise to a new and dangerous economic form: surveillance capitalism. Industrialization in the nineteenth century had to crush the natural concept of beauty in order to produce the orderly structures of capitalist market exchange. Similarly, the new capitalism based around relentless aggregation and algorithmic exploitation of data necessarily undermines protection of privacy, which resists the transformation of personal information into raw material for corporate exploitation. Zuboff explains how the battles now underway over the power and role of digital platforms are not just conflicts over regulation and antitrust (although they are that), but fundamental conflicts about the very structures of power in our society.

The Internet's transformation from source of creative innovation to agent of domination may have been avoidable, but the seed of surveillance capitalism were present from the early days.

Finally, my contribution, *The Siren Song*, aims forward. If the original *Digital Tornado* was an analysis in 1997 based on a vision of 2007 or 2017, what would a similar exercise look like today? One of the most plausible scenarios for how newer technologies might disrupt and reconstitute the Internet economy is based on blockchain and related mechanisms. Because of their fundamental decentralization, enforced through cryptography, these technologies hold out the promise of resisting the centralization of control that Zuboff highlights. The problem is that the power of blockchain to create trust without reliance on trusted third parties depends on immutable transactions. And that means prospectively limiting human freedom of action. Like Frischmann and Selinger, I worry about replacing human judgment with relentlessly logical machines, although my focus is more practical than normative. Immutability inevitably creates the possibility of catastrophe, unless paired with imperfect governance mechanisms that keep humans in the loop. There is still no free lunch.

THE CHOICES WE FACE

In the third decade of the twenty-first century, as in the last decade of the twentieth, our approach to technology can emphasize the safety of the familiar or the protean creativity of the new, but each choice brings complications. Those who warned that a lightly regulated Internet would produce harmful consequences were not wrong, nor are those who point out that for all the current problems, Internet-based platforms still generate economic and social benefits for much of the world's population.

History, even recent history, is a collection of narratives we create to give coherence to events. The US government in the 1990s might have taken a different line toward the Internet, being more radically deregulatory or (more likely) imposing more traditional rules on unfamiliar and threatening new systems. We can only speculate on the counterfactual present that would have produced.

The final line of *Digital Tornado* was the following: "In the long run, the endless spiral of connectivity is more powerful than any government edict."[13] The intervening years have demonstrated both the truth of that prediction, and its incompleteness. The Internet did shape the world in incredibly significant ways, in spite of resistance of governments and private actors. Yet both also found ways to rein it in, or even bend the Internet to serve their aims. Some of the edicts the Internet overran were mechanisms to protect privacy, prevent harassment, protect consumers, and other desirable initiatives. Not all forms of self-reinforcing growth are healthy; some

---

[13]   *Digital Tornado*, at 84.

are cancerous. From the vantage point of 2017, the speculative optimism of 1997 seems both prescient and naïve.

The next twenty years are likely to witness similarly surprising development patterns. The raw number of individuals touched by the Internet will not grow by two orders of magnitude again, because we have nearly run out of unconnected people (although pockets without access remain a problem). Yet how people experience connectivity will change. The social consequences will continue to evolve as the networks of machines grow in numbers and sophistication.

My hope is that this volume contributes to our collective understanding of the next turnings of the endless spiral of connectivity.

Kevin Werbach
Philadelphia, PA
October 2019

Prelude

Digital Tornado: The Internet and Telecommunications Policy (1997) Selected Excerpts

Kevin Werbach
Federal Communications Commission Office of Plans and Policy
Working Paper #29 (March 1997), at www.fcc.gov/Bureaus/OPP/
working_papers/oppwp29.pdf.

BACKGROUND

The Internet, from its roots a quarter-century ago as a military and academic research tool, has become a global resource for millions of people. As it continues to grow, the Internet will generate tremendous benefits for the economy and society. At the same time, the Internet poses significant and difficult questions for policy makers. This working paper examines some of these emerging issues at the intersection of technology, law, economics, and public policy.

The United States federal government has long been involved in the development of the Internet. Through research grants, and by virtue of its status as the largest institutional user of computer services in the country, the federal government played a central role in bringing what we now call the Internet into being. Just as important, the federal government has consistently acted to keep the Internet free of unnecessary regulation and government influence. As the Internet has matured and has grown to support a wide variety of commercial activity, the federal government has transitioned important technical and management functions to the private sector. In the area of telecommunications policy, the Federal Communications Commission (FCC) has explicitly refused to regulate most online information services under the rules that apply to telephone companies.

Limited government intervention is a major reason why the Internet has grown so rapidly in the United States. The federal government's efforts to avoid burdening the Internet with regulation should be looked upon as a major success, and should be continued. The Telecommunications Act of 1996 (1996 Act) adopts such a position. The 1996 Act states that it is the policy of the United States "to preserve the vibrant and competitive free market that presently exists for the Internet and other interactive computer services, unfettered by Federal or State regulation,"[1] and the FCC

---

[1] Telecommunications Act of 1996, Pub. L. No. 104–104, 110 Stat. 56, *to be codified at* 47 U.S.C. §§ 151 *et. seq* (1996 Act), at § 230(b)(2). Hereinafter, all citations to the 1996 Act will be to the 1996 Act as codified in the United States Code.

has a responsibility to implement that statute. The draft "Framework for Global Electronic Commerce" developed by the White House with the involvement of more than a dozen federal agencies, similarly emphasizes the need to avoid unnecessary government interference with the Internet.[2]

This working paper addresses three overlapping telecommunications policy areas that relate to the Internet: law, economics, and public policy. Legal questions arise from the difficulty in applying existing regulatory classifications to Internet-based services. Economic questions arise from the effects of Internet usage on the telecommunications infrastructure, and the effects of the telecommunications infrastructure on the Internet. Public policy questions arise from the need to maximize the public benefits that the Internet brings to society.

The Internet is a fluid, complex entity. It was designed to route around obstacles, such as failures at central points of the network, and it may respond in unexpected ways to pressures placed on it. It has developed largely without any central plan, especially in the past several years as the US government has reduced its management role. It overcomes any boundaries that can be drawn, whether rooted in size, geography, or law. Because the Internet represents an ever-growing interconnected network, no one entity can control or speak for the entire system. The technology of the Internet allows new types of services to be layered on top of existing protocols, often without the involvement or even the knowledge of network providers that transmit those services. Numerous users can share physical facilities, and the mix of traffic through any point changes constantly through the actions of a distributed network of thousands of routers.

The chaotic nature of the Internet may be troubling for governments, which tend to value stability and certainty. However, the uncertainty of the Internet is a strength, not a weakness. With decentralization comes flexibility, and with flexibility comes dynamism. Order may emerge from the complex interactions of many uncoordinated entities, without the need for cumbersome and rigid centralized hierarchies. Because it is not tied to traditional models or regulatory environments, the Internet holds the potential to dramatically change the communications landscape. The Internet creates new forms of competition, valuable services for end users, and benefits to the economy. Government policy approaches toward the Internet should therefore start from two basic principles: avoid unnecessary regulation, and question the applicability of traditional rules.

Beyond these overarching themes, some more specific policy goals can be identified. For the FCC in particular, these include the following.

Promote competition in voice, video, and interactive services.

In passing the 1996 Act, Congress expressed its intent to implement a "pro-competitive deregulatory national communications policy." The Internet provides

---

[2] *A Framework for Global Electronic Commerce*, available on the World Wide Web, at www.white house.gov.

both a space for innovative new services, as well as potential competition for existing communications technologies. The FCC's role will be to ensure that the playing field is level, and that efficiency and market forces drive competition.

Facilitate network investment and technological innovation.

The Internet encourages the deployment of new technologies that will benefit consumers and produce jobs. The Commission should not attempt to pick winners, but should allow the marketplace to decide whether specific technologies become successful. By eliminating regulatory roadblocks and other disincentives to investment, the FCC should encourage both incumbents and new entrants to develop innovative solutions that transcend the capabilities of the existing network.

Allow all citizens to benefit from advanced technologies.

The communications revolution should benefit all Americans. In an age of new and exciting forms of interactive communications, the FCC should ensure that entities such as schools and libraries are not left behind. However, the mechanisms used to achieve this goal should be consistent with the FCC's broader policies of competition and deregulation.

This working paper is intended to explore issues and to facilitate discussion, not to propose specific government actions. Many proponents of the Internet's development are wary of any government actions directed toward the Internet. Government, however, has been intimately involved with the Internet since the network's beginnings. Government decisions – such as the FCC's directive that Internet service providers not be subject to interstate access charges, and the widespread requirement by state regulators that local calls be available at flat monthly rates – continue to shape Internet development. Moreover, policy decisions are best made with knowledge and comprehension of their potential implications.

The goal of this paper, therefore, is to promote greater understanding, on the part of both government and the private sector, of the unique policy issues the Internet raises for the FCC and similar agencies. The discussion of a topic is not a suggestion that government regulation in that area is necessary or desirable. On the contrary, a fundamental position of this paper is that government should work to avoid unnecessary interference with the Internet's development.

Government may influence the evolution of the Internet in many ways, including directly regulating, participating in technical standards development, providing funding, restricting anti-competitive behavior by dominant firms, facilitating industry cooperation otherwise prohibited by antitrust laws, promoting new technologies, encouraging cooperation between private parties, representing the United States in international intergovernmental bodies, and large-scale purchasing of services. The FCC and other government entities may also play a useful role simply by raising the profile of issues and stimulating debate. A better understanding of the relationship between the Internet and telecommunications policy will facilitate intelligent decision-making about when and to what extent any of these government actions are appropriate.

THE ENDLESS SPIRAL OF CONNECTIVITY

Government officials, pundits, and market researchers often compare the Internet to established communications technologies such as telephony and broadcasting. These efforts are understandable. "Traditional" technologies have well-defined usage characteristics, growth patterns, and market behavior. Moreover, the Internet physically "piggybacks" on other networks, in particular the wireline telephone infrastructure.

Drawing analogies between the Internet and traditional media makes it easier to decide whether existing bodies of law or regulation apply to new Internet-based services. Thus, for example, the debate over the constitutionality of the Communications Decency Act (CDA), which seeks to restrict the transmission of indecent material over the Internet, has often boiled down to a conflict of analogies. Opponents of the CDA have compared the Internet to a telephone network, while supporters often describe the Internet as similar to broadcasting. Because telephone carriers are generally not legally responsible for the content routed over their networks, but broadcasters may be subject to fines for transmitting inappropriate material, the choice of analogy can predetermine the legal outcome.

Although such analogies are appealing, most break down upon closer analysis of the unique characteristics of the Internet. The Internet is substitutable for all existing media. In other words, the Internet potentially poses a competitive threat for every provider of telephony, broadcasting, and data communications services. At the same time, Internet-related businesses are substantial customers of existing telephony, broadcasting, and data companies. The Internet creates alternate distribution channels for pre-existing content, but more importantly, it permits delivery of new and hybrid forms of content. The Internet is one of many applications that utilize the existing telephone network. However, from another perspective, the telephone, broadcasting, and cable networks are simply nodes of the larger network that is the Internet.

Thus, the Internet is fundamentally different from other communications technologies. In most cases, simply mapping the rules that apply to other services onto the Internet will produce outcomes that are confusing, perverse, or worse. Any attempt to understand the relationship between the Internet and telecommunications policy must therefore begin with the distinguishing aspects of the Internet.

HOW THE INTERNET IS UNIQUE

The distinctiveness of the Internet derives in large part from its technical architecture, which is described in greater detail in Section II. The Internet functions as a series of layers, as increasingly complex and specific components are superimposed on but independent from other components.[3] The technical protocols that form the foundation

---

[3] Tony Rutkowski, former Executive Director of the Internet Society, has written a more detailed discussion of the implications of Internet architecture for the development of the network. *See*

of the Internet are open and flexible, so that virtually any form of network can connect to and share data with other networks through the Internet. As a result, the services provided through the Internet (such as the World Wide Web) are decoupled from the underlying infrastructure to a much greater extent than with other media. Moreover, new services (such as Internet telephony) can be introduced without necessitating changes in transmission protocols, or in the thousands of routers spread throughout the network.

The architecture of the Internet also breaks down traditional geographic notions, such as the discrete locations of senders and receivers. The Internet uses a connectionless, "adaptive" routing system, which means that a dedicated end-to-end channel need not be established for each communication. Instead, traffic is split into "packets" that are routed dynamically between multiple points based on the most efficient route at any given moment. Many different communications can share the same physical facilities simultaneously. In addition, any "host" computer connected directly to the Internet can communicate with any other host.

A further distinguishing characteristic of the Internet is its fractal nature. Fractals are derived from the branch of mathematics known as chaos or complexity theory. Fractals exhibit "self-similarity"; in other words, a roughly similar pattern emerges at any chosen level of detail. Internet traffic patterns most clearly demonstrate the Internet's fractal tendencies. For traditional communications networks (including the telephone network), engineers have over many years developed sophisticated statistical models to predict aggregate usage patterns. Researchers have shown that usage of the Internet follows not the traditional "poisson" pattern, but rather a fractal distribution.[4] In other words, the frequency of Internet connections, the distribution between short and long calls, and the pattern of data transmitted through a point in the network tend to look similarly chaotic regardless of the time scale.

The fractal nature of the Internet confounds regulatory and economic models established for other technologies. However, as chaos theorists have shown, fractals have valuable attributes. In a fractal entity, order emerges from below rather than being dictated from above. The fact that the Internet does not have an easily-identifiable hierarchy or any clear organizational structure does not mean that all behavior is random. Many small, uncoordinated interactions may produce an aggregate whole that is remarkably persistent and adaptable.

Finally, the Internet has thus far not been regulated to the same extent as other media. The Communications Act of 1934 (Communications Act), which created the Federal Communications Commission to oversee telephony and radio broadcasting, is more than sixty years old. By contrast, Internet service providers, and other companies in the Internet industry, have never been required to gain regulatory approval for their actions.

Anthony M. Rutkowski, "Internet as Fractal: Technology, Architecture, and Evolution," in *The Internet as Paradigm* (Aspen Institute 1997).

[4] *See* Amir Atai and James Gordon, *Impacts of Internet Traffic on LEC Networks and Switching Systems* (Bellcore 1996); Vadim Antonov, *ATM: Another Technological Mirage*, available on the World Wide Web, at www.pluris.com/ip_vs_atm/.

THE FEEDBACK LOOP

If the Internet is not like any other established communications technology, what then is it? On one level, the Internet is whatever anyone wants it to be. It is plastic, decentralized, and constantly evolving network. Any simple concept to describe the Internet will necessarily be incomplete and misleading.[5] Such templates are useful, however, to promote greater understanding of aspects of the Internet that may not otherwise be obvious.

For purposes of this paper, I believe it is valuable to understand the Internet as a feedback loop. A feedback loop occurs when the output of a system is directed back into the system as an input. Because the system constantly produces fuel for its own further expansion, a feedback loop can generate explosive growth.[6] As the system expands, it produces more of the conditions that allow it to expand further. All networks are feedback loops, because they increase in value as more people are connected.[7] The Internet, however, is driven by a particularly powerful set of self-reinforcing conditions.

Figure 1 describes some of the interrelated factors that build upon each other to foster the growth of the Internet. Some "supply" factors (such as the availability of higher-capacity networks) permit an expansion of demand (for example, by allowing bandwidth-intensive services such as high-resolution video transmission). Like a digital tornado, the vortex continues, as the new level of demand creates the need for additional capacity, and so forth.[8] The Internet feedback loop is a fundamentally positive force, because it means that more and more services will be available at lower and lower prices. So long as effective self-correcting mechanisms exist, the Internet will overcome obstacles to its future growth.

Understanding the underpinnings of the Internet feedback loop is necessary to craft policies that facilitate, and do not hinder, its continuation. There are four primary factors that support the growth of the Internet:

DIGITALIZATION AND "DEEP CONVERGENCE"

As described above, the Internet exhibits characteristics of several media that had previously been distinct. Networks carry three types of information – voice, video, and data – and those categories are further subdivided into areas such as pre-recorded vs. live or real-time presentation, and still vs. moving images. Historically, these different

---

[5] For a thorough explication of various metaphors for the Internet, including the now well-worn notion of the "Information Superhighway" coined by Vice President Albert Gore, see Mark Stefik, *Internet Dreams: Archetypes, Myths, and Metaphors* (1996).

[6] For an extended discussion of the significance for feedback loops and control mechanisms as they relate to new technologies, see Kevin Kelly, *Out of Control: The New Biology of Machines, Social Systems, and the Economic World* (1994).

[7] *See infra* section (IV)(B).

[8] The tornado metaphor has been used by Paul Saffo, Eric Schmidt, and others to describe the Internet.

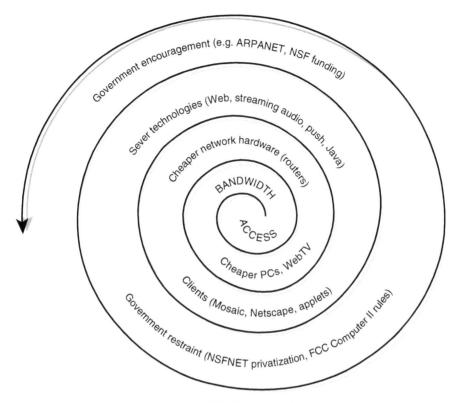

FIGURE 1: The Internet Spiral

forms of information have used different delivery vehicles. The telephone network delivered voice, private corporate networks delivered data, and broadcast networks delivered video. Each service was tightly coupled to a specific form of infrastructure – the telephone network used copper wires to reach subscribers, broadcast television used the airwaves, cable television used coaxial cable, and so forth.

"Convergence" means that those lines are blurring. However, convergence is often understood in a shallow manner, as simply the opportunity for owners of one type of delivery system to compete with another type of delivery system, or as the opportunity for content owners to deliver their content using different technologies. In reality, convergence is something far more fundamental. "Deep convergence" is driven by a powerful technological trend – digitalization. Digitalization means that all of the formerly distinct content types are reduced to a stream of binary ones and zeroes, which can be carried by any delivery platform.[9] In practical terms, this means not only that specific boundaries – between a telephone network and a cable system,

---

[9] See *Digitization and Competition* (Computer Systems Policy Project 1996).

for example – are blurred, but also that the very exercise of drawing any such boundaries must be fundamentally reconsidered or abandoned.

Digitalization has been occurring for decades. The long-distance telephone network in the United States is now almost entirely comprised of digital switches and fiber optic transmission links. These digital facilities, however, have been optimized to transport a single service – voice. The Internet, by contrast, can transmit any form of data. Internet protocols are sufficiently flexible to overcome the boundaries between voice and other services. Innovators can develop new services and immediately load them onto the existing Internet infrastructure. Convergence creates new markets, and new efficiencies, because particular services are no longer locked into specific forms of infrastructure.

MOORE'S LAW AND METCALFE'S LAW

As George Gilder has most clearly articulated, the two technological "laws" that most impact the growth of the Internet are Moore's Law and Metcalfe's Law.[10] Moore's Law holds that the maximum processing power of a microchip, at a given price, doubles roughly every eighteen months. In other words, computers become faster at an explosive rate, or conversely, the price of a given level of computing power decreases at that same dramatic rate. Metcalfe's Law says that the value of a network is equivalent to the square of the number of nodes. In other words, as networks grow, the utility of being connected to the network not only grows, but does so exponentially.

Moore's Law and Metcalfe's Law intersect on the Internet. Both the computers through which users access the Internet, and the routers that transmit data within the Internet, are subject to the price/performance curve described by Moore's Law. At the same time, advances in data transmission technology have expanded the capacity of the Internet's backbone networks. As the bandwidth available through the network continues to grow, Moore's Law states that the price of obtaining a given level of bandwidth continues to drop, while Metcalfe's Law dictates that the value of a connection increases exponentially. The ratio of the cost of Internet access to the value it provides plummets over time. And as it plummets, connectivity and higher-bandwidth connections become that much more important, generating more usage and more capital to upgrade the network.

THE MAGNETISM OF MONEY AND MINDS

Moore's Law and Metcalfe's Law describe the technological forces that push the growth of the Internet, but there are also business forces that exert a powerful influence. In a capitalist economy, the "invisible hand" of the market dynamically

---

[10] *See, e.g.,* George Gilder, "The Bandwidth Tidal Wave," *Forbes ASAP,* December 5, 1994.

redirects capital where it is most highly valued, without any direct outside intervention. Companies that demonstrate superior potential for generating future revenues more easily attract investment, and for public companies, see their stock prices rise. Other companies in the same industry sector often see increases in their stock prices as well, as investors seek to repeat the pattern of the first company and to capitalize on economic trends.

As money flows into a "hot" sector, so do talented people seeking to obtain some of that money by founding or working at a company in that sector. The presence of so many top minds further attracts capital, reflecting a synergistic process I call "the magnetism of money and minds." This trend promotes the availability of financing to spur the future growth of the Internet.

COMPETITION

Competition enables both the dynamic allocation of capital and talent, as well as the constant innovation in technology that leads to deep convergence and falling prices. In a competitive market, companies must constantly invest and innovate, or risk losing out to competitors. Intel CEO Andy Grove has observed that in the computer industry there are only two kinds of companies: the quick and the dead. Even those companies with strong positions must always look over their shoulder, because customer loyalty vanishes in the face of superior alternatives.

The benefits of competition are evident in the computer industry, where companies must constantly improve their products to remain successful. Competition in the Internet context means that many different providers of hardware, software, and services vie for customers. In a competitive market, providers that can offer superior service or prices are more likely to succeed. Technological innovations that lower costs or allow new service options will be valuable to providers and consumers alike.

THREATS TO THE CONTINUED SPIRAL

If the Internet truly operates like a feedback loop, why is government intervention necessary?

There are many ways the Internet spiral could be derailed. Any of the underlying drivers of Internet growth could be undermined. Moving toward proprietary standards or closed networks would reduce the degree to which new services could leverage the existing infrastructure. The absence of competition in the Internet service provider market, or the telecommunications infrastructure market, could reduce incentives for innovation. Excessive or misguided government intervention could distort the operation of the marketplace, and lead companies to expend valuable resources manipulating the regulatory process.

Insufficient government involvement may also, however, have negative consequences. Some issues may require a degree of central coordination, even if only to establish the initial terms of a distributed, locally-controlled system. A "tragedy of the commons" situation may arise when all players find it in their own self-interest to consume limited common resources. The end result, in the absence of collective action, may be an outcome that no one favors. In addition, the failure of the federal government to identify Internet-related areas that should not be subject to regulation leaves open opportunities for state, local, or international bodies to regulate excessively and/or inconsistently.

HOW GOVERNMENT SHOULD ACT

The novel aspects of the Internet require government policies that are sensitive to both the challenges and the opportunities of cyberspace. Three principles should guide such government decision-making.

Scalability, Not Just Stability

Rather than seeking to restrain the growth of the Internet, government should encourage it. As long as the underpinnings of the network support further expansion, and self-correcting mechanisms can operate freely, the Internet should be able to overcome obstacles to further development. Additional capital and innovation will be drawn to any challenge due to the prospect of high returns. In addition, a focus on scalability directs the attention of policy makers to the future of the network, rather than its current configuration. Given the rapid rate at which the Internet is changing, such a forward-looking perspective is essential. The "growth" of the Internet means more than an increase in the number of users. It also means that the network will evolve and change, becoming an ever more ubiquitous part of society.

Nevertheless, stability remains important. The Internet must achieve a sufficient level of reliability to gain the trust of consumers and businesses. However, even such stability requires an architecture that is built to scale upward. Otherwise, periods of calm will inevitably be followed by crashes as the Internet continues to grow.

Swim with the Current

The economic and technological pressures that drive the growth of the Internet should not be obstacles for government. Rather, government should identify ways to use those pressures to support the goals that government hopes to achieve. In telecommunications, this means using the pricing signals of the market to create incentives for efficiency. In a competitive market, prices are based on costs, and the firm that can provide a service for the lowest cost is likely to succeed. Such competitive pressures operate far more effectively, with lower administrative costs, than direct government mandates.

Similarly, government should look for mechanisms that use the Internet itself to rectify problems and create opportunities for future growth. For example, new access technologies may reduce network congestion, as long as companies have proper incentives to deploy those technologies. Filtering systems may address concerns about inappropriate content. Competition from Internet services may pressure monopolies or outdated regulatory structures. Government agencies should also use the Internet themselves to receive and disseminate information to the public.

The Network, not Networks

The Internet is a network, but so are AT&T, TCI, and NBC. The FCC's goal should not be to foster the development of any one of those networks individually, but to maximize the public benefits that flow from the Network that encompasses all of those networks and many more. With the growth of competition and the elimination of traditional regulatory, technological, and economic boundaries, networks are more likely than ever to be interdependent, and a policy that benefits one network may have a detrimental effect on others. For example, a mandate that Internet service providers be entitled to connect to the telephone network for free might stimulate Internet use, but telephone companies might be forced to increase their rates or offer lower quality service to recover the increased cost of supporting such connections.

Although government should support the growth of the Internet, this support need not involve explicit subsidies that are not independently justified as a matter of public policy and economics. Instead, government should create a truly level playing field, where competition is maximized and regulation minimized.

HOW THE INTERNET WORKS

Basic Characteristics

Just as hundreds of millions of people who make telephone calls every day have little conception of how their voice travels almost instantaneously to a distant location, most Internet users have only a vague understanding of how the Internet operates. The fundamental operational characteristics of the Internet are that it is a distributed, interoperable, packet-switched network.

A **distributed** network has no one central repository of information or control, but is comprised of an interconnected web of "host" computers, each of which can be accessed from virtually any point on the network. Thus, an Internet user can obtain information from a host computer in another state or another country just as easily as obtaining information from across the street, and there is hierarchy through which the information must flow or be monitored. Instead, routers throughout the network regulate the flow of data at each connection point. By contrast, in a centralized network, all users connect to single location.[11] The distributed nature of the Internet gives it robust survivability characteristics, because there is no one point of failure for the network, but it makes measurement and governance difficult.

An **interoperable** network uses open protocols so that many different types of networks and facilities can be transparently linked together, and allows multiple services to be provided to different users over the same network. The Internet can run over virtually any type of facility that can transmit data, including copper and fiber optic circuits of telephone companies, coaxial cable of cable companies, and various types of wireless connections. The Internet also interconnects users of thousands of different local and regional networks, using many different types of computers. The interoperability of the Internet is made possible by the TCP/IP protocol, which defines a common structure for Internet data and for the routing of that data through the network.

A **packet-switched** network means that data transmitted over the network is split up into small chunks, or "packets." Unlike "circuit-switched" networks such as the public switched telephone network (PSTN), a packet-switched network is "connectionless."[12] In other words, a dedicated end-to-end transmission path does (or circuit) not need to be opened for each transmission.[13] Rather, each router calculates the best routing for a packet at a particular moment in time, given current traffic patterns, and sends the packet to the next router. Thus, even two packets from the same message may not travel the same physical path through the network. This mechanism is referred to as "dynamic routing." When packets arrive at the destination point, they must be reassembled, and packets that do not arrive for whatever reason must generally be re-sent. This system allows network resources to be used more efficiently, as many different communications can be routed simultaneously over the same transmission facilities. On the other hand, the inability of the sending computer under such a "best effort" routing system[14] to ensure that sufficient bandwidth will be available between the two points creates difficulties for services that require constant transmission rates, such as streaming video and voice applications.[15]

---

[11] In some cases, centralized networks use regional servers to "cache" frequently accessed data, or otherwise involve some degree of distributed operation.

[12] Some newer technologies, such as asynchronous transfer mode (ATM) switching, allow for the creation of "virtual circuits" through the Internet, which allow traffic to follow a defined route through the network. However, information is still transmitted in the form of packets.

[13] In actuality, much of the PSTN, especially for long-distance traffic, uses digital multiplexing to increase transmission capacity. Thus, beyond the truly dedicated connection along the subscriber loop to the local switch, the "circuit" tied up for a voice call is a set of time slices or frequency assignments in multiplexing systems that send multiple calls over the same wires and fiber optic circuits.

[14] In a "best effort" delivery system, routers are designed to "drop" packets when traffic reaches a certain level. These dropped packets must be resent, which to the end user is manifested in the form of delay in receiving the transmission.

[15] "Streaming" voice and video applications are those in which the data available to the receiving user is updated as data packets are received, rather than waiting until an entire image or sound file is downloaded to the recipient's computer.

The Internet Today

As of January 1997 there were over sixteen million host computers on the Internet, more than ten times the number of hosts in January 1992.[16] Several studies have produced different estimates of the number of people with Internet access, but the numbers are clearly substantial and growing. A recent Intelliquest study pegged the number of subscribers in the United States at 47 million,[17] and Nielsen Media Research concluded that 50.6 million adults in the United States and Canada accessed the Internet at least once during December 1996 – compared to 18.7 million in spring 1996.[18] Although the United States is still home to the largest proportion of Internet users and traffic, more than 175 countries are now connected to the Internet.[19]

According to a study by Hambrecht & Quist, the Internet market exceeded one billion dollars in 1995, and is expected to grow to some 23 billion dollars in the year 2000. This market is comprised of several segments, including network services (such as ISPs); hardware (such as routers, modems, and computers); software (such as server software and other applications); enabling services (such as directory and tracking services); expertise (such as system integrators and business consultants); and content providers (including online entertainment, information, and shopping). The Internet access or "network services" portion of the market is of particular interest to the FCC, because it is this aspect of the Internet that impacts most directly on telecommunications facilities regulated by the Commission. There are now some 3,000 Internet access providers in the United States,[20] ranging from small start-ups to established players such as Netcom and AT&T to consumer online services such as America Online.

Internet Trends

Perhaps the most confident prediction that can be made about the Internet is that it will continue to grow. The Internet roughly doubled in users during 1995, and this trend appears to be continuing.[21] Figure 2 shows one projection of the growth in residential and business users over the remainder of the decade. Estimates suggest as many as half a billion people will use the Internet by the year 2000.[22]

---

[16] Network Wizards Internet Domain Survey, January 1997.

[17] *See* "US on-line population reaches 47 million – Intelliquest survey results," *Internet IT Informer*, February 19, 1997, available on the World Wide Web, at www.mmp.co.uk/mmp/informer/netnews/HTM/219n1e.htm.

[18] *See* Julia Angwin, "Internet Usage Doubles in a Year," *San Francisco Chronicle*, March 13, 1997, at B1.

[19] Network Wizards Internet Domain Survey, January 1997, available on the World Wide Web, at www.nw.com/zone/WWW/top.html.

[20] Boardwatch Directory of Internet Service Providers (Fall 1996).

[21] *See* "Market Size," *CyberAtlas*, available on the World Wide Web, at www.cyberatlas.com/market.html.

[22] Paul Taylor, "Internet Users 'Likely to Reach 500m by 2000,'" *Financial Times*, May 13, 1996, at 4.

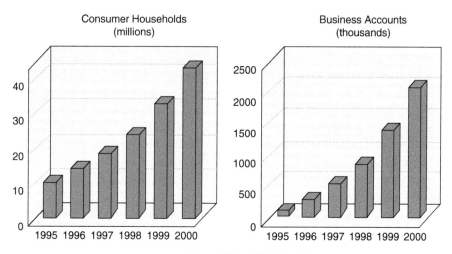

FIGURE 2: Internet Growth Projections

As the Internet grows, methods of accessing the Internet will also expand and fuel further growth. Today, most users access the Internet through either universities, corporate sites, dedicated ISPs, or consumer online services. Telephone companies, whose financial resources and network facilities dwarf those of most existing ISPs, have only just begun to provide Internet access to businesses and residential customers. Cable companies are also testing Internet access services over their coaxial cable networks, and satellite providers have begun to roll out Internet access services. Several different forms of wireless Internet access are also being deployed.

At the same time as these new access technologies are being developed, new Internet clients are also entering the marketplace. Low-cost Internet devices such as WebTV and its competitors allow users to access Internet services through an ordinary television for a unit cost of approximately $300, far less than most personal computers. Various other devices, including "network computers" (NCs) for business users, and Internet-capable video game stations, promise to reduce the up-front costs of Internet access far below what it is now. These clients promise to expand greatly the range of potential Internet users. Moreover, as Internet connectivity becomes embedded into ordinary devices (much as computer chips now form the brains of everything from automobiles to microwave ovens), the Internet "market" will expand even more.

Bandwidth will continue to increase to meet this new demand, both within the Internet backbones and out to individual users. There is a tremendous level of pent-up demand for bandwidth in the user community today. Most users today are limited to the maximum speed of analog phone lines, which appears to be close to the 28.8 or 33.6 kbps supported by current analog modems, but new technologies promise tremendous gains in the bandwidth available to the home.[23] In addition, the backbone circuits of the Internet are now being upgraded to OC-12 (622 Mbps) speeds, with far greater speeds on the horizon.[24] With more bandwidth will come more services, such as full-motion video applications. Virtually every one of the challenges identified in this paper will become more acute as bandwidth and usage increase, and as the current limitations of the Internet are overcome. Thus, even though some of the questions that the Internet poses are of limited practical significance today, policy makers should not wait to consider the implications of the Internet.[25]

Throughout the history of the Internet, seemingly insurmountable obstacles have been overcome. Few people would have expected a network designed for several dozen educational and research institutions to scale to a commercial, educational, and entertainment conduit for tens of millions of users, especially with no means of central coordination and administration. Governments should recognize that the Internet is different from traditional media such as telephony and broadcasting, although lessons can be learned from experience in dealing with those technologies. At the same time, the Internet has always been, and will continue to be influenced by the decisions of large institutions and governments. The challenge will be to ensure that those decisions reinforce the traditional strengths of the Internet, and tap into the Internet's own capability for reinvention and problem-solving.

CATEGORY DIFFICULTIES

The FCC has never directly exercised regulatory jurisdiction over Internet-based services. However, the rapid development of the Internet raises the question of whether the language of the Communications Act of 1934 (as amended by the Telecommunications Act of 1996), or existing FCC regulations, cover particular services offered over the Internet.

Governments act by drawing lines, such as the jurisdictional lines that identify which governmental entity has authority over some activity, or the service classifications that differentiate which body of law should be applied in a particular case. Governments traditionally determine the treatment of new services by drawing

---

[23] Several manufacturers are beginning to deploy 56kbps modems. *See* "U.S. Robotics Launches the New Battle – 56kbps Modems," *Boardwatch*, January 1997. This technology provides higher downstream transmission rates, but requires ISPs to have digital connections to the local exchange network. The throughput of these modems under real-world conditions will depend on the nature of each user's connection, and will usually be lower than 56 kbps. In addition, current FCC technical rules governing line power may limit the maximum connection speed of these modems to 53kbps.

[24] MCI, for example, currently plans to upgrade its backbone to OC-48 speed (2.5 Gbps) by 1998.

[25] Of course, widespread penetration of new, higher-bandwidth services may take far longer than some breathless commentators predict today. *See* Jonathan Weber, "Internet Video: Idea Whose Time Will Come ... Slowly," *Los Angeles Times*, May 13, 1996, at B8. Although policy makers and regulators should be aware of the possibilities that the Internet created, concrete actions should not be taken based on mere speculation about the potential impact of a service.

analogies to existing services. For example, the FCC regulates long-distance tele-phony, but does not regulate dial-up remote access to corporate data networks. ISPs almost exclusively receive calls from their subscribers, but so do retailers taking catalog orders or radio stations holding call-in promotions. Dial-up access to the Internet resembles, but differs from, other types of connections.

There are reasons to believe that a simple process of drawing analogies to familiar services will not be appropriate for the Internet. The Internet is simultaneously local, national, and global, and is almost infinitely plastic in terms of the services it can support. As a result, it confounds any attempt at classification. Failure to consider such category difficulties is, however, itself a form of line drawing. As long as some communications services are subject to regulatory constraints, legal boundaries will be necessary. New approaches may therefore be necessary to avoid inefficient or burdensome results from existing legal and regulatory categories.

TOWARD A RATIONAL APPROACH

The primary goal of this paper is to identify issues, not to offer specific policy recommendations. It is important to remember that, despite the tremendous atten-tion given to the Internet in the past few years, it remains orders of magnitude smaller in terms of usage and revenues than the voice telephone network in the United States. Many of the questions raised here will answer themselves as service providers fine-tune their business models and as the communications industry evolves. Once competition is sufficiently well-developed, regulation may become largely unnecessary. At some point, companies will be disciplined more strongly by market forces than by the dictates of regulators. Nonetheless, some thoughts about how to address the categorization challenges raised in this section are appropriate.

So long as some services are regulated, a line-drawing process must take place. When Internet services are involved, this line drawing will be inherently messy and imprecise. However, even the premise that Internet services should not be regulated requires a precise assessment of what constitutes an "Internet" service. With the increasing prevalence of hybrid services, joint ventures, and alternative technolo-gies, such distinctions will always be difficult. No matter how sophisticated the regulator, companies in the marketplace will devise clever means of avoiding regulatory restrictions. No matter how well-intentioned the regulator, government intervention in the private sector can have unexpected and unfortunate consequences.

Thus, government should apply blunt instruments that achieve underlying goals, rather than struggling for an elegant or precise solution that will cover every case. Wherever possible, market forces should be harnessed to take the place of direct regulatory intervention. Although new services like Internet telephony and stream-ing video may create legal headaches, these developments are positive ones that government should encourage. Such new technologies are valuable both because of the new options they represent for consumers, but also because of the potential competitive pressure they may exert on incumbent providers.

The first task of government policy towards these new Internet-based services should therefore be to identify those areas where regulation is clearly not appropriate. By distinguishing these "easy cases," government can provide greater certainty to the private sector that regulation will not be extended to the theoretical boundaries of statutory authority. For example, when a company such as Vocaltec sells retail software that allows end users to make voice phone calls through the Internet, and nothing more, it makes little sense to classify that company as a telecommunications carrier subject to federal and state regulation. Such software providers merely enable end users to utilize a functionality through the network, much like companies that sell fax machines. They do not themselves transport telecommunications traffic. Similarly, an ISP should not be classified as a telecommunications carrier simply because some of its users choose to use Internet telephony software to engage in voice calls. By stating that such companies are not subject to the Communications Act, the FCC could eliminate fear and uncertainty, while still leaving room to analyze the harder questions.

The next step should be to identify relatively simple and flexible structures that achieve underlying policy goals. The initial assumption ought to be that new Internet-based services should not be subject to the regulatory constraints of traditional services. Government policy should be sensitive to the fact that technology is changing rapidly, and that the Internet landscape a few years in the future may look very different than it does today. Market forces may lead to the creation of differentiated classes of service, with users paying higher rates for higher quality, thus de facto distinguishing between different types of service offerings, without any intervention by the government.

The analytical process must work in both directions. Government should think not only about the regulatory treatment of new services, but about the implications of those new services for the regulatory treatment of existing services. If a competitive imbalance exists because a new technology is not subject to the same regulatory constraints as a competing older technology, the answer should be reduced regulation of the older technology. Of course, such deregulation should be dependent on the existence of sufficient competition to police the actions of incumbents. The ultimate objective, however, should be less regulation for all, rather than more regulation for some.

CONCLUSION

This working paper has reviewed many difficult and complex issues that have arisen as the Internet has grown to prominence. I have attempted to identify government policy approaches that would have a positive influence on the development of the Internet. This final section seeks to place the challenges described throughout this paper into a broader context.

The Internet and Competition in Telecommunications

The movement toward deregulation and local competition in telecommunications in the United States may be the single most significant development for the future of the Internet. The decisions that the FCC, state regulators, and companies make about how to create a competitive marketplace will determine the landscape in which the Internet evolves. The shape of local competition will influence what types of companies are able to provide Internet access to what categories of users, under what conditions, and at what price. The removal of barriers between different industries – such as the prohibition on BOCs offering in-region long-distance service – will accelerate the convergence that is already occurring as a result of digitalization and other technological trends.

Internet providers are potentially both substantial customers of circuit-switched voice carriers, and competitors to them. It is ultimately in the interests of both ISPs (who depend on the PSTN to reach their customers) and LECs (who derive significant revenue from ISPs) to have pricing systems that promote efficient network development and utilization. If the costs of Internet access through incumbent LEC networks increase substantially, users will have even stronger incentives to switch to alternatives such as competitive local exchange carriers, cable modems, and wireless access.

Dial-up Internet access today tends to be priced on a flat-rated basis, for both the PSTN portion of the connection and the transmission of packets through Internet backbones. By contrast, interexchange telephone service tends to be charged on a per-minute basis.[26] However, both networks run largely over the same physical facilities. There is some evidence that Internet and long-distance pricing are beginning to move towards each other.[27] This paper has discussed some of the arguments about usage pricing for Internet connections through the PSTN; similar debates are occurring among Internet backbone providers in response to congestion within the Internet. With the development of differentiated quality of service mechanisms on Internet backbones, usage pricing seems likely to become more prevalent on the Internet, although usage in this context may be measured by metrics other than minutes.

In the telephone world, flat-rated pricing appears to be gaining ground. The FCC established the subscriber line charge (SLC), because the fixed costs it represented were more efficiently recovered on a flat-rated basis. The *Access Reform* proceeding raises questions about whether other usage-sensitive charges (such as the Transport Interconnection Charge and the Carrier Common Line Charge) should be replaced with flat-rated charges, and there was substantial debate in the *Interconnection* proceeding about whether LEC switching capacity should be sold on a flat-rated basis in the form of a "switch platform." Pressure toward flat-rated pricing is also arising for business

---

[26] Outside the United States, local telephone service is usually charged on a per-minute basis as well.
[27] *See generally* "Too Cheap to Meter?," *The Economist*, October 19, 1996, at 23.

reasons – for example, Southwestern Bell has reportedly considered offering a flat-rated regional long-distance plan when it receives interLATA authorization. Customers in the US seem to prefer the certainty of flat-rated pricing even where it winds up costing more for their particular level of usage.

There are, of course, important differences in the architectures of the Internet and the public switched telephone network. However, both of these architectures are evolving. There will not be one universal pricing structure for the Internet or the telephone network, for the simple reason that there will not be one homogenous network or one homogenous company running that network. Technology and business models should drive pricing, rather than the reverse.

Today, the vast majority of Internet users and ISPs must depend on incumbent LECs for their connections to the Internet. These incumbent LECs have huge investments in their existing circuit-switched networks, and thus may be reluctant, absent competitive pressure, to explore alternative technologies that involve migrating traffic off those networks. The economics of the Internet are uncertain, since the market is growing and changing so rapidly. Competition will enable companies to explore the true economics and efficiencies of different technologies. The unbundling mandated by the 1996 Act will allow companies to leverage the existing network to provide new high-bandwidth data services.

Competition can lead to instability or confusion, especially during periods of transition. Monopolies provide certainty of returns that, by definition, cannot be achieved in a competitive market. With many potential players, forecasting the future of the industry can be difficult. Companies must choose between different technologies and business models, and those companies that do not choose wisely will see the impact on their bottom lines.

Yet, as the Internet demonstrates, uncertainty can be a virtue. The Internet is dynamic precisely because it is not dominated by monopolies or governments. Competition in the Internet industry, and the computer industry that feeds it, has led to the rapid expansion of the Internet beyond anything that could have been foreseen. Competition in the communications industry will facilitate a similarly dynamic rate of growth and innovation.

The Right Side of History

The legal, economic, and technical underpinnings of the telecommunications infrastructure in the United States have developed over the course of a century, while the Internet as a service for consumers and private businesses is less than a decade old, and the national framework for competition in local telephone telecommunications markets was adopted scarcely more than a year ago. Challenges that seem insurmountable today may simply disappear as the industry and technology evolve.

As significant as the Internet has become, it is still near the beginning of an immense growth curve. America Online, the largest ISP, has grown from under a million subscribers to eight million in roughly four years. But those eight million subscribers represent only a fraction of the eighty million households served by AT&T. The revenues generated by the Internet industry, although growing rapidly, pale in comparison to those generated by traditional telephony. Only about 15 percent of the people in the United States use the Internet today, and less than 40 percent of households even have personal computers. A decade from now, today's Internet may seem like a tiny niche service. Moreover, as Internet connectivity is built into cellular phones, television sets, and other household items, the potential number of Internet hosts will mushroom beyond comprehension. Computers are now embedded in everything from automobiles to cameras to microwave ovens, and all of these devices may conceivably be networked together. The Internet may exert the greatest influence on society once it becomes mundane and invisible.

The growth potential of the Internet lends itself to both pessimistic and optimistic expectations. The pessimist, having struggled through descriptions of legal uncertainties, competitive concerns, and bandwidth bottlenecks, will be convinced that all these problems can only become worse as the Internet grows. The optimist, on the other hand, recognizes that technology and markets have proven their ability to solve problems even faster than they create them.

The global economy increasingly depends on networked communications, and communications industries are increasingly shifting to digital technologies. Bandwidth is expanding, but so is demand for bandwidth. None of these trends shows signs of diminishing. As long as there is a market for high-speed connections to the Internet, companies will struggle to make those high-speed connections available in an affordable and reliable manner. Once a sufficiently affordable and reliable network is built, new services will emerge to take advantage of it, much as the World Wide Web could take off once the Internet had reached a certain level of development.

Difficulties and confusion may arise along the way, but improvements in communications technology will continue to provide myriad benefits for individuals, businesses, and society. In the long run, the endless spiral of connectivity is more powerful than any government edict.

PART I

Networks

1

The Regulated End of Internet Law, and the Return to Computer and Information Law?

Christopher T. Marsden[*]

This chapter is both a retrospective, and also even a requiem, for the 'unregulation' argument in Internet law in the past twenty-five years, and a prospective on the next twenty-five years of computer (or cyber) law,[1] in which many of the expert treatises of the 1990s need to be dusted down and reabsorbed.[2]

The global communications network connected by the Internet Protocol has transformed the consumer/prosumer and small business experience of electronic communication.[3] The Internet is not a lawless, special unregulated zone; it never was.[4] Now that broadband Internet is ubiquitous, mobile, and relatively reliable in urban and suburban areas, it is being regulated as all mass media before it. The major gatekeepers are regulated for the public good and public interest, whether that be access providers through infrastructure sharing, electronic privacy, cybersecurity and network

---

[*] I wish to thank the contributors to this edited collection and its editor, the panelists and participants at the Wharton School symposium "After the Digital Tornado" on 10 November 2017, and participants at the Georgetown Technology Law Review symposium on 23 February 2018 on "Platform Law," especially Julie Cohen and Mireille Hildebrandt. I also wish to thank the contributors and participants at the Münster Institute for Information and Telecommunications Law twentieth anniversary symposium in Berlin, Germany on 15 July 2017, especially Bernd Holznagel, and the contributors and participants at the eleventh annual Gikii symposium in Winchester, England, on 15 September 2017, especially Lilian Edwards, Andres Guadamuz, Paul Bernal, Daithi MacSithigh, and Judith Rauhofer. All errors and omissions remain my own.

[1] Eastham, Laurence (2011) *Interview with SCL's New President, Richard Susskind*, Society for Computers and Law, 23 August, at www.scl.org/articles/2191-interview-with-scl-s-new-president-richard-susskind. See also Susskind, Richard (2018) *Sir Henry Brooke – A Tribute*, Society for Computers and Law, at www.scl.org/articles/10221-sir-henry-brooke-a-tribute.

[2] A good introduction is Reed, Chris (2010) *Making Laws for Cyberspace*, Oxford: Oxford University Press, especially at pp. 29–47.

[3] See generally for European law, Edwards, Lilian (ed., 2018) *Law, Policy, and the Internet*, Oxford: Hart Publishing; for US law, Goldman, Eric (2018) *Internet Law Cases and Materials*. For an annotated bibliography of classic academic legal writing, see Marsden, Chris (2012) *Internet Law*, Oxford Bibliographies Online, New York: Oxford University Press.

[4] For early UK cases, see Athanasekou, P. E. (1998) Internet and Copyright: An Introduction to Caching, Linking and Framing, *Journal of Information, Law and Technology* (JILT); Opinion of Lord Hamilton in *The Shetland Times Ltd* v. *Dr Jonathan Wills and Zetnews Ltd*. Court of Session, Edinburgh 24 October 1996, at www.linksandlaw.com/decisions-87.htm.

neutrality regulation, or the social media, e-commerce and search giants through various duties of care including those for notice and rapid action – in many cases, requiring takedown of allegedly illegal material in a day or even an hour,[5] and notification of breach of security and privacy to the customer.[6] An Internet law expert arriving in a time machine from the mid-1990s would find all this quite shocking.

We have now come full circle from computer law prior to the Internet's explaining the importance of robotics, cybernetics, and Electronic Data Interchange (EDI) in the 1980s; to an explanation of the Internet's impact on the law in the 1990s that ranged across the entire syllabus including constitutional law and jurisprudence;[7] to more specialist examinations of law in such areas as intellectual property and telecommunications in the 2000s; to a realization that the future was delayed not denied and that cyberlaw is vital to understanding regulation of platforms, of artificial intelligence and robotics, of blockchains, of automated vehicles, and of disinformation in our democracies.

The 2020s will finally be the decade of cyberlaw, not as 'law of the horse', but as digital natives finally help bring the law syllabus, legal practice, and even legislatures into the Information Society.

In the first part of the chapter, I explain how the cyberlawyers of the 1990s dealt with regulation of the then novel features of the public Internet. Internet law was a subject of much interest in the 1990s in the US, and some specialist interest in UK and Europe.

In Part 2, I explain the foundational rules for the adaptation of liability online initially focused on absolving intermediaries of legal responsibility for end user-posted content. This exceptionalist approach gradually gave way. While some US authors are hamstrung by a faith in the myth of the superuser and somewhat benign intentions of corporations as opposed to federal and state government, there has been a gradual convergence on the role of regulated self-regulation (or co-regulation)[8] on both sides of the Atlantic.[9]

In Part 3, I argue that the use of co-regulation has been fundamentally embedded since European nations began to enforce these rules, with limited enforcement in

---

[5] European Commission (2017) Communication on Tackling Illegal Content Online: Towards an Enhanced Responsibility of Online Platforms; European Commission (2018) Recommendation on Measures to Effectively Tackle Illegal Content Online, published 1 March.

[6] Belli, Luca and Zingales, Nicolo (eds. 2017) *Platform Regulations: How Platforms Are Regulated and How They Regulate Us*, FGV Direito Rio, Brazil, at https://bibliotecadigital.fgv.br/dspace/handle/10438/19402.

[7] An excellent review is provided by chapters 1–3 in Murray, Andrew and Reed, Chris (2018) *Rethinking the Jurisprudence of Cyberspace*, Cheltenham: Edward Elgar.

[8] Holznagel, Bernd and Hartmann, Sarah (2017) Do Androids Forget European Sheep? – The CJEU's Concept of a 'Right to Be Forgotten' and the German Perspective, in Russel Miller (ed.) *Privacy and Power – A Transatlantic Dialogue in the Shadow of the NSA-Affair*, Cambridge: Cambridge University Press, pp. 586–614.

[9] See, for instance, Frischmann, Brett, M. (2005) An Economic Theory of Infrastructure and Commons Management, Minnesota Law Review, Vol. 89, 917–1030, at https://ssrn.com/abstract=588424, discussed in Marsden, Chris (2017) *Network Neutrality: From Policy to Law to Regulation*, Manchester: Manchester University Press.

Return to Computer and Information Law? 37

which judges and regulators stated that business models largely focused on encouraging illegal posting would not be protected. Settled policy on liability, privacy, trust, encryption, open Internet policies against filtering, were arrived at as a result of expert testimony and exhaustive hearings.

Finally, in Part 4, I argue that hanging those policies on a whim results in potentially catastrophic results in terms of untying the Gordian knots of intermediary safe harbour, privacy, copyright enforcement, and open Internet European regulations.

It is often forgotten that the Werbach's 'Digital Tornado' paper[10] heralded a model of limited state regulation, but very substantial responsible collective self-regulation ('consensus and running code') within transnational law.[11] When that pact was broken by 4Chan script kiddies and two billion Facebook users, it moved regulation away from the responsible collectivism of the pioneers' Internet.

There were three views of regulation in 1997: the type of self-regulation I have described; a belief in state regulation by those existing vested interests in broadcast, telecommunications and newspapers; and a third view that state regulation was inevitable as the Internet became ubiquitous but needed to be as reflexive and responsive as could be maintained with human rights responsibilities.

The perspective of today allows us to rethink the apparent triumph of the first view. If 2018 can in retrospect be seen as the year that the 'Tech Bros' view of regulation faltered and was replaced (to some extent) by state and supranational intervention, then the third option, of what I describe as co-regulation, appears to be supplanting that self-regulation option.[12] The state intervention was most notable in both scale and scope in European Union law, for data protection, consumer/prosumer protection, and also for competition enforcement.

PART 1: 1990S' HISTORY OF INTERNET LAW

The Internet was developed in the 1960s at a group of research institutes in the United States and the United Kingdom.[13] The Internet is a network of approximately 50,000

---

[10] Werbach, Kevin (1997) Digital Tornado: The Internet and Telecommunications Policy, Federal Communications Commission Office of Plans and Policies Working Paper 29. Washington, FCC.

[11] See most recently, Mahler, Tobias (2019) *Generic Top-Level Domains: A Study of Transnational Private Regulation* (Elgar Studies in Law and Regulation) Cheltenham: Edward Elgar. See also Marsden, Chris (forthcoming) Transnational Information Law, in Peer Zumbansen (ed.) *Oxford Handbook of Transnational Law*, Oxford: Oxford University Press.

[12] For co-regulation, see Senden, Linda A. J. (2005) Soft Law, Self-regulation and Co-regulation in European Law: Where do they Meet?, *Electronic Journal of Comparative Law*, Vol. 9, No. 1, January 2005, at https://ssrn.com/abstract=943063; Marsden, Chris (2011) *Internet Co-Regulation*, Cambridge: Cambridge University Press. Historically, see the Max Planck Institute study: Collin, Peter (2016) Justice without the State within the State: Judicial Self-Regulation in the Past and Present, *Moderne Regulierungsregime*, Vol. 5, IX, 373.

[13] Clark, David D., Field, Frank, and Richards, Matt (2010) *Computer Networks and the Internet: A Brief History of Predicting Their Future*, CSAIL Working Paper, at http://groups.csail.mit.edu/ana/People/DDC/Working%20Papers.html; first international links were from the United States to Norway, see

autonomous systems, which are interconnected by the Internet Protocol. The Internet became an information network of critical mass in the 1990s with the rise of Bulletin Board Services (BBS),[14] still more so with the growth of commercial Internet service providers (ISPs) in the late 1980s, and eventually a mass market artefact with the development of the World Wide Web ('WWW') and release of commercial web browsers in 1993–1994. The Internet developed as a self-regulated academic network,[15] and its emergence as a commercial platform that would rapidly permeate through society was largely unpredicted.[16] Kahin and Nesson explained that the development of the Internet was bottom up and self-regulatory, and explored the emerging tensions as other nation-states began to assert a regulatory role.[17]

Internet growth, together with its increasing commercial exploitation, was accompanied by an explosive growth in United States' scholarship. In 1993, Reidenberg explained that information had become an international commodity, ill served by existing legal frameworks poorly adapted due to their focus on the tangible aspects of information-intensive products and insufficient attention to the intangible aspects of information content.[18] Reidenberg extended the argument that technology can create an environment in the absence of legal rules in his ground-breaking conception of *lex informatica*. In the absence of *ex ante* sovereign power and legal rules, technology can symbiotically create de facto commercial regulation in much the same way as the mediaeval *lex mercatoria*.[19] He extensively spelled out the use of technology as a parallel form of regulation.

Building on Reidenberg's insights, Johnson and Post made the classic argument for the Internet as a borderless self-regulatory medium that should be permitted to develop with less of the state-imposed restrictions that impeded the growth and development of earlier media.[20] The growth of the application of law to its

---

Brown, Ian (ed., 2012) *Research Handbook on Governance of the Internet*, Cheltenham: Edward Elgar, chapter 1.

[14] Goldman, Eric S. (1994) Cyberspace, the Free Market and the Free Marketplace of Ideas: Recognizing Legal Differences in Computer Bulletin Board Functions, *Hastings Comm/Ent Law Journal*, Vol. 16, 87.

[15] Clark, David D. and Blumenthal, Marjory S. (2011) The End-to-End Argument and Application Design: The Role of Trust, *Federal Communications Law Journal*, Vol. 16, 357–70.

[16] De Sola Pool, Ithiel (1983) *Technologies of Freedom*, Harvard: Harvard University Press. Pool analyzed the confrontation between the regulators of the new communications technology and the First Amendment, presciently forecasting the legal conflict that the Internet created between freedom of expression and government control/censorship. See also Kahin, Brian and Keller, James H. (eds., 1997) *Coordinating the Internet*, Cambridge, MA: MIT Press.

[17] Kahin, Brian and Nesson, Charles (eds., 1997) *Borders in Cyberspace: Information Policy and the Global Information Infrastructure*, Cambridge, MA: MIT Press.

[18] Reidenberg, Joel (1993) Rules of the Road for Global Electronic Highways: Merging the Trade & Technical Paradigms, *Harvard Journal of Law and Technology*, Vol. 6, 287, at http://jolt .law.harvard.edu/articles/pdf/vo6/o6HarvJLTech287.pdf.

[19] Reidenberg, Joel (1998) Lex Informatica: The Formulation of Information Policy Rules through Technology, *Texas Law Review*, Vol. 76, 553–93.

[20] Johnson, D. and Post, D. (1996) Law and Borders: The Rise of Law in Cyberspace, *Stanford Law Review*, Vol. 48, 1367–75.

emergence was also unpredictable, although Johnson and Post argued for an 'exceptionalism' to permit this globalized unregulated medium to grow unfettered by state censorship, which they saw as both normatively and substantively unjustified. They drew on United States' constitutional law and history in the argument. They suggest a structured, principled, and internationally acceptable manner for national legislators to respond to the Internet. Lessig, while rejecting excessive state intervention, warned that self-regulation could lead to an Internet controlled by corporate interests.[21] Lessig argued that state forbearance was rapidly resulting in private regulation by new monopolies, to supplement the existing regulation by technical protocols.

Although cyber-exceptionalism became the dominant viewpoint among scholars, it was not without its opponents. Goldsmith made a legal positivist stand against the Post-Johnson Internet exceptionalism, seeing as both normatively and substantively flawed any 'claim that cyberspace is so different from other communication media that it will, or should, resist all governmental regulation'.[22] He asserted that it can be regulated, including via conflict of laws rules, although this is not a normative position on whether law should utilize its tools to regulate the Internet. In an early trans-Atlanticist article arguing against Internet exceptionalism and reactive national Internet regulation, Mayer-Schönberger and Foster argued that the global information infrastructure limits both absolutists and regulators.[23] The emerging internationalization of the Internet would lead to both jurisdictional conflicts as well as a clash of rights principles, as foreseen by Mayer-Schönberger and Foster. Samuelson argued persuasively that legislators must ensure that the impending rule making for the Internet is proportional in both economic and human rights terms to the needs and demands of users, as well as coordinated internationally.[24] Samuelson accepted the rise of the state, the need for sovereign intervention, and the efficiency self-regulation had provided, in arguing for principles for legislating on the Internet.

There have been extensive discussions as to the provenance of a field termed 'Internet' or 'cyber' law since the mid-1990s. As the law was colonizing the metaphorical "cyberspace" – communications between computer users over the Internet – most of the most authoritative and pioneering legal scholarship with regard to the new medium dates to the 1990s. Several offline subjects have themselves incorporated large literatures from their digital form, including intellectual property, non-networked computer law, telecommunications, privacy, cybercrime,

---

[21] Lessig, Lawrence (2006) *Code and Other Laws of Cyberspace*, New York: Basic Books. Revised 2nd ed. titled *Code v2.0*, at http://codev2.cc/.

[22] Goldsmith, Jack L. (1998) Against Cyberanarchy, *University of Chicago Law Review*, Vol. 65, 1199.

[23] Mayer-Schönberger, Viktor and Foster,Teree E. (1997) A Regulatory Web: Free Speech and the Global Information Infrastructure, *Michigan Telecommunications and Technology Law Review*, Vol. 3, 45, at www.mttlr.org/volthree/foster.pdf.

[24] Samuelson, P. (2000) Five Challenges for Regulating the Global Information Society, in Chris, Marsden (ed.) *Regulating the Global Information Society*, Routledge: London.

and media content regulation. As the Internet was 'born global' but first became widely deployed in the United States, much of the literature has a bias in that direction.

Many argue that the effects of digital information retrieval on the law applies across all areas with some relevance, especially for intellectual property, and that Internet law should be considered part of the law of contracts, competition, the Constitution, and so on, with narrow exceptions for such issues as legal informatics, and telecommunications law, which are being transformed by technology, and therefore cannot remain distinct[25]. Easterbrook famously argued along these lines that there is no field of 'Internet law', any more than there is the 'law of the horse'.[26] Lessig responded that the transformative effects of the Internet on law, in areas including free expression, privacy, and intellectual property, are such that it offers lawyers a radically new route to thinking about private regulation and globalization, the limits of state action, as well as a powerful metaphor for explaining these wider changes to law students.[27] Sommer dismissed Lessig's claims regarding the exceptionalism of cyberlaw, arguing that 'a lust to define the law of the future' is dangerous, and can create bad taxonomy and bad legal analysis.[28]

Academics have constantly argued that the lack of general academic expertise and the emergence of the field mean that Internet law is a necessary short-term distinct study area, which may eventually be reintegrated into its constituent parts, as an inevitable eventual assimilation. Kerr explained two divergent views of Internet law. The first is an internalized expert view of the law, the second a technophobic view. Kerr concluded that two perspectives will converge and evolve, as more people understand the underlying technologies involved, and the useful middle ground.[29] In a survey essay into the origins of the Internet law debate, Guadamuz argued that several new fields are emerging from the study of computers and law, including legal informatics, artificial intelligence (AI) and law, and that Internet law can provide new insights into established fields that provide contemporary context for the theoretical study of several subjects, and the profession's development as a whole.[30] Guadamuz argued that the 'Attack of the Killer Acronym' was preventing accessibility to Internet law for the wider legal profession, clients (and faculty).

---

[25] Marsden, C. (2010) *Network Neutrality: Towards a Co-Regulatory Solution*, London: Bloomsbury, at 216–19.

[26] Easterbrook, Frank H. (1996) *Cyberspace and the Law of the Horse*, Chicago: University of Chicago Legal Forum, 207.

[27] Lessig, Lawrence (1999) The Law of the Horse: What Cyberlaw Might Teach, *Harvard Law Review*, Vol. 113, 501.

[28] Sommer, Joseph H. (2000) Against Cyberlaw, *Berkeley Technology Law Journal*, Vol. 15, 3, at www .law.berkeley.edu/journals/btlj/articles/vol15/sommer/sommer.html.

[29] Kerr, Orin S. (2003) The Problem of Perspective in Internet Law, *Georgetown Law Journal*, Vol. 91, 357, at http://ssrn.com/abstract=310020.

[30] Guadamuz, Andrés (2004) Attack of the Killer Acronyms: The Future of IT Law, *International Review of Law, Computers & Technology*, Vol. 18, No. 3, 411–24.

Larouche later argued that the object of information law has mutated, scope for public intervention has been rolled back, implementation of any form of public intervention has been made more difficult, and that information law has seen its main topics expropriated by more traditional topics. The law syllabus is being digitized, literally (e-books, e-syllabi, e-libraries). He predicted the end of Internet law as a subject and the abstraction of information law to move away from a specific technology (except telecoms, media law). As a result, he argued that a 'future information law' will be radically amended.[31] Goldman argued for an Internet law that can be taught using new pedagogical elements employed on a survey-type course, and argued against Easterbrook that the volume of Internet-specific legislation and case law means that common law cannot provide a sufficient grounding for students to understand the transformations wrought by Internet law.[32]

Specialization happened to some extent, with e-commerce part of standard contract law, platform dominance in competition law, digital copyright (and patent) law, cybercrime in criminal law, and so on, as Murray described.[33] Some of the more interesting specialist Internet law academic literature from the 1990s (and early 2000s) has also stood the test of time,[34] for instance, on network effects,[35] cyberlaw, and control by code or *lex informatica*,[36] free and open source software and control of the online environment,[37] network neutrality and the regulation of intermediaries by their networked environment,[38] and the creation of monopoly gatekeepers resisting yet also predicting the dominance of Google, Amazon, Facebook, Apple, and Microsoft (GAFAM).[39] Internet law has been approached as a private and public law, with policy perspectives from law and economics as well as sociolegal studies. The overviews that best introduce the topic to general readers contain contributions that provide both a commercial and a public law perspective. Some important

---

[31] Larouche, Pierre (2008) On the Future of Information Law as a Specific Field of Law, TILEC Discussion Paper No. 2008-020, at http://ssrn.com/abstract=1140162.

[32] Goldman, Eric (2008) Teaching Cyberlaw, Santa Clara University School of Law Legal Studies Research Papers Series Working Paper No. 08-57, at http://ssrn.com/abstract=1159903.

[33] Murray, A. (2013) Looking Back at the Law of the Horse: Why Cyberlaw and the Rule of Law are Important, *SCRIPTed*, Vol. 10, No. 3, 310, at http://script-ed.org/?p=1157.

[34] See, for instance, Marsden, Chris (2012) *Oxford Bibliography of Internet Law*, New York: Oxford University Press.

[35] Lemley, Mark and McGowan, David (1998) Legal Implications of Network Economic Effects, *California Law Review*, Vol. 86, 479, at https://papers.ssrn.com/sol3/papers.cfm?abstract_id=32212.

[36] Lessig, Lawrence (1999) *Code and Other Laws of Cyberspace*, New York: Basic Books.

[37] Benkler, Yochai (2002) Coase's Penguin, or Linux and the Nature of the Firm, *Yale Law Journal*, Vol. 112, 369, at www.benkler.org/CoasesPenguin.html.

[38] Wu, Tim (2003) When Code Isn't Law, *Virginia Law Review*, Vol. 89, 679, at papers.ssrn.com/sol3/papers.cfm?abstract_id=413201.

[39] Zittrain, Jonathan (2006) The Generative Internet, *Harvard Law Review*, Vol. 119, 1974, at papers.ssrn.com/sol3/papers.cfm?abstract_id=847124.

contributions have focused on US law and policy,[40] and relatively few works provide a trans-Atlantic context.[41]

The world has changed less than we think it has in the last generation, and the battle between tyranny and freedom is eternal and geographical.[42] Both the twenty-first-century Internet and the nineteenth-century telegraph are controlled by the Five Eyes (the Anglo-American powers and their former colonies in Singapore and Oceania). While the reach of international human rights law was severely limited in the nineteenth century, largely a matter of humanitarian aspects of the law of war and the extraterritorial application of domestic anti-slavery laws by the hyper-power Great Britain, we now live in what are claimed to be more enlightened times. The cabling of the planet for the Internet uses much the same undersea telegraph lanes and developments from those technologies. The first Internet link outside North America was to Norway (as part of the North Atlantic Treaty Alliance) in 1973. We have wired Africa and have an interplanetary Internet. Geography matters, and so does territorial sovereignty. Information flows through those cables, and whoever controls the cables controls the information. The tapping of telegraph lines and blocking of encrypted messages was de rigueur in the Victorian era but this policy has been challenged under international human rights law in the twenty-first century.

The likelihood that multistakeholder civil society is able to exercise useful scrutiny and control over hyper-power politicians and their obedient corporate clients or partners may appear remote, and the call for international norms for human rights law quixotic. It could mark what some might call a tectonic shift in governance of communications. Cables may girdle the Earth in only 66.8 light milliseconds, but we continue to observe covert Internet surveillance in the shadowy half-light of governance of the corporations and surveillance agencies that have for so long controlled our information.[43]

PART 2: A VERY SHORT INTERNET LIABILITY LEGISLATIVE HISTORY

These foundational rules for the adaptation of liability online focused on absolving faultless (and low fault, the line is shifting) intermediaries of liability for end user-posted

---

[40] Lemley, Mark, Menell, Peter S., Merges, Robert P., and Samuelson, Pamela (2011) *Software and Internet Law*, Gaithersburg, MD: Aspen Law & Business, 4th ed.; Thierer, Adam (ed., 2003) *Who Rules the Net? Internet Governance and Jurisdiction*, Washington, DC: Cato Institute.

[41] Yaman, Akdeniz, Walker, Clive, and Wall, David (eds., 2001) *The Internet, Law and Society*, London: Longman; Edwards, Lilian and Waelde, Charlott (eds., 2009) *Law and the Internet*, 3rd ed., Oxford: Hart Publishing; Marsden, Chris (ed., 2000) *Regulating the Global Information Society*, London: Routledge; Hedley, S. (2006) *The Law of Electronic Commerce and the Internet in the UK and Ireland*, London: Routledge-Cavendish.

[42] Marsden, Chris (2004) Hyperglobalized Individuals: the Internet, Globalization, Freedom and Terrorism, *Foresight*, Vol. 6, No. 3, 128–40.

[43] Marsden, Chris (2014) Hyper-Power and Private Monopoly: the Unholy Marriage of (Neo) Corporatism and the Imperial Surveillance State, *Critical Studies in Media Communication*, Vol. 31, No. 2, 100–108, at www.tandfonline.com/doi/full/10.1080/15295036.2014.913805.

content. More than two decades after *ACLU* v. *Reno* and the 'Information Superhighway' metaphor of Al Gore and Bill Clinton's first term is as useful a time as any to look back to the future. Settled policies were arrived at as a result of expert testimony and exhaustive hearings, on liability, privacy, trust, encryption, open Internet policies against filtering. Changing those policies now may result in potentially catastrophic untying of the Gordian knots of intermediary safe harbour, privacy, copyright enforcement, and open Internet European regulations.

The legislation that underpins intermediary liability was introduced in an extraordinary 'dot-com' boom in the period 1996–1999, frequently dated to start on 12 April 1996, when Yahoo! underwent an initial public offering, shares making 270 per cent profit for investors on a single day. The growth of Yahoo! reflects the heady valuations of Internet stocks in the period with its peak at \$118.75 a share on 3 January 2000 crashing to \$8.11 on 26 September 2001 – lower than the price of its IPO.[44] The rise and fall of broader telecoms stocks (the Internet's infrastructure plumbing) of about forty-two months was documented by Malik as amounting to an excessive valuation of about \$750 billion.[45] A regulatory outcome of the large-scale fraud, accounting irregularity, and generalized lack of regulation in that period is the lack of proper investigation to learn the lessons of that boom and bust beyond the Sarbanes-Oxley Act 2002.[46] This may have contributed in small part to the failure of regulation, and far greater losses, of the 'Great Recession' of 2008–2009 and the 'Age of Austerity' that followed.[47]

Two myths need rebutting to understand the 'self-regulatory settlement' of Internet law. The first is that the United States settled on self-regulation and a hands-off approach. While this was the spirit of the Digital Tornado paper, it was very much unreflective of the 104th Congress that voted through the *Communications Decency Act* as part of the *Telecommunications Act 1996*.[48] In the US, liability regimes have differed according to speech-based and copyright-based liabilities. *Communications Decency Act* 1996 s.230 provides that 'No provider or user of an interactive computer service shall be treated as the publisher or speaker of any information provided by another information content

---

[44] Odlyzko, Andrew (2003) *Pricing and Architecture of the Internet: Historical Perspectives from Telecommunications and Transportation*, December 29, at www.dtc.umn.edu/»odlyzko. For Yahoo! rise and fall, see https://en.wikipedia.org/wiki/Yahoo!#Expansion.

[45] See, generally, Malik, Om (2003) *Broadbandits: Inside the \$750 Billion Telecom Heist*, Wiley & Sons.

[46] Pub. Law No. 107-204, 15 U.S.C. §§ 7201 et seq. (2003).

[47] Wren-Lewis, Simon (2015) The Austerity Con, *London Review of Books*, Vol. 37, No. 4, 9–11. UK neoliberal austerity lasted until 2018, in contrast to the US under President Obama's stimulus programme from 2010. For a US perspective, see Paul Krugman (2015) The Austerity Delusion, *The Guardian*, 29 April, at www.theguardian.com/business/ng-interactive/2015/apr/29/the-austerity-delusion; Romano, Roberta (2004) *The Sarbanes-Oxley Act and the Making of Quack Corporate Governance*, New York University Law and Economics Working Paper 3, at http://lsr.nellco.org/nyu_lewp/3.

[48] 47 U.S.C. § 230. See Cannon, Robert (1996) The Legislative History of Senator Exon's Communications Decency Act: Regulating Barbarians on the Information Superhighway, *Federal Communications Law Journal*, Vol. 51, 74.

provider.'[49] This language might shield ISPs from liability for subscriber copyright infringement as well. However, Section 230(e)(2) specifically states: 'Nothing in this section shall be construed to limit or expand any law pertaining to intellectual property.' Section 230 established the concept of limited liability.[50] The *Digital Millennium Copyright Act 1998* s.512 laid out detailed rules for copyright infringement and the action required of intermediaries when notice of infringement, as paid out in DMCA, was sent. The introduction on 30 June 1995 of the *Internet Freedom and Family Empowerment Act* to amend the omnibus *Telecommunications Act of 1934*, was designed in part to mandate filters against adult pornography in all United States' households, and the eventual law as amended was voted through 420–4 on 4 August 1995,[51] remaining the federal law until part struck down in the famous *ACLU v. Reno* Supreme Court case on 26 June 1997.[52]

This non-filtered Internet regime, which arrived by accident as a result of constitutional convention, has been developed over time, and maintains a significant degree of difference from the gradually less permissive intermediary regime now permitted in the European Union.[53] Note that the 105th and 106th Congress were largely obsessed with attempting to impeach President Clinton for perjury, related to a sexual misconduct that was first publicized via that unrestricted Internet that Congress had attempted to control in 1995–7.[54] Attempts to reform the law in the period 2000 onwards were partially successful in restricting government-funded Internet services in for instance libraries, e.g. *Children's Internet Protection Act 2001*,[55] although statutes such as *Child Online Protection Act 1998* were struck down by the Supreme Court.[56]

There is thus a patchy history of US federal legislators attempting to restrict Internet harms and place restrictions on Internet access, struck down by the Supreme Court defending individual liberty against censorship.[57] In the absence of an active Supreme Court, Europe's lawmakers have faced fewer restrictions on controlling the Internet, although the liability regime is only modestly different. As Holznagel indicates, US courts have applied 'safe harbour' provisions to widely

---

[49]   47 U.S.C. § 230(c)(1).
[50]   The Communications Decency Act was Part V of the Telecommunications Act of 1996, in which S.222 deals with privacy and transparency.
[51]   On the roll call vote, see www.congress.gov/amendment/104th-congress/house-amendment/744.
[52]   *ACLU v. Reno*, 521 U.S. 844, overturned s.223. Rappaport, Kim L. (1997) In the Wake of *Reno v. ACLU*: The Continued Struggle in Western Constitutional Democracies with Internet Censorship and Freedom of Speech Online, *American University International Law Review*, Vol. 13. 765.
[53]   Guadamuz, Andres (2018) Chapter 1: Internet Regulation, inLilian Edwards (ed.) *Law, Policy and the Internet*, Oxford:Hart/Bloomsbury Publishing.
[54]   DrudgeReport Archives (1998), *Newsweek Kills Story On White House Intern*, 17 January, at www .drudgereportarchives.com/data/2002/01/17/20020117_175502_ml.htm.
[55]   Upheld in *United States v. American Library Association*, 539 U.S. 194 (2003).
[56]   *Ashcroft v. American Civil Liberties Union*, 542 U.S. 656 (2004).
[57]   Goldman, Eric (2018) *An Overview of the United States' Section 230 Internet Immunity*, in Giancarlo Frosio (ed.) *Oxford Handbook of Online Intermediary Liability*, at https://ssrn.com/abstract=3306737.

protect Internet service providers (ISPs), even where [a] it was aware of unlawful hosted content; [b] if it had been notified of this by a third party; [c] if it had paid for the data.[58] According to Yen: '[T]he general philosophy motivating these decisions – namely, that the liability against ISPs for subscriber libel would result in undesirable censorship on the Internet – remains vitally important in assessing the desirability of ISP liability.'[59] Despite multiple recent proposals to amend the limited liability safe harbour of s.230 Communications Decency Act to counter 'revenge porn', disinformation and terrorist content, the broad exemption from liability for ISPs has continued into 2020.[60] Frydman and Rorive see courts as 'in line with the legislative intent . . . applied the immunity provision in an extensive manner'.[61]

The second myth that needs exposing is that Europe was entirely reactive to the US Internet liability regime. While it is true that European telecoms were only formally liberalized in 1998, moves to regulate liability for online services predate the public Internet. European consumer Internet use roughly dates to 1998, with the opening of the Telecoms Single Market, and broadband to 2000, with the Local Loop Unbundling Regulation. However, a high-level group of experts led by Professor Luc Soete was set up in May 1995 to advise the European Commission on 'social and societal changes associated with the Information Society', which set out over one hundred initial policy suggestions in January 1996, including the infamous 'bit tax' to prevent e-commerce eroding the local tax base.[62] Among these suggestions was a recommendation to investigate further 'appropriate ways in which the benefits of the Information Society can be more equally distributed between those who benefit and those who lose'. Given the upheavals of the 'zero hours' precariat economy of the 2010s, and the scandals of Apple, Amazon, Alphabet, Facebook and other multinationals' failure to pay tax on in-country activities, the bit tax may be returning in 2020.[63]

In the German Teleservices Act of 1997[64] and *Bavaria* v. *Felix Somm* (Compuserve) case,[65] Germany showed that it wished to see a similar limited liability regime to that in the US. This led with British support to adoption of the

---

[58] Holznagel, B. (2000) Responsibility for Harmful and Illegal Content as Well as Free Speech on the Internet in the United States of America and Germany, in C. Engel and H. Keller (eds.) *Governance of Global Networks in Light of Differing Local Values*, Nomos: Baden Baden.

[59] Yen, Alfred (2000) Internet Service Provider Liability for Subscriber Copyright Infringement, Enterprise Liability and the First Amendment, *Georgetown Law Journal*, Vol, 88, 1.

[60] Holznagel, supra note 58.

[61] Frydman, B. and Rorive, I. (2002) Regulating Internet Content Through Intermediaries in Europe and the USA, *Zeitschrift fur Rechtssoziologie* Bd.23/H1, July 2002, Lucius et Lucius.

[62] CORDIS (1996) *The 'Bit Tax': The Case for Further Research*, at https://cordis.europa.eu/news/rcn/6988/en. The bit tax is a tax on the transmission of information by electronic means – literally, on bits.

[63] Dickson, Annabelle (2018) *UK to Introduce 'Google Tax' in 2020*, Politico, 29 October, at www.politico.eu/article/uk-to-bring-in-digital-services-tax-in–2020/.

[64] Also known as the Information and Communications Services Act (*Informations- und Kommunikationsdienstegesetz – IuKDG*). See IRIS Legal Observations of the European Audiovisual Observatory, IRIS 1997-8:11/16, at http://merlin.obs.coe.int/iris/1997/8/article16.en.html.

[65] Bender, G. (1998) *Bavaria* v. *Felix Somm*: The Pornography Conviction of the Former CompuServe Manager, IJCLP Vol. 1, at www.digital-law.net/IJCLP/1_1998/ijclp_webdoc_14_1_1998.html.

Electronic Commerce Directive of 2000, creating the Digital Single Market in e-commerce. 1999 seems very late in the dot-com boom – but the legislative history of the ECD is directly traceable to 16 April 1997, months before the Teleservices Act was finally ratified. The coordination of US and European lawmaking came in the International Ministerial Conference 'Global Information Networks: Realizing the Potential' in Bonn (then the German capital city) on 6–8 July 1997, which addressed 'international policy-making amongst others for electronic commerce with a view to adopting a Ministerial Declaration'.[66] As with the US Telecommunications Act 1996, it was an eighteenth-month legislative process.

'Safe harbour' protection of ISPs from liability was only implemented on 17 January 2002, when the ECD came into force. Article 12 protects the ISP where it provides 'mere conduit' with no knowledge of, or editorial control over, content or receiver ('does not initiate [or] select the receiver'). Benoit and Frydman establish that it was based on the 1997 German Teleservices Act, albeit with 'slightly more burden on the ISPs in comparison with the former German statute'.[67] Where ISPs provide hosting services, under Article 14, they are protected from liability, in two ways:

1. the provider does not have actual knowledge of illegal activity or information and, as regards claims for damages, is not aware of facts or circumstances from which the illegal activity is apparent; or
2. the provider, upon obtaining such knowledge or awareness, acts expeditiously to remove or to disrupt access of the information.

Like the proverbial three blind monkeys, ISPs and web hosting services should 'hear no evil, see no evil, speak no evil'.[68] As mere ciphers for content, they are protected; should they engage in any filtering of content, they become liable. Thus masterly inactivity except when prompted by law enforcement is the economically most advantageous policy open to them. Frydman and Rorive state 'undoubtedly the Directive seeks to stimulate coregulation'. It does this by formally permitting national courts to override the safe harbour in the case of actual or suspected breach, of national law, including copyright law.

Whereas in the US, the absolute speech protection of the First Amendment and procedural concerns mean that Notice and Take Down is counter-balanced by 'put back' procedures, in Europe, where no such protection of free speech exists, speech freedom is qualified by state rights. In both jurisdictions, Notice and Take Down regimes cause Frydman and Rorive to state that: '[T]his may lead to politically correct or even economically correct unofficial standards that may constitute an

---

[66] See IP/97/313 Brussels, 16 April 1997: *Electronic Commerce: Commission presents framework for future action*, at http://europa.eu/rapid/press-release_IP-97-313_en.htm?locale=en.

[67] Frydman and Rorive, supra note 61, at 54.

[68] Marsden, C. (2011) Network Neutrality and Internet Service Provider Liability Regulation: Are the Wise Monkeys of Cyberspace Becoming Stupid? *Global Policy*, Vol. 2, No. 1, 1–12.

informal but quite efficient mechanism for content-based private censorship.'[69] It is clear that the economic incentive for ISPs is simply to remove any content notified, otherwise do nothing to monitor content, and let end users, the police and courts, and ultimately the ethics of the content providers decide what is stored and sent over their access networks. Frydman and Rorive state that: 'Business operators should never be entrusted with . . . guidelines defining the limits of the right to free speech and offering procedural guarantees against censorship . . . which belong to the very core of the human rights of a democratic people.'[70] That is nevertheless the situation that ISP Codes of Conduct seek to self-regulate.

Could a stronger case be made to make ISPs responsible for a class of their content, where it serves their commercial benefit? This is an idea that was suggested in the 1990s, before the CDA and ECD supplanted the idea. It has returned in the US with Balkin and Zittrain's concept of information fiduciaries,[71] adapted to Europe in Perrin and Woods' recent work on duty of care.[72]

Vicarious liability tests the ability to benefit and control [i] the right and ability to supervise and [ii] a financial direct interest. This tends to make ISPs choose not to monitor even for law enforcement. The financial direct benefit is interesting in view of the 'killer application' for broadband deployment in the 2000s: Did this include peer-to-peer if the access charges received by the ISP is based on traffic i.e. adverts on portal or bandwidth usage? ISPs arguably benefitted from the existence of copyright infringement on the Internet. Thousands of users desired Internet service precisely because it offers free access to copyrighted materials. As Yen argued, an ISP (like the *Polygram* trade show operator[73]) could make copyright compliance part of its system rules and then monitor for violations.[74] The *Viacom* v. *YouTube* case in 2010 failed to fully establish the burden in such cases.[75]

Similar controversies have arisen beyond content and intellectual property. The landmark 2000 French criminal case of *Yahoo* v. *LICRA*, confirmed that US multinationals must conform to national criminal law on hate speech.[76] With regard to privacy, in 2000, the Europeans and US published the 'safe harbour' agreement.

---

[69] Frydman and Rorive, supra note 61, at 56.

[70] Ibid at 59.

[71] Balkin, Jack andZittrain, J. (2016) *A Grand Bargain to Make Tech Companies Trustworthy?* The Atlantic, October, https://perma.cc/WW5N-98UZ.

[72] Perrin, W. and Woods, L. (2018) *Harm reduction in social media – what can we learn from other models of regulation?* Carnegie Trust, www.carnegieuktrust.org.uk/blog/harm-reduction-social-media-can-learn-models-regulation/. For criticism, see Smith, Graham (2018) *Take care with that social media duty of care*, Inforrm Blog, 23 October, https://inforrm.org/2018/10/23/take-care-with-that-social-media-duty-of-care-graham-smith/.

[73] *Polygram International Publishing* v. *Nevada/TIG, Inc.*, 855 F. Supp. 1314, 1317-18 (D. Mass. 1994).

[74] Yen, supra note 59, at 19.

[75] *Viacom International, Inc.* v. *YouTube, Inc.*, No. 07 Civ. 2103, US District Court for the Southern District of New York, settled in 2013.

[76] Reidenberg, J. (2005) Technology and Internet Jurisdiction, *University of Pennsylvania Law Review*, Vol. 153, 1951, at http://ssrn.com/abstract=691501.

Negotiated from 1998, it was always legal nonsense if sound policy, and was struck down by the European Court of Justice in *Schrems* in 2015.[77] Its replacement, the 'privacy shield', is equally a sticking plaster over trans-Atlantic differences, and may also be struck down. While this chapter will not describe any of the data protection law developments over the last 25 years, it is noteworthy that the Data Protection Directive[78] was continually attacked as unsuitable for the Internet that it was not expressly designed to regulate,[79] so the new General Data Protection Regulation is already subject to much attack for its failure to regulate artificial intelligence and robotics, yet again technologies for which it was not expressly designed ... but may be adapted.[80]

PART 3: THE DEVELOPMENT OF CO-REGULATION

The early period of frenetic legislative activity in 1997–2001 matched the growth of the Internet sector in Europe, which was very small and not officially measured until 1998, when it grew from 9 per cent to over 42 per cent in 2002 in the United Kingdom, for example.[81] This unprecedented growth of a single electronic medium was driven by broadband, mobile and Wifi-enabled Internet access as well as the growth of social media: seven in ten Europeans were using the Internet by 2010.[82] By the end of 2017, 86 per cent of European Union citizens used the Internet, with 433 million users, and 252 million users of Facebook within that number and approximately 400 million Google users.[83]

---

[77] Case C-362/14.

[78] 95/46/EC.

[79] For which, see the Electronic Privacy Directive 2002/58/EC, which specifically regulates personal data protection on electronic networks.

[80] Regulation EU 2016/679 of the European Parliament and of the Council of 27 April 2016 on the protection of natural persons with regard to the processing of personal data and on the free movement of such data, and repealing Directive 95/46/EC (General Data Protection Regulation) OJ L119. See Veale, Michael and Edwards, Lilian (2018) Clarity, Surprises, and Further Questions in the Article 29 Working Party Draft Guidance on Automated Decision-Making and Profiling,*Computer Law & Security Review*, Vol. 34, No. 2, 398–404, at http://dx.doi.org/10.2139/ssrn.3071679. See also O'Conor M. (2018) GDPR Is for Life Not Just 25th of May, *Computers and Law*, 18 April, at www.scl.org/blog/10192-gdpr-is-for-life-not-just-the-25th-of-may.

[81] Office of National Statistics (2012) *Internet Access – Households and Individuals, 2012, Figure 1: Households with Internet Access, 1998 to 2012*, at www.ons.gov.uk/ons/rel/rdit2/internet-access–households-and-individuals/2012/chd-figure-1.xls.

[82] OECD (2017) *Digital Economy Outlook*, OECD: Paris, at www.oecd.org/internet/ieconomy/oecd-digital-economy-outlook-2017-9789264276284-en.htm.

[83] Eurostat (2018) *Archive: Internet Access and Use Statistics – Households and Individuals*, Revision as of 15:34, 28 March, at https://ec.europa.eu/eurostat/statistics-explained/index.php?title=Internet_access_and_use_statistics_households_and_individuals&oldid=379591.Using a group of various official statistics, the best current source is Internet World Stats (2017) *Internet User Statistics, Facebook & 2017 Population for the 28 European Union member states*, at www.internetworldstats.com/stats9.htm.

The European Commission has conducted continuous monitoring of Internet self-regulation throughout the twenty-first century. A 2004 report for the European Commission concluded:

> An imperfect self-regulatory solution may be better than no solution at all, and we must not raise our standards so high that self-regulation is never attempted. But there are limits to how much imperfection can be tolerated, and for how long. If self-regulatory codes and institutions are insufficiently transparent and accountable, and if they do not observe accepted standards of due diligence, they will lose the trust of the public and fail. There is a danger that some aspects of internet self-regulation fail to conform to accepted standards. We recommend co-regulatory audit as the best balance of fundamental rights and responsive regulation.[84]

The development of Internet regulation has been scrutinized in real time as it developed. Self-regulation continues, and even in the absence of any new laws we would expect the development of the Internet not to be static.[85] Legislative impact assessments of Internet law that ask, 'What happens if we do nothing?', do not involve stasis. The zero option is that the Internet continues to develop.[86] Self-regulation is viewed as making standards and practices across industry that the European Commission, or a Member State, views agnostically in legislative terms (or pre-legislative, given the focus on areas that are emerging and which are not yet regulated), but which intends to monitor to analyse the extent to which the self-regulation approaches the standards of 'representativeness' that co-regulation is meant to demonstrate as a best practice. The Commission's insistence that this is not an inevitable journey is backed by its actions in such areas as technical standard setting.

The largest European Internet companies are United States based. Half of the world's ten largest public companies by capitalization are computer technology, Internet-based advertising, media and e-commerce conglomerates: Google (trading as Alphabet Inc.), Apple, Facebook, Amazon, and Microsoft (GAFAM). Apple is in the global top twenty corporations by revenues, with two Internet access providers in the top thirty (AT&T and Verizon). Large Internet companies have very high profit margins driven in part by their avoidance of high sales taxes, corporate taxes and transfer pricing, as well as merger activity. The European Commission explained

---

[84] Directorate-General for Communications Networks, Content and Technology (European Commission), Programme in Comparative Law and Policy (2004) *Self-Regulation of Digital Media Converging on the Internet: Industry Codes of Conduct in Sectoral Analysis*, Final Report of IAPCODE Project for European Commission DG Information Society Safer Internet Action Plan, 30 April, Section 12.7, at https://publications.europa.eu/en/publication-detail/-/publication/b7c998d9-75d6-464d-9d91-d59aa90a543c/language-en.

[85] Marsden, C. (2017) *How Law and Computer Science Can Work Together to Improve the Information Society: Seeking to remedy bad legislation with good science*, Communications of the ACM, Viewpoint: Law and Technology.

[86] Marsden C., Cave, J. and Simmons, S. (2008) *Options for and Effectiveness of Internet Self- and Co-Regulation*, TR-566-EC. Santa Monica, CA: RAND Corporation.

that: 'Google's search engine has held very high market shares in all EEA countries, exceeding 90% in most. It has done so consistently since at least 2008.'[87] Regulation by states of the failings of those private actors is in general much slower, with the Google competition breach investigated from November 2010 until a record fine was finally issued in June 2017. The actors that enforce regulation on the Internet are thus young but globally successful multinationals, an unprecedented group of private actors regulating speech and commerce on a communications medium. In 2017, the European Commission found all these companies guilty of anticompetitive conduct:

- Apple in Ireland, and Amazon in Luxembourg, had received illegal state aid of respectively €13 billion and €1.5 billion.
- Google abused its dominance through its search business, EC imposing a €2.4 billion fine.
- Facebook had flagrantly breached the terms of its merger with WhatsApp in 2014, with an EC fine of €110 million imposed in May 2017.
- Previously dominant software and Internet company Microsoft had been found guilty of abusing its dominance three times since 2007; fined a total of €2.2 billion.

This total of fines is a record for any sector, as are the individual instances of fines. To give a sense of the scale of mergers by the companies in that period, they made 436 acquisitions worth a total $131 billion in the decade to June 2017.[88] These private actors operate with enormous scale and scope, yet they are legally regulated exactly as small commercial websites. The size and scale of their operations make their regulation more difficult than the equivalents in other industries – for instance, the infamous 'Seven Sisters' energy companies whose regulation inspired both energy and, to some extent, environmental law.[89] Such regulation between states and firms has been termed 'para-diplomacy',[90] and it is constantly engaged in by the GAFAM group.

Major platforms (now including Google, Yahoo!, Facebook, Microsoft) and access providers formed a self-regulatory group, the Global Network Initiative (GNI), in 2008 to respond to government demands for better enforcement. GNI members publish transparency reports which can be audited by the board of GNI,

[87] European Commission (2017) Antitrust: Commission Fines Google €2.42 Billion for Abusing Dominance as Search Engine by Giving Illegal Advantage to Own Comparison Shopping Service, Factsheet, Brussels, 27 June 2017, at http://europa.eu/rapid/press-release_MEMO-17-1785_en.htm.

[88] European Commission (2017) Speech by Johannes Laitenberger, Director-General for Competition, *EU competition law in innovation and digital markets: fairness and the consumer welfare perspective*, at http://ec.europa.eu/competition/speeches/text/sp2017_15_en.pdf.

[89] Sampson, Anthony (1973) *The Sovereign State of ITT*, New York: Stein and Day.

[90] Stopford, John and Strange, Susan (1991) *Rival States, Rival Firms*, Cambridge: Cambridge University Press; Duchacek, Ivo D. (1984) The International Dimension of Subnational Self-Government, *Publius: The Journal of Federalism*, Vol. 14, No. 4, 5–31, at https://doi.org/10.1093/oxfordjournals.pubjof.a037513.

Return to Computer and Information Law?

an example of self-regulation by a group.[91] Google first published a report in 2010, and reported in 2018 almost 4 billion annual copyright removal requests as compared to 495,000 annual "right to be forgotten" delisting requests and only 16,000 annual government content requests (affecting 221,000 websites), demonstrating that its most substantial enforcement actions are carried out on behalf of copyright owners.[92] Facebook, Twitter (since 2012), Amazon (since 2015) and others also produce annual transparency reports.[93]

Co-regulation was noted by United States Congress in 2002 to describe certain aspects of European regulation: 'government enforcement of private regulations'.[94] It actually came from Australia.[95] The European adventure in co-regulation in wider consumer protection legislation, as well as standards setting, was made detailed in 2002,[96] and became official policy in December 2003, with the Inter-Institutional Agreement on Better Law-Making (IIA), which defines co-regulation.[97] Although a non-legislative act, the IIA is virtually a constitutional document in European law, and its importance cannot be over-estimated, as it agrees the rules of engagement of the European Parliament, Council of Ministers and Commission.[98] The Commission confirms that forms of regulation short of state regulation 'will not be applicable where fundamental rights or important political options are at stake or in situations where the rules must be applied in a uniform fashion in all Member States'.

De jure co-regulation involves legislation that tells the industry 'regulate or else'. The UK *Digital Economy Act 2010* included two specific elements of co-regulation, for the domain name authority (Nominet) and audiovisual media services online (the Authority for Television on Demand). De facto co-regulation exists where the regulators have used their powers of extreme persuasion. It is an area in which the industry players are very aware that the regulator has power. There can be de facto co-regulation taking place alongside de jure co-regulation.

The Commission in 2005 analysed co-regulation in terms of 'better regulation'.[99] This was immediately made part of internal EC practice in the Impact Assessment

---

[91] Global Network Initiative (2018) *2017 Annual Report*, at https://globalnetworkinitiative.org/global-network-initiative-annual-report-2017-reinforcing-a-global-standard/ and https://globalnetworkinitiative.org/about-gni/.

[92] https://transparencyreport.google.com/copyright/overview – noting many companies have such reports, linking to 42 others (some have since merged or discontinued reports).

[93] See, for instance, https://transparency.twitter.com/ and https://aws.amazon.com/blogs/security/privacy-and-data-security/.

[94] H. Rept. 107–803 – *Legislative Review Activities of the Committee On International Relations* 107th Congress (2001-2002). See, generally, for US Internet co-regulation, Weiser, P. (2009) The Future of Internet Regulation, *U.C. Davis Law Review*, Vol. 43, 529–90.

[95] Marsden, *Internet Co-Regulation*, supra note 12.

[96] See COM/2002/275, COM/2002/0278, COM 2002/704.

[97] Inter-Institutional Agreement on Better Law-Making (OJ C 321, 31.12.2003), pp. 1–5.

[98] European Union (2016) *Better Regulation*, at www.consilium.europa.eu/en/policies/better-regulation/.

[99] COM/2005/97.

Guidelines,[100] which the Commission must follow before bringing forward a new legislative or policy proposal.[101] Price and Verhulst (2005) contained significant focus on AOL and internal self-organization.[102] They identified even then increasing realism in recognizing competition problems, emerging monopolies, and dominance. Verhulst and Latzer provided excellent analysis of the types of co-regulation beginning to develop and their institutional path dependency.[103] They identify five types of regulation, short of statutory agency-led regulation:

- Co-regulation,
- State-supported self-regulation,
- Collective industry self-regulation,
- Single company self-organization,
- Self-help/restriction by users including rankings to impose restrictions on access to content.

Note the direction of travel: both bottom-up transformations from self- into co-regulatory bodies, and top-down delegation from regulation into co- but not self-regulation. Also note examples of 'zombie' self-regulation – where no one will declare the patient dead or switch off the life support machine. I described these as 'Potemkin' self-regulators, where there was a website and the appearance of a regulator but few resources, no physical address containing offices and little or no apparent adjudication and enforcement.[104] We should note the gains and losses in the lifecycle of regulation – will self-regulation ossify if it stays true to its principles of self-regulation? If ossification were to result, would it matter other than to self-regulatory purists if a mature self-regulator were then to be made into a co-regulator? UK converged communications regulator Ofcom's own managerial and regulatory analysis of co- and self-regulation arrives at similar conclusions.[105]

The EC has made it pragmatic to fund standards and ex ante support self-regulation in cases where the US would simply ex post regulate via competition law. This leads to substantial US–European differences of approach, which may create 'transatlantic competition of standardization philosophies ... [in] consumer protection systems'.[106]

---

[100] SEC /2005/791.

[101] This is now codified in the new Interinstitutional Agreement between the European Parliament, the Council of the European Union and the European Commission on Better Law-Making OJ L 123, 12.5.2016, pp. 1–14, at https://eur-lex.europa.eu/legal-content/EN/TXT/PDF/?uri=OJ:L:2016:123: FULL&from=EN.

[102] Price M. and Verhulst, S. (2005) *Self-Regulation and the Internet*, Amsterdam: Kluwer.

[103] Latzer, Michael, Price, Monroe E., Saurwein, Florian, Verhulst and Stefaan G. (2007) *Comparative Analysis of International Co- and Self-Regulation in Communications Markets*, Research report commissioned by Ofcom.

[104] Marsden, *Internet Co-Regulation*, supra note 12, at pp. 60, 147, 222.

[105] Ofcom (2008) *Identifying Appropriate Regulatory Solutions: Principles for Analysing Self- and Co-Regulation*, 10 December.

[106] Newman Abraham, L. and Bach,David (2004) Self-Regulatory Trajectories in the Shadow of Public Power: Resolving Digital Dilemmas in Europe and the United States, *Governance: An International Journal of Policy, Administration, and Institutions*, Vol. 17, No. 3, July 2004, 388.

Examples of co-regulation have become frequent in this field in the 2000s, notably in data privacy, domain name governance, content filtering, Internet security, and network neutrality, as well as standard setting and social network privacy regulation.[107] Both soft law and soft enforcement play a vital regulatory role which legal positivists would be in danger of overlooking by a failure to consider the law in its co-regulatory context.

A Beaufort scale of co-regulation was developed for the European Commission based on the Beaufort scale of wind speed (from calm to hurricane).[108] The wind in this case is the degree to which the government was breathing on the forms of self-regulation that were taking place. Zero was a state of calm, which would be an entirely technical standards body whose standards were formed totally within the technical community, such as the Internet Engineering Task Force, up to a state of storm, which could be the forms of co-regulation that were formalized in the Digital Economy Act. Between zero and eleven, there is a lot of room for us to see different elements of influence that have been exerted. That wind is blowing a lot more strongly from European governments and from parliaments towards trying to achieve something much closer to co-regulation than to self-regulation. There are three alternatives:

1. not to regulate, but the world develops without regulation
2. to regulate all the platforms that legislators are concerned about
3. to regulate only the dominant platforms.

It is this regulatory dilemma that I consider in the final part of the chapter.

PART 4: BACK TO THE FUTURE OF CYBERLAW IN THE UBIQUITOUS NETWORKED COMPUTING ERA

Internet lawyers are widening their horizons and returning to the broader notion of being information lawyers whose interests extend beyond a public IP network. The end of the special place for Internet law, and its absorption into media law, has been prematurely announced. It is not only the European institutions that are becoming excited about more Internet regulation, driven in part by self-preservation and the rise of disinformation ('fake news' – sic). Reed and others question how we regulate AI[109] and dominance of the 'surveillance-industrial' state in these post-Snowden /Schrems/GDPR times, pushing digital law into even constitutional studies.[110] These are exciting times to be an information lawyer.

---

[107]   Froomkin, A. Michael, Wrong Turn in Cyberspace: Using ICANN to Route Around the APA and the Constitution, *Duke Law Journal*, Vol. 50, 17, at www.law.miami.edu/~froomkin/articles/icann .pdf.

[108]   Marsden, Cave and Simmons, supra note 86.

[109]   Reed, Chris (2018) *How Should We Regulate Artificial Intelligence?* Philosophical Transactions of the Royal Society, A 2018 376 20170360.

[110]   See, for instance, Frischmann, Brett M. (2005) An Economic Theory of Infrastructure and Commons Management, *Minnesota Law Review*, Vol. 89, 917–1030, https://ssrn.com/abstract=588424.

To put a damp squib on too much recurrent techno-optimism or cynicism, I argue that most arguments for regulating the Internet and cyber-technologies today remain old wine in new bottles.[111] The United Kingdom regulator Ofcom has called for more regulation, and potentially a new regulator, of the Internet.[112] Most developed legal systems have lots of legal regulators of information, even if none of those is entirely shiny, new, and 'cyber'. There is the UK Information Commissioner, Electoral Commission, Ofcom itself, the Advertising Standards Authority, and others. There are technical support institutions such as National Cyber Security Centre,[113] and a variety of non-governmental organizations such as the Nuffield Foundation-supported Ada Lovelace Foundation, the Turing Institute, and venerable Foundation for Information Policy Research.[114] In constructing what I call 'OffData', a regulator of electronic communications and content,[115] we need to learn the lessons of previous regulatory mergers both inside (OfCom) and outside (OfGem) communications. We need to recall what is known about sectoral regulation. UK Ofcom was set up almost twenty years ago as a result of technological convergence between broadcasting and telephony,[116] but deliberately constructed not to regulate Internet content. It is now required to so do. This is not a moment for unique solution peddling or an ahistorical view of the need to extend competences beyond a privacy, a security, a sectoral competition, and a communications regulator.

While information law is maturing, and the old Internet law/cyberlaw nomenclature may be fading, what we do as lawyers dealing with computers and their impact on society is growing more important. Some of the new ideas about regulating the Internet and artificial intelligence (AI) betray a naive faith in technology companies' intentions towards law enforcement. It is now the job of grizzled, veteran information lawyers to help policy makers understand how to make better laws for cyberspace.[117] Hildebrandt explains the scale and scope that can create disinformation problems in social media platforms:

[111]   Marsden, C. (2018) *Oral Evidence to Lords Communications Committee, "The internet: to regulate or not to regulate?"* Parliamentlive.tv, 24 April, at https://parliamentlive.tv/Event/Index/4fac3ac3-3408-4d3b-9347-52d567e3bf62.

[112]   White, Sharon (2018) *Tackling online harm – a regulator's perspective*: Speech by Sharon White to the Royal Television Society, 18 September, at www.ofcom.org.uk/about-ofcom/latest/media/speeches/2018/tackling-online-harm.

[113]   Merging CESG (the information security arm of GCHQ), the Centre for Cyber Assessment (CCA), Computer Emergency Response Team UK (CERT UK) and the cyber-related responsibilities of the Centre for the Protection of National Infrastructure (CPNI).

[114]   See www.cl.cam.ac.uk/~rja14/fipr-20th.html.

[115]   Marsden, C. (2018) Prosumer Law and Network Platform Regulation: The Long View Towards Creating Offdata, *Georgetown Technology Law Review*, Vol. 2, No. 2, pp. 376–98.

[116]   Oftel (1995) *Beyond the Telephone, the TV and the PC*: Consultation Document. Note further consultations were released, the last in 1998 – seen as a forerunner to the agenda on convergent communications for government and eventually Ofcom. See Barnes, Fod (2000) Commentary: When to Regulate in the GIS? A Public Policy Perspective, chapter 7, pp. 117–24 in Marsden, C. ed. (2000) *Regulating the Global Information Society*, New York: Routledge.

[117]   See Kroll, Joshua A., Huey, Joanna, Barocas, Solon, Felten, Edward W., Reidenberg, Joel R., Robinson, David G. and Yu, Harlan (2017) Accountable Algorithms, *University of Pennsylvania Law Review*, Vol. 165, at https://ssrn.com/abstract=2765268. See also Reed, supra note 2.

Due to their distributed, networked, and data-driven architecture, platforms enable the construction of invasive, over-complete, statistically inferred, profiles of individuals (exposure), the spreading of fake content and fake accounts, the intervention of botfarms and malware as well as persistent AB testing, targeted advertising, and automated, targeted recycling of fake content (manipulation).[118]

Some of the claims that AI can 'solve' the problem of disinformation ('fake news') do just that. Limiting the automated execution of decisions (e.g. account suspension) on AI-discovered problems is essential in ensuring human agency and natural justice: the right to appeal. That does not prevent Internet platform operators' suspension of 'bot' accounts at scale, but ensures the correct auditing of the system processes deployed.[119]

Technological solutions to detect and remove illegal/undesirable content have become more effective, but they also raise questions about who is 'judge' in determining what is legal/illegal, desirable/undesirable in society. Underlying AI use is a difficult choice between different elements of law and technology, public and private solutions, with trade-offs between judicial decision making, scalability, and impact on users' freedom of expression. Public and private actors have suggested that AI could play a larger role in future identification of problematic content – but these systems have their own prejudices and biases. It is worth restating that neither law nor technology is neutral: they both embody the values and priorities of those who have designed them ('garbage in, garbage out').

Does the use of AI that employs algorithmic processes to identify 'undesirable' content and nudge it out of consumers' view, provide a means for effective self-regulation by platforms? The UK Parliament Artificial Intelligence Committee reported on some of these issues in 2017.[120] There are an enormous number of false positives in taking material down. It is very difficult for AI to tell the difference between a picture of fried chicken and a Labradoodle, simply because of the nature of the attempts by algorithms to match these things.[121] It will need human intervention to analyse these false positives. AI can be deployed, but Google and Facebook are employing 50,000 more people because they recognize that there will have to be a mixture in

---

[118] Hildebrandt, Mireille (2018) Primitives of Legal Protection in the Era of Data-Driven Platforms, Georgetown Technology Law Review, Vol. 2, 252, at 253 footnote 3.

[119] See Marsden, Chris and Meyer, Trisha (2019) Regulating Disinformation with Artificial Intelligence (AI): The Effects of Disinformation Initiatives on Freedom of Expression and Media Pluralism, Report for Panel for the Future of Science and Technology (STOA), Scientific Foresight Unit of the Directorate for Impact Assessment and European Added Value, Directorate-General for Parliamentary Research Services (EPRS) of the Secretariat of the European Parliament.

[120] House of Lords (2017) AI Select Committee: AI Report Published, at www.parliament.uk/business/committees/committees-a-z/lords-select/ai-committee/news-parliament-2017/ai-report-published/ (note the report is published in non-standard URL accessed from this link).

[121] Reddit poster (2017) Artificial Intelligence Can't Tell Fried Chicken from Labradoodles, at www.reddit.com/r/funny/comments/6h47qr/artificial_ intelligence_cant_tell_fried_chicken/.

order to achieve any kind of aim.[122] Artificial intelligence and algorithms cannot be the only way to regulate content in future.[123]

'Mechanical Turks' are people employed – subcontracted, typically – to carry out these activities,[124] in parts of the world where their own cultural understanding of the content they are dealing with may not be ideal.[125] One of the problems is that they are responding to a perceived need to remove more content, rather than addressing fair process and due process. Subcontracting to people on very low wages in locations other than Europe is a great deal cheaper than employing a lawyer to work out whether there should be an appeal to put content back online. The incentive structure will be for platforms to demonstrate how much content they have removed.

Transparency and explanation are necessary, but remain a small first step towards greater co-regulation.[126] Veale et al. have explained how to move beyond transparency and explicability to replicability: to be able to run the result and produce the answer that matches the answer they have.[127] The greater the transparency, the greater the amount of information you give to those users who do not read the terms of service online: the degree to which that helps is limited. Prosumers are told: 'If you do not agree to the effectively unilateral terms of service you may no longer use Facebook.' A better approach would be the ability to replicate the result achieved by the company producing the algorithm. Algorithms change all the time, and the algorithm for Google search, for instance, is changed constantly. There are good reasons to keep that as a trade secret. Replicability would be the ability to look at the algorithm in use at the time and, as an audit function, run it back through the data to produce the same result. It is used in medical trials as a basic principle of scientific inquiry. It would help to have more faith in what is otherwise a black box that prosumers and regulators have to trust. The European Commission has used the overarching phrase 'a fair deal for consumers'.[128]

[122] www.fastcompany.com/40563782/how-a-i-anxiety-is-creating-more-jobs-for-humans.
[123] Discussed by Marietje Schaake MEP in April at www.theguardian.com/commentisfree/2018/apr/04/algorithms-powerful-europe-response-social-media.
[124] Hara, Kotaro, Adams, Abi, Milland, Kristy, Savage, Saiph, Callison-Burch, Chris and Bigham, Jeffrey (2017) *A Data-Driven Analysis of Workers' Earnings on Amazon Mechanical Turk*. arXiv:1712.05796, Conditionally accepted for inclusion in the 2018 ACM Conference on Human Factors in Computing Systems (CHI'18) Papers program.
[125] YouTube Transparency Report (2018), at https://transparencyreport.google.com/youtube-policy/overview.
[126] Edwards, Lilian and Veale, Michael (2017) *Slave to the Algorithm? Why a "Right to Explanation" is Probably Not the Remedy You are Looking for*, at https://ssrn.com/abstract=2972855; Erdos, David (2016) European Data Protection Regulation and Online New Media: Mind the Enforcement, *Gap Journal of Law and Society*, Vol. 43, No. 4, 534–64, at http://dx.doi.org/10.1111/jols.12002.
[127] Veale, Michael, Binns, Reuben and Van Kleek, Max (2018) *The General Data Protection Regulation: An Opportunity for the CHI Community?* (CHI-GDPR 2018), Workshop at ACM CHI'18, 22 April 2018, Montreal, Canada, arXiv:1803.06174.
[128] Vestager, M. (2018) *Competition and a Fair Deal for Consumers Online*, Netherlands Authority for Consumers and Markets Fifth Anniversary Conference, The Hague, 26 April, at https://ec.europa.eu/commission/commissioners/2014-2019/vestager/announcements/competition-and-fair-deal-consumers-online_en.

Platform regulation is a new version of an existing regulated problem, with potentially dramatic negative effects on democracy and media pluralism.[129] In tackling disinformation (and other undesirable uses of online communication, as the history of electoral and defamation reform shows), not only the effectiveness of the technological measures needs to be considered, but also raising awareness of the individual and social responsibility for the provision and appreciation of verifiable truthful content, by independent platforms rather than a single central authority. Media pluralism and literacy go hand in hand with any technological intervention.

I predict that 2020 will see the implementation of hard law requiring 'notice and action' within one hour of complaints about illegal content online.[130] The vigorous action on social network regulation has not happened, in spite of urging from national and European politicians in view of terrorist content, sexual abuse, fake news, and the other vile elements of human society manifested on the Internet. European regulators continue to rely more on corporate social (ir)responsibility than hard law. The European Commission record fine for Google is being appealed, but it will have to accept some kind of co-regulation of its vertically integrated advertising in time.

I explained in the Introduction to this chapter that Werbach's Digital Tornado, along with Reidenberg's conception of *lex informatica*, heralded a model of limited state but very substantial responsible collective self-regulation. Hard law, in the shape of the proposed European Digital Services Act to be introduced in 2020, will continue in the 2020s to be accompanied by Codes of Conduct and other self- or co-regulatory measures. At the time of writing, the world was plunging into a deep economic and social depression due to the pandemic, with broadband connectivity and Internet platforms ever more vital. Even as legislatures introduce hard law to combat their particular favourite online harm, continued emphasis will focus on giant platforms' self-regulatory practices. Cyberlaw has become mainstream in the most dramatic manner imaginable.

---

[129] A recent Bird & Bird study for the European Commission evaluated the first triennial review of Net Neutrality in Regulation 2015/2120 – its conclusions were that the lack of enforcement to date means it is too early to tell how useful it will be. But zero rating is more controversial in developing nations, not least because the use of zero rated WhatsApp in data-poor Brazil appears to have helped swing the Presidential election of Bolsonaro: Belli, Luca (2018) *WhatsApp Skewed Brazilian Election, Proving Social Media's Danger to Democracy*, The Conversation, 5 December, at https://theconversation.com/whatsapp-skewed-brazilian-election-proving-social-medias-danger-to-democracy-106476.

[130] Marsden, C. (2019) *Predictions 2019: Professor Chris Marsden*, Society for Computers and Law, at www.scl.org/articles/10379-predictions-2019-professor-chris-marsden.

2

Networks, Standards, and Network-and-Standard-Based Governance

Julie E. Cohen[*]

The Net interprets censorship as damage and routes around it.
— John Gilmore, Interview, *Time Magazine*

INTRODUCTION

This chapter, adapted from a forthcoming book on the evolution of legal institutions in the networked information society, situates the disruptive effects of networked digital technologies within a longer process of institutional change catalyzed by the gradual emergence of an informationalized global political economy. Over the last half century, institutions for transnational economic governance have multiplied. The landscape of world trade agreements and enforcement processes has grown increasingly complex. New structures for transnational regulation of economic activity have emerged that seem to operate according to their own rules in ways influenced by states but not controlled by them. Other new institutions, created to govern the Internet and its constituent protocols and processes, do not operate based on state representation at all. This chapter juxtaposes the various governance processes and treats them explicitly as iterations of a new – or, more precisely, emergent – networked legal-institutional form.[1] It also considers the relationship(s) between that institutional form and new platform entities that wield enormous de facto power – though not (yet) formally acknowledged sovereign authority – based on their control of infrastructures and protocols for networked, social communication.

Although networked governance institutions differ from one another in many ways, they share a common structure: They are organized as networks constituted around standards. Each of the scholarly literatures that has grown up around the various institutions described in this chapter has grasped some essential aspects of

---

[*] My thanks to Laura DeNardis, Paul Ohm, Greg Shaffer, and Kevin Werbach for their helpful comments and to Jade Coppieters, Natalie Gideon, Sherry Safavi, and Tom Spiegler for research assistance.

[1] Julie E. Cohen (2019), *Between Truth and Power: Legal Constructions of Informational Capitalism*, New York: Oxford University Press.

the network-and-standard dynamic but not that of others. Legal scholars who study transnational business regulation have interrogated the political legitimacy of networked governance processes, and they also have explored the political issues surrounding the development of international technical standards. Even so, they have paid less attention to the ways that standards bind networks together, and so the two conversations do not fully join up.[2]

Legal scholars who study "code as law" have explored how technical standards structure the markets organized around them, and they also have raised persistent, serious concerns about the relationships between and among automated enforcement, lock-step conformity, and authoritarian modes of governance. They have tended, however, to situate standards processes within market-based governance frameworks and to understand code's mandatory nature as illustrating how code *differs from* law. Consequently, they have not taken network-and-standard-based governance seriously as a new legal-institutional type.[3] And, for the most part, the different scholarly communities have not engaged in much dialogue with one another.

To posit networked governance institutions as an emergent category of legal institutions is, of course, to beg some basic questions about what makes an institution distinctively legal. One traditional set of answers has to do with the ways that the outcomes produced by such institutions are linked to rulemaking and enforcement authority. Another traditional set of answers is more explicitly normative: what makes an institution distinctively legal is its adherence to regular procedural rules and associated rule-of-law values. Communities are accountable only to themselves and markets may mete out consequences that seem arbitrary. According to a thick conception of what makes a legal institution, law's authoritarian bite is (or should be) mitigated by procedural fairness and conformance with principles of public reason.[4]

---

[2] On networked governance, see, for example, John Braithwaite (2006), "Responsive Regulation and Developing Economies," *World Development* 34(5): 884–898; Kal Raustiala (2002), "The Architecture of International Cooperation: Transgovernmental Networks and the Future of International Law," *Virginia Journal of International Law* 43(1): 1–92; Anne Marie Slaughter (2004), *A New World Order*, Princeton, NJ: Princeton University Press. On standards in transnational governance, see, for example, Panagiotis Delimatsis, ed. (2015), *The Law, Economics, and Politics of International Standardization*, New York: Cambridge University Press; Harm Schepel (2005), *The Constitution of Private Governance: Product Standards in the Regulation of Integrating Markets*, Portland, OR: Hart Publishing.

[3] See, for example, Lawrence Lessig (1998), *Code and Other Laws of Cyberspace*, New York: Basic Books; Joel R. Reidenberg (1998), "Lex Informatica: The Formulation of Information Policy Rules through Technology," *Texas Law Review* 76(3): 553–593. For a brief flirtation with the idea of Internet governance processes as "hybrid" code- and law-based institutions, see Laurence B. Solum (2009), "Models of Internet Governance," in *Internet Governance: Infrastructure and Institutions*, eds. Lee A. Bygrave and Jon Bing, New York: Oxford University Press, pp. 48–91.

[4] For a summary and analysis of the major strands of Anglo-American rule-of-law theorizing, see Richard H. Fallon, Jr. (1997), "'The Rule of Law' as a Concept in Constitutional Discourse," *Columbia Law Review* 97(1): 1–56. For a broader comparative discussion, see Mireille Hildebrandt (2016), *Smart Technologies and the End(s) of Law: Novel Entanglements of Law and Technology*, Northampton, MA: Edward Elgar, pp. 133–156.

As we are about to see, network-and-standard-based governance institutions satisfy each of these definitions in some respects while challenging them in others. For some, that means they are not law at all, but I think that answer is too pat. The shift to a networked and standard-based governance structure poses important challenges both to the realizability of rule-of-law values and to traditional conceptions of the institutional forms that those values require, but the rule-of-law constructs that legal theorists traditionally have articulated are themselves artefactual – outgrowths of the era of text-based communication and of accompanying assumptions about the feasible mechanisms for formulation, justification, and transmission of claims of authority that are now rapidly being outpaced by sociotechnical change.[5] If the new governance institutions are to serve the overarching values that traditionally have informed thicker versions of rule-of-law thinking, both institutions and constructs will need to adapt. Here, I lay some groundwork for that project.

The first part of the chapter provides an overview of the rich and varied assortment of transnational, networked governance arrangements. The next part identifies five important features of the network-and-standard-based legal-institutional form that challenge traditional understandings of how legal institutions – institutions constrained by the rule of law – ought to operate. The final part of the chapter provides a brief introduction to information platforms and the functions they perform and considers whether platforms are best understood as stakeholders or as emergent information-era sovereigns.

NETWORKS AND STANDARDS IN TRANSNATIONAL GOVERNANCE

The processes of world trade regulation, transnational business regulation, and Internet governance span many different subject areas and involve many different participants and interests. The institutions through which those forms of regulation are conducted also vary considerably from one another in terms of their rules for membership and participation. Some assign membership and participation rights to nation states while others operate differently, and some are more highly formalized than others. Even so, juxtaposing the various institutions and processes also reveals equally important ways in which they resemble one another: They are organized as networks, the networks are constituted around standards designed to facilitate and structure flows of economic and communicative activity, and the formulation and administration of those standards reflect the increasing influence of private economic power.

The global logics of production and extraction that have become characteristic of informational capitalism rely heavily on governance arrangements for facilitating crossborder flows of trade. Norms of liberalization do not simply relate to manufactured goods or even to crossborder flows of raw materials and intermediate inputs to

---

[5] Hildebrandt, cited in note 4, pp. 174–185.

more complex products. Following the important Uruguay Round of negotiations, which produced the World Trade Organization (WTO), the General Agreement on Trade in Services (GATS) and the protocol on Trade-Related Aspects of Intellectual Property Rights (TRIPS), liberalization imperatives relating to services, information, and intellectual goods have emerged as separate, powerful logics driving the articulation and expansion of trade obligations.[6] The Uruguay Round also produced two important agreements on international technical standardization that have generated increasing momentum toward scientific (and quasi-scientific) rationalization of liberalization rules.[7]

For many decades, the multilateral regime organized around the framework established under the General Agreement on Tariffs and Trade was the principal source of trade liberalization standards, but a series of rapid and pronounced shifts in the institutional structure of world trade governance began to occur in the mid-1990s. As noted earlier, the Uruguay Round produced several new multilateral instruments and a powerful new enforcement body, the WTO, which began operations in 1995. Following the Uruguay Round, however, the process of reaching new agreements under the established multilateral framework has ground to a halt, and trade negotiators have shifted their efforts toward framing and securing new bilateral free trade agreements. The thickening network of bilateral agreements has in turn shaped proposals for new multilateral and regional instruments.[8] Although the initial impetus for the turn toward bilateral and multilateral agreements negotiated outside the WTO framework came from the United States and other developed economies, the so-called Washington Consensus on trade liberalization has begun to fragment and other significant initiatives have emerged. For example, the Regional Coalition for Economic Participation (RCEP) has launched an effort to negotiate a new, pan-Asian trade protocol.

In parallel with the changes in institutional structure, the landscape of world trade governance and world trade activism also has broadened to include a more heterogeneous assortment of actors and interests. In particular, transnational corporations and business associations wield increasing de facto power in setting trade policy priorities. In part, that power flows through traditional channels of influence; powerful economic actors have long enjoyed privileged access to national policymakers and have learned to exploit that access to demand stronger and more effective

---

[6] For two very different perspectives on the origins and effects of trade liberalization logics, see William J. Drake and Kalypso Nicolaidis (1992), "Ideas, Interests, and Institutionalization: 'Trade in Services' and the Uruguay Round," *International Organization* 46(1): 37–100; Jane Kelsey (2008), *Serving Whose Interests? The Political Economy of Trade in Services*, New York: Routledge-Cavendish, pp. 76–88.

[7] See, generally, Delimatsis, ed., cited in note 2.

[8] For a sampling of perspectives on these developments, Todd Allee and Andrew Legg (2016), "Who Wrote the Rules for the Trans-Pacific Partnership?," *Research and Politics* July–September 2016: 1–9; Kyle Bagwell, Chad P. Bown, and Robert W. Staiger (2016), "Is the WTO Passé?," *Journal of Economic Literature* 54(4): 1125–1231; Nitsan Chorev and Sarah Babb (2009), "The Crisis of Neoliberalism and the Future of International Institutions: A Comparison of the IMF and the WTO," *Theory and Society* 38(5): 459–484.

protection for their global supply chains.[9] But global logics of production and extraction also translate into new networked models of influence that flow outside state-sanctioned channels, and assertions of corporate interest also have prompted experimentation with new forms of dispute resolution that allow corporations to assert claims directly against states.[10] Meanwhile, exploiting the same networked connectivity that has facilitated global concentrations of economic power, civil society groups have worked to challenge asserted failures of transparency and accountability, building alliances with one another and coordinating their efforts for maximum effect.[11]

The landscape of transnational economic governance also includes a large and varied group of regulatory arrangements, some well-established and others more emergent, that extend through and around the boundaries of nation states. Some arrangements originate with the United Nations (UN) or its member agencies. Others are cooperative ventures among national regulators or among other entities that play well-established quasi-regulatory roles. For example, financial regulators and central bankers engage in extensive, cooperative crossborder governance of financial market activities, and data protection regulators work collaboratively on various policy issues.[12] Other regulatory arrangements involve UN officials or national regulators in collaboration with private industry oversight bodies and trade associations.

As in the case of world trade, pervasive and crosscutting themes in both the theory and the practice of transnational regulation are the increasing importance of standard-setting activities and the growing power of private "stakeholders."[13] The universe of standard-making activities is large and diverse and comprises a thickening network of "soft law" that structures and coordinates economic conduct. Many of the UN's standard-making initiatives are structured as public–private collaborations.[14] Additionally, in 1996, the UN adopted a consultative process intended to give civil society organizations and other nongovernmental organizations (NGOs) a formal

---

[9] See Christopher Ingraham, "Interactive: How Companies Wield Off-the-Record Influence on Obama's Trade Policy," *Washington Post*, February 8, 2014, https://perma.cc/UPN6-DHKD.

[10] Joachim Pohl, Kekeletso Mashigo, and Alexis Nohen (2012), "Dispute Settlement Provisions in International Investment Agreements: A Large Sample Survey," OECD Working Papers on International Investment 2012/02, https://perma.cc/VN6T-GT64.

[11] Margaret E. Keck and Kathryn Sikkink, eds. (1998), *Activists Beyond Borders: Advocacy Networks in International Politics*, Ithaca, NY: Cornell University Press, pp. 1–43.

[12] Chris Brummer (2012), *Soft Law and the Global Financial System*, New York: Cambridge University Press; Charles D. Raab (2011), "Networks for Regulation: Privacy Commissioners in a Changing World," *Journal of Comparative Policy Analysis: Research and Practice* 13(2): 195–213.

[13] See, generally, Mark Raymond and Laura DeNardis (2015), "Multistakeholderism: Anatomy of an Inchoate Global Institution," *International Theory* 7(3): 572–616.

[14] Benedicte Bull and Desmonde McNeill (2007), *Development Issues in Global Governance: Public-Private Partnerships and Market Multilateralism*, New York: Routledge, pp. 1–22; Marco Schäferhoff, Sabine Campe, and Christopher Kaan (2009), "Transnational Public-Private Partnerships in International Relations: Making Sense of Concepts, Research Frameworks, and Results," *International Studies Review* 11(3): 451–474.

avenue for providing input into its policymaking processes. Business NGOs have been especially active users of that process.[15] Transnational corporations engage in standard making to facilitate their own operations and those of their global supply chains, and industry associations may work to coordinate those activities.[16] In the domain of financial governance, private transnational associations spanning fields from securities to insurance to accounting perform a wide variety of governance functions.[17]

Also notably, the outputs of both private and public–private standard-making processes have begun to migrate into the domain of world trade. In particular, new bilateral and multilateral trade agreements covering labor, environmental regulation, and corporate social responsibility often refer to such standards.[18] As a result, standard-making activities constitute a new and fruitful avenue for private economic actors wanting to shape the formulation of trade provisions intended to delineate the appropriate reach of domestic protective mandates.

A final important site of transnational legal-institutional entrepreneurship is the Internet and its constituent protocols and processes. The most prominent governance arrangements for the Internet are formally non-state-based and multistakeholder-oriented. The Internet Engineering Task Force (IETF), a voluntary membership organization of computer technologists, oversees the continuing evolution of the Internet's foundational standards for information transmission, and the Internet Corporation for Assigned Names and Numbers (ICANN), a not-for-profit transnational governance corporation chartered under California law, oversees governance of the domain name system. An assortment of other organizations – some formally multilateral and some private – also play important roles, however. For example, the International Telecommunications Union, a UN-affiliated body, superintends standards for wireless telephony, and the Institute of Electrical and Electronic Engineers, a technical professional organization, coordinates the evolution of standards for wireless interconnection. The databases that map human-readable domain names to network addresses are maintained by a small group of entities – including

---

[15] Melissa J. Durkee (2017), "Astroturf Activism," *Stanford Law Review* 69(1): 201–268; Melissa J. Durkee (2018), "International Lobbying Law," *Yale Law Journal* 127(7): 1742–1826.

[16] Klaas Hendrik Eller (2017), "Private Governance of Global Value Chains from Within: Lessons for Transnational Law," *Transnational Legal Theory* 8 (3): 296–329; Li-Wen Lin, "Legal Transplants through Private Contracting: Codes of Vendor Conduct in Global Supply Chains as an Example," *American Journal of Comparative Law* 57(3) (2009): 711–744; Schepel, *The Constitution of Private Governance*, cited in note 2.

[17] Heather McKeen-Edwards and Tony Porter (2013), *Transnational Financial Associations and the Governance of Global Finance: Assembling Wealth and Power*, New York: Routledge.

[18] See, for example, Jordi Agusti-Panareda, Franz Christian Ebert, and Desiree LeClerq (2015), "ILO Labor Standards and Trade Agreements: A Case for Consistency," *Comparative Labor Law and Policy Journal* 36(2): 347–380; Orr Karassin and Oren Perez (2018), "Shifting between Public and Private: The Reconfiguration of Global Environmental Regulation," *Indiana Journal of Global Legal Studies* 25(1): 97–130; Kevin Kolben (2011), "Transnational Labor Regulation and the Limits of Governance," *Theoretical Inquiries in Law* 12(2): 403–437.

universities, research consortia, government entities, and a few private corporations – pursuant to contracts with the Internet Assigned Numbers Authority, an entity for many years overseen by the US Department of Commerce and now administered by an affiliate of ICANN.[19]

Technical standard making is front and center in Internet governance, but Internet governance arrangements also play more substantive and comprehensive roles in the governance of global networked communications, and do so via increasingly elaborate institutional structures.[20] Under pressure from a diverse mix of global stakeholders, ICANN has developed regularized pathways for participation, including formal consultative procedures for national governments and civil society organizations.[21] At its inception, the IETF was a self-selected community of volunteers that rejected "kings, presidents, and voting" in favor of "rough consensus and running code."[22] Today, although membership remains voluntary and policy-making consensus-based, it comprises two principal divisions made up of over one hundred working groups, overseen by two steering groups and advised by two different boards. Working groups follow elaborate protocols for documenting their activities, communicating with other groups, and reporting to the steering groups and advisory boards. There is a process (so far, never used) for administrative appeals. At the same time, as in the cases of trade and transnational economic regulation, private economic power also plays a highly visible role in Internet governance. Private technology firms are well-represented in myriad working groups and steering committees, and as the Internet's constitutive liberalization norms have been filtered through the lens of multistakeholder-based institutional design, they have produced institutional responses optimized to the needs of the most active and well-resourced stakeholders.[23]

NETWORKS, STANDARDS, AND THE RULE OF LAW: FIVE PROBLEMATICS

A *network* is a mode of organization in which hubs and nodes structure the flows of transactions and interactions. Some commentators have characterized structures for

---

[19] On the complexity of assemblages for Internet namespace and protocol governance, see generally Laura DeNardis (2014), *The Global War for Internet Governance*, New Haven, CT: Yale University Press, pp. 45–55, 63–76.

[20] For comprehensive refutations of the view that Internet governance is a purely technical activity, see Laura DeNardis (2009), *Protocol Politics: The Globalization of Internet Governance*, Cambridge, MA: MIT Press; DeNardis, cited in note 19; Milton Mueller (2004), *Ruling the Root: Internet Governance and the Taming of Cyberspace*, Cambridge, Mass: MIT Press. See also Roger Cotterrell (2012), "What Is Transnational Law?," *Law and Social Inquiry* 37(2): 500–524.

[21] On the evolving civil society role, see Stefania Milan and Niels ten Oever (2017), "Coding and Encoding Rights in Internet Infrastructure," *Internet Policy Review* 6(1). On the involvement of governments and on ICANN's design more generally, see Raymond and DeNardis, cited in note 13.

[22] Andrew L. Russell (2006), "'Rough Consensus and Running Code' and the Internet-OSI Standards War," *IEEE Annals of the History of Computing* 28(3): 48–61.

[23] DeNardis, cited in note 19, pp. 70–71, 226–230; Raymond and DeNardis, cited in note 13.

networked participation and governance as radically democratizing, while others have worried that the absence of definite chains of command undermines democratic accountability.[24] Important recent books about power and global political economy by David Singh Grewal and Manuel Castells explore the importance of networked organization for political economy generally, articulating new theoretical models of networked social, political, and communication power.[25] Network-and-standard-based governance arrangements, however, are not simply networks; they are also institutions.[26] This section seeks to identify with greater precision the various points of mismatch between the rule-of-law tradition in legal theory and the operation of the network-and-standard-based legal-institutional form. It begins by reconsidering two points of conventional wisdom about network organization and its relationship to legal power.

First, the assertion that network organization is inherently more democratic than other forms of organization because it facilitates the expression and circulation of dissenting views is open to serious question. It is true that, because network organization is nonhierarchical, even an enormously powerful hub cannot prevent information from flowing around it through other nodes.[27] Within networked governance arrangements, however, the ability to navigate interruptions works most reliably to the benefit of the powerful. The same networked affordances that enable the dissident to evade the censor also enable economically or politically dominant parties to circumvent inconvenient negotiating stalemates and avoid inconvenient but localized regulatory burdens. *Within networked governance arrangements, power interprets regulatory resistance as damage and routes around it.*

Second, the observation that network organization is nonhierarchical can be somewhat misleading. From an internal perspective, network organization around a standard imposes a form of hierarchical ordering that inheres in the standard itself. If other networks organized around other standards are available that may not matter much. But a standard invested with legal significance is not *just* a standard because

---

[24] Well-known expressions of network optimism include Yochai Benkler (2006), *The Wealth of Networks: How Social Production Transforms Markets and Freedom*, New Haven, CT: Yale University Press; Anupam Chander (2013), *The Electronic Silk Road: How the Web Binds the World Together in Commerce*, New Haven, CT : Yale University Press; Joshua Cohen and Charles F. Sabel, "Global Democracy?," *N.Y.U. Journal of International Law & Politics* 37(4): 763–797. More measured evaluations include Jack Goldsmith and Tim Wu (2008), *Who Controls the Internet? Illusions of a Borderless World*, New York: Oxford University Press; Laurence R. Helfer (2004), "Regime Shifting: The TRIPs Agreement and New Dynamics of International Intellectual Property Lawmaking," *Yale Journal of International Law* 29(1): 1–84; Anna di Robilant (2006), "Genealogies of Soft Law," *American Journal of Comparative Law* 54(3): 499–554.

[25] David Singh Grewal (2008), *Network Power: The Social Dynamics of Globalization*, New Haven, CT: Yale University Press; Manuel Castells (2009), *Communication Power*, New York: Oxford University Press.

[26] See, generally, Milton L. Mueller (2010), *Nations and States: The Global Politics of Internet Governance*, Cambridge, MA: MIT Press, pp. 41–46.

[27] On network organization generally, see Albert-Laszlo Barabasi (2002), *Linked: The New Science of Networks*, Cambridge, MA: Perseus Publishing.

participants lack the authority to depart from it. So too with a standard, such as the basic Internet protocol, that exacts universal adherence as a practical matter. Network organization under conditions of legally or practically mandated standardization may be quite exacting as to the forms of compliance, and it also may afford new opportunities for the exercise of economic and political power. From the perspective of traditional legal theory, this point is easy to miss because legal theory traditionally has drawn a distinction between rules and standards that drives in the opposite direction. Within that scholarly tradition, "rules" are granular and demand precise compliance, while "standards" are more flexible and are fleshed out via norms and interpretative conventions.[28] Network organization under conditions of legally or practically mandated standardization is a different creature entirely.

The powerful critiques of transnational governance arrangements that have emerged within legal scholarship still have not fully assimilated the hybridity of the network-and-standard-based legal-institutional form. Both the ability of power to route around inconvenient regulatory resistance and the relocation of authority into the standard strain traditional accounts of *law*, reliably eliciting institutional features that seem very different from those that a system of the rule of law would require. The same developments also strain conventional understandings of *standards* and *standardization*, reliably foreclosing the kinds of pathway that facilitate competition, correction, and stabilization in the contexts where standards are more usually studied. It has become vitally important to understand the ways that the intersecting vectors of governance, law, and standardization are transforming one another. This section identifies five important directions for inquiry, which relate to the nature of standard-making authority, the available pathways for contesting and changing the reigning standard, the available pathways for coopting governance mechanisms to advance authoritarian political and geopolitical interests, the mechanisms for political accountability, and the vernaculars in which mandatory standards are articulated, applied, and contested.

Dominance as Hegemony: The Problem of Unchecked Authority

One distinctive characteristic of emergent global networked legal-institutional arrangements is the way that network-and-standard-based organization reshapes the exercise of lawmaking authority. Within such arrangements, a dominant party's ability to shape policy is both more absolute than it typically is within more traditional legal settings and more immediate than it typically is in technology standards markets. When instituted against a background of vastly unequal geopolitical power, network organization under conditions of mandated standardization has resulted in policy hegemony relatively unchecked by political or structural constraints.

---

[28] Duncan Kennedy (1976), "Form and Substance in Private Law Adjudication," *Harvard Law Review* 89(8): 1685–1778; Pierre Schlag (1985), "Rules and Standards," *UCLA Law Review* 33(2): 379–430.

In democratic societies with rule-of-law traditions, legal institutions are recognizable as such in part because of their adherence to regular, reasoned processes for making policy and for contesting policy choices. This is not to suggest that such processes always work perfectly or even well. But certain high-level constraints on institutional behavior – in particular, principles of separation of powers and procedural due process and commitments to giving reasons for official actions – also have been widely acknowledged in democratic societies.

Dominance in technology standards markets confronts different kinds of limit. Although networks do exhibit lock-in effects, various forms of competition remain possible (we will consider those forms more closely in the next section).[29] Additionally, in paradigmatic, discrete technology standards markets, the connection between market dominance and policy dominance tends to be indirect. The standards governing such matters as the layout of a typewriter keyboard or the arrangement of prongs on an appliance plug are thoroughly agnostic as to their users' political beliefs and policy commitments. Many contemporary disagreements over technology policy arise precisely because the emergence of networked information and communications technologies has set protocol and policy on converging paths.

Network-and-standard-based legal-institutional arrangements connect protocol and policy directly to one another and eliminate separation between them. Within such arrangements, the point of mandated standardization is exactly to specify the kinds of flow that must, may, and may not travel via the network. The policy is the standard and vice versa, and that equivalence sets up the two interlocking dynamics that produce policy hegemony. On one hand, a dominant network enjoys network power – which David Grewal defines as the self-reinforcing power of a dominant network and Manuel Castells explains as a power that is "exercised not by exclusion from the networks, but by the imposition of the rules of inclusion" – simply by virtue of its dominance.[30] On the other, if a particular hub within a dominant network exercises disproportionate control over the content of the standard, then networked organization will amplify that hub's authority to set policy and legally mandated standardization will amplify it still further.

Developments in the domains of world trade governance and transnational business regulation over the second half of the twentieth century mapped straightforwardly to this lock-in-based theoretical model (we will consider some more recent anomalies in the next section), enabling the consolidation of US policy hegemony across a wide and varied set of domains.[31] The case of Internet governance is more complicated. US observers, in particular, tend to think that Internet governance

---

[29] On network lock-in, see Michael L. Katz and Carl Shapiro (1985), "Network Externalities, Competition, and Compatibility," *American Economic Review* 75(3): 424–440.

[30] Grewal, cited in note 25, pp. 4–8; Castells, cited in note 25, p. 43.

[31] See generally John Braithwaite and Peter Drahos (2000), *Global Business Regulation*, New York: Cambridge University Press.

processes have avoided the worst excesses of US policy hegemony precisely because of their sui generis, multistakeholder design. As noted earlier, however, private technology companies, including especially the dominant US technology firms, wield considerable influence within Internet governance processes, and the turn to multistakeholderism reflects a long-standing and largely bipartisan preference in the United States for a strong private-sector role in Internet governance.[32] It is unsurprising, then, that the responses of marquee institutions such as ICANN and the IETF to the policy problems that have repeatedly bedeviled them – from privacy and surveillance to content regulation and censorship to intellectual property enforcement to network security – have tended to reflect the particular norms of flow enshrined in US information law and policy.

Legal Standards Wars: The Problem of Regulatory Arbitrage

A second striking characteristic of emerging global network-and-standard-based legal-institutional arrangements relates to the mechanisms available for changing a governing standard. On one hand, mandated standardization intensifies lock-in to the current standard by foreclosing many of the pathways for change that ordinarily would exist. On the other, it incentivizes efforts at regulatory disintermediation by those favoring a different or modified standard, and those efforts may gain purchase to the extent that the network remains accessible via new points of interconnection.

It is useful to begin by considering the mechanisms through which standards can change over time in market settings. Carl Shapiro and Hal Varian distinguish between evolution and revolution, with the former consisting of gradual change while maintaining backward compatibility with the original standard and the latter involving a sharp, disjunctive break between new and old standards.[33] Such changes may be implemented cooperatively, or two (or more) parties may seek conflicting changes, as in the case of the Blu Ray and HD DVD standards for digital video storage and playback, which maintained backward compatibility with the regular DVD format but were incompatible with one another. If the parties cannot agree on which course is best, a standards war may ensue.

In struggles to shape the future of a legally mandated standard, the mandatory structure of networked legal-institutional arrangements narrows the universe of possible outcomes. Gradual evolution is most feasible when it moves in directions that are compatible with the dominant standard's underlying policy commitments. In theory, gradual retrenchment from the hegemonic norm is also possible; in practice, however, one cannot fall below the threshold level of compliance that the standard requires unless there is cooperative agreement to extend forgiveness.

---

[32] Kal Raustiala (2016), "Governing the Internet," *American Journal of International Law* 110(3): 491–503; see also Raymond and DeNardis, cited in note 13.

[33] Carl Shapiro and Hal R. Varian (1999), "The Art of Standards Wars," *California Management Review* 41(2): 8–32.

Revolution against a background of mandated standardization is more difficult still. Absent cooperative agreement to depart from the dominant standard, revolutionary change – or, in the language of technologists, forking the standard – requires not only confidence in one's installed base but also willingness to court diplomatic or even geopolitical instability. In the domain of world trade, disjunctive changes without backward compatibility risk starting trade wars; in the various domains of transnational business regulation, departure or threatened departure from agreed conventions can roil markets and create diplomatic incidents. Internet governance institutions have powerful norms against forking network standards. When such proposals have originated – generally from states that are geopolitical outsiders – they have commanded little support and have been unable to generate momentum.[34] A systemic shock can create impetus for a mutually agreed disjunctive break; so, for example, the 2008 financial crisis generated the momentum required to tighten standards for measuring bank capital adequacy.[35] Absent such a shock, however, revolutionary change is unlikely.

Standards wars can be horizontal or vertical, however, and this means that even dominant standards are characterized by their potential amenability to disintermediation by a rival standard that sits closer to the relevant activity. So, for example, although Microsoft's Windows operating system still dominates the personal computing market, it is no longer the most important interface for those wishing to market applications to personal computer users. Web browsers provide an alternative interface for many applications, as do social networks and mobile operating systems. More recently still, the "Internet of things" and the emergent market for smart home assistants have opened new channels for companies seeking to become the intermediary of choice for as many online interactions as possible.

Networked governance arrangements organized around legally mandated standardization are similarly vulnerable to disintermediation by adjacent governance arrangements. So, for example, when developing nations began to balk at additional extensions to the TRIPS agreement that they saw as benefiting developed economies, US trade negotiators simply routed around the WTO, negotiating new bilateral and multilateral agreements incorporating the stronger provisions they wanted to see enshrined as new network standards. Developing nations fought back, gradually organizing around a proposed "development agenda" for the World Intellectual Property Organization (WIPO), a constituent body of the United Nations. The WIPO Development Agenda thereby briefly became an entry in an intellectual property standards war. Developing nations' effort at "regime shifting" enjoyed only temporary success, however, because developed countries returned to WIPO in

---

[34] See, generally, Daya Kishan Thussu (2015), "Digital BRICS: Building a NWICO 2.0?", in *Mapping BRICS Media*, eds. Kaarle Nordenstreng and Daya Kishan Thussu, New York: Routledge, pp. 242–263; see also Tracy Staedter, "Why Russia Is Building Its Own Internet," *IEEE Spectrum*, January 17, 2018, https://perma.cc/6UU4-NNJG.

[35] See Brummer, cited in note 12, pp. 233–265.

force and asserted their own interests.[36] Meanwhile, the copyright industries of the Global North have appropriated regime-shifting tactics to their own ends, working to introduce interdiction mandates directly into arrangements for Internet governance.[37]

As a different example, consider evolving arrangements for governance of cross-border transfers of personal information. The European Union has worked to export its high standards for personal data protection to the rest of the world, whereas parties seeking greater liberalization – including especially dominant global platform firms headquartered in the US – have shifted their emphasis toward inserting strengthened mandates for crossborder flow into bilateral and multilateral trade agreements, including especially agreements involving the Asian nations that are increasingly significant players in the emerging crossborder data servicing economy.[38] Privacy NGOs have worked to thwart trade workarounds for data protection obligations, but that project has become more difficult as the center of gravity has shifted into trade governance, which had not traditionally been a focus of transnational privacy activism, and toward Asia, where civil society organizations focused on privacy and data protection have not traditionally had a significant presence. And here again, Internet governance has emerged as an important focus of regime shifting efforts; for example, even European data protection authorities have largely acquiesced in ICANN's continuing failure to require adequate privacy protections for WHOIS registry data.[39] Each of these developments destabilizes settled expectations about where authority to regulate crossborder transfers of personal data resides and about what the reigning standard requires.

In theory, at least, a system of the rule of law is not supposed to work this way. An important principle associated with the ideal of the rule of law is that legal rules should be applied consistently, and the ideal of consistency in turn implies a degree of constancy. In fact, those ideals have been under siege since the complex legal ecologies of the late twentieth century began to offer a wider and more complex

[36] Laurence R. Helfer (2004), "Regime Shifting: The TRIPs Agreement and New Dynamics of International Intellectual Property Lawmaking," *Yale Journal of International Law* 29(1): 1–84.

[37] Annemarie Bridy, (2017) "Notice and Takedown in the Domain Name System: ICANN's Ambivalent Drift into Online Content Regulation," *Washington and Lee Law Review* 74 (3): 1345–1388; Peter Bright, "DRM for HTML5 Finally Makes It as an Official W3C Recommendation," *ArsTechnica*, September 18, 2017, https://perma.cc/Z9P6-2JLW.

[38] For analyses of the interplay between data protection and multilateral trade instruments, see Svetlana Yakovleva and Kristina Irion (2016), "The Best of Both Worlds? Free Trade in Services, and EU Law on Privacy and Data Protection," *European Data Protection Law Review* 2(26): 191–208; Graham Greenleaf (2017), "Free Trade Agreements and Data Privacy: Future Perils of Faustian Bargains," in *Transatlantic Data Privacy Relations as a Challenge for Democracy*, eds. Dan Svantesson and Dariusz Kloza, Antwerp: Intersentia, pp. 181–212; Graham Greenleaf (2018), "Looming Free Trade Agreements Pose Threats to Privacy," *International Report: Privacy Laws & Business* 152: 123–127.

[39] Stephanie E. Perrin (2018), "The Struggle for WHOIS Privacy: Understanding the Standoff between ICANN and the World's Data Protection Authorities," unpublished dissertation, Faculty of Information, University of Toronto, pp. 243–253.

array of possibilities for regulatory arbitrage than those within which the rule-of-law ideal was first articulated. Even so, in domestic settings each strategy confronts built-in limits. At the end of the day, there is an institutional actor with the power to exercise jurisdiction over the challenged conduct, to superintend a reasoned but finite process of contestation, and to say what the law is. Relative to that benchmark, the new networked governance arrangements manifest both frustrating path dependence and a destabilizing failure of finality.

Network Power and Moral Hazard: The Problem of the Authoritarian End Run

A third distinctive attribute of global network-and-standard-based governance arrangements is a particular kind of moral hazard that concerns the relative importance of economic and political liberalization. As economic liberalization has become the primary driver of innovation in transnational legal ordering, and the overriding importance often ascribed to facilitating flows of crossborder economic activity sets up the conditions for a dynamic that I will call the authoritarian end run. In brief, an authoritarian regime wishing to stint its liberalization obligations in the interest of maintaining its political control often may do so with impunity because of the dominant network's interest in maintaining and consolidating its economic dominance.

Recall that network power operates by harnessing and disciplining the desire for inclusion. That mechanism presents tradeoffs for the policy hegemon – the party that enjoys dominant hub status – as well as for other network participants. Simply put, there are downsides to sanctioning or expelling members for standards violations, and those downsides may lead both the policy hegemon and other network participants to overlook certain types of infraction – especially those that can plausibly be characterized as purely domestic in scope – to preserve flows of goods, services, and information across borders and within corporate supply chains. So, for example, developed nations historically have been willing to minimize the importance of certain labor practices in developing countries, to overlook local restrictions on religious and press freedoms, and to excuse certain endemic forms of gender discrimination.[40]

To the extent that the authoritarian end run entails subverting the dominant standard for purposes dictated by conflicting political goals, it is broadly consistent with the dynamic of the legal standards war described in the previous section, but it is also different. In the short term, it is not an exit strategy but rather a shirking strategy available to entities lacking the power or the motivation to provoke a standards war. In the longer term, it is a strategy for alternative network making around standards that blend elements of economic liberalization with elements of

---

[40] Anu Bradford and Eric A. Posner (2011), "Universal Exceptionalism in International Law," *Harvard International Law Journal* 52(1): 3–54, 36.

mercantilist central planning and political control. Above all else, authoritarian states seek to control unwanted flows of information within and across their borders.

In principle, any state with sufficient economic and geopolitical power can wield what Manuel Castells calls network-making power – or the power to constitute its own network by establishing alternative conditions of interconnection.[41] In the contemporary geopolitical landscape, the principal author of the authoritarian end run is China. Chinese trade policy and information technology policy have emerged as powerful and mutually reinforcing components of a larger strategy for pursuing dominance of standards for global economic and technical exchange. The Chinese program for physical infrastructure development, now known in English as the Belt and Road initiative, seeks to facilitate flows of labor, goods, and raw materials across continents and oceans under conditions that advance Chinese economic interests.[42] The Chinese information technology sector has grown rapidly and now includes two firms that rank among the world's twenty largest: search and social networking firm Tencent and e-commerce giant Alibaba.[43]

As the Chinese information technology sector has matured and turned toward new markets, affordances for both economic development and state control of communications infrastructure play key roles. Tencent, Alibaba, and other Chinese platform companies have begun to make inroads in developing markets across Asia, Africa, and the Middle East, and Chinese hardware manufactures like Huawei and Xiaomi sell equipment ranging from backbone servers to mobile phones across the developing world. In terms of development, capabilities for mobile payment, banking, and credit have driven rapid penetration within populations hungry for modernization.[44] For client states inclined to control information flows to their own populations, meanwhile, Chinese firms' relative willingness to work with host governments to implement filtering and surveillance in their own markets is a selling point.[45] The combined result of these technology policy initiatives is "a geopolitical enclave in which computational architectures and informational actors are coming together into what could be deservedly termed the Red Stack" – a networked communications infrastructure offering the ability to layer

[41] Castells, cited in note 25, pp. 45–46.
[42] Yiping Huang (2016), "Understanding China's Belt & Road Initiative: Motivation, Framework and Assessment," *China Economic Review* 40: 314–321; Dane Chamorro, "Belt and Road: China's Strategy to Capture Supply Chains from Guangzhou to Greece," *Forbes*, December 21, 2017, https://perma.cc/4LYV-EFNW.
[43] PwC, "Global Top 100 Companies by Market Capitalisation," March 31, 2017, 35, https://perma.cc/8TNB-TBCA.
[44] McKinsey Global Institute, "China's Digital Economy: A Leading Global Force," August 2017, https://perma.cc/X4BD-75TB; Charles Arthur, "The Chinese Tech Companies Poised to Dominate the World," *Guardian*, June 3, 2014, https://perma.cc/W7TP-E89Z.
[45] Samm Sacks, "Beijing Wants to Rewrite the Rules of the Internet," *Atlantic*, June 18, 2018, https://perma.cc/YFY8-KYM5.

separation and control on top of the underlying connectivity afforded by the basic Internet protocols.[46]

The authoritarian end run has an ambivalent relationship to the rule of law. On one hand, both Chinese trade policy and Chinese technology policy emphasize centralized control by state institutions. One byproduct of China's accession to membership in the WTO and its movement toward greater economic liberalization has been modernization of domestic courts and other formal governance institutions along the lines that the WTO's obligations require. To the extent that concerns about the rule of law in the era of networked governance hinge on the disintegration of sovereign authority, one might argue that some components of the Chinese strategy address those concerns. On the other, the rule-of-law construct that Chinese global governance initiatives enshrine is thin, emphasizing regularity and predictability over transparency and contestability – features that Chinese Internet policy, in particular, works to eliminate.

Extreme Multistakeholderism: The Problem of Public Accountability

A fourth striking characteristic shared by the processes described in this chapter is their unusual mechanisms for political accountability. Emergent networked governance arrangements are strikingly inhospitable to traditional mechanisms for instilling accountability within legal institutions, and they have invited powerful new variations on rent seeking by nonstate actors. That development marks the emergence of a new model of public participation in governance, which I will call extreme multistakeholderism. It is amenable to practice by those entities or coalitions that are both sufficiently well-resourced to monitor governance processes unfolding concurrently at multiple sites and sufficiently well-connected to gain access to processes and documents that may be shrouded in secrecy.

In theory, many of the transnational regulatory processes described in this chapter incorporate delegation-based accountability mechanisms.[47] In the US for example, trade policy is the domain of the executive, and the executive in turn is accountable to the Senate and to the voting public. Interventions in transnational business regulatory processes also emanate from the executive branch and its constituent agencies and commissions. In practice, however, both trade policy processes and transnational regulatory processes are far more accountable to special interests than to their official constituencies. In the U.S., members of the industries affected by trade agreements sit on trade advisory councils that operate outside the purview of open-government laws, and new "fast-track" procedures have been devised to move newly ratified agreements through the congressional approval process; both

---

[46] Gabriele de Seta, "Into the Red Stack," *Hong Kong Review of Books*, April 17, 2018, https://perma.cc/J5VD-7SH3.

[47] Ruth W. Grant and Robert O. Keohane (2005), "Accountability and Abuses of Power in World Politics," *American Political Science Review* 99(1): 29–43.

arrangements are thought to be justified by the executive's broad authority to conduct diplomatic relations with foreign countries.[48] Transnational regulatory processes are procedurally entrepreneurial and may also incorporate substantial privatization components, so the traditional mechanisms for executive branch accountability tend not to reach them directly. The courts, for their part, are inclined to regard both trade policy choices and transnational regulatory undertakings as nonjusticiable because they involve matters committed to the discretion of political actors.[49]

Internet governance processes that rely on delegation-based accountability work differently and somewhat better. The particular form of incorporation chosen for ICANN – that of a Californian public benefit corporation – imposes a set of accountability mandates that include both stakeholder representation and transparency obligations. ICANN has adopted a variety of measures to keep its constituencies informed, some taken from the corporate toolkit (e.g., quarterly performance calls) and others from the transnational governance toolkit (e.g., multilingual reporting).[50] In practice, however, the stakeholder-based model for public input has produced – and was intended to produce – a significant policy tilt toward relatively well-resourced interests concerned chiefly with protection of trademarks and other intellectual property and more recently also concerned with access to the rich trove of personal information contained in WHOIS domain registry databases.[51]

The other traditional mechanism for political accountability involves direct participation. Some Internet standards governance arrangements adopt this model, but here too underlying patterns of power and access can operate to impede participatory democracy. Although membership in the IETF and a number of other technical professional organizations active in Internet standard making is exercised on an individual basis, as a practical matter participation is heavily corporatized. The World Wide Web Consortium, a private membership organization that oversees the development of the Web's hypertext protocols, has different tiers of membership for different types of stakeholder, with large technology corporations paying the highest fees and wielding corresponding levels of clout.

From a theoretical perspective, these developments are unsurprising. Within networked governance arrangements, one would expect both assertions of power and assertions of counterpower to exhibit returns to scale.[52] The lengthy, intricate, and globally distributed nature of transnational legal-institutional processes sets an effective lower bound on the kinds of entity that can participate effectively. The

---

[48] Margot E. Kaminski (2014), "The Capture of International Intellectual Property Law through the U.S. Trade Regime," *Southern California Law Review* 87(4): 977–1052.

[49] For an illustrative discussion, see Golan v. Holder, 565 U.S. 302, 335–336 (2012).

[50] ICANN, "Accountability and Transparency," https://www.icann.org/resources/accountability.

[51] Mueller, *Ruling the Root*, cited in note 20; DeNardis, *The Global War for Internet Governance*, cited in note 19; Perrin, cited in note 39.

[52] In general, the innovations that "go viral" within networks are those originating from more connected nodes within the network. See Barabasi, cited in note 27, pp. 131–135.

affordances of networked media and communication infrastructures offset geographical limits to some extent but also favor those best positioned to make use of them to coordinate interventions across multiple, farflung sites. Civil society organizations too have learned to play the multistakeholder game, forming transnational networks that enable them to pool their resources and act cooperatively, but corporate actors and business NGOs, including the International Chamber of Commerce and the International Trademark Owners Association, have followed suit, mobilizing the comparatively greater resources of their memberships to shift policymaking efforts into more congenial arenas.[53]

The flipside of procedures guaranteeing both orderly contestation and finality is a political culture prepared to honor their requirements and abide by their results. The political culture of extreme multistakeholderism is different. The rewards flow to those who can access the most up-to-date information and marshal it most effectively on a global playing field. Those who lack comparable resources are doomed to play catch-up, continually pursuing a threshold of influence that remains out of reach.

Technocracy and Its Discontents: The Problem of Publicly Available Law

A final distinctive attribute of emergent arrangements for global business governance and global network governance is their highly technocratic character. Some legal scholars who study transnational regulatory processes have worried that those processes lend themselves to capture by elites.[54] It is helpful to understand that tendency as bound up with essential but imperfectly assimilated sociotechnical shifts. The mandated standards around which networked legal institutions are organized exemplify an approach that scholars who study sociotechnical assemblages for financial regulation have called the numericization of governance.[55] They are developed via expert proceedings and encoded in lengthy, highly technical specifications whose implementation requires ongoing supervision by cadres of managerial elites.

The particular expert register in which transnational governance is conducted varies from setting to setting. In the Internet governance context, the language of governance is produced by and for computer scientists and engineers. In world trade governance and transnational financial regulation, the language of governance is predominantly economic and, particularly in financial governance settings, highly quantitative. Environmental and food and drug regulatory processes incorporate

---

[53] Durkee, "Astroturf Activism," cited in note 15.

[54] For an especially compelling articulation of this worry, see David Kennedy (2014), "Law and the Political Economy of the World," in Grainne de Burca, Claire Kilpatrick, and Joanne Scott, eds., *Critical Legal Perspectives on Global Governance: Liber Amicorum David M. Trubek*, Portland, OR: Hart Publishing, pp. 65–102.

[55] Hans Krause Hansen and Tony Porter (2012), "What Do Numbers Do in Transnational Governance?," *International Political Sociology* 6(4): 409–426.

technical vernaculars from fields such as climate science, marine ecology, and epidemiology. In other transnational settings, the prevailing vernacular is more generally managerial. For example, detailed operational standards geared to the rhythms of organizational processes and to the benchmarks and reporting conventions used by professional auditors are increasingly common features of transnational environmental and labor regulation.[56]

In each case, reliance on technical vernaculars produces both some obvious entry barriers and some less obvious obstacles to broadly democratic policymaking. Even where participation in network governance processes is formally open to all comers, as in the case of the IETF's working groups, the learning curve for those without appropriate technical facility is often steep. Civil society organizations in particular have struggled to attain technical parity with their better-resourced counterparts in the business and technology communities.[57] Expertise is required, as well, to understand the ways in which methods and analytical commitments that are ostensibly technical also implicate, reflect, reinforce, and sometimes predetermine policy commitments. Disentangling fact from value and understanding the social construction of technology are perennial problems in science and technology policy, but network organization under mandated standardization exacerbates them.[58] As substantive policy choices are folded into mandated standards, they become more and more difficult to disentangle, and certain types of especially incommensurable concern – for example, concerns relating to development of capabilities for human flourishing and protection of fundamental rights – may seem to disappear altogether.[59]

A corollary is that, as technocratic oversight of regulatory functions becomes more solidly entrenched, the (explicit or implicit) political commitments of the expert regulators themselves may become more difficult to identify, contest, and dislodge. So, for example, the pathbreaking "end-to-end" design of technical protocols for the Internet reflected solid technical judgment about robustness to certain kinds of disruption and also encoded the generally libertarian commitments of the original Internet pioneers. As a result, although the Internet overall is extraordinarily resistant

---

[56] For a detailed example, see Kernaghan Webb (2015), "ISO 26000 Social Responsibility Standard as 'Proto Law' and a New Form of Global Custom: Positioning ISO 26000 in the Emerging Transnational Regulatory Governance Rule Instrument Architecture," *Transnational Legal Theory* 6(2): 466–500.

[57] Timothy H. Edgar (2017), *Beyond Snowden: Privacy, Mass Surveillance, and the Struggle to Reform the NSA*, Washington, DC: Brookings Institution Press, p. 123.

[58] See, generally, Sheila Jasanoff (1990), *The Fifth Branch: Science Advisers as Policymakers*, Cambridge, MA: Harvard University Press.

[59] See Sakiko Fukuda-Parr (2011), "The Metrics of Human Rights: Complementarities of the Human Development and Capabilities Approach," *Journal of Human Development and Capabilities* 12(1): 73–89; Sakiko Fukuda-Parr and Alicia Yamin (2013), "The Power of Numbers: A Critical Review of MDG Targets for Human Development and Human Rights," *Development* 56(1): 58–65; AnnJanette Rosga and Margaret Satterthwaite (2009), "The Trust in Indicators: Measuring Human Rights," *Berkeley Journal of International Law* 27(2): 253–315.

to disruptions of service, it has proved extraordinarily hospitable to other kinds of threat that exploit networked interconnection.[60] The discourses of risk management and cost-benefit analysis that play increasingly important roles in financial and environmental regulation charge can fail to reckon adequately with certain kinds of large systemic threat.[61] In the domain of world trade, the leading theoretical models generally have viewed liberalization as an unqualified good and have tended to discount evidence suggesting that it is also important to provide for equitable distribution and domestic capability building.[62]

An important element of the rule-of-law ideal is commitment to publicly accessible rules and publicly accessible reasoning about the justifications for official decisions. From that perspective, network organization under mandated standardization creates a paradox: Effective control of highly informationalized processes requires governance institutions capable of responding in kind, but the very process of optimizing regulatory controls to highly informationalized processes makes governance arrangements more opaque and less accountable to broader global publics.

PLATFORMS AS EMERGENT TRANSNATIONAL SOVEREIGNS?

So far, the discussion has presumed that, within networked governance arrangements, nonstate entities act as stakeholders but only sovereign states function as policy hubs. But that implicit division of roles ignores both the leveling effects of network logics and the amenability of standards to disintermediation. Commentators have long puzzled over the undeniable fact that, although they are nominally stakeholders in transnational networked governance processes, transnational corporations speak with increasingly independent voices in their relationships with sovereign states and also wield considerable governance authority of their own over globally distributed labor and supply chains.[63] Dominant global platform firms – firms that have attained positions as dominant intermediaries within the

---

[60] For a prescient early treatment of this problem, see Jonathan Zittrain (2008), *The Future of the Internet—And How to Stop It*, New Haven, CT: Yale University Press, 36–57.

[61] See, for example, Frank Ackerman, Lisa Heinzerling, and Rachel Massey (2005), "Applying Cost-Benefit to Past Decisions: Was Environmental Protection Ever a Good Idea?," *Administrative Law Review* 57(1): 155–192; Kenneth A. Bamberger (2010), "Technologies of Compliance: Risk and Regulation in a Digital Age," *Texas Law Review* 88(4): 669–740; James Fanto (2009), "Anticipating the Unthinkable: The Adequacy of Risk Management in Finance and Environmental Studies," *Wake Forest Law Review* 44(3): 731–756.

[62] William Krist (2013), *Globalization and America's Trade Agreements*, Washington, DC: Woodrow Wilson Center Press with Johns Hopkins University Press; Erik Reinert (2007), *How Rich Countries Got Rich ... and Why Poor Countries Stay Poor*, New York: Carroll & Graf.

[63] See, for example, Claudio Grossman and Daniel D. Bradlow (1993), "Are We Being Propelled Towards a People-Centered Transnational Legal Order?," *American University Journal of International Law and Policy* 9(1): 1–26; Gunther Teubner (2011), "Self-Constitutionalizing TNCs? On the Linkage of 'Private' and 'Public' Corporate Codes of Conduct," *Indiana Journal of Global Legal Studies* 18(2): 617–38.

emerging global, networked information and communications infrastructure – push both tendencies to new extremes.

Over the last several decades, the platform has emerged as the core organizational logic of the political economy of informationalism. In other work, I have explored the intertwined functions that platforms provide – intermediation between would-be counterparties and techniques for rendering users legible – and explained how those functions afford unprecedented control of commercial and social interaction.[64] From an economic perspective, platforms represent infrastructure-based strategies for introducing friction into networks. Platforms provide services that participants view as desirable and empowering, thereby generating and enabling participants to leverage network externalities. At the same time, they use a combination of legal boilerplate and technical protections to assert ownership and control of user data, to police access by app developers and potential competitors, and to maintain their algorithms for search, user profiling, and ad targeting as valuable trade secrets. Those strategies work to pull users closer and keep would-be competitors further away, generating the rich-get-richer dynamics that have produced dominant platforms and continually reinforce their preeminence.

As a result of their enormous and growing power over the conditions of information exchange, platforms are unmatched by other transnational corporations in the extent of the authority they wield over the day-to-day experiences and activities of their users. Here again, the distinctions developed by Manuel Castells in his exploration of communication power in the networked digital era are useful for explicating the various kinds of power that platforms possess. By virtue of their privileged and infrastructural access to flows of information, platforms wield both network power – which, as we have seen, inheres in the self-reinforcing power of a dominant network and by extension in its standards – and network-making power – or the power to constitute the network and perhaps to reconstitute it along different lines by altering the conditions for interconnection.[65]

From the traditional international relations perspective, it makes no sense to speak of platforms or any other private corporations as sovereigns. Within the Westphalian international legal order, a sovereign state is, most minimally, an entity with a defined territory and a permanent population, the authority to govern its territory, and the capacity to enter into relations with other states.[66] Platform firms own premises within the territories of nation states and provide services to citizens of those states. Unlike state sovereigns, they lack authority to use physical force to assert the primacy of their laws or defend the sanctity of their borders.

Yet the growing practical sovereignty of platforms over many aspects of their users' everyday lives blurs the boundaries that the traditional criteria impose. The network power and the network-making power of platforms are rooted in the very

---

[64] Julie E. Cohen (2017), "Law for the Platform Economy," *U.C. Davis Law Review* 51(1): 133–204.
[65] Castells, cited in note 25, pp. 45–46.
[66] See Convention on Rights and Duties of States art. 1, December 26, 1933, T.S. No. 88.

considerations of territory, population, and enforcement authority that platforms supposedly lack. Both technically and experientially, platform territories are clearly demarcated spaces.[67] Google and Facebook also operate substantial privatized Internet "backbone" infrastructures – the interconnection facilities that link different pieces of the Internet together.[68] Dominant platforms such as Facebook, Google, and Apple have user populations that number in the billions, vastly eclipsing the populations of all but the largest nation states.[69] The logic of platform membership is a network logic that relies on lock-in, and it persistently undercuts the strategies of exit and voice through which users police more ordinary commercial relationships. The benefits of membership accrue most visibly and predictably to users who maintain permanent and consistent membership. In part for that reason and in part because of the way that platform protocols mediate access to platform territories, the enforcement authority of platforms is real and immediate. Platform protocols structure the forms and flows of permitted conduct – e.g., sponsored search results, Facebook "likes" and "tags," Twitter retweets – and enable swift imposition of internal sanctions that may range from content removal to account suspension or cancellation.[70]

Sovereign authority also must be recognized as such by other sovereigns, and here the picture is muddier. On one hand, the dominant US platform firms actively and theatrically resist both incursions by nation states on their governance authority and various kinds of national and local regulation. On the other, platform firms have at times pursued more collaborative relationships with governments on both matters of national security and law enforcement and matters of technology policy more generally.[71] As noted earlier, Chinese platform firms have more systematically collaborated with government authorities both at home and abroad. On the global stage, platforms firms increasingly practice both diplomacy and transnational networked policymaking in the manner of sovereign actors. Facebook's privacy team travels the world meeting with government officials to determine how best to satisfy their concerns while continuing to advance Facebook's own interests, much as

---

[67] On the spatial dimension of user experiences of the Internet, see Julie E. Cohen (2007), "Cyberspace as/and Space," *Columbia Law Review* 107(1): 210–255.

[68] DeNardis, *The Global War for Internet Governance*, cited in note 19, pp. 45–55.

[69] Facebook, "Newsroom: Company Info," https://perma.cc/5RC7-ZPGG (2.13 billion monthly active users as of December 2017); Xavier Harding, "Google Has 7 Products with 1 Billion Users, Popular Science," February 1, 2016, https://perma.cc/2ZYC-LU5C; Credit Suisse, "Apple Inc. (AAPL.OQ) Company Update," p. 1 (2016) (estimated 588 million users as of April 2016), https://perma.cc/TK8F-JTKW.

[70] See Tarleton Gillespie (2017), "Governance of and by Platforms," in Jean Burgess, Alice Marwick, and Thomas Poell, eds., *The SAGE Handbook of Social Media*, Thousand Oaks, CA: Sage, pp. 254–278; Kate Klonick (2018), "The New Governors: The People, Rules, and Processes Governing Online Speech," *Harvard Law Review* 131(6): 1598–1670.

[71] David Dayen, "The Android Administration: Google's Remarkably Close Working Relationship with the Obama White House, in Two Charts," *The Intercept*, April 22, 2016, https://perma.cc/QL5K-VT7Y.

a secretary of state and his or her staff might do.[72] Speaking at a recent network security conference, Microsoft's president sketched a vision of a future in which platform firms function as "a trusted and neutral digital Switzerland," safeguarding private communications against all types of sovereign incursion.[73]

In short, networked legal-institutional form allows for the possibility of nonstate but functionally sovereign power, and platforms represent an (arguable and emergent) example of such power. Concentrated stakeholder control of the networked communications infrastructure can produce and perhaps is beginning to produce an inversion of law- and policymaking authority, through which certain very powerful platform stakeholders become policy hubs in their own right. Theories of international relations that deny the possibility of private sovereignty are ill-equipped to respond to that possibility. Reconceptualizing transnational governance in a way that accounts for the network-making power of dominant platforms has become an increasingly important project.

CONCLUSION

Taking networks and standards seriously as organizing principles for a new legal-institutional form provides a helpful framework for understanding various features of transnational governance arrangements that have perplexed scholars across a number of disciplines. If what such institutions do is not "just" governance – if they represent an emergent form of law for the informational economy, and an increasingly important one – the disconnects between network-and-standard-based governance and rule-of-law ideals point to the beginning of an important institutional design project directed toward rendering them more accountable to global networked publics. That project also must contend with the growing practical sovereignty of platforms and with the challenges such sovereignty poses for the practical realization of rule-of-law aspirations within networked information environments.

---

[72] Mike Swift, "Facebook to Assemble Global Team of 'Diplomats,'" *San Jose Mercury News*, May 20, 2011, https://perma.cc/396G-SUGX; Gwen Ackerman, "Facebook and Israel Agree to Tackle Terrorist Media Together," *Bloomberg*, September 12, 2016, https://perma.cc/E4UU-SRVF; My Pham, "Vietnam Says Facebook Commits to Preventing Offensive Content," *Reuters*, April 27, 2017, https://perma.cc/FN45-XLNY; Adam Taylor, "Denmark is Naming an Ambassador Who Will Just Deal with Increasingly Powerful Tech Companies," *Washington Post*, February 4, 2017, https://perma.cc/PCV3-L2J3.

[73] Kate Conger, "Microsoft Calls for the Establishment of a Digital Geneva Convention," *TechCrunch*, February 14, 2017, https://perma.cc/78Q3-Q38S.

3

Tech Dominance and the Policeman at the Elbow

Tim Wu[*]

INTRODUCTION

What drives the "digital tornado," to use the evocative phrase coined by Kevin Werbach to describe the fierce, concentrated winds of technological change? One school of thought, neo-libertarian at its core, sees it as an entirely private process, driven by brave scientists, risk-taking entrepreneurs, and the capital markets. If government is relevant, it is merely through the guarantee of property rights and contract; otherwise it does best by staying out of the way.

But what if powerful firms seek to slow down, modulate, or co-opt the winds of change? The view just described takes this as an inherently hopeless task, for it is axiomatic that the rate of technological change is always accelerating, so that any firm or institution dependent on a given technology is therefore automatically doomed to a rapid obsolescence. Even well-meaning laws designed to catalyze innovation, at best, merely risk interfering with a natural progression toward a better technological future, hindering "the march of civilization." As the general counsel of Standard Oil once put it, government cannot control the aggregation of private power: "You might as well endeavor to stay the formation of the clouds, the falling of the rains, or the flowing of the streams."[1]

This view, which was widely held in the early 2000s through the 2010s, has great relevance for the antitrust law, the subject of this chapter, and particularly, the parts of the law concerned with monopolization. For if we can indeed assume that the rate of technological innovation is always accelerating, it follows that there can be no such thing as lasting market power, the concern of the law. The dominant firm, necessarily dependent on an older technology, will be quickly surpassed and replaced by a new firm. In its strongest version, it suggests that the antimonopoly portions of the antitrust law are obsolete.

---

[*] This essay benefited from comments by Kevin Werbach, discussions with Randy Picker, and an illuminating conversation with Bill Gates.

[1] Quoted in Tim Wu, *The Curse of Bigness* (2018).

Over the 1980s through 2010s, a series of powerful anecdotes supported this narrative, so much so that it became a broadly accepted wisdom. After all, IBM, in the 1970s and 1980s, once thought lord of everything, was bested by a college dropout named Bill Gates and a few of his buddies. Microsoft, in turn, was ravaged by a series of garage startups with goofy names like Yahoo!, Google, and Facebook. AOL rose and then fell like a rocket that fails to achieve orbit, as did other firms, such as MySpace, Netscape, and so on. The chaos and rapid change made it obvious to many that there could be no such thing as a lasting monopoly. A three-year old firm was middle-aged already; a five-year old firm almost certainly near death, for "barriers to entry" were a twentieth-century concept. The best, indeed the only thing the antitrust law should do is to stand well back and watch.

But what if the supposed new order itself were itself just a phase? What if the assumption of constant accelerating technological change is wrong – or a function of market structure? As these questions may suggest, this chapter joins the challenge to the narrative described. I say join because it is a larger conversation, not to be settled with one single chapter. The contribution of this chapter is to examine a foundational part of the narrative – the erosion of IBM's dominance in the 1970s and the case of *United States* v. *IBM*.

Why focus on IBM? The decline of IBM's dominance over the 1980s has long been a foundational part of the story that we described in the introduction, one that casts the "new economy" as an exception to the usual rules of industrial organization. As the story goes, IBM, bested by Microsoft, Compaq, Dell, Intel, and other competitors, serves as strong proof that lasting monopoly in unachievable in high-tech industries. Even the mighty IBM could not hold out, given the inevitable challenge from new inventions and innovators.

Unfortunately, that account tends to overlook the fact that IBM was not subject only to the forces of technological change, but also faced significant legal challenges, targeted directly at the exercise of monopoly power. This chapter suggests, with the benefit of decades of hindsight, that subjecting IBM to an antitrust lawsuit and trial actually catalyzed numerous transformational developments key to the growth and innovation in the computing industries. The undeniable fact is that the "policeman at the elbow" can and does change conduct. The IBM case put a policeman at the elbow of the world's dominant computer firm during a crucial period of change and development in the technology industries. This, I suggest, aided an ongoing process of transformational or Schumpeterian innovation.[2] Contrary to conventional wisdom, I also think that *United States* v. *IBM* is a valuable guide to enforcement policy in the technology-centered industries. This chapter, in short, is a revisionist history of the *IBM* case, one that casts serious doubt on the narrative of law's irrelevance in aiding technological change.

---

[2] I elaborate this theory in Tim Wu, *The Master Switch* (2010), at pp. 138, 158.

The goal is not just to give the *IBM* case its due among those who study law and technology, but also to rehabilitate its reputation within antitrust law, where, it is given, conventional wisdom has not been kind. *United States* v. *IBM* has been cast as among antitrust's lowest moments, and among the Justice Department's greatest mistakes. Robert Bork memorably dubbed the litigation "Antitrust's Vietnam"; Joseph Lopatka termed it a "monument to arrogance"; while an appellate judge quipped that it "went on longer than World War II and probably cost as much."[3] Lasting from 1969 through 1982, the case included a six-year trial; the government's presentation took 104,000 pages of transcript, while for its part, IBM called 856 witnesses and cited 12,280 exhibits. Yet after years of trial, the Justice Department withdrew the case in 1982, without settlement or judicial remedy. The failure of the case to reach a verdict added ammunition to a Reagan-era movement against antitrust's "big case" tradition.[4] This has yielded, for many, one lasting "lesson" from *IBM*: that "big antitrust" – the industry-clearing Section 2 cases – should be used sparingly, at best, given the costs and potential for failure.

This chapter challenges the conventional wisdom and suggests that the IBM lawsuit and trial, despite never reaching a verdict, actually catalyzed numerous transformational developments key to the growth and innovation of the computing industries.

I do not seek to defend everything about the IBM trial. It is admittedly difficult, if not impossible, to defend the manner in which the Justice Department and court managed the litigation and allowed it to last so long. It is also true, as the critics have charged, that the government could have had a clearer theory from the outset. However, in spite of the lack of a remedy, the historic materials made available since the litigation have made it clear that the antitrust case did substantially change IBM's behavior in specific ways. Perhaps the most important was the case's role in pushing IBM to unbundle its software offerings from its hardware, and therefore to leave room for the birth of an independent software industry. While the effects are less direct, the case seems to have also influenced the manner of IBM's PC launch and its conduct thereafter. These developments appear to have at least contributed to the thriving of an independent computer software industry, and later, to a new market for competing, IBM-compatible personal computers, as well as a slew of related, independent industries in storage, processing, printing, modems, and otherwise. During this period, IBM's avoidance of exclusive contracts and its failure to acquire or seek control of obvious targets (like Microsoft itself) all suggest a firm with "antitrust phobia," and thereby one that allowed competition to flourish.

Of course, there were a great number of other factors in the late 1970s affecting the software and hardware industries, and there is no claim here that the IBM antitrust

---

[3] Steven Brill, What to Tell Your Friends About IBM, *American Lawyer* (April 1982), 1.

[4] *See* Gary L. Reback, *Free the Market!: Why Only Government Can Keep the Marketplace Competitive* (2009); William E. Kovacic, *Failed Expectations: The Troubled Past and Uncertain Future of the Sherman Act as a Tool for Deconcentration*, 74 *Iowa L. Rev.* 1105 (1989).

litigation drove everything that happened during this era. However, many of the existing narratives are too quick to assume that the developments were "inevitable," or, alternatively, all the byproduct of the particular genius of Bill Gates, a favorite thesis of the Microsoft-centered books. As discussed earlier, it is well understood by legal scholars that both firms and individuals may behave differently when enforcement is more likely, especially "with a policeman at the elbow."[5] The operating theory of this chapter is that a pending monopolization case, which focuses on exclusionary and anticompetitive acts and scrutinizes efforts to dominate new industries, may affect firm conduct in recognizable ways. And the thesis is that the policeman standing at the elbow of the dominant computing firms during the 1970s and early 1980s had an important impact on the development of the software and personal computing industries.

This reexamination of IBM also has important implications for antitrust enforcement policy, for an enforcer interested in "big cases" in the tech industries filed under Section 2 of the Sherman Act. To say that antitrust has, in the late 2010s, regained relevance is to state the obvious. For since the turn of the millennium, when it seemed that market power was indeed always going to be fleeting, the tech industries have consolidated into a much smaller number of "big tech" firms. The question, therefore, of when to bring a big tech case and against whom has returned to first-order importance.

This chapter suggests three things. First, that government lawyers should look for situations where it appears that a single firm is sitting as gatekeeper on what might, plausibly, be several innovative industries, and where breakups or lesser remedies might therefore unleash substantial growth. Specifically, beyond the usual search for monopoly power and anticompetitive practices, enforcers should be looking for "bundled" or "tied" markets that have the potential to be those nascent industries. The presence of stunted cottage industries might suggest an underlying potential. Second, the IBM case suggests the importance of a credible threat – that is, an investigation that seeks dissolution or other important remedies – so as to induce actual changes in conduct and deter anticompetitive behavior. Finally, the IBM case cautions enforcers to be concerned, but not overly concerned with the costs of investigation and trial, which are multimillion dollars questions, when there are billions and possibly trillions at stake.

BACKGROUND: THE COMPANY AND THE MARKET

The predecessor firm to International Business Machines was founded in 1911, as a manufacturer of machines for tabulating and data processing. By the 1960s, IBM

---

[5] For a recent account of the influence of a high probability of law enforcement over compliance with the law, *see* Aaron Chalfin and Justin McCrary, *Criminal Deterrence: A Review of the Literature*, 55 J. Econ. Lit 5 (2017) (reviewing effects of increased law enforcement on crime); *see also* Robert C. Ellickson, *Order Without Law: How Neighbors Settle Disputes*, pp. 147–148 (1991) (dismissing extreme view of "legal peripheralism").

had become a dominant manufacturer of general purpose, or "mainframe" computers designed to be used by corporations, government agencies, and other large institutions. "Big Blue" was, by then, the largest computer manufacturer in the world. By 1971, IBM had grown to 258,662 employees and $7.2 billion in annual revenues, and its IBM System/360 was the nation's, indeed the world's, most successful computer line.[6] It was a proud company, and its anthem went as follows:

> EVER ONWARD – EVER ONWARD!
> That's the spirit that has brought us fame!
> We're big, but bigger we will be
> We can't fail for all can see
> That to serve humanity has been our aim!

During the 1960s, the "mainframe" was the dominant computer design – one large computer, covered with blinking lights, designed to handle the most challenging tasks, or to serve many users at once. There was no such thing as a personal computer: At that point the cheapest computers sold by IBM cost over $100,000, and the more expensive units were priced in the millions.

IBM's design philosophy was characteristic of the era of its greatest success – it embodied the system design thinking of the 1950s and 1960s, which favored centralized, fully integrated designs, of which AT&T "Bell System" was the exemplar.[7] Hence, IBM's mainframe computers integrated, or bundled, all hardware, software and peripherals in one package. Of particular interest to us, software was not made available for sale or lease as an independent product: It was a service provided to buyers of IBM hardware.

IBM was not without competitors. The mainframe market was lucrative, and by the mid-1960s, IBM faced competition from seven smaller firms (the "seven dwarfs"), with their own mainframes, such as Burroughs, Univac, NCR, CDC, GE, RCA, and Honeywell. Firms like Univac typically targeted the lower end of the mainframe market, and attempted to win consumers with lower prices. In the early parts of mainframe history, all of the computers offered for sale were incompatible: That is, a firm usually bought all of its computers and peripheries from either IBM or Univac, for the computers were incapable of working together. Later, some firms began to offer peripheral hardware, like disk drives, designed to be "plug-compatible" with IBM's System/360 mainframes, which meant one could plug the peripherals into IBM's machines. Finally, other firms, like Control Data, focused on superior performance, and in particular, the supercomputer market, crafting computers faster (and even more expensive) than IBM's offerings.

---

[6] Daniela Hernandez, Tech Time Warp of the Week: 50 Years Ago, IBM Unleashed the Room-Sized iPhone, *Wired* (June 27, 2014), https://www.wired.com/2014/06/tech-time-warp-ibm-system360/.

[7] The centralized design ideology is described in Wu, supra note 2, at pp. 45–60.

THE CASE

Over the 1960s, there were long-standing complaints that IBM was maintaining its mainframe monopoly and scaring people away from supercomputers using anticompetitive, predatory, and unethical practices. IBM and its management had faced antitrust complaints before: Tom Watson Sr., IBM's longtime CEO, was convicted of criminal violations of antitrust back in 1913 (when he worked for NCR), and actually sentenced to prison.[8] What's more, in 1956, IBM entered into a consent decree with the Justice Department surrounding its leasing practices.[9]

Matters came to a head when, in 1968, rival Control Data sued IBM in a private antitrust action, focusing on its predatory conduct in the supercomputer and mainframe markets.[10] In 1969, after a long investigation, the Justice Department filed its own suit, also charging IBM with monopoly maintenance in violation of Section 2 of the Sherman Act.[11] According to the Justice Department, IBM had undertaken "exclusionary and predatory conduct" to maintain its dominant position in "general purpose digital computers."[12] That was a market, according to the government's estimates, in which IBM took some 70 percent of annual revenue.

Most important for our purposes were the government's allegations surrounding software.[13] IBM was accused of tying software to "related computer hardware equipment" for a single price in a manner that the Justice Department alleged to be anticompetitive. IBM, it was alleged, also gave away software for free for "the purpose or with the effect of . . . enabling IBM to maintain or increase its market share."[14]

Beyond the software practices, the government also accused IBM of predatory practices. In particular, it accused IBM of developing specific "fighting machines" designed not to make a profit but rather to intimidate would-be competitors. It also accused IBM of vaporware practices, that is, announcing "future production and marketing [of certain products] when it believed or had reason to believe that it was unlikely to be able to produce and market such products within the announced time frame."

For these violations, the government sought divestiture – that is, a full breakup of IBM into constituent parts. In that sense, the case was a classic example of the "big case" tradition in antitrust, in the model of the Northern Securities or Standard Oil litigation, whose goal was to restructure the industry entirely.[15]

---

[8] Kevin Maney, *The Maverick and His Machine: Thomas Watson, Sr. and the Making of IBM* (2003).

[9] Ibid at p. 423.

[10] James Cortada, *IBM: The Rise and Fall and Reinvention of a Global Icon*, pp. 332–333 (2019).

[11] The Complaint is reprinted in the appendix of Franklin M. Fisher et al., *Folded, Spindled and Mutilated: Economic Analysis and U.S. v. IBM*, 353 (1983).

[12] Plaintiff's Statement of Triable Issues (dated Sep. 23, 1974), *United States* v. *IBM*, 69 Civ. 200 (S.D.N.Y. 1969).

[13] *See* Amended Complaint, *U.S* v. *IBM*, 69 Civ. 200, ¶ 19(a) (S.D.N.Y. 1969).

[14] Plaintiff's Statement, supra note 12.

[15] *See* Wu, supra note 1.

After some six years of discovery, the case finally went to trial in 1975. The early stages of the trial were somewhat complicated by the fact that IBM was also defending the private antitrust lawsuit brought by Control Data, the manufacturer of supercomputers. At the beginning, Control Data actively cooperated with the Justice Department, and had accumulated a massive database of alleged predatory acts perpetrated by IBM and its salesmen over the 1960s. It was information from this file that the Justice Department hoped to deploy in its lawsuit. However, in 1973, Control Data settled with IBM, and agreed to hand over its file.[16] IBM immediately destroyed (in some accounts burned) the files, thereby setting back the Justice Department's discovery.

During the trial, IBM put on a vigorous defense, and spent untold millions of 1970s' dollars defending the case.[17] The judge, David Edelstein, permitted the calling of a seemingly unlimited number of witnesses, for indefinite periods of time. One government witness testified for more than six months. Other trial days consisted of reading of depositions into the record.[18] Many of these details were chronicled by legal writer Steven Brill, in a scathing piece that portrayed the entire trial as a complete fiasco, or, in his words, "a farce of such mindboggling proportions that any lawyer who now tries to find out about it ... will be risking the same quicksand that devoured the lawyers involved in the case."[19] The trial continued for an astonishing six years, until the Justice Department finally rested in 1981.[20]

But here we are interested less in the trial itself, and more in the effects of the litigation on IBM's conduct and decision making. For during the lengthy trial and its aftermath, there is little dispute among business historians and journalists that IBM's management was influenced by the very fact of being under investigation and being on trial. As Don Waldman writes, "the filing and prosecution of the antitrust case affected IBM's business behavior for the next twenty years."[21] Furthermore, as he writes, "lawyers gained control over even the most technical elements of IBM's business."[22] William Kovacic concurs: "DOJ's law-suit exacted a high price from IBM. Along with the private lawsuits, the DOJ case caused IBM to elevate the role of lawyers in shaping commercial strategy and seems to have led the firm to pull its competitive punches."[23] Reporter Paul Carroll, in his insider account *Big Blues*, gave a detailed portrayal of the effects of efforts to avoid strengthening the antitrust

---

[16] James Cortada, *IBM: The Rise and Fall and Reinvention of a Global Icon*, p. 333 (2019).

[17] Ibid at p. 331.

[18] *See* Fisher, supra note 7, at 16.

[19] Brill, supra note 2, at 1.

[20] Peter Behr, IBM, Justice Rests Cases In Historic Antitrust Trial, *Wash. Post* (June 2, 1981), available at https://www.washingtonpost.com/archive/business/1981/06/02/ibm-justice-rests-cases-in-historic-anti trust-trial/5cc16dbo-8e7f-4763-a17d-fdfb6fefo464/?noredirect=on.

[21] Don Waldman, IBM, in *Market Dominance: How Firms Gain, Hold, Or Lose it and the Impact on Economic Performance*, p. 140 (David Ira Rosenbaum, ed., 1998).

[22] Ibid.

[23] Andrew I. Gavil, William E. Kovacic, Jonathan B. Baker, Antitrust Law in Perspective: Cases, Concepts, and Problems in Competition Policy 1112 (2008).

case by producing evidence of market share or anticompetitive conduct: "Lawyers, who were developing a stranglehold on the business, decided what could be said at meetings. No one could talk about IBM's market share, or if they did, they'd talk in meaningless terms, describing the market for word processors as though it included everything from the supercomputer on down to paper and pencils. Executives couldn't do any competitive analysis. Developers weren't allowed to buy a competitor's machine; they were just supposed to know what was in it."[24]

Critics have emphasized the sheer size of the case, which did last an astonishing thirteen years, at the end of which, the Reagan Administration simply dropped the case.[25] Was it, then, all just a waste of resources? That's no trip to the county courthouse, and no one can defend how the Justice Department managed the litigation, which became as bloated as a 1970s' muscle car. On the other hand, consider the stakes: The computer and software industries were already bringing in billions in revenue and today are collectively worth trillions of dollars, encompassing many of the most valuable companies on earth. Small effects on this industry would and did have major long-term effects. Neither was the IBM case, as G. David Garson writes, "without its effects" for the early computing industry.[26]

EFFECTS AND IMPACT

It is one thing to suggest that the IBM trial may have caused IBM to behave more cautiously, evade obvious anticompetitive conduct, and generally avoid strengthening Justice's case. Among other things, that may simply have weakened IBM as a competitor. But it seems more important to point out specific decisions and outcomes that seem to have been strongly influenced by the "antitrust phobia" resulting from being the subject of a Sherman Act case designed to break up the company. In this section I focus on three key moments: (1) IBM's unbundling of software from hardware, (2) its entry into the microcomputer market, IBM PC, in partnership with Microsoft and others, and (3) its pattern of non-acquisitions in the aftermath of the PC's success.

Unbundling and the Rise of an Independent Software Industry

The clearest impact of the antitrust case was its contribution to the rise of an independent software industry. This development is no small matter, given that software today is a $1.2 trillion-dollar industry in the US ($3 trillion globally), employing 2.5 million people. However, most of the legal and economics critics of

---

[24] Paul Carroll, Big Blues: The Unmaking of IBM 57 (1994).
[25] Cortada, supra note 16, at p. 346.
[26] G. David Garson, Public Information Technology and E-governance: Managing the Virtual State 229 (2006).

The Policeman at the Elbow   89

the IBM litigation have, unaccountably, failed to acknowledge the case's contribution to the software industry.

In the 1960s, it was IBM's practice, and the practice of most other mainframe manufacturers, to "bundle" software with hardware.[27] That is, software was sold as a service that was tied to the sale of its hardware – the IBM mainframe unit came with a contract by which IBM programmers wrote software customized to the needs of the customer. Any prepackaged software was meant merely to illustrate for the customer what software might look like, like a model home for a prospective customer.[28] There were those within IBM who also thought that there might be a profitable market for packaged software, but they were unable to persuade the firm to break from its traditional practices.[29] The software industry itself was a "small, offbeat, almost cottage industry" and there was, interestingly, little customer demand for independent software.[30]

In the late 1960s, as it became apparent that the Justice Department was planning on bringing an antitrust lawsuit, IBM's legal team began to conclude, as a legal matter, that the software–hardware tie would be difficult to defend. A key figure was IBM's general counsel, Burke Marshall, who "saw bundling as a glaring violation of antitrust law" and suggested that, if forced to defend the tie, IBM "would lose."[31] Faced with this assessment, and hoping for a quick settlement, IBM President and CEO Thomas Watson Jr. made the decision, late in 1968, to begin the process of unbundling IBM's software offerings from its hardware offerings.[32] While the unbundling decision was made before the formal filing of complaint, it was an effort to avoid the complaint's being filed; such efforts to settle preemptively as is common in antitrust practice.[33] If there was once some controversy over why IBM unbundled, Watson's description of the decision, in his autobiography, coupled with the writings of other IBM insiders, seems to have settled the matter.

[27] In antitrust jargon, bundling and tying are differentiated by the idea that tying is non-optional, while a bundle allows the customer to buy the constituent products separately, or in a (usually cheaper) bundle. However, in business usage, the two terms are used interchangeably, and in this piece "bundling" is used as a synonym for "tying."

[28] Burton Grad, A Personal Recollection: IBM's Unbundling of Software and Services 24. *IEEE Annals of the History of Computing* 64, 66 (2002).

[29] Ibid at p. 67.

[30] Stanley Gibson, Software Industry Born with IBM's Unbundling, *Computerworld*, 6 (June 19, 1989).

[31] Thomas J. Watson Jr. and Peter Petre, *Father, Son & Co.: My Life at IBM and Beyond* (1990). There were also some within IBM who thought that the firm was missing out on an opportunity to make money in software. *See* Grad, supra note 28, at p. 65.

[32] There was, at some point, controversy over what caused IBM to unbundle software. In 1983, Fisher, McKie, and Mancke disputed the argument that it was antitrust pressure, and suggested that cutting the costs of support was the primary motive. *See* Franklin M. Fisher, James W. McKie, and Richard B. Mancke, *IBM and the U.S. Data Processing Industry: An Economic History* (1983). However, later admission in Watson's autobiography and corroboration by insiders like Grad seems to have ended the controversy.

[33] For example, in the 2010s, when under FTC investigation, Google preemptively abandoned several practices that investigators had deemed anticompetitive. *See* https://www.vox.com/2017/12/27/16822150/google-ftc-yelp-scraping-antitrust-ftc.

On June 23, 1969 – sometimes called the "independence day" for the software industry – IBM, for the first time, made seventeen applications independently available for lease (not yet for sale). With the first release of prepackaged software products by the world's dominant computer firm, the world of computing was never the same again. Richard Lilly, founder of a prominent 1970s software firm, said in 1989, "It created the industry we're in."[34]

Consistent with Lilly's statement, most experts agree that IBM's unbundling was one key factor in the development of an independent software industry.[35] Nonetheless, a few caveats are in order. First, it is not that IBM was the first firm to release software as a product – there were others, albeit very few. By becoming the largest firm to enter the industry itself, IBM played a role in validating the idea that software could be a product at all, and also the idea that software was valuable. Second, it is also true that there were other factors necessary for the birth of a software industry. One was IBM's own development of the 360-mainframe architecture, which was a standardized platform; another, the rise of the minicomputer, a smaller and cheaper alternative to the mainframe. Nonetheless, in its action, IBM both gave life to the industry and, critically, reconceptualized what software was. Its unbundling, as Martin Campbell-Kelly writes, transformed "almost overnight the common perception of software from a free good to a tradable commodity."[36] The decision also had important consequences for IBM, both in terms of what it was and what it could control. As Burton Grad, of IBM, writes: "As a consequence of unbundling, IBM unquestionably became the largest supplier of computer software and services during the 1970s and 1980s. However, it never could control that business in the same way that it had (and has) dominated the mainframe hardware market."[37] The ongoing antitrust suit, moreover, prevented IBM from rebundling and risking new liability. Hence, the suit and the unbundling helped create the model of computing that drove development through the 1970s and beyond – the concept of a *platform* for which *applications* are developed.

Estimating the economic importance of this development – and the contribution of IBM's unbundling – is not easy, if only because the transformation was so far reaching. An important fact, however, is that the impact was not felt all at once. Hardware continued to be more important than software, and even into the 1980s, the software industry remained relatively small. One economic analysis suggests that "in 1987, the receipts of U.S. software programming service companies (SIC 7371) were $14.2 billion, the receipts for computer integrated systems design (SIC 7373) were $7.1 billion, and the receipts from prepackaged software (SIC 7372) sales were

---

[34] Gibson, supra note 30, at p. 6.

[35] *See*, e.g., Grad, supra note 28; *see also* W. Edward Steinmueller, The U.S. Software Industry: An Analysis and Interpretive History, in *The International Computer Software Industry: A Comparative Study of Industry Evolution and Structure* (David C. Mowery ed., 1995).

[36] Martin Campbell-Kelly, Development and Structure of the International Software Industry, 1950–1990, 24 *Bus. & Econ. History* 73, 88 (1995).

[37] Grad, supra note 28, at p. 71.

$5.9 billion."[38] Other developments, like the triumph of the personal computer over all aspects of business computing, were yet to come. Yet by the 2010s, providers of software, even narrowly construed, were responsible for over a trillion dollars in US revenue, and broadly construed, far more of the world's economic activity. In the words of Marc Andreessen, "software is eating the world."[39]

We cannot know for sure whether, without IBM's decision, software would have become unbundled anyhow – that it was, in some way, the natural order of things. But it seems hard to deny that the antitrust case sped that development. And the failure to take account of the significance and effect of IBM's unbundling of its software is a major flaw in many of the critiques of the IBM litigation. Take, for example, the work of economic historians Robert W. Crandall and Charles L. Jackson and their highly skeptical analysis of the effects of the IBM antitrust litigation, published in 2011, on the computing industry. The two do mention that unbundling was among the Justice Department's goals, yet fail to even mention that it actually achieved this goal. That omission allows them to make the incorrect conclusion that: "It is difficult to see how an antitrust action brought in 1969 and dismissed in 1982 could have been a major contributor"[40] to dramatic changes in the industry.

* * *

If unbundling succeeded in transforming the history of computing, unfortunately for Watson and IBM, it failed in its goal of mollifying the Justice Department, which persisted with other claims of predation and anticompetitive behavior. It seems that the Justice Department continued to litigate based on its large collection of potentially predatory activities – in particular, related to pricing and misleading consumers about IBM's forthcoming supercomputers (a vaporware strategy). The persistence of the lawsuit led to its influence over another transformational development: The arrival of the personal computer.

The Personal Computer and Microsoft

Another major development that occurred during the pendency of the IBM antitrust lawsuit was the development of the personal computer industry. While Apple and competitors Commodore and Tandy may have ignited the market with the successful launch of the first mass market personal computers, IBM would come to play a central role by developing and releasing the IBM PC, the personal computer whose design would come to dominate the market, with its radically modular, or

---

[38] Steinmueller, supra note 35, at p. 7.

[39] Marc Andreessen, Why Software is Eating the World, *Wall St. J.* (August 20, 2011), available at https://a16z.com/2016/08/20/why-software-is-eating-the-world/.

[40] Robert W. Crandall and Charles L. Jackson, Antitrust in High-Tech Industries, 38 *Rev. Ind. Organ.* 319, 327 (2011).

open, design. This section examines the influence of IBM's "antitrust phobia" over the core decisions made during this period.

There are two dominant, and conflicting, narratives surrounding the development of the personal computer. The first lionizes IBM's rapid creation of a personal computer that would come to dominate the new industry. The second describes a blundering IBM, and credits Bill Gates for his brilliant outwitting of a myopic and foolish IBM based on an inability of the latter to understand the future. It isn't hard to see the contradiction: If IBM was too stupid or backward to understand the personal computer market, how did it come to dominate it in just a few years? And if Bill Gates had such a brilliant sense of the future, why did he only grudgingly come to understand the potential in selling a standardized operating system? But most mysterious of all: Once the IBM PC began to take off, why was it so inert in the defense of its position? Why, for example, did it decline to acquire control of the companies critical to the PC, as IBM's philosophy of centralized control would suggest? The point of this section is not to suggest that the traditional narrative is entirely wrong, but that it is incomplete. Particularly when it comes to Microsoft, it implies that IBM was simply too bone-headed to appreciate the future, rather than, potentially, concerned about its fate in the antitrust trial, and later, the possibility of reigniting antitrust litigation. There were so many dogs that did not bark during the launch of the PC and its aftermath, many of which are consistent with a fear that too aggressive a posture might yield renewed antitrust pressures based on the monopolization of the PC markets or software.

A moment, first, on the IBM PC itself and its significance. IBM, as already discussed, was the great champion of the mainframe computer – "big iron," the monster machines designed to serve the needs of an entire business unit. (To be fair, mainframes were actually much smaller than the computers of the 1950s, which sometimes took up entire buildings, and were employed mainly by the military, but that is another matter.) Priced in the millions of dollars, they were obviously not intended for home usage. In the late 1960s through the 1970s, however, a number of researchers, particularly those associated with Xerox's Palo Alto Research Center, and hobbyists like Steve Jobs and Steve Wozniak, had come up with the idea of a "personal" computer, intended for individual usage or for small businesses. A group of firms, led by Apple and its introduction of the Apple II, and also including Commodore, Atari, Sinclair, Tandy, and others, had by the 1970s proved both that personal computers could be produced for less than $2,000, and that there was a market for them.

IBM had experimented with smaller, entry-level computers, but they were generally smaller versions of its mainframes, and still priced way beyond the reach of any individual. In 1980, with the success of Apple and others, IBM decided to enter the microcomputer market in earnest. In an impressive twelve months, it had introduced the IBM PC, coupled with an advertising campaign featuring Charlie Chaplin's "Little Tramp." More powerful than the Apple II or Commodore 64,

The Policeman at the Elbow 93

and soon the beneficiary of a "killer app" in the VisiCalc and then Lotus 1–2-3 spreadsheet program for businesses, the PC would soon become the best-selling personal computer in history to that point, and the dominance of its design had a profound influence on the subsequent history of computing.

What made that design so interesting is that the IBM PC was built in a manner unlike any other IBM product, a fact that would have enormous long-term consequences for the industry. As suggested earlier, IBM, whose system design traditions dated from the 1950s, has been among the champions of a fully integrated system design. Like AT&T, the company whose design philosophy was the most similar, IBM had long believed that the best products required that every component and service be provided in-house. Its practice of bundling, stated differently, was not limited to software; it included all hardware as well – it tended to source all of its hardware and software from itself.

The first IBM PC, however, was an extraordinarily radical break from that design, with a modular, open design philosophy that was essentially the opposite of IBM's closed and centralized philosophy. The IBM PC team (as we shall see, an experimental subunit of IBM proper) selected a hard drive manufactured by Seagate, a printer made by Epson, and a processor made by Intel, instead of using its own hardware. Most importantly over the long term, an operating system provided by the company then named "Micro-Soft," then a small startup, headed by one Bill Gates who was just twenty-four at the time and lacking a college degree. Gates, for his part, did not, in fact, write the operating system, but acquired it from a partner (Seattle Software) to whom he paid a license of $25,000 (reportedly, he didn't mention to Seattle Software that the customer was IBM, or that it had paid him $700,000).[41] In the end, when the PC came out, only the keyboard, screen, motherboard, and its hardware BIOS (Basic Input Output System) were actually produced by IBM's internal divisions. Of those, only the BIOS was proprietary.

There is one competitive detail of particular importance in the story of the IBM PC. When IBM contracted with Microsoft to provide the main operating system for the computer,[42] it neither bought the rights to the software nor required an exclusive license. The agreement was, instead, nonexclusive, leaving Microsoft free to sell its MS-DOS to other computer manufacturers as well. This nonexclusivity was a crucial factor in facilitating competition in the market for IBM-compatible PCs (like Compaq, or Dell). But this is something of a tangent. The question this chapter is trying to assess is what role, if any, the antitrust investigation played in influencing IBM's original design and subsequent strategic conduct. Unlike unbundling, the causation is much more diluted, but no less important.

---

[41] Mat Honan, Bill Gates Spent the Best Money of His Life 30 Years Ago Today, *Gizmodo* (July 27, 2011).

[42] The IBM PC was actually offered with three operating systems, but Microsoft's was the cheapest ($40) and may have been the default, for it quickly became the dominant choice. Eric G. Swedin and David L. Ferro, *Computers: The Life Story of a Technology*, p. 95 (2007).

First, we do need return back to the original 1969 software unbundling and its effect on the development of the personal computer. Among the effects of IBM's prior unbundling decision was to create the conditions for the platform/application model that would become the foundation of the personal computer industry. Burton Grad, again, writes that "[u]nbundling mainframe software established a framework for the independent microcomputer software industry's later growth, which followed the model of separately priced offerings by major software suppliers."[43] In other words, perhaps the larger influence of unbundling in 1969 was setting a model for firms like Microsoft, VisiCalc, and Lotus (the last two being among the first spreadsheet producers) to follow, which were a major factor in the success of the IBM PC. The unbundling also made possible Microsoft, which we shall discuss in greater detail in a moment.

The second matter was the question of how IBM would come to enter the market for personal computers. A dominant view is that the industry had too little revenue to attract or interest a mighty firm like IBM. However, there is evidence that, as early as the mid-1970s, IBM management, including its chairman, had gained interest in low-cost, entry-level computers, based on the accurate perception that lower-cost computers would come to be important, and also that rival Xerox might dominate that market. (Xerox had developed an advanced personal computer, the Alto, by 1973, that even had a graphical user interface, but had kept it for internal use, and did not bring a computer to market until the mid-1980s.) IBM considered the acquisitions that might help it forestall the emergence of competitors, but that path was discouraged by its lawyers, who were at that point involved in every level of decision making. For example, IBM considered the acquisition of Atari, and later considered working with Atari to produce its PC, but never did so – whether out of antitrust concerns or not, is unclear.

The IBM PC's production was also influenced by IBM's internal restructuring. By the late 1970s, both in the hope of promoting innovation, and also in anticipation of a potential breakup, IBM had divided the firm. Frank Cary, IBM's CEO, created a separate division to contain all of IBM's non-mainframe businesses, and it was in this division that the PC was launched. More specifically, IBM created a series of independent business units designed to be innovative and also potential survivors of a breakup, just as AT&T concentrated its choice assets (or so it thought). It was one of these, the "entry level computing" division based in Boca Raton, Florida, that both proposed and then built the IBM PC (codenamed *Project Chess*).

It is this team that made the decisions to create the modular and open design already discussed. That decision, in turn, is said to have been somewhat inspired by both Wozniak's Apple II design as well as the *Chess* team's desire to get around IBM's slow-moving methodical culture and arrive to market quickly and cheaply. The evidence leaves little doubt that this was the primary reason behind the design.

---

[43] Grad, supra note 28, at p. 71.

As Bill Lowe, the first head of the PC team, later said: "[A]t IBM it would take four years and three hundred people to do anything, I mean it's just a fact of life. And I said no sir, we can provide with product in a year. ... To save time, instead of building a computer from scratch, [the team] would buy components off the shelf and assemble them – what in IBM speak was called 'open architecture.' IBM never did this."[44] Lowe explained that "the key decisions were to go with an open architecture, non-IBM technology, non-IBM software, non-IBM sales and non-IBM service."

But while speed was surely a predominant factor in the design, it does not provide an explanation for everything. It fails to explain certain matters, like the crucial agreement to a nonexclusive license for Microsoft's PC-DOS (an exclusive contract would not have been slower), and to leave Microsoft with full control of the source code. Those who have studied that agreement and its creators have tended to focus on Bill Gates' side of the story, and attribute to him great savvy and foresight, based mainly on his own testimony.[45] While seeing the potential in the operating system and in nonexclusivity deserves enormous credit, it doesn't explain why IBM would agree to such a thing. It takes two parties to reach agreement, and as a small firm negotiating with the dominant computing power, it is safe to say that Microsoft would not necessarily have the final say. We also have the fact that IBM made an offer to buy a competing operating system, CP/M, outright.[46] What is lacking is a reason for IBM's non-assertion of its market power, and the implicit assumption that IBM was simply too stupid or short-sighted is an inadequate explanation.

The studies of IBM's side of the deal and its motivations for agreeing to non-exclusivity are fewer, but more important for our purposes. Joseph Porac, in a comprehensive study of the deal, suggests a variety of factors. One was that IBM did not want to manage the code or develop the operating system itself, having had several bad experiences with doing so in recent years. But the other leading reason, according to Porac, was "antitrust phobia." As he writes: "[A] reluctance to over-control small companies that could become potential competitors [was an] offshoot of the company's antitrust phobia. Signing a nonexclusive contract with Microsoft that was clearly to Microsoft's benefit was one way of avoiding any future claim that IBM was dominating the personal computer market."[47] His assertion is echoed by Charles Ferguson and Charles Morris, who write: "[B]ecause of the still-pending antitrust action, IBM was wary of owning operating system software for fear of suits

---

[44] Robert X. Cringely, "Triumph of the Nerds: The Rise of Accidental Empires," *PBS* (June 1996), http://www.pbs.org/nerds/part2.html.

[45] Walter Isaacson, The Innovators: How a Group of Hackers, Geniuses, and Geeks Created the Digital Revolution 360 (2015).

[46] Eric G. Swedin and David L. Ferro, Computers: The Life Story of a Technology 95 (2007).

[47] Joseph F. Porac, *Local Rationality, Global Blunders, and the Boundaries of Technological Choice: Lessons from IBM and DOS, in Technological Innovation: Oversights and Foresights* 129, 137 (Raghu Garud et al. ed., 1997).

from software writers" for "IBM was extremely sensitive to even the appearance of having an unfair advantage over a small supplier."[48]

It is difficult, in the final analysis, to deny that IBM's antitrust lawyers strongly influenced elements of the legal and technical design of the IBM PC, for it was essentially antitrust-proof. Indeed, after IBM's successful rise to dominance in the PC market, there was some complaining about "IBM dominance" but no serious antitrust scrutiny or assertion that the firm had employed tying or other exclusionary strategies. The avoidance of even a hint of exclusivity in the design is notable. It is the non-assertion of market power or obvious failures to protect itself from competition that suggest a firm exceptionally intent on avoiding anything that might strengthen the antitrust case against it. Unfortunately for IBM, but fortunately for the economy, the very design of the PC made it much harder for IBM to control the PC market.

The Non-Acquisitions, and More Dogs that Did Not Bark

In 1984, after the success of its PC, IBM was unquestionably the world's dominant computer firm. In fact, at that point, IBM was the world's single most valuable company, its stock price rising to $79 billion by the end of that year. It had upended the personal computer industry, and achieved, for a while, a dominant market share in that market. The last point we consider, in terms of the lasting effects of antitrust scrutiny, was IBM's astonishing failure to take some of the classic measures used by a monopolist to defend its market position.

As already suggested, IBM entered the market in a manner that can only be described as unusually and exceptionally stimulating to competition, and indeed in a manner that breathed life into firms and nascent industries. The level of competition ended up being much greater than IBM could possibly have anticipated. Some of this was surely a blunder on the part of IBM. A key matter was IBM's assumption that its ownership of the BIOS code would protect it from those seeking to create 100 percent IBM compatibles, based on the premise that it might use copyright infringement lawsuits to block any direct copies. However, Compaq and other firms effectively reverse-engineered and cloned IBM's BIOS, using clean-lab techniques (that is, its engineers had no access to the relevant code).[49] This development, which IBM clearly did not anticipate, created a major breach in the barriers to competition it thought it had, and yielded a flourishing PC market from the 1980s onward.

---

[48] Charles H. Ferguson and Charles R. Morris, Computer Wars: The Post-IBM World 26, 71 (1993). *See also* Eli M. Noam, Media Ownership and Concentration in America 187 (2009).

[49] For a description of one firm's cloning techniques, *see* James Langdell, *Phoenix Says Its BIOS May Foil IBM's Lawsuits*, PC NEWS (Jul. 10, 1984), available at https://books.google.com/books?id=Bwng8NJ5fesC&lpg=PA56&ots=_i5pxGorF7&dq=ibm+pc+program+use+extra+bios+chip&pg=PA56&hl=en#v=onepage&q&f=true.

The Policeman at the Elbow

An easier way to protect its dominance would have been control over Microsoft's DOS,[50] and we have already discussed IBM's decision not to insist that the Microsoft's DOS be exclusive to IBM, or even partially exclusive. That single decision, as many have noted, might have ensured a far longer domination of the PC market for the firm. But even if this might have been, in part, at least an oversight, it is hard to explain IBM's subsequent non-acquisition of PC-DOS, of Microsoft, or even of a share of Microsoft, without crediting some concern of renewed antitrust problems.

In the 1990s, reporters first revealed that, in fact, IBM was offered various opportunities to buy Microsoft or its software. In 1980, according to the *Wall Street Journal*, Microsoft offered to let IBM buy its operating system outright, an opportunity that IBM declined, for the reasons discussed above. Later, in 1986, after the IBM PC had successfully taken over personal computing, Bill Gates offered IBM the opportunity to buy 10 percent of Microsoft.[51] There is some reason to think that, while surely the price would have been steep, IBM might have even have tried to acquire Microsoft in its entirety. IBM – still the most valuable firm in the world – demurred, concerned that its purchase would reignite antitrust concerns by being seen as "throwing its weight around."[52] Paul Carroll reports Bill Lowe of the PC team stating that "IBM didn't want to be seen as dominating the PC market too thoroughly."[53]

Given the runaway success of the PC, it was also plausible that an IBM that was behaving more like Facebook, Microsoft, or other less inhibited giants would have sought to either acquire or clone the other units, including hard drive manufacturer Seagate, and Epson. However, it made no efforts whatsoever to acquire these actors, which would go on to earn most of the profits in the PC industry.

* *

The various design decisions surrounding the IBM PC and IBM's subsequent failure to defend its position are of such great importance over the long term for both the computer industry and the entire high-tech economy that they must be carefully examined.[54] We have already noted that the nonproprietary design left the market open to challengers to the IBM PC, which manufactured cheaper but compatible computers, also using MS-DOS. Over the long run, this development would erode IBM's early dominance. But more generally, an important consequence was the fostering of a whole series of new and independent industries: an industry for hard

---

[50] A contrasting theory, not explored further, is that exclusivity would have hindered the spread of the PC platform, or perhaps made CP/M rivals more successful.

[51] Don E. Waldman, The Rise and Fall of IBM, in *Market Dominance: How Firms Gain, Hold, or Lose It and the Impact on Economic Performance*, p. 141 (David Ira Rosenbaum ed., 1998).

[52] Ibid.

[53] Carroll, supra note 24, at p. 57.

[54] *See*, e.g., Jimmy Maher, The Complete History of the IBM PC, Ars Technica (July 31, 2017), https://arstechnica.com/gadgets/2017/06/ibm-pc-history-part-1/.

drives and other forms of storage, another for processors and memory, and, of course, the market for personal computer software. It is true that these industries existed previously, but their growth was catalyzed by the IBM PC and its later competitors. It is interesting to contrast the PC, in this respect, with Apple, the previous leader, which was slightly less open than IBM, and with the launch of the Apple Macintosh, retreated to an entirely closed architecture with most components manufactured by Apple. In an alternative universe without IBM, had some version of the Apple Macintosh became the dominant business computer, it is very possible that the storage and software industries, in particular, would have been greatly reduced in independence and significance.

LESSONS FOR ENFORCERS

Today, the concentration of the high-tech industries has become, one again, a matter of major public concern. That's why the IBM case merits careful study by enforcers, for it was the first major tech antitrust case of the computing era, and a neglected member of the big three cases of the late twentieth century (IBM, AT&T, and Microsoft). Close study of the case offers guidance and insight into what might be the dynamic justifications for bringing a major antitrust lawsuit in the 2020s.

IBM was just one company. Yet, in retrospect, it was sitting atop what turned out to be an enormous number of important industries, from software through storage, processing and operating systems. The subsequent flourishing of the industries that were once in areas controlled, or potentially controlled, by IBM has unquestionably transformed the modern economy.

Given the complexity of any historical period, it is almost always impossible to claim that one factor – one leader, one case, one invention, or one critical decision – changed everything. However, it is not impossible to claim a contribution or a catalyst. And even if we don't know what would have happened in the absence of antitrust – if, in fact, software might have been unbundled anyhow, or the PC might have developed more or less the same – there is good reason to believe that the pervasive evidence of antitrust phobia hastened the outcome.

If an enforcer wanted to duplicate the catalytic effects of the IBM case, what would he or she do? A close look at the history recommends that antitrust enforcers, particularly when thinking about big Section 2 cases, should spend time thinking about what industries or potential future markets and industries the dominant firm sits on top of or can potentially control the development of. The intuition is that there is a difference, say, between a shoe monopoly and monopoly on sidewalks, given that the latter might be an input into and entwined in so many other businesses. This suggests that antitrust enforcers should, when considering cases, begin by thinking about how many markets are influenced or dependent on the product or service.

The Policeman at the Elbow 99

A similar logic suggests prioritizing Sherman 2 cases where the problem isn't just competition in the primary market, but where competition in adjacent markets looks to be compromised or threatened. The long cycles of industrial history suggest that what are at one point seen as adjacent or side industries can sometimes emerge to become of primary importance, as in the example of software and hardware. Hence, the manner of how something is sold can make a big difference. In particular, "bundling" or "tying" one product to another can stunt the development of an underlying industry. Even a tie that seems like "one product" at the time the case is litigated, as, for example, software and hardware were in the 1960s, or physical telephones and telephone lines, might contribute to such stunting. If successful, an antitrust prosecution that breaks the tie and opens a long-dominated market to competition may serve to have very significant long-term effects.

While all things are clearer in retrospect, the existence of a cottage or nascent industry might serve as a clue that, in fact, a vibrant industry might emerge from breaking the tie. If some firms manage to survive even in the presence of a tie, that suggests the possibility that there is far more potential there. In the example of the software industry, as we've suggested, the concept of prepackaged software existed, and a scattering of firms sold it and made a profit thereby. That pattern suggested plenty of room to grow, even if it would take many years for premade software to develop into the thriving industry it became.

A last lesson that might be gleaned from the IBM litigation is this: If the government wants to spur a change in conduct, it should seek maximum remedies in the cases it brings. In *IBM*, the Justice Department brought a complaint seeking dissolution – a full structural remedy. IBM's concern about such a remedy had a major effect on its thinking and decision making, and seemed to yield the antitrust phobia that proved important over the 1970s. That suggests that the Justice Department cannot induce improved behavior without making credible threats of punishment at the outset of the case. In particular, there is a risk that a case that begins seeking a mere consent decree might not have any real effect on firm conduct.

A full discussion of what should go into case selection is beyond the scope of this or perhaps any article. But the final caveat or warning is this: While I think it is correct to suggest that the costs of litigation should not be fetishized – although the millions matter less when there are billions at stake – one thing that does matter are the effects on the company itself. IBM was, arguably, a reduced entity during the antitrust case (although it remained extremely profitable, and actually quadrupled its stock price). Knowing that the effect of litigation is to damage the firm, the enforcer needs to have some confidence that the damage will be salutary – that is, it will yield room for competitors to take the ball and run with it. While "do not harm" cannot be the mantra of antitrust enforcement, no one should seek outcomes that make things worse. And this is what makes timing all important, and suggests that enforcement policy will always be a matter requiring, above all, good judgment and a clear eye toward what one hopes to achieve.

PART II

Algorithms

4

Who Do We Blame for the Filter Bubble? On the Roles of Math, Data, and People in Algorithmic Social Systems

Kartik Hosanagar and Alex P. Miller

INTRODUCTION

Algorithms are playing an increasingly important role in the modern economy and, more recently, civic life. Online search engines, digital media, and e-commerce websites have long made use of recommendation systems to filter, sort, and suggest the products and media we consume on the internet. However, with the rise of social media and scientific developments in artificial intelligence research, algorithms have started to impact how decisions are made in entirely new domains. The influence of algorithms can be found in the structure of our social networks, whom we marry, what news articles we see, and what jobs we get.

As algorithmic suggestions and decisions have proliferated, so too has an awareness – and, increasingly, wariness – about the impact that algorithms are having on society. This has included specific concerns about racial disparities in the predictive accuracy of recidivism prediction instruments (Angwin et al. 2016), gender bias in how digital job advertisements are placed (Lambrecht and Tucker 2016), the ability of dynamic pricing algorithms to discriminate indiscriminately (Miller and Hosanagar 2019), the role of news-filtering algorithms in polarizing our political discussions (Pariser 2014), and a general concern about the ethics of using the unprecedented power of artificial intelligence for private and governmental surveillance (Tufekci 2017; Zuboff 2019). All of this attention has led to an increased scrutiny of not just the institutions behind these technologies, but also the mathematics of the specific algorithms driving these systems and the decisions of the people engineering them.

As such, articulating and understanding the roles that algorithms play in shaping our society is no longer an academic exercise. In April 2019, a group of US Senators proposed the "Algorithmic Accountability Act" (AAA), in which they raised concern about the potential for "automated decision systems" to exhibit bias and discrimination (among concerns such as privacy and security) (Booker 2019). Their proposed remedy would require firms to conduct "impact assessments" of their internal algorithms and security systems. Despite the inherent complexities involved in assessing the impact of *algorithmic social systems*, this process may soon be a legally required undertaking for many organizations. As we begin to debate, study, legislate, and influence the role of algorithms in our society, it is essential to have a common (and commonsense) characterization of how algorithmic social systems function. What are the inputs of these systems? What influence do these inputs have on outcomes of interest?[1] What properties, rules, or dynamics of these systems generalize across different contexts?

In this chapter, we introduce a framework for understanding and modeling the complexities of algorithmic social systems. While some commentators have directly implicated "algorithms," "machines," "software," and "math" as the primary source of concern in many systems, we believe this language masks what are sometimes the most important dynamics for determining outcomes in these systems (Eubanks 2018; Knight 2017; O'Neil 2017). Algorithms do not emerge out of thin air; their impact is driven by not just the mathematics behind them, but also the data that feed them, and the systems they interact with. We use this framework to propose a description of algorithmic systems being comprised of three fundamental factors: The underlying data on which they are trained, the logic of the algorithms themselves, and the way in which human beings interact with these systems (see Figure 3). Each of the individual factors in these systems plays an important role and can, in various circumstances, have the largest responsibility in determining outcomes. Furthermore, as we will demonstrate concretely, the interactions between the various components can also have significant impact, making targeted interventions difficult to evaluate ex ante and cross-context comparisons difficult to generalize between different circumstances.

As researchers attempt to study algorithmic social systems and lawmakers get closer to drafting legislation that regulates the inputs and outputs of these systems, we believe it is important to consider the challenges of ascribing blame, liability, and responsibility in the many circumstances in which automated decisions play a significant role. Our framework provides a scaffolding on which analysis of any algorithmic social system can be conducted. While we advocate for nuance and rigor in the assessment of algorithmic systems, we are not suggesting that such

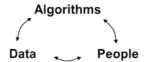

FIGURE 3: The results of algorithmic systems can be attributed to their underlying data, the mathematical logic of the algorithms, and the way people interact with these factors.

---

[1] In the various specific cases cited above, such outcomes may include a measurement of racial disparities in algorithmic predictions, gender disparities in automated ad viewership, selective partisan exposure in online news consumption, or pricing inequities.

systems are simply too complex to understand, analyze, or influence. Indeed, the purpose of our framework is to encourage researchers, policymakers, and critics to (first) identify each of three components – data, algorithms, and people – when discussing the prospect of intervening in an algorithmic social system and (second) ensure the responsibilities and intended consequences of such interventions are well-articulated for each of the system's components. This framework provides a principled starting point for modeling the key factors involved with complex algorithmic systems.

CASE STUDY: FILTER BUBBLE

To illustrate the utility of our framework for understanding the impact of algorithms in a particular context, we focus our attention on a hotly debated topic in the social sciences in recent years: The phenomenon of "filter bubbles" and the role that algorithms have played in creating them.[2] In the United States,[3] social media and search engines are increasingly prominent sources of news, with up to two-thirds of Americans relying on social media for news in their daily lives (Moon 2017). However, many commentators have raised concerns about the way in which these news platforms fragment our social fabric: Because psychometric algorithms at large tech companies are able to learn users' preferences over time, the more people use these tools, the less likely it is that they will come across articles from perspectives that are different from their own (Pariser 2014; The Economist 2017). The Obama Administration raised concern about this phenomenon in their 2016 White House Report on "Big Data", in which they specifically referred to algorithms "that narrow instead of expand user options" as being a "hard-to-detect flaw" in the design of personalized services (Obama 2016). Especially given the scholarship on the increase in political polarization in the United States over the last several decades, we are at a moment when shared values and information environments are already under threat (Sunstein 1999; Achenbach and Clement 2016). Any role that algorithms and technology platforms play in increasing social fragmentation – for example, by exclusively serving conservative news to conservative users and liberal news to liberal users – is worth investigating and understanding.

[2] We do not discuss the difference in ideological fragmentation between users who consume news online vs. offline. In the studies reviewed here, the counterfactual comparisons are between users in different regimes of online news consumption (e.g., different algorithmic choices, or different channel choices which have varying degrees of algorithmic curation). It is possible (even likely) that the effect of consuming news online – in which the mere act of choosing one's news sources or friends depending on our behavioral preferences – causes more fragmentation relative to consuming news through traditional offline channels (newspaper, TV, radio, etc.). This discussion, however, is beyond the scope of the current essay.

[3] While this discussion may be relevant for considering filter bubble effects in other countries, we mostly discuss the context of the United States in this essay. One implication of this simplification is that, because the US is largely a two-party political system, "political fragmentation" can be considered (in a simplistic model) to be synonymous with "polarization."

Such an understanding will be necessary if our goals – as individuals, scholars, activists, and policymakers – are to mitigate the negative consequences of online filter bubbles. The importance of developing a clear understanding of online platforms' roles in the filter bubble phenomenon is underscored by a recent legislative proposal, introduced on the floor of the United States Senate in November 2019, named the "Filter Bubble Transparency Act" (FBTA). Separate from the Algorithmic Accountability Act, and designed specifically with the consumers of social media and political news in mind, this legislation has a stated purpose of guaranteeing Americans the right to "engage with a [media] platform without being manipulated by algorithms driven by user-specific data" (US Senate 2019).

In their attempts to legislate the use of personal data by internet platforms, the authors of the bill distinguish between two types of "user-specific" data: That which were "expressly provided by the user to the platform" for the purpose of an "algorithmic ranking system," and that which were not. The bill specifies that platforms are allowed to use the list of accounts that someone subscribes to on social media to determine what content they will see. However, any filtering, ordering, or ranking of someone's content feed – outside of chronological ordering – would require that platforms show "a prominently placed icon" near their content feeds. This icon would serve two primary purposes: (1) inform users that their feeds are being filtered based on their user-specific behavioral data and (2) allow users to select between an algorithmically ranked feed and a chronological feed.[4]

Given the name of the bill itself, the implicit assumption of these regulations is that requiring platforms to be more transparent and giving users the option to avoid algorithmic filtering will alleviate some problems associated with digital filter bubbles. But to what extent are these assumptions true? In an effort to enrich our understanding of how this and other potential interventions might affect users' online browsing behaviors, we review relevant research on the roles of people, data, and algorithms in determining filter bubble effects on social media and content aggregation platforms.

REVIEW OF RELATED LITERATURE

We review several empirical studies that attempted directly to compare the effects *between* different factors in our framework applied to digital media platforms. These studies give us some insight into how significant each of the factors are in determining the extent of the filter bubble effect by attempting to quantify the political diversity of internet users' media consumption.

We begin by considering research on users of Facebook, the largest social media network in the world and often the focus of discussions about digital filter bubbles.

---

[4] The way Twitter currently accomplishes this with a small icon in the upper right-hand corner of their app is explicitly called out as a good example of how this might work.

While much of the platform's data are kept proprietary, researchers at Facebook published a large-scale study of real-user behavior in 2015 (Bakshy, Messing, and Adamic 2015). By looking at the behavior of 10.1 million active Facebook users in the US who self-reported their political ideology ("conservative," "moderate," and "liberal"), the researchers analyzed how the social network influences its users' exposure to diverse perspectives. The researchers then calculated what proportion of the news stories in these users' newsfeeds was crosscutting, defined as sharing a perspective other than their own (for example, a liberal reading a news story with a primarily conservative perspective).

To evaluate the impact of Facebook's newsfeed algorithm, the researchers identified three factors that influence the extent to which we see crosscutting news. First, who our friends are and what news stories they share; second, among all the news stories shared by friends, which ones are displayed by the newsfeed algorithm; and third, which of the displayed news stories we actually click on. Note that this systematic approach to decomposing the impact of the newsfeed algorithm is similar to the data-algorithm-people framework we proposed earlier. In the context of a social media newsfeed, the primary data that feed into Facebook's algorithm are the articles shared by one's network. The algorithm then chooses which articles to display, from which individual users select a subsample of articles to click on and read. Each of these steps interacts in a dynamic process that determines the intensity of our ideological segregation.

By systematically comparing the extent to which exposure to crosscutting news is affected by each step in this filtering process, the researchers were able to quantify how much each factor affected the ideological diversity of news consumption on Facebook. If the second step – the newsfeed algorithm itself – is the primary driver of the echo chamber, this would suggest that Facebook's design choices and the specific logic of its filtering algorithms play a significant role in driving online polarization. By way of contrast, if the first or third steps are more responsible for the filter bubble, it would suggest that the data and ways we interact with algorithmic suggestions are more significant than the algorithms themselves. Of course, this would not absolve Facebook from all responsibility in the development of filter bubbles, but it would suggest that focusing on algorithms specifically as the primary driver of polarization would be a parochial way of understanding the problem.

Interestingly, it is this latter hypothesis that was borne out by Facebook's study. The researchers found that if users acquired their news from a randomly selected group of Facebook users, nearly 45 percent of stories seen by liberals and 40 percent seen by conservatives on Facebook would be crosscutting. However, because users come across stories from their self-selected network of friends, the researchers found that only 24 percent of news stories shared by liberals' friends were crosscutting and about 35 percent of stories shared by conservatives' friends were crosscutting. The friends people choose to associate with on Facebook play a dramatic role in reducing the diversity of news we see on the platform (relative to what is shared by the broader

US population). Because we are more likely to be connected to friends with interests similar to our own (a phenomenon known as "homophily"), the news items those friends share are more likely to agree with our preexisting ideological positions than a random sample of news items across Facebook (McPherson et al. 2001).

The study also found that the newsfeed algorithm did reduce the proportion of crosscutting news stories (to 22 percent for liberals and 34 percent for conservatives). However, the magnitude of this reduction was significantly smaller than that attributable to the self-selection process in the first step. Facebook's algorithm does exacerbate the filter bubble, but not by much. The last step in the filtering process – the extent to which we actually click on crosscutting news stories – further reduces the ideological diversity of our news. But again, the magnitude of this effect is modest: The final proportion of crosscutting news stories we click on is 21 percent for liberals and 30 percent for conservatives (see Figure 4).

Given that the research cited above was conducted in-house by Facebook social scientists, critics may be skeptical of these findings. However, the results described above are consistent with another recent study on the topic of filter bubbles. Using an independently gathered dataset on web-browsing behavior, Flaxman, Goel, and Rao (2016) were able to isolate the impact of social media on news consumption patterns relative to other channels, such as news aggregators, search engines, and direct referrals (e.g., through bookmarks or typing specific websites into the browser's address bar).

While this cross-channel comparison is different from the specific filtering effects of Facebook's newsfeed analyzed by Bakshy et al., there are important similarities in the high-level findings. Flaxman et al. compare ideological exposure between four different channels of online news consumption, with varying levels of algorithmic influence: direct referrals (visits to self-selected news sites, with mostly editorial

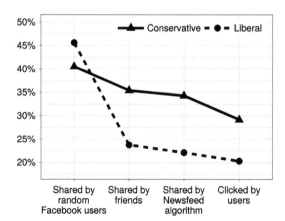

FIGURE 4: Summarized results of "Exposure to ideologically diverse news and opinion on Facebook" (based on data presented in Science, 2015).

curation), news aggregators (whose recommendations are almost entirely driven by algorithmic selection), and search engines and social media (both of which are influenced by users' choices themselves – what they search for and who they befriend – and algorithmic curation). In this research, the authors find interesting nuances around the differences between news and opinion articles and the importance of defining what metrics we use to quantify ideological polarization. But among their primary findings is that "the vast majority of online news consumption is accounted for by individuals simply visiting the home pages of their favorite, typically mainstream news outlets."

While it is not possible to disentangle the specific effects of algorithmic selection vs. the effects of homophily in social networks in this study, we can compare the researchers' findings between pure algorithmic curation (on news aggregators) and self-initiated browsing behaviors (through direct referrals). It turns out that, particularly for "hard news," the algorithmically curated news feeds had content that was less ideologically polarized, resulting in users being exposed to more crosscutting content on these platforms than their personal browsing behaviors. As before, this research suggests that individuals' own ideological preferences – and how those preferences translate into behavior in social networks and online browsing behaviors – play a larger role in the filter bubble effect than the results of algorithmic curation.

Another related set of studies, from our research group in 2010 and 2014, evaluated media consumption patterns of more than 1,700 iTunes users (Fleder et al. 2010; Hosanagar et al. 2014). We measured the overlap in media consumed by users – in other words, the extent to which two randomly selected users listened to any overlapping set of songs. If users were fragmenting due to algorithmic recommendations, the overlap in consumption across users would decrease after they start receiving recommendations. However, in our findings, we found that recommendation algorithms increased the average overlap of digital media consumption. This increase occurred for two reasons. First, users simply consumed more media when an algorithm found relevant media for them. If two users consumed twice as much media, then the chance of them consuming common content also increased. Second, algorithmic recommendations helped users explore and branch into new interests. While one might be concerned that these new interests were fragmented across many genres, our evidence suggests recommendation algorithms systematically push users toward more *similar* content. This is partially due to the fact that these algorithms exhibit a popularity bias, whereby products that are already popular are more likely to be recommended (Fleder and Hosanagar 2009). Because algorithms tend to push different people toward the same content, even after controlling for the volume-effect of recommendations, the algorithm had the effect of increasing consumption overlap among users. In aggregate, this means that algorithms increase the probability that you share a musical interest with another random user in the system. That the effects of algorithms can appear to increase fragmentation in one context (social media) and decrease it in another (digital media) suggests we need to be careful about making cross-context generalizations in this discussion. We will revisit (and attempt to provide insight into) this observation in a simulation analysis below, but we now discuss several recent studies that address an important limitation of research discussed thus far.

While all of the aforementioned studies are useful for illuminating the empirics of media consumption patterns on the internet, their research questions are, fundamentally, ones that *compare* the effects of data, people, and algorithms on fragmentation. This is different from asking what the effects would be if we were to counterfactually manipulate these factors (while attempting to hold others constant). In particular, an important component of these systems not explicitly discussed yet is that the design, logic, and mathematics of recommendation algorithms can have significant effects on fragmentation. This is demonstrated by Garimella et al. (2017), who designed an algorithm specifically to reduce users' political polarity by exposing them to diverse content. Further, recent game-theoretic work on the digital filter bubbles – which models the dynamics of network formation, the economic incentives of content producers, and horizontal differentiation among user preferences – also suggests that different algorithm designs can both enhance and mitigate filter bubble effects in different contexts (Berman and Katona 2019).

Despite their insights, a limitation of these studies is that they were not able to study how their proposed interventions behave in the wild. However, there are some studies in which the specific roles of different recommendation algorithms are evaluated in close-to-real-world environments. Graells-Garrido et al. (2016) experimentally changed the graphical interface of a Chilean Twitter service designed to surface and recommend new content for its users to read. The authors randomly assigned users to different variations of the site's graphical interface and different versions of the service's recommendation algorithm. Interestingly, while the algorithm the authors designed to increase users' network diversity was successful in exposing users to more politically diverse accounts, it performed worse than a (homophilic) baseline algorithm in getting users to accept its recommendations. This finding points to the importance of considering the downstream effects on all components of this algorithmic social system; simply changing one factor (algorithm design) may be offset by the differential way that other factors respond (e.g., people's uptake of a new algorithm's recommendations).

This point is also demonstrated by a study that attempted not to change the algorithms used on social media platforms, but rather by directly increasing the political diversity of users' social graph (an intervention on the *data* component in our framework). In this work, researchers incentivized Twitter users to follow a bot account that reshared posts from accounts of elected officials and opinion leaders of the political party opposite from their own (Bail et al. 2018). While this intervention expanded the political diversity the accounts users followed, this exposure to opposing opinions actually reinforced users' original political identities, causing liberals to hold more liberal views and conservatives to have more conservative views.

We have so far looked at studies that have counterfactually changed users' recommendation algorithms and network structures, but what about the effects of attempting to change people's behaviors directly? Indeed, implicit in the transparency requirement proposed in the FBTA is the assumption that the behavior of the people using social media and content platforms would be different if they had more information. Informing users that their feeds are being algorithmically filtered might cause them to become more aware of the things they click, like, and react to, or opt to use a different (perhaps purely chronological) type of content filtering.

While we know little about the targeted effects of this specific type of transparency on social media users' browsing behavior, we can look at some research that has attempted similar behavioral interventions. In Gillani et al. (2018), researchers recruited Twitter users to use a "social mirror" application that was designed to reveal the structure and partisanship of each participant's social network. By being made aware of the homogeneity of their network, the authors hypothesized that they could "motivate more diverse content-sharing and information-seeking behaviors." Unfortunately, the results of the study were largely null, indicating that even behavioral interventions specifically designed to mitigate filter bubble effects have limited effects. If nothing else, this research points to the likelihood that the transparency component of the FBTA's proposal will have little effect on changing consumer behavior on digital content platforms.

THE INTERACTION BETWEEN ALGORITHMS AND DATA

Taken together, the research discussed above demonstrates that the algorithms, underlying data, and human behaviors all have roles to play in the fragmentation debate. Especially when analyzing individual aspects of a single algorithmic social system, our three-factor framework provides useful context for understanding the dynamics at play between users, their data, and the algorithms they interact with. However, the juxtaposition of findings from the two separate contexts analyzed in this research – digital music and political news – highlights an important phenomenon: In some contexts, algorithmic recommendations can (modestly) increase fragmentation, while in other contexts, algorithms decrease fragmentation. This is not necessarily the understanding portrayed in some popular press, which has suggested that algorithms are a (if not *the*) primary culprit to blame for filter bubbles (Gupta 2019; Hern 2017; Lazer 2015). There are many factors varying across the studies cited above, but this simple observation about the apparent heterogeneity in algorithmic effects suggests that discussions of digital filter bubbles without systematic and contextual nuance may lead us to make simplistic conclusions.

In line with this observation, we wish to highlight the need for rigor and caution in applying policy changes or recommendations *across* different contexts. As US legislators edge closer to directly intervening in the way online platforms recommend and curate digital media, it is important to recognize the challenges associated with crafting regulations that accomplish their intended goals. To illustrate these complexities, we will show specifically how the interactions between the various factors in algorithmic systems can play significant roles in system outcomes. In particular, we will show how applying the same (relatively minor) changes to the underlying logic of a recommendation algorithm in different contexts can have dramatically different results on the users' emergent level of fragmentation. In addition to contextualizing the seemingly contradictory findings of the research cited earlier, this analysis demonstrates that, especially when several factors are changing simultaneously between contexts, one-size-fits-all approaches for addressing concerns about the digital filter bubble will likely fail.

SIMULATION ANALYSIS

The research cited above suggests that complex interactions between the factors in an algorithmic social system may exist, but the contexts are too disparate for any systematic analysis. Ideally, we would like to experimentally vary the nature of the data, people, and algorithms in these environments to understand how they may interact. This motivates the development of a simulation framework, which we outline below. To make our rhetorical case for the importance of interaction effects across different contexts, we will only have to vary two of the three factors (the specific mathematics of the algorithms that determine which media are recommended and the underlying data that serve as inputs to the algorithms). But we emphasize how in between most real-world systems, all three factors will vary simultaneously, only adding to the complexities involved in making any unilateral policy recommendations across contexts.

Our framework is designed to capture many of the most important dynamics of how recommendation algorithms and consumers interact through time. In particular, we will model a set of consumers with idiosyncratic preferences, interacting with an online media platform in which their consumption patterns are influenced by the platform's recommendations (similar to how news is recommended on Facebook or books and movies are recommended on Amazon). As with recommendation algorithms in real life, the recommendations one user receives in our simulation are also influenced by the consumption patterns of other users on the platform. This introduces a complex set of dynamics that make it difficult to predict a priori how one algorithm will affect system outcomes compared to another. As mentioned, we will study how this system evolves under different assumptions about the internal logic of the recommendation algorithm and the nature of the data on which these algorithms are trained.[5] We will specifically compare how two different recommendation algorithms affect fragmentation in environments that are more or less polarized. While there are many ways to describe "fragmentation," in this setting we use a measure of "overlap" between users' media consumption patterns. In our context, overlap will measure the extent to which a user in one ideological group consumes the same content as users from an alternative ideological group (roughly based on the conservative-liberal dichotomy in American politics). We discuss precisely how our simulation works in more detail below.

Simulation Setup

Our simulation is built around a two-dimensional "ideal point model" (Kamakura 1986). The two dimensions represent two abstract product attributes in this market. To capture the notion of political polarity, we will think of the X-dimension in our analysis as being analogous to one's location on a scale from progressive to conservative. The Y-dimension can then be thought of as representing an abstract auxiliary attribute associated with digital media. (In the real world, these may be target age group, degree of sensationalization, writing style, etc.) An example of the data that serve as input to this model is shown in Figure 5. The preference of an individual consumer is represented by their position in this space (their "ideal point"); the products available for consumption in this market are also characterized

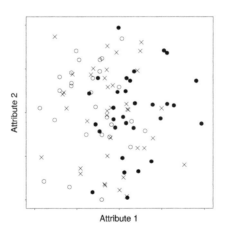

FIGURE 5: Sample draw of consumers and items

---

[5] There are other ways of operationalizing the factors in our system, but in this analysis we think of users' empirical distribution of preferences as the relevant "data" component of this system. This represents how the ambient characteristics that describe people's preferences can vary across contexts, not necessarily how the data used to represent these preferences vary (which is another way algorithmic systems may differ). The way in which they make decisions about which media to consume – their decision function in our simulation – can be thought of as the way in which "people" interact with this system; in our simulations, this decision function is constant across environments.

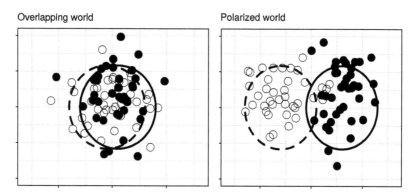

FIGURE 6: Sample draws of consumer ideal points in overlapping (left) and polarized (right) contexts

by their coordinates in attribute space. This system allows us to model consumer utility as a function of the distance between their ideal point and the item they consume. In this model, users probabilistically consume items that are closer to them with a higher chance than they consume items that are further away.[6]

We first describe how we manipulate the ambient data-generating process for our simulation. In particular, we will vary the degree of underlying polarization present in the political environment. This manipulation is designed to account for the fact that some forms of media (like political news) may be inherently more fragmented/clustered along item attributes than others. To model this in our simulation, we first divide consumers into two nominal groups: White and black. In one set of simulations, we will assume that there is very little difference in political preferences among these two groups; but in another set of simulations, we will assume that these two groups' preferences follow a bimodal distribution, with white congregating around one extreme and black congregating around the opposite extreme. We label these initial conditions as "overlapping" and "polarized", respectively (see Figure 6). Effectively, these two different preference distributions help create two very different input datasets of media preferences for training our system's recommendation algorithms.

One of the primary motivations for the use of recommendation systems in practice is that it is not possible for consumers to perform an exhaustive search of the item space. This means that – at least initially – consumers should only be aware of a subset of products in the market. We capture this in our model by only allowing consumers to purchase products in their "awareness set." Initially, this set includes only products that are either close to the consumer in attribute space or close to the origin. This

---

[6] Formally, we use a random utility model in which the probability that an item is purchased by a user is equal to the softmax of that item's distance in attribute space, with respect to the set of products in the user's awareness set.

reflects the notion that consumers are likely to be aware of items in their own "neighborhood" and those that are most popular in the market overall.[7] Because consumers are not aware of all items in the market, we will use a recommendation algorithm to add items into each consumer's consideration set over time.

Importantly, by performing this analysis via simulation, we can vary the *both* the ambient data environment of different contexts *and* the nature of an algorithm's internal logic. Further, we can do this in more systematic ways than the empirical studies described earlier were able to do. The first algorithm we will use is the classic, nearest-neighbor collaborative filter ("people like you also bought X"). This is a deterministic algorithm that first selects the ten "most similar" users to a particular focal user (using mathematical definitions of "similarity" based on historical purchases), and then recommends the most popular item among this set of neighbors. We will then use an extension of the collaborative filter that uses stochastic item selection: Rather than recommending the most popular item in each neighborhood, as is done by the classical method, the stochastic algorithm recommends each item with a probability that is proportional to its popularity among a user's most similar neighbors. This algorithm is designed to mitigate the problem of "popularity bias" in collaborative filters alluded to earlier; for our purposes, the stochastic collaborative filter provides a small twist on the classical algorithm that allows us to investigate how different algorithms behave in and interact with different contexts.

In keeping with our interest in analyzing polarization in digital media consumption, we will use this simulation framework to measure how each combination of empirical context and algorithm logic affects aggregate measures of fragmentation between white and black consumer types. We do this by operationalizing the notion of "commonality" or "overlap" by first constructing a network in which each consumer is a node and edges are added between two nodes whenever two users consume the same item (see Figure 7). Thus, users who consume similar items will have stronger ties in this network than users who do not share any mutually consumed items. Our final quantitative measure of overlap will be the percentage of edges in the entire network that are between users of different types (i.e., we count the number of connections between white and black users, and divide this by the total number of connections in the network).[8]

---

[7] It is not entirely necessary to use the origin as the location of the most popular items in the market. So long as the awareness "neighborhood" used is identical across consumers, this region will contain products that, by construction, most users know about. However, by using the origin specifically for this location, we capture the notion that "mass market" media is typically not going to be extreme in any particular ideological dimension, much in the same way that traditional broadcast news networks in past decades were more likely to be nonpartisan.

[8] There are indeed many measures of overlap/polarization that we could choose to study, including ones that are more local to individual users. However, for the purposes of this analysis, we are most interested in demonstrating that small changes in underlying data structures and algorithms can have complex and unpredictable interactions on system-level outcomes (such as cross-type edge percentage).

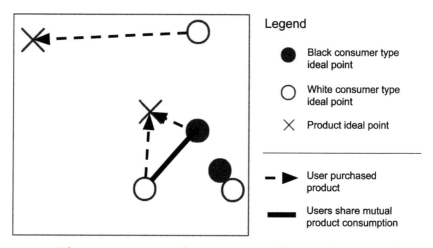

FIGURE 7: When two users consume the same item, we add a network connection between them. We measure the number and proportion of edges between users of different types.

In summary, we have a 2-by-2 experimental setup (overlapping vs. polarized context; classical vs. stochastic collaborative filter) that we carry out according to the following procedure:

1. Overlapping vs. polarized preference distribution chosen.
2. Deterministic vs. stochastic collaborative filtering algorithm chosen.
3. Consumer and item positions drawn in attribute space (according to assumption about preference distribution made in step 1).
4. Consumers initially made aware of small subset of items.
5. Each user is recommended an item by adding it to their awareness set (recommended items are selected based on each users' consumption history, according to the algorithm selected in step 2).
6. Each user probabilistically selects one item to consume from their awareness set, with higher weights given to those items that are closer to the user in attribute space.
7. Recommendation algorithm updates nearest neighbor calculations based on new consumption data.
8. Steps 5–7 repeat for 500 iterations.
9. Polarization metrics calculated for co-consumption network between consumers.

SIMULATION RESULTS AND DISCUSSION

We have plotted the numeric results of our simulations in Figure 8, in which we have graphed the proportion of cross-type edges (our measure of overlap/commonality) for each of the four experimental conditions.

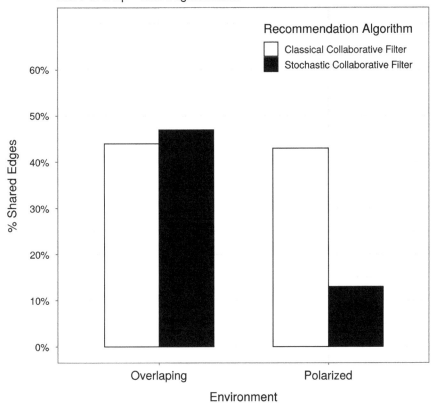

FIGURE 8: Proportion of cross-type edges (measure of overlap) in 2-by-2 simulation experiment

First, note how moving from a classical to stochastic collaborative filter (comparing colors within groups) has differential effects depending on the underlying data distribution. In the polarized world, the stochastic algorithm *decreases* commonality among dissimilar users (the proportion of cross-type edges goes from 43 percent to 13 percent), whereas this same change in the world with overlapping groups *increases* commonality (the proportion of cross-type edges goes from 44 percent to 47 percent). Similarly, when we hold the algorithm constant (comparing across groups for the same colors), moving from the polarized world to the overlapping world has a marginal effect on commonality when the classical algorithm is used, but this shift has a substantial effect on commonality when the stochastic algorithm is used.

These observations demonstrate that understanding the impact of either data or algorithms requires us to consider their effects *jointly*, with a focus on how they interact with one another. While this is a simple simulation in a microenvironment with several artificial assumptions, the implications of these results should inform our macro-discussion about echo chambers (and algorithmic systems) generally. Indeed, even in this simplistic, simulated world in which only a small number factors are varying, we observe complex interactions between data and algorithms. In real-world environments, the algorithms are more opaque, the data are more massive, and users exhibit more complex patterns of behavior. All of these factors only increase the complexity of the social system and suggest a need for an even greater appreciation of the intricacies associated with the interactions between all factors involved. On the whole, we believe these results suggest that, if policymakers are not careful about recognizing the distinct dynamics at play in different media contexts, they run the risk of exacerbating problems in one context while attempting to fix them in another.

While these interactions may indeed be complex, our framework provides a basis for understanding how the same changes in one context can have opposing effects in a different context (as we observed in the previously discussed studies on newsfeed and digital music fragmentation). We hope our simulation highlights both the importance of using a systematic framework for understanding algorithmic effects and – due to the presence of potentially significant interactions between factors in algorithmic systems – the importance of not overgeneralizing findings from one context or implementing policies that indiscriminately affect systems with differing characteristics.

CONCLUSION

In sum, the framework we propose here provides a way to decompose and contextualize current concerns around the negative impacts of algorithmic suggestions and decisions. We apply the framework to look at the growing concerns that social newsfeed algorithms are driving increased political polarization. We find that algorithms can play a role but focusing exclusively on them while ignoring the manner in which data, algorithms and people interact can paint an incomplete, and even misleading, picture when attempting to understand the effects of each component across different contexts. By systematically decomposing the causes of filter bubbles, we are able to provide a more complete characterization of the problem and facilitate the development of meaningful policy changes for moving forward.

As we attempt to engineer our algorithmic systems, the algorithms themselves certainly deserve a high degree of scrutiny. But it is important to not forget the role of other components of the system. As our analysis has shown, the same algorithm can have dramatically different effects depending on the context in which it is applied, and the same input data can have varying results depending on the algorithm that is acting on the data.

We conclude by suggesting that adding more context – both *sociological* and *technological* – to these discussions provides the most meaningful way forward for ensuring algorithms have a positive effect on society. By decomposing, quantifying, and ultimately understanding the complex dynamics that exist between humans and algorithms, we will be able to more efficiently diagnose, inform, and improve these systems. In this chapter, we have suggested a starting place for this process, which is for researchers to focus on both the individual roles of and the interactions between people, data, and algorithms in algorithmic social systems. We argue that, if we are to successfully steer these systems toward socially beneficial outcomes, it will be critical to appreciate the complexities between these systems and to avoid reaching for simplistic generalizations about the dynamics at play within them.

REFERENCES

Achenbach, Joel and Scott Clement. 2016. "America Really Is More Divided Than Ever." *Washington Post.* https://www.washingtonpost.com/national/america-really-is-more-divided-than-ever/2016/07/17/fbfebee6-49d8-11e6-90a8-fb84201e0645_story.html.

Angwin, Julia, Jeff Larson, Surya Mattu, and Lauren Kirchner. 2016. "Machine Bias." ProPublica. https://www.propublica.org/article/machine-bias-risk-assessments-in-criminal-sentencing.

Bail, Christopher A., Lisa P. Argyle, Taylor W. Brown, John P. Bumpus, Haohan Chen, M. B. Fallin Hunzaker et al. 2018. "Exposure to Opposing Views on Social Media Can Increase Political Polarization". *Proceedings of the National Academy of Sciences,* 115, no. 37: 9216–21.

Bakshy, Etyan, Solomon Messing, and Lada A. Adamic. 2015. "Exposure to Ideologically Diverse News and Opinion On Facebook." *Science* 348 (6239): 1130–32.

Berman, Ron and Zsolt Katona. 2019. "Curation Algorithms and Filter Bubbles in Social Networks." NET Institute Working Paper No. 16–08. https://ssrn.com/abstract=2848526 or http://dx.doi.org/10.2139/ssrn.2848526.

Booker, Cory. 2019. "Booker, Wyden, Clarke Introduce Bill Requiring Companies to Target Bias in Corporate Algorithms" [Press release]. *Senate.gov.* https://www.booker.senate.gov/?p=press_release&id=903.

Economist, The. 2017. "Once Considered a Boon to Democracy, Social Media Have Started to Look Like its Nemesis". *The Economist.* https://www.economist.com/news/briefing/21730870-economy-based-attention-easily-gamed-once-considered-boon-democracy-social-media.

Eubanks, Virginia. 2018. *Automating Inequality: How High-Tech Tools Profile, Police, and Punish the Poor.* London: St. Martin's Press.

Flaxman, Seth, Sharad Goel, and Justin M. Rao. 2016. "Filter Bubbles, Echo Chambers, and Online News Consumption." *Public Opinion Quarterly* 80 (S1): 298–320.

Fleder, Daniel and Kartik Hosanagar. 2009. "Blockbuster Culture's Next Rise or Fall: the Impact of Recommender Systems on Sales Diversity." *Management Science* 55, no.5: 697–712.

Fleder, Daniel, Kartik Hosanagar, and Andreas Buja. 2010. "Recommender Systems And Their Effects On Consumers: The Fragmentation Debate." In *11Th ACM Conference On Electronic Commerce (EC '10),* 229–230. Cambridge, Massachusetts: Association for Computing Machinery. https://dl.acm.org/citation.cfm?id=1807378.

Garimella, Kiran, Gianmarco De Francisci Morales, Aristides Gionis, and Michael Mathioudakis. 2017. "Factors in Recommending Contrarian Content on Social

Media." *Proceedings of the 2017 ACM on Web Science Conference*, pp. 263–6. Association for Computing Machinery.

Gillani, Nabeel, Ann Yuan, Martin Saveski, Soroush Vosoughi, and Deb Roy. 2018. "Me, My Echo Chamber, and I: Introspection on Social Media Polarization." *Proceedings of the 2018 World Wide Web Conference*. International World Wide Web Conferences Steering Committee.

Graells-Garrido, Eduardo, Mounia Lalmas, and Ricardo Baeza-Yates. 2016. "Data Portraits and Intermediary Topics: Encouraging Exploration of Politically Diverse Profiles." *Proceedings of the 21st International Conference on Intelligent User Interfaces*. Association for Computing Machinery.

Gupta, Alisha H. 2019. "Are Algorithms Sexist?" *New York Times*. https://www.nytimes.com/2019/11/15/us/apple-card-goldman-sachs.html.

Hern, Alex. 2017. "How Social Media Filter Bubbles and Algorithms Influence the Election." *The Guardian*. https://www.theguardian.com/technology/ 2017/may/22/social-media-election-facebook-filter-bubbles.

Hosanagar, Kartik, Daniel Fleder, Dokyun Lee, and Andreas Buja. 2014. "Will The Global Village Fracture Into Tribes? Recommender Systems and Their Effects on Consumer Fragmentation." *Management Science* 60 (4): 805–823.

Kamakura, Wagner A., and Rajendra K. Srivastava. 1986. "An Ideal-Point Probabilistic Choice Model for Heterogeneous Preferences". *Marketing Science* 5, no. 3: 199–218.

Knight, Will. 2017. "Biased Algorithms Are Everywhere, and No One Seems to Care." *MIT Technology Review*. https://www.technologyreview.com/s/ 608248/biased-algorithms-are-everywhere-and-no-one-seems-to-care/.

Lambrecht, Anja and Catherine E. Tucker. 2016. "Algorithmic Bias? An Empirical Study Into Apparent Gender-Based Discrimination in the Display of STEM Career Ads." *SSRN Electronic Journal*. doi:10.2139/ssrn.2852260.

Lazer, David. 2015. "The Rise of the Social Algorithm". *Science* 348, no. 6239: 1090–91.

McPherson, Miller, Lynn Smith-Lovin, and James M. Cook. 2001. "Birds of a Feather: Homophily in Social Networks". *Annual Review of Sociology* 27, no. 1: 415–44.

Miller, Alex P. and Kartik Hosanagar. 2019. "How Targeted Ads and Dynamic Pricing Can Perpetuate Bias." *Harvard Business Review*. https://hbr.org/2019/11/how-targeted-ads-and-dynamic-pricing-can-perpetuate-bias.

Moon, Angela. 2017. "Two-Thirds of American Adults Get News from Social Media: Survey." *U.S.* https://www.reuters.com/article/us-usa-internet-socialmedia/two-thirds-of-american-adults-get-news-from-social-media-survey-idUSKCN1BJ2A8.

Obama White House. 2016. "Big Data: A Report on Algorithmic Systems, Opportunity, and Civil Rights." Executive Office of the President.

O'Neil, Cathy. 2017. *Weapons of Math Destruction*. New York: B/D/W/Y Broadway Books.

Pariser, Eli. 2014. *The Filter Bubble: How The New Personalized Web Is Changing What We Read and How We Think*. New York: Penguin Books.

Sunstein, Cass R. 1999. "The Law of Group Polarization". *SSRN Electronic Journal*. doi:10.2139/ssrn.199668.

Thune, John. 2019. "Bipartisan 'Filter Bubble' Bill Would Give Consumers More Control Over What They View Online" [Press release]. *Senate.gov*. https://www.thune.senate.gov/public/index.cfm/2019/11/thune-bipartisan-filter-bubble-bill-would-give-consumers-more-control-over-what-they-view-online.

Tufekci, Zeynep. 2017. *We're Building a Dystopia Just to Make People Click On Ads*. Video. New York City: TED.

US Senate. 2019, November. "Thune, Colleagues Introduce Bipartisan Bill to Increase Internet Platform Transparency and Provide Consumers With Greater Control Over Digital Content" [Press release]. *Senate.gov*. https://www.thune.senate.gov/public/index.cfm/press-releases?ID=E1595915-69A3-456B-8CBA-0237F28AB4A3.

Zuboff, Shoshana, 2019. *The Age of Surveillance Capitalism: The Fight for a Human Future at the New Frontier of Power*. New York: Public Affairs.

5

Regulating the Feedback Effect

Viktor Mayer-Schönberger

A century and a half ago, Karl Marx wrote about markets becoming concentrated over time – the fundamental genetic defect that would eventually lead to capitalism's demise and spur the proletarian revolution.[1] Today, his dire prediction seems to ring true. While business dynamism has been stagnant for years, a few firms grow fast, amass astonishing profits, and capture a huge share of the market.[2]

Just in the fall of 2017, Apple – already the world's most valuable company by market capitalization – announced an increase in profits of 19 percent. Google/ Alphabet's profits grew by an even stronger 33 percent, and Facebook topped both with an increase in profits of 79 percent. Each of these three has also cornered an enormous portion of a market. Apple is the world's largest smartphone producer by revenue, Google dominates online search with a market share of well over 80 percent globally, and Facebook rules the social media platform market, with over 2 billion users worldwide in 2017.

They are not the only ones. Digital markets, in particular, seem to move swiftly towards concentration. The market for domain names is cornered by GoDaddy, Netflix controls more than 75 percent of the US video streaming market, and Amazon accounts for 43 percent of US online retail sales.[3]

---

[1] Karl Marx, *Capital* (Penguin Classic 1992); but see also Joseph A. Schumpeter, *Capitalism, Socialism, and Democracy*, 3rd ed. (Harper Perennial Modern Classics 2008).

[2] On stagnant business dynamics, see Ryan A. Decker et al., *Declining Dynamism, Allocative Efficiency, and the Productivity Slowdown*, Finance and Economics Discussion Series 2017–019 (Board of Governors of the Federal Reserve System 2017); on profit concentration see David Autor et al., *The Fall of Labor Share and the Rise of Superstar Firms*, NBER Research Working Paper 23396 (May 2017); David Autor et al., *Concentrating on the Fall of the Labor Share*, NBER Working Paper 23108 (January 2017), Simcha Barkai, *Declining Labor and Capital Shares*, http://home.uchicago.edu/~barkai/doc/BarkaiDecliningLaborCapital.pdf.

[3] On GoDaddy's market share see Andrew Allemann, *Go Daddy Marches Toward $1 Billion, DomainName Wire*, August 17, 2010; on Amazon's share of online retail sales in the US, see *Amazon Accounts for 43 Percent of US Online Retail Sales*, Business Insider, February 2, 2017; on Netflix market share see Sara Perez, *Netflix Reaches 75 percent of US Streaming Service Viewers*, TechCrunch, April 20, 2017.

Unsurprisingly, a growing number of commentators has called for strengthening existing antitrust and competition laws to ensure that the concentration process is slowed, or at the very least does not lead to uncompetitive behavior by market-dominating firms.[4]

In this chapter, I suggest that these concerns are well-warranted, but that the remedies proposed are ill-suited to address the challenge we face. This is because while we see market concentration, the reason for that concentration has shifted, rendering much of the existing regulatory toolkit to ensure competitive markets essentially ineffective. In its place, I suggest a novel regulatory measure – the progressive data-sharing mandate – that is specifically designed to tackle the very concentration dynamic we witness.

The first part of this chapter describes the concentration process in greater detail, and how the dynamic is fueled by a new driver. I then explain why this novel driver – the feedback effect – cripples market competition differently than existing drivers, and thus requires novel regulatory measures. In the second part, I put forward such a measure, carefully tailored to address the crippling dynamic that leads to market concentration, and map out the consequences of such a measure should it be enacted.[5]

A CLOSER LOOK AT MARKET CONCENTRATION

Markets become concentrated when one or a small number of market participants enjoy a significant cost differential in offering products or services. There are many drivers for such a concentration dynamic, but the most prominent and well-analyzed are so-called scale effects. Scale effects signify the downward slope of marginal costs to produce or sell a particular good the more a particular actor sells.

Scale effects manifest themselves in various forms. For instance, buyers of large volumes can often negotiate discounts and thus get better deals than those purchasing smaller quantities. Fixed costs, too, are less onerous when they are spread across many goods rather than just a few. That's why it is costlier per good sold for Microsoft to operate its retail stores than for Apple. Many scale effects aren't consumed once a company has reached a certain size, but continue to be present as they grow and deliver improvements to a company's bottom line. As Ford Model Ts came off the assembly line almost a century ago and sales increased steadily over time, Ford was able to continue to lower cost year after year, largely because of the focus on exploiting scale effects in every aspect of manufacturing and sales.

---

[4] For instance, Columbia cyberlaw professor Tim Wu (*The Curse of Bigness: Antitrust in the New Gilded Age* (Columbia 2018)) and Harvard economist Kenneth Rogoff (*Has Big Tech Gotten Too Big for Our Own Good?*, *MarketWatch*, July 11, 2018) see the digital superstars as clearly being too big and too powerful.

[5] This is based on Viktor Mayer-Schönberger and Thomas Ramge, *Reinventing Capitalism in the Age of Big Data* (Basic Books 2018); see also Viktor Mayer-Schönberger and Thomas Ramge, *A Big Choice For Big Tech*, 97(5) *Foreign Affairs* 48 (September 2018).

Because smaller competitors do not reap similar benefits of scale, they have to produce at higher cost. This provides large players with an advantage in the market that they can convert into higher profits or, through lower prices, an increase in demand and thus market share. The resulting dynamic, at least in principle, is that through scale effects bigger players grow bigger, while smaller competitors wither away.

Of course, this theory does not always pan out in practice. Some large players are badly managed, become complacent, and lose their ability to produce the goods the market wants. Large firms have the scale advantage, but it often comes with a lack of flexibility and an inability to adjust swiftly to changes in the marketplace. In general, however, scale effects do lead to market concentration. Economists have been worrying about the negative effects for competitive markets for decades.

More recently, a further effect has led to much discussion. Termed the network effect, it is present whenever additional customers joining a particular service increase the utility of that service to everyone else using it.[6] It is often associated with digital networks and the Internet. Every additional person using Facebook, for example, improves the utility Facebook has for other users as they can reach more people through the service. But network effects are not an invention of the digital age. They already were a key driver leading to the consolidation of telephone networks (and thus concentration of network operators) in the early twentieth century, and even before that in the concentration of railroad networks.[7]

Network effects are particularly beneficial for the companies that provide the respective service, because apart from accommodating additional users, they need not actively do anything for the utility of their service to improve. Unlike with scale effects, for instance, firms do not have to renegotiate sourcing contracts to reap the benefits.

Network effects offer another advantage to scale effects, at least in theory: They grow more quickly with an increase in size than the often more linear scale effects. This is true even though in practice the increases in utility are not evenly spread, and certainly do not simply grow by the square of the number of users, as a particularly popular formulation of a certain type of network effect, "Metcalfe's law" seems to suggest.[8]

These qualities have made network effects the focus of many startups, and an important driver for substantial entrepreneurial successes. Particularly social

[6] See e.g. Oz Shy, The Economics of Network Industries (Cambridge University Press 2001); David Easley and Jon Kleinberg, Networks, Crowds and Markets (Cambridge University Press 2010), 449–478.

[7] On the evolution of US telephone networks, see Richard R. John, Network Nation: Inventing American Telecommunications (Harvard University Press 2010).

[8] For a description of Metcalfe's law see Carl Shapiro and Hal R. Varian, Information Rules (1999); on why this is flawed, see, e.g., Bob Briscoe, Andrew Odlyzko and Benjamin Tilly, Metcalfe's Law is Wrong, IEEE Spectrum (July 2006), https://spectrum.ieee.org/computing/networks/metcalfes-law-is-wrong.

network services, such as Facebook, Twitter, and LinkedIn have greatly benefitted from them, much as in the 1990s telecom providers and mobile phone equipment producers profited from the network effects of the GSM mobile phone standard. This has propelled network effects into public prominence.

Scale and network effects are not exclusive. In digital markets, often both of them are at play. Amazon profits from scale effects thanks to the huge volume of orders it fulfills, but also from network effects as it offers its customers a community to review and share information about products. Google can spread its indexing cost for its search engine across billions of users every day, but its shared document standards and interfaces (e.g., Google Docs) also create a sticky global network of activity.

For consumers, scale and network effects often have positive consequences. In competitive markets, lowering the cost of production per unit will result in lower prices, saving consumers a bundle. And an improving utility of a particular service, thanks to network effects, is a benefit for all of its customers.

Unfortunately, scale and network effects also help companies to increase their market shares, as they can produce more cheaply than smaller competitors or, thanks to network effects, offer a superior service. Combined, scale and network effects have facilitated a concentration process in countless markets around the world, reducing, at times even eliminating robust competition. Without sufficient competition, large firms can extract extra rents from customers.

Over time, this dynamic would cripple markets if there weren't a powerful counterforce that enabled new entrants to successfully compete with large incumbents and at times even to topple them. This counterforce is innovation.

Three quarters of a century ago, economist Joseph Schumpeter emphasized the disruptive force of innovation – of new products or production processes (or markets).[9] Innovative companies with ground-breaking ideas are able to overtake existing players, and in doing so preserve competition in the marketplace. Economies of scale, as well as network effects, are kept in check by the might of innovation, resulting in a dynamic balance that enhances consumer welfare.

Even (or perhaps particularly) in the context of digital markets, there is ample evidence that innovation has been the key driver that enabled new entrants to unseat dominating incumbents. 3G and LTE pushed aside GSM, Facebook dethroned MySpace, Google replaced Yahoo! as the online search champion, and Apple's operating system now runs on more digital devices than Microsoft's Windows. In our digital economy, too, innovation has provided the much needed antidote to market concentration.

Schumpeter feared that eventually innovation would become concentrated in a few large companies, because of their ability to attract talent and create a suitable environment for stimulating and bringing to market new ideas.[10] So far, fortunately, this has

---

[9] Schumpeter, supra note 1.
[10] Id.

not happened. Quite the contrary: Large companies often become unwieldy, with many hierarchies and entrenched processes that are difficult to adapt, and with ossified structures that stunt innovation and scare away talent, leaving new entrants with ample opportunities to compete against established players.[11]

Quite obviously, the counterforce of innovation is strongest in sectors that experience quick and substantial technical change. Unsurprisingly therefore, the Internet seemed to usher in an especially disruptive phase of innovation, with lowered cost of entry and an amazing variety of new ideas. Unlike Henry Ford, new data startups do not require huge amounts of capital to build factories, neither do they today even need huge server farms (as Google and Amazon did) to build out a new innovative idea. Digital disruptors can use digital platforms and infrastructures available to them often at commodity price. Until 2010, Twitter was renting cloud assets for its service rather than having built its own. And Uber, Lyft, and Didi Chuxing did not have to design and build digital devices to connect their drivers to their services; they are smartly piggybacking on existing smart phone infrastructure.[12]

Away from the realm of the digital economy, however, the innovation story has become a bit less impressive in recent years. Innovation economists have been pointing to the great deceleration in business dynamism outside of a small number of high-tech fields as an indication that our ability to disrupt through innovation in many sectors is actually stalling.[13] But at least in high-tech, encompassing an ever-increasing share of the economy, the innovation engine seemed as capable of disruption as ever. Unfortunately, and dramatically, this is changing, and the change is linked to a shift in the nature of innovation.

Since the beginning of humanity, innovation has been tied to the inventiveness of the human spirit. The ability to innovate rested on new ideas generated by human creativity and ingenuity – ideas that could then be translated into superior products and services or production processes. The romantic image of the single idea that changes the world overnight might rarely have been true, but persistent entrepreneurs have been able to shape markets and society. Because, at least in principle, such novel and valuable ideas can come from any human being, the capacity to innovate is not limited to large organizations with deep pockets. Sometimes, the tinkerer in the garage outsmarts armies of corporate researchers, whose

---

[11] A useful overview is Jan Fagerberg, David C. Mowery and Richard R. Nelson, The Oxford Handbook of Innovation (Oxford University Press 2005).

[12] This strategy of repurposing the existing smart phone infrastructure is not limited to ride-hailing and ride-sharing; it plays a central role in the ongoing displacement of existing payment infrastructures such as conventional credit cards with smart phone-based systems such as Apple Pay, Google Pay or Alipay; the same strategy is at play when it comes to health applications that innovatively utilize some of the many sensors found on smart phones to detect anything from irregular sleeping patterns to early signs of Parkinsons and heart problems.

[13] See, e.g., Ryan A. Decker et al., Declining Dynamism, Allocative Efficiency, and the Productivity Slowdown, FEDS Working Paper No 2017–019 (2017); David Autor et al., The Fall of Labor Share and the Rise of Superstar Firms (2019), https://economics.mit.edu/files/12979.

preconceived notions of what works and how may cloud their ability to – in the words of Steve Jobs – see the world differently.

The story of innovation has been tied to human originality, and – at least in more recent decades – to the small startup Davids upending slow and stodgy Goliaths. Although this narrative may be mythical and naïve, innovation unquestionably has acted as a powerful counterforce to scale-based concentration effects. But innovation's positive role in ensuring competitiveness hinges on it being equally available (at least in principle) to organizations and players of any size.

The world is abuzz with talk about artificial intelligence and machine learning. The labels may conjure up alarming visions of humanoid robots roaming the world. The reality, however, is more sanguine – and more troubling. What is termed AI or machine learning isn't a system that acquires abstract knowledge by being fed general rules. Machine learning denotes the ability to analyze massive amounts of data and uncover statistical patterns in them, devising algorithms that capture and replicate these patterns. Importantly, as new data points become available, the analysis is redone, and the resulting algorithm adjusted. Incrementally, the system "learns." It captures an ever more comprehensive slice of reality, and thus more accurately reflects the essence of the phenomenon in question.

We already see such systems popping up everywhere in the digital realm. Google's services – from online search and spell-check to language translation, from voice recognition all the way to autonomous driving – are continuously improving because of the gigantic stream of data available to Google. And Google isn't alone. Apple's Siri and Amazon's Alexa are improving because of data-driven machine learning, and so are the music recommendations presented by Spotify and the products recommended on Alibaba. Every additional data point so gathered is an opportunity to automatically learn from and adapt the system. And the more data points gathered the faster machines learn, producing innovation.

Whether it is a data-driven system defeating some of the world's best poker players, or a system diagnosing skin cancer with precision equal or better than the average dermatologist, the principle is always the same: Automated learning from the analysis of huge amounts of training and feedback data.[14] As the ability of machines to collect and analyze data comprehensively and increasingly unsupervised has grown dramatically, the source of innovation has been shifting from humans to systems of data and software. Yesterday's innovator was a human with bold ideas; tomorrow's equivalent are those capturing and feeding the most data into their learning systems.

Of course, humans will continue to invent, and human-based innovation is far from over. But data-driven innovation offers a few advantages that human

[14] On AI playing poker Olivia Solon, *Oh the Humanity! Poker Computer Trounces Humans in Big Step for AI*, Guardian, January 30, 2017; see also Mayer-Schönberger and Ramge, Reinventing Capitalism, 59–62; on IBM Watson diagnosing types of skin cancer better than the average dermatologist, *Computer Learns to Detect Skin Cancer More Accurately Than Doctors*, Guardian, May 29, 2018.

innovation can't easily replicate. It scales well, while human innovation doesn't so easily. It can be formalized and thus incorporated in organizational processes while standardizing the human innovation process is far more difficult; human ingenuity is unpredictable. And, arguably most importantly, data-driven machine-based innovation is less inhibited by human imagination – by the questions we humans ask as much as by the questions we don't ask; by the tensions we sense, and by what we seem deaf to.

Of course, the data that AI systems use to learn from isn't devoid of biases and errors, leading to biased decisions.[15] But the hope is that with comprehensive data from diverse sources, some of these distortions are flattened out.[16] At the very least, they are less constraining than the biases of a small number of humans in a conventional innovation lab, subject to "group-think."[17] With fewer constraints due to human preconceptions, data-driven machine-based innovation is less encumbered by traditional thinking and conventional beliefs. This is not to suggest that data-driven innovation is always better than human innovation; only that in the future human innovation will no longer be always the most relevant game in town.

As the source of innovation shifts at least partially from human ingenuity to data analyzed by machine learning systems, those with access to much data have most of the raw material to translate into innovative insights. Here, too, having the raw material does not necessarily equate with the ability to employ it successfully. Some companies will fail in the innovation drive despite having all the data, because of their shortcomings in setting up and maintaining appropriate systems and processes to learn from it.[18] But the reverse is even more true: Without data, even the best AI company will falter. In short, having access to data is *the crucial* (albeit not sufficient) condition for innovative success in the data age.

Due to this change in the nature of innovation, the emerging market dynamic pits large incumbent companies with substantial scale economies and network effects on the one hand against smaller startups with needs for lots of data to learn from. This in itself is already problematic: Companies with lots of data will hardly let entrepreneurs have access to their data troves, when they realize that access to data is a source of innovation (and thus competitive success). This likely inhibits small startups to turn themselves into disruptive innovators. The result is a market that may still be competitive and innovative among the larger firms, but no longer easy to enter for newer, smaller players.

---

[15] For a particularly pessimistic view, see, e.g., Cathy O'Neil, Weapons of Math Destruction: How Big Data Increases Inequality and Threatens Democracy (Broadway Books 2016).

[16] See Viktor Mayer-Schönberger and Kenneth Cukier, Big Data (HMH 2013).

[17] There is a rich literature on group think, with the term itself made popular by Irving Janis, Groupthink: Psychological studies of policy decisions and fiascoes (HMH 1983).

[18] It is said that up to 85 percent of data being collected in North America and Europe is shockingly underutilized; see, e.g., Pedro Hernandez, *Enterprises are Hoarding 'Dark' Data: Veritas*, Datamation, October 30, 2015, https://www.datamation.com/storage/enterprises-are-hoarding-dark-data-veritas.html

The situation is far more damning, however, when we look at the kind of data that will lead to innovation advantages. Most of the digital superstar firms aren't conventional manufacturing behemoths, neither are they exploiters or traders of natural resources. They are data-rich marketplaces with smart recommendation and other decision-assistance systems to aid market participants in their transaction decisions.[19] For these marketplaces, innovation lies in the ability to better match transaction partners: to help them in discovery and selection, as well as the process of decision making. If these companies want to innovate a better decision assistant, they need not any kind of data, but data about preferences and transactions – precisely the kind of data available to these digital superstars. It is data that offers feedback to the superstars about market activities from which to learn. Amazon's recommendation engine is getting better and better with each additional data point collected through a customer's interaction on Amazon's website. Spotify's choice of music gets better with each feedback from one of its listeners, much as each time you let Siri proceed with what she understood to be your request, Siri's underlying voice recognition system learns to understand human speech.

Not simply any kind of data, but *feedback* data is the raw material that lets these superstar companies innovate and offers customers a superior experience on their marketplaces. It's no surprise that eBay, a major long-established marketplace, is investing heavily into data and machine learning, because it, too, needs to tap into the innovative power of the feedback data streams it has access to if it wants to compete successfully against the other superstars.[20] Neither is it astonishing that shopping curation service Stitch Fix, one of the latest digital unicorns, employs many dozens of data analysts to mature its machine-learning systems that translate rich feedback data from multiple channels, including through photos posted online, into its innovative curation service.[21]

These digital superstars are innovating, but such innovation is no longer acting as a counterforce to market concentration. Instead, it's fed by valuable feedback data that only large data-rich markets collect in huge quantities. This makes firms that operate data-rich marketplaces and smart decision assistants (and who already benefit from scale and network effects) the most innovative as well. The *feedback effect* aligns innovation with market concentration, and shapes markets and the economy much as scale and network effects already do. The result is an unprecedented impulse towards larger and more powerful firms that could lead to a dramatic restructuring of our economy.

But the feedback effect isn't only pushing market concentration, undermining competition, and ultimately leading to higher prices and dangerously powerful oligopolies. It, perhaps surprisingly, also makes the superstar firms that use the

---

[19] On such data-rich markets, see Mayer-Schönberger and Ramge, Reinventing Capitalism, 59–85.

[20] Mayer-Schönberger and Ramge, Reinventing Capitalism, 69–70.

[21] See, e.g., Ryan Mac, *Stitch Fix: The $250 Million Startup Playing Fashionista Moneyball*, Forbes, June 1, 2016; see also https://algorithms-tour.stitchfix.com.

feedback effect extensively for innovation, as well as their customers, shockingly vulnerable to systemic failure. As AI systems learn from data and get better and better in assisting participants in a superstar's marketplace, more and more customers will be attracted to such a market. As a result, everyone may be using the same decision assistant. In such a context, any hidden errors and biases in the decision assistant will affect and potentially cripple every participant's decision making. It's akin to the danger of a brake in one's car malfunctioning due to a manufacturing defect – and the realization that everyone else's car uses the same faulty brake, too. This single point of failure undermines decentralized decision making, the very quality of markets that makes them so resilient and successful. In turn, this structural defect in the marketplace will make the superstar firm that runs the marketplace deeply vulnerable as well, because an error in decision assistance may now bring down the entire company.

Thus, superstar firms utilizing data-driven machine learning find themselves in a highly uncomfortable position. On the one hand, their exploitation of the feedback effect creates a unique and dangerous vulnerability. On the other hand, without data-driven innovation they will no longer be able to compete. Faced with the imminent threat of competition versus the potential danger of a systemic vulnerability, most firms will likely opt to tackle the former rather than focus on the later. Long-term, this will lead to a problematic situation, not just for their customers but for the companies as well.

POLICY RESPONSES

Market concentrations aren't new. By themselves, in most instances they aren't seen as problematic, at least from a consumer welfare perspective. As long as players even with very high market share don't exploit their position – for example by raising prices beyond what would be acceptable in a competitive market – regulatory measures are usually deemed unnecessary. Consequently, in competition law, the focus in recent years has been on constraining anticompetitive *behavior*.[22]

This poses a unique challenge in the context of the feedback effect. Companies exploiting the feedback effect, especially as detailed in the previous section, aren't behaving illicitly as defined by conventional competition regulation. They are simply utilizing the resources available to them, in the form of feedback data, to advance innovation. Companies have no obligation under existing competition law to make it easy for their rivals – large or small, established or new – to compete

---

[22] The focus on behavior in competition law in the US is evident even in works critical of the rise of digital superstars, such as Ezrachi and Stucke, Virtual Competition: The Promise and Perils of the Algorithm-Driven Economy (Harvard University Press 2016); one may believe that European competition law may be different, given its distinct historical trajectory, but as David J. Gerber (Law and Competition in Twentieth Century Europe (Oxford University Press 2001) points out, at least on this issue it is not; it, too, is focused on behavior.

against them. Only when they cross a red line into illegal behavior will they be stopped. Hence, one could argue that feedback effects even if resulting in market concentration aren't problematic in themselves, and do not require regulatory attention.

The flaw in this argument is the focus on consumer welfare, narrowly defined. Until now, competition law could be focused on such a narrow scope of consumer welfare, because innovation, which acted as a crucial counterforce to scale and network effects, was founded on human ingenuity. Nobody, not even the largest player in the market, could hope to have a monopoly on the human mind to have new ideas. At least in theory, therefore, the biggest incumbent could be dethroned by an innovative startup with an ingenious idea, so long as the incumbent did not engage in deliberately anticompetitive manipulation of the market. In practice, of course, large players have been able to use their market power to capture a disproportionate slice of human talent. But that has not precluded others from having great ideas, and bringing them to market, at least in sectors with relatively low barriers to entry.

Therefore, policymakers have not felt the need to worry about market concentration inhibiting innovation, at least not in the highly dynamic sector of digital technologies with its fast pace of innovation and comparatively low barriers to entry. With data-driven machine learning turning into a prime engine for innovation, this is no longer the case. Those with access to data in general, and feedback data in particular, now enjoy a massive advantage over others. This concentrates innovative activity among the largest players in a market and reduces the breadth and diversity of innovation.

Some may argue that a concentration of innovation activity isn't bad in itself. High-tech areas such as chip manufacturing, despite being highly concentrated, have been subject to continued innovation in recent years. The truth is, however, that low barriers to entry have always been the hallmark of strong and sustained innovation. It may be true that chip manufacturing is concentrated, but the advances in computer chips over the past two decades (if not longer) do not primarily stem from advances in chip manufacturing coming from the few remaining large chip fabs, but from innovation in tooling for chip manufacturing, and even more importantly from chip design – a far less concentrated area with far lower financial barriers to entry. A similar argument could be made for the innovation dynamic in biotech, and the crucial role of CRISPR in enabling genetic engineering at relatively low cost.[23] As it turns out, the most recent trajectories of high-tech innovation offer ample evidence for diversity and against concentration.

There is a decisive further reason for being concerned about the concentration of innovative activity. As detailed in the previous section, feedback-data-driven

---

[23] See, e.g., Juan Enriquez and Steve Gullans, Evolving Ourselves: Redesigning the Future of Humanity–One Gene at a Time (Portfolio 2016).

machine learning concentrates innovation among superstar firms that operate data-rich markets and offer smart decision assistance. The resulting single points of failure create vulnerabilities for the entire market, including market participants. Just consider a failure of the recommendation system in an app store market for one of the two big smart phone ecosystems: It could prompt hundreds of millions of consumers worldwide to download apps they don't need or want, and that perhaps are even nefarious, irrespective of any illegal or uncompetitive behavior of the market provider.

Massive market failures and the resulting potential for huge losses in consumer welfare, could, perhaps should turn into a valid concern for policymakers. But because this dynamic involves no illicit behavior by market participants, current competition law fails to protect against it.[24] Worse, even if competition law were triggered by data-driven innovation, it offers no suitable remedies. Behavioral remedies fail when the problem lies in the very dynamic of data-driven innovation. For instance, prohibiting or greatly constraining data-rich companies to utilize their data troves to gain novel insights, makes little sense: it would stifle innovation, limit the insights gleaned from data, and reduce data's overall utility, which likely translates into a reduction in overall consumer welfare and market efficiency.

In light of the limitations of behavioral remedies and the huge power of the most well-known superstar firms, the so-called GAFA – Google (technically a unit of the holding company Alphabet), Amazon, Facebook, and Apple – some have suggested that these firms should be broken up, much like AT&T, to prevent their controlling such large shares of the market.[25] This seems a blunt and draconian remedy, and it's unclear how such a remedy could be anything more than a temporary fix. Given the underlying drivers of market power (scale, network, and feedback effects), market concentration after such a breakup would likely continue anew.

This calls for different and novel policy measures – both new triggers for regulatory action, and new remedies – that are more carefully crafted to address the root cause of the problem: the shift in the source of innovation. Expanding on work by Jens Prüfer and colleagues on search engines, I suggest a progressive data-sharing mandate.[26]

The principle of such a mandate is straightforward: Every company with a share above a certain threshold – for instance 10 percent – in a market has to let other market participants have access to a subset of the data it has collected and uses in its

---

[24] See, e.g., Ariel Ezrachi and Maurice Stucke, Virtual Competition.

[25] For example, US Senator Elizabeth Warren has called for GAFAs to be broken up (Elizabeth Warren, *Here's How We Can Break Up Big Tech*, Medium, March 8, 2019, https://medium.com/@teamwarren/heres-how-we-can-break-up-big-tech-9ad9e0da324c).

[26] Jens Prüfer and Christoph Schrottmüller, *Competing with Data*, TILEC Discussion Paper 2017–006 (February 16, 2017); see also Cedric Argenton and Jens Prüfer, *Search Engine Competition with Network Externalities*, 8 Journal of Competition Law 73 (2012).

Regulating the Feedback Effect

data-driven machine learning systems. The higher the market share of a particular company, the larger the slice of the data that it has to share.[27]

Data would be depersonalized to avoid any undue privacy risks[28] and the data shared would be chosen randomly from the full dataset.[29] Technically, access would happen through an appropriate API – and without a regulator in the middle to eliminate any unnecessary slowdown.[30] The task of the regulator would be to ensure and enforce compliance, and to categorize companies based on market share.

Importantly, every competitor would be granted access to the appropriate slice of the data. For instance, in a market with two large players commanding 30 and 40 percent of the market and many small players below the 10 percent threshold, not only the small players would get access to a slice of the data of the big players. Each of the big players would be entitled to access a slice of the other big player.

This setup has a number of advantages. Every market participant could continue to utilize the data available to it; unlike a monetary redistribution through a tax, the progressive data-sharing mandate does not "rob" the large players of the ability to innovate. But by granting access to other especially smaller players, it enables these smaller players to amass large enough data sets to use in data-driven machine learning, and thus to stay innovative. It also facilitates competition in the market by helping smaller players without inhibiting the ability of large players to utilize data as well. Every player benefits from access to data, but smaller players benefit more so – relatively speaking – than larger players. In short, the idea builds on the unique quality of data to be used multiple times by different parties without losing its value.

The progressive data-sharing mandate is also narrowly tailored to tackle the problem in question. If the challenge is the shift in the source of innovation to data, enabling access to data spreads the raw material of innovation. The policy also

---

[27] The then leader of the German social democratic party SPD, Andrea Nahles, advocated a more comprehensive model of progressive data sharing that would be limited to companies above a certain market share threshold, but require all firms above a certain simple minimum threshold of revenue or customers to be included. Termed "data-for-all" law, the proposal aimed not only to curb the information power of the digital superstars, but to stimulate data-driven innovation in Germany, especially among its numerous smaller and medium-sized enterprises. See Digitaler Fortschritt durch ein Daten-für-Alle-Gesetz, SPD, https://www.spd.de/aktuelles/daten-fuer-alle-gesetz/.

[28] A lot of data is actually not personal data at all, but data gathered from sensors measuring aspects of reality, like vibrations of jet engines or temperatures of machines in a factory; and while I do not want to downplay the privacy challenge, much of the remaining personal data can be depersonalized, although this demands skills and requires effort as well as the appropriate depersonalization strategy. Recent advances in cryptography have made effective depersonalization even of large data sets or highly personal data possible, and new technologies are becoming available that expand the depersonalization toolkit, like fully homomorphic encryption (for an overview see Frederick Armknecht et al., *A Guide to Fully Homomorphic Encryption*, https://eprint.iacr.org/2015/1192.pdf).

[29] Random choice of data ensures against strategic gaming in the choice of data being shared, either from the requester or the provider of data.

[30] When the US Department of Justice demanded that Google enable access to data it got through the acquisition of travel back-office service provider ITA, Google established access through an API.

does not negate the effort expended by large data collectors, as competitors gain access to only a randomly chosen subset of the data trove and not all of it. Crucially, this measure protects not only market competition, it also ensures a diversity of players based on a diversity of data sets. As the data subset provided to competitors is randomly selected, each player will have a somewhat different data source to learn from. This means that, for instance, not only multiple recommendation engines will be possible, but that the data used to train each such engine differs from one another, preventing the likelihood of systemic weaknesses.

Won't the large data-using superstars battle such a mandate, thereby dooming its chance for legislative success? Not necessarily. To be innovative in the context of data-rich markets will require access to lots of relevant feedback data. But even though data is the prime component for success, it is not the only one. Google's chief economist Hal Varian has said as much, when he highlighted the differentiating power of algorithms, especially regarding the most appropriate machine learning tools.[31] This suggests that large companies that have superb data analytics and machine learning capabilities continue to be well-placed to extract innovation out of data. Hence, they may see giving data access to smaller competitors as less of a ruinous threat, especially compared with some of the regulatory alternatives – like breakups – being discussed.

Moreover, mandating data sharing isn't an entirely novel policy measure. Its principle of enabling data access is embedded in a number of regulatory measures that have been enacted around the world. In the US and the European Union for instance, the legal right of phone subscribers to keep their phone numbers as they switch operators essentially disappropriated phone companies from valuable assets in the name of lowering switching cost.[32] It resulted in an increase in competition in the phone markets, and improved consumer welfare. Perhaps emboldened by this success, the European Union later passed legislation to let bank customers get access to their bank account data in machine-readable form.[33] This was intended not only to lower switching cost (and enhance competition in the banking sector), but also to create a wide stream of informational raw material that innovative fintechs can avail themselves of to enter the market. The goal is a diverse and innovative ecosystem of financial insight driven by drastically enhanced access

---

[31] *Data Is Giving Rise to a New Economy*, The Economist, May 6, 2017.

[32] In the US, mobile phone number portability was enacted as part of the Telecommunications Act 1996 and codified as 47 U.S.C. § 251(b)(2); in the European Union it is Article 30 of the Universal Service Directive (Directive 2002/22/EC of the European Parliament and of the Council of 7 March 2002 on universal service and users' rights relating to electronic communications networks and services, OJ L 108, 24.4.2002, 51–77); similar legislation exists in many other nations around world.

[33] Directive (EU) 2015/2366 of the European Parliament and of the Council of 25 November 2015 on payment services in the internal market, amending Directives 2002/65/EC, 2009/110/EC and 2013/36/EU and Regulation (EU) No 1093/2010, and repealing Directive 2007/64/EC, OJ L 337, 23.12.2015, 35–127, also referred to as the Payment Services Directive 2 (PSD2).

to data. And finally and most dramatically, the EU's General Data Protection Regulation[34], which came into force in 2018, explicitly mandates "data portability" – the right of individuals to get all personal data from a data processor in machine-readable form.[35] It's phone number portability and bank account portability spread across the board and applied to all personal data.

There is an important difference, however, between data portability and the progressive data-sharing mandate. Data portability's immediate aim is a rebalancing of informational power away from large data processors and towards individuals. Only if individuals then make their "portable data" accessible to other processors can the market concentration process be halted. The health of market competition thus hinges on the behavior of individuals, who do not all have strong incentives to share their data.[36] Moreover, because their data contains personal identifiers – it's the unaltered personal dataset – individuals have to trust data processors each time they share their data with them. This puts an unfair burden on individuals and results in an unfortunate disincentive for data sharing.

Data portability is simply not predictable and sustainable enough a policy measure to ensure competition and diversity in markets. But it is, no doubt, a powerful case in point that even legislative mandates that constrain the power of large data processors can get enacted – and in this case even on a pan-European level. This bodes well for the chances of a progressive data-sharing mandate.

CONCLUSIONS

In the past, markets have remained competitive in significant part because scale and network effects have been counterbalanced by innovation. Competition law could thus be focused on uncompetitive behavior, and not on market concentration in general. As the source of innovation shifts from human ingenuity to data-driven machine learning, behavioral constraints are no longer sufficient to protect competition.

The situation is exacerbated when the raw material of innovation in digital decision assistance is feedback data, collected and used by the providers of both

---

[34] Regulation (EU) 2016/679 of the European Parliament and of the Council of 27 April 2016 on the protection of natural persons with regard to the processing of personal data and on the free movement of such data, and repealing Directive 95/46/EC (General Data Protection Regulation), OJ L 119, 4.5.2016, 1–88.

[35] Art 20 GDPR: "The data subject shall have the right to receive the personal data concerning him or her, which he or she has provided to a controller, in a structured, commonly used and machine-readable format and have the right to transmit those data to another controller without hindrance from the controller to which the personal data have been provided, where: the processing is based on consent pursuant to point (a) of Article 6(1) or point (a) of Article 9(2) or on a contract pursuant to point (b) of Article 6(1); and the processing is carried out by automated means."

[36] This is essentially a "collective action problem", as described by Mancur Olson (The Logic of Collective Action: Public Goods and the Theory of Groups (Harvard University Press 1971)) and highlights negative externalities of such an individuals-based approach.

markets and digital assistants. Then, in addition to worries about a concentration of innovation, we may also face a single point of failure, exposing the market itself to a structural vulnerability.

The progressive data-sharing mandate is the policy measure I propose to address this unique situation. It is narrowly tailored to spread access to the raw material of innovation, with incentives for data utilization and renewed competition based on the ability to tease valuable insights from the raw data. While novel as a competition measure, it is based on principles of lowering switching cost and enhancing competition that are well-rooted in existing policy practices. If enacted, the progressive data-sharing mandate will act as a powerful antidote to market concentration, foster broad innovation, and prevent systemic vulnerabilities of online markets.[37]

---

[37] The idea of a data-sharing mandate has cropped up in a number of legislative and regulatory proposals, especially in Europe. For instance, in May 2019, the European Commissioner for Competition, Margrethe Vestager called for data-sharing (see John Detrixhe, *Instead of Breaking Up Facebook, the EU May Force It to Share Its Data*, Quartz, May 17, 2019, https://qz.com/1622036/break-up-facebook-eus-margrethe-vestager-favors-making-it-share-data-instead/); similar suggestions were put forward on a national level: in May 2019 the Dutch government sent a letter to the Dutch parliament on amending competition policy and opined: "The responsible competition authority must be given the power to take ex ante action if a platform risks gaining a position where it becomes impossible for businesses or consumers to avoid it. For example, it should be possible to impose obligations on a platform to share data with other companies", https://www.government.nl/latest/news/2019/05/27/dutch-government-change-competition-policy-and-merger-thresholds-for-better-digital-economy; in March 2019 the UK Digital Competition Expert Panel wrote "Active efforts ... to make data available for competitors, offering benefits to consumers and also facilitating the entry of new businesses", https://assets.publishing.service.gov.uk/government/uploads/system/uploads/attachment_data/file/785547/unlocking_digital_competition_furman_review_web.pdf; in 2018 the Swiss Expert Group on the Future of Data Use and Data Security suggested that the Swiss government should consider a data-sharing mandate for non-personalized data, https://www.newsd.admin.ch/newsd/message/attachments/53591.pdf.

6

Shaping Our Tools: Contestability as a Means to Promote Responsible Algorithmic Decision Making in the Professions

Daniel N. Kluttz, Nitin Kohli, and Deirdre K. Mulligan[*]

INTRODUCTION

Offering a "barously brief" distillation of Marshall McLuhan's writings, John M. Culkin expanded on one of McLuhan's five postulates, *Art Imitates Life*, with the now-famous line, *We shape our tools and thereafter they shape us.*[1] This fear of being shaped and controlled by tools, rather than autonomously wielding them, lies at the heart of current concerns with machine learning and artificial intelligence systems (ML/AI systems). Stories recounting the actual or potential bad outcomes of seemingly blind deference and overreliance on ML/AI systems crowd the popular press. Whether it is Facebook's algorithms allowing Russian operatives to unleash a weapon of mass manipulation, trained on troves of personal data, on electorates in the US and other countries; inequitable algorithmic bail decisions placing people of color behind bars while whites with similar profiles are sent home to await trial; cars in autonomous mode driving their inattentive could-be-drivers to their death; or algorithms assisting Volkswagen in routing around air quality regulations, there is a growing sense that our tools, if left unchecked, will undermine our choices, our values, and our public policies.

If we fail to grapple with the significant challenges posed by ML/AI systems designed to automate tasks or aid decision making, things may get much worse. At risk are potential decreases in human agency and skill,[2] both over- and under-reliance on decision support systems,[3] confusion about

---

[*] Titles in alphabetical order.

[1] Culkin, J. M. 1967. "A Schoolman's Guide to Marshall McLuhan." *The Saturday Review*, March 1967, 51–53, 70–72.

[2] Lee, John D., and Bobbie D. Seppelt. 2009. "Human Factors in Automation Design." In *Springer Handbook of Automation*, edited by Shimon Nof, pp. 417–36. Springer: Berlin (detailing how automation that fails to attend to how it redefines and restructures tasks, and the behavioral, cognitive, and emotional responses of operators to these changes, produce various kinds of failure, including those that arise from deskilling due to reliance on automation).

[3] Goddard, Kate, Abdul Roudsari, and Jeremy C. Wyatt. 2012. "Automation Bias: A Systematic Review of Frequency, Effect Mediators, and Mitigators." *Journal of the American Medical Informatics*

responsibility,[4] and diminished accountability.[5] Relatedly, as technology reconfigures work practices, it also shifts power in ways that may misalign with liability frameworks, diminishing humans' agency and control but still leaving them to bear the blame for system failures.[6] Automation bias, power dynamics, belief in the objectivity and infallibility of data, and distrust of professional knowledge and diminished respect for expertise – all coupled with the growing availability of ML/AI systems and services – portend a potential future in which we are *ruled by our tools*.

Designing a future in which our tools help us reason and act more effectively, efficiently, and in ways aligned with our social values – i.e., creating the tools that help us act responsibly – requires attention to system design and governance models. ML/AI systems that support us, rather than control us, require designs that foster in-the-moment human engagement with the knowledge and actions systems produce, and governance models that support ongoing critical engagement with ML/AI processes and outputs. Expert decision-support systems are a useful case study to consider the system properties that could maintain human engagement and the governance choices that could ensure they emerge.

We begin by describing three new challenges – design by data, opacity to designer, and dynamic and variable features – posed by the use of predictive algorithmic systems in professional, expert domains. Concerns about inscrutable bureaucratic rules and privatization of public policy making (and the specific opacity that technology can bring to either) apply to predictive machine learning systems generally, but we suggest there are distinctive challenges posed by such predictive systems. We then briefly explore transparency and explainability, two policy objectives that current scholarship suggests are antidotes to such challenges. We show how conceptions of transparency and explainability differ along disciplinary lines (e.g., law, computer science, social

---

Association 19 (1): 121–27(reviewing literature on automation bias in health care clinical decision support systems); Bussone, A., S. Stumpf, and D. O'Sullivan. 2015. "The Role of Explanations on Trust and Reliance in Clinical Decision Support Systems." In *2015 International Conference on Healthcare Informatics*, 160–69, p. 160 (discussing research findings on automation bias and self-reliance).

[4] For an overview of research on technology-assisted decision making and responsibility, see Mosier, Kathleen L., and Ute M. Fischer. 2010. "Judgment and Decision Making by Individuals and Teams: Issues, Models, and Applications." *Reviews of Human Factors and Ergonomics* 6 (1): 198–256.

[5] Nissenbaum, Helen. 1994. "Computing and Accountability." *Commun. ACM* 37 (1): 72–80; Simon, Judith. 2015. "Distributed Epistemic Responsibility in a Hyperconnected Era." In *The Onlife Manifesto: Being Human in a Hyperconnected Era*, edited by Luciano Floridi, pp. 145–59. Cham, CH: Springer International Publishing.

[6] Jones, Meg Leta. 2015. "The Ironies of Automation Law: Tying Policy Knots with Fair Automation Practices Principles." *Vanderbilt Journal of Entertainment & Technology Law* 18 (1): 77–134; Elish, Madeleine C. 2016. "Moral Crumple Zones: Cautionary Tales in Human-Robot Interaction." In *We Robot 2016 Working Paper*, 1–26. University of Miami (exploring how humans take the brunt of failures in sociotechnical systems, acting as "moral crumple zones" and absorbing a disproportionate amount of responsibility and liability, and arguing for reapportioning responsibility and liability in relation to actual control and agency).

Shaping Our Tools 139

sciences) and identify limitations of each concept for addressing the challenges posed by algorithmic systems in expert domains.

We then introduce the concept of contestability and explain the particular benefits of contestable ML/AI systems in the professional context over and above transparent or explainable systems. This approach can be valuable for an algorithmic handoff in a highly professionalized domain, such as the use of predictive coding software – a particular e-discovery tool – by lawyers during litigation. Current governance frameworks around the use of predictive coding in the form of professional norms and codified rules and regulations have their limitations. We argue that an approach centered around contestability would better promote attorneys' continued, active engagement with these algorithmic systems without relying so heavily on retrospective, case-specific, and costly legal remedies.

THE LIMITATIONS OF EXISTING APPROACHES TO PROTECTING VALUES

Technical systems containing algorithms are shaping and displacing human decision making in a variety of fields, such as criminal justice,[7] medicine,[8] product recommendations,[9] and the practice of law.[10] Such decision-making handoffs have been met with calls for greater transparency and explainability about system-level and algorithmic processes. The delegation of *professional* decision making to predictive algorithms – models that predict or estimate an output based on a given input[11] – creates additional issues with respect to opacity in machine learning[12] and to more general concerns with bureaucratic inscrutability[13] and privatization of public power.[14]

---

[7] Angwin, Julia, Jeff Larson, Surya Mattu, and Lauren Kirchner. 2016. "Machine Bias." *ProPublica*, May 23, 2016. https://www.propublica.org/article/machine-bias-risk-assessments-in-criminal-sentencing.

[8] See, e.g., Faggella, Daniel. 2018. "Machine Learning Healthcare Applications – 2018 and Beyond." *TechEmergence*. March 1, 2018. https://www.techemergence.com/machine-learning-healthcare-applications/; see generally, Berner, Eta S., ed. 2016. *Clinical Decision Support Systems: Theory and Practice*. 3rd ed. Health Informatics. New York: Springer.

[9] As an example, see Netflix's recommendation engine: https://medium.com/netflix-techblog/netflix-recommendations-beyond-the-5-stars-part-1-55838468f429.

[10] Ashley, Kevin D. 2017. Artificial Intelligence and Legal Analytics: New Tools for Law Practice in the Digital Age. Cambridge: Cambridge University Press.

[11] James, G., D.Witten, T. Hastie, and R. Tibshirani. (2013). *An Introduction to Statistical Learning*. New York: Springer.

[12] Burrell, Jenna. 2016. "How the Machine 'Thinks': Understanding Opacity in Machine Learning Algorithms." *Big Data & Society* 3 (1): 1–13 (describing three forms of opacity: corporate or state secrecy; technical illiteracy; and complexity and scale of machine-learning algorithms).

[13] Freeman, Jody. 2000. "Private Parties, Public Functions and the New Administrative Law Annual Regulation of Business Focus: Privatization." *Administrative Law Review* 52: 813–58.

[14] Citron, Danielle Keats. 2008. "Technological Due Process." *Washington University Law Review* 85 (6): 1249–313. ("Agencies inadvertently give rulemaking power to computer programmers who can, and do, alter established policy when embedding it into code." "Because the policies embedded in

Three Challenges Facing Algorithmic Systems in Expert Domains

We identify three challenges facing the use of predictive algorithms in expert systems. First, such predictive algorithms are not designed by technologists in the traditional sense. Whereas engineers of traditional expert systems explicitly program in a set of rules, ideally from the domain knowledge of adept individuals, predictive algorithms supplant this expert wisdom by deriving a set of decision rules from data.

Predictive algorithms can be partitioned into two categories: (1) those focused on outcomes that do not rely too heavily on professional judgment (e.g., was an individual readmitted to the hospital within thirty days of their visit?) versus (2) those focused on outcomes that are more tailored toward emulating the decisions made by professionals with specific domain expertise (e.g., does this patient have pneumonia?). Specifically, the first example can be deemed either true or false simply via observation of admit logs, regardless of professional training. The second example, by way of contrast, is distinct from the first in that it requires medical expertise to make such a diagnosis. In the strictest sense, expert systems fall into the second category,[15] and as such, inferences of such rules via predictive algorithms create unique challenges for the transfer of expertise from both individuals to the algorithm, and from the algorithm to individuals.

The second challenge is one of opacity. In many ways, this issue is induced by the first. While certain classes of predictive algorithms lend themselves to ease of understanding (such as logistic regression and shallow decision trees), other classes of model make it difficult to understand the rules inferred from the data (such as neural networks and ensemble methods). Unlike expert systems, where domain professionals can review and interrogate the internal rules, the opacity of certain algorithms prevents explicit examination of these decision rules, leaving experts to infer the model's underlying reasoning from input–output relationships.

Last, these algorithms are case-specific and evolving. They will not necessarily make the same decision about two distinct people in the same way at the same point in time, neither will they necessarily make the same decision about the same individual at varying points in time. This plasticity creates challenges for understanding and interrogating a model's behavior, as input–output behavior can vary from case to case and can vary over time.

Transparency: Perspectives and Limitations

Due to the challenges described above, algorithmic handoffs have been met with calls for greater transparency.[16] At a fundamental level, transparency refers to some

---

code are invisible, administrators cannot detect when the rules in an automated system depart from formal policy.")

[15] See Todd, Bryan S. 1992. *An Introduction to Expert Systems*. Oxford: Oxford University Computing Laboratory.

[16] Brauneis, Robert, and Ellen P. Goodman. 2018. "Algorithmic Transparency for the Smart City." *Yale Journal of Law & Technology* 20: 103–76, p. 108.

Shaping Our Tools 141

notion of openness or access, with the goal of becoming informed about the system. However, the word "transparency" lends itself to the question: *What* is being made transparent?

Given the growing role that algorithmically driven systems are poised to play across government and the private sector, we should exercise care in choosing policy objectives for transparency. A trio of federal laws – two adopted in the 1970s due to fears that the federal government was amassing data about citizens – exemplify three policy approaches to transparency relevant to algorithmic systems. Together, the laws aim to ensure citizens "know what their Government is up to,"[17] that "all federal data banks be fully and accurately reported to the Congress and the American people,"[18] that individuals have access to information about themselves held in such data banks, and that privacy considerations inform the adoption of new technologies that manage personal information. These approaches can be summarized as relating to (1) scope of a system, (2) the decision rules of a process, and (3) the outputs.

The Privacy Act of 1974,[19] which requires notices to be published in the Federal Register prior to the creation of a new federal record-keeping system, and section 208 of the E-Government Act of 2002,[20] which requires the completion of privacy impact assessments, exemplify the scope perspective. These laws provide notice about the existence and purpose of data-collection systems and the technology that supports them. For example, the Privacy Act of 1974 requires public notice that a system is being created and additional information about the system, including its name and location, the categories of individual and record maintained in the system, the use and purpose of records in the system, agency procedures regarding storage, retrieval, and disposal of the records, etc.[21] The first tenet of the Code of Fair Information Practices, first set out in a 1973 HEW (Health, Education, Welfare) Report[22] and represented in the Privacy Act of 1974 and data-protection laws the world over, stipulates in part that "there must be no personal-data record-keeping systems whose very existence is secret."[23] With the Privacy Act of 1974, the transparency theory is one of public notice and scope. Returning to our previous question of "what is being

---

[17] US Dept. of Justice v. Reporters Committee, 489 U.S. 749, 773 (1989).
[18] Ware, W. H., 1973. Records, Computers and the Rights of Citizens (No. P-5077). Santa Monica, CA: RAND Corporation.
[19] 5 U.S.C. § 552a (2014).
[20] Pub. L. No. 107–347, § 208, 116 Stat. 2899 (Dec. 17, 2002).
[21] 5 U.S.C. § 552a(e)(4); *see also* United States Department of Health, Education, and Welfare. 1973. "Report of the Secretary's Advisory Committee on Automated Personal Data Systems, Records, Computers, and the Rights of Citizens." MIT Press (discussing purpose and provisions of Privacy Act).
[22] US Department of Health, Education, and Welfare. "Report of the Secretary's Advisory Committee on Automated Personal Data Systems: Records, Computers, and the Rights of Citizens," 1973, at § III. Safeguards for Privacy.
[23] The full Code of Fair Information Practices can be found at https://epic.org/privacy/consumer/code_fair_info.html.

made transparent," in this approach to transparency, it is precisely the existence and scope being made available.

Unlike the scope aspect of transparency, the decision-rules aspect is not concerned with whether or not such a system exists. Rather, this view of transparency refers to tools to extract information about how these systems function. As an example, consider the Freedom of Information Act (FOIA), a law that grants individuals the ability to access information and documents controlled by the federal government.[24] The transparency theory here is that the public has a vested interest in accessing such information. But instead of disclosing the information upfront, it sets up a mechanism to meet the public's demand for it. As such, FOIA allows for individuals to gain access to the decisional rules of these systems and processes. Similarly, the privacy impact assessment requirement of the E-Government Act of 2002 provides transparency around agencies' consideration of new technologies, as well as their ultimate design choices.

Last, several privacy laws allow individuals to examine the inputs and outputs of systems that make decisions about them. Under this perspective, transparency is not the end goal itself. Rather, transparency supports the twin goals of ensuring fair inputs and understanding the rationale for the outputs by way of pertinent information about the inputs and reasoning. The laws all entitle individuals to access information used about them and to correct or amend data. Some of the privacy laws in this area also entitle individuals to receive information about the reasons behind negative outcomes.[25] For example, under the Equal Credit Opportunity Act, if a candidate's credit application is rejected, the credit bureau must provide the key reasons for the decision.[26] Thus, this type of transparency refers to notice of how a particular decision was reached. These forms of transparency are aimed at individual, rather than collective, understanding; they provide, to a limited extent, insight into the data and the reasoning – or functioning – of systems.

Within the computer science literature, transparency is similar to the functional and outputs perspective presented in law. That is, transparency often refers to some notion of openness around either the internals of a model or system, or around the outputs. Typically, less focus is given to disclosing the subjective choices that were invoked during the system design and engineering process or to system inputs.

The social sciences and statistics, however, take a more comprehensive perspective on transparency. Transparency in these disciplines not only captures the ideas from law and computer science, but also means disclosures about how the data was gathered, how it was cleaned and normalized, the methods used in the analysis, the choice of hyperparameters and other thresholds, etc., often in line with the goals of

---

[24]   5 U.S.C. § 553 (2016).

[25]   See, e.g., The Equal Credit Opportunity Act (ECOA), 15 U.S.C. § 1691 et seq., as implemented by Regulation B, 12 C.F.R. §1002.9. *See also* The Fair Credit Reporting Act (FCRA), 15 U.S.C. § 1681 et seq.

[26]   15 U.S.C. § 1691(d).

reproducibility.[27] The sweep of transparency reflects an understanding that these choices contribute to the methodological design and analysis. This more holistic approach to transparency acknowledges the effect that humans have in this process (reflected in decisions about data, as well as behaviors captured in the data), which is particularly pertinent for predictive algorithms.

Current policy debates, and scientific research, center around explainability and interpretability. Transparency is being reframed, particularly in the computer science research agenda, as an instrumental rather than final objective of regulation and system design. The goal is not to lay bare the workings of the machine, but rather to ensure that users understand how the machines are making decisions – whether those decisions be offering predictions to inform human action or acting independently. This reflects both growing recognition of the inability of humans to understand how some algorithms work even with full access to code and data, but also an emphasis on the overall system – rather than solely the *algorithm* – as the artifact to be known.

Explainability: Perspectives and Limitations

Explainability is an additional design goal for machine-learning systems. Driven in part by growing recognition of the limits of transparency to foster human understanding of algorithmic systems, and in part by pursuit of other goals such as safety and human compatibility, researchers and regulators are shifting their focus to techniques and incentives to produce machine-learning systems that can explain themselves to their human users. Such desires are well-founded in the abstract. For the purposes of decision making or collaboration, explanations can act as an interface between an end-user and the computer system, with the purpose of keeping a human in the loop for safety and discretion. Hence, explanations invite questioning of AI models and systems to understand limits, build trust, and prevent harm. As with transparency, different disciplines have responded to this call to action by operationalizing both explanations and explainability in differing ways.

One notable use of explanations and explainability comes from the social sciences. Miller[28] performed a comprehensive literature review of over 200 articles from the social sciences and found that explanations are causal, contrastive, selective, and social. What is pertinent from this categorization is how well the paradigms invoked in predictive algorithms (machine learning, artificial intelligence, etc.) fall within social understandings of explanations. Machine learning raises difficulties for all four of Miller's attributes of explanations.

---

[27] Miguel, Edward, Colin Camerer, Katherine Casey, Joshua, Cohen, Kevin M. Esterling, Alan Gerber, Rachel Glennerster, et al. 2014. "Promoting Transparency in Social Science Research." *Science* 343 (6166): 30–31.

[28] Miller, Tim. 2017. "Explanation in Artificial Intelligence: Insights from the Social Sciences." *ArXiv:1706.07269 [Cs]*, June. http://arxiv.org/abs/1706.07269.

For concreteness and clarity, imagine we have a predictive algorithm that classifies a patient's risk for breast cancer as either low risk, medium risk, or high risk. In this scenario, a causal explanation would answer the question: "Why was the patient classified as high risk?" Alternatively, a contrastive explanation would answer questions of the form, "Why was the patient classified as high risk as opposed to low risk or medium risk?" As such, explanations of the causal type require singular scope on the outcome, whereas contrastive explanations examine not only the predicted outcome, but other candidate alternatives as well.

With respect to machine learning, this distinction is important and suggestive. Machine learning is itself a correlation box. As such, the *output itself should not be interpreted as causal*. However, when individuals ask for *causal explanations* of predictive algorithms, they are not necessarily assuming that the underlying data mechanism is causal. Rather, the notion of causality is seeking to understand what caused the algorithm to decide that the patient was high risk, not what caused the patient to be high risk in actuality. Thus, causal explanations can be given of a model built on correlation. However, the fact that they can be produced doesn't mean that causal explanations further meaningful understanding of the system.

Contrastive explanations are a better fit for machine learning. The very paradigm of machine learning – classification models – are built in a contrastive manner. These models are trained to learn to pick the "best" output given a set of inputs – or equivalently stated, the model is taught to discern an answer to a series of input questions based on the fixed set of alternatives available. Combining these insights, it follows that requiring causal explanations for classification models is inappropriate for determining why a model predicted the value it did. Contrastive explanations, which provide insight into the counterfactual alternatives that the model rejected as viable, transfer more knowledge about the system, than causal ones.

Regardless of whether the type of explanation is causal or contrastive, Miller argued that explanations in the social sciences were selective. That is, explanations tend to highlight a few key justifications rather than being completely exhaustive. Consider the case of a doctor performing a breast cancer-screening test in the absence of a predictive algorithm. When relaying the rationale of their diagnosis to a patient, a doctor would provide sufficient reasons for their decision to justify their answer. Now, consider the state of the world where a handoff has been made to the predictive model. Suppose the model being used relies on 500 features. When explaining why the model predicted the outcome it did, it is indeed unreasonable to assume that providing information about all 500 features would practically relay any information about why the model made the choice it did. As such, requiring explanations of predictive models requires honing into the relevant features of a decision problem, which may differ from patient to patient and may vary over time.

On the aspect of explanations being social, Miller noted that explanations are meant to transfer knowledge from one individual to another. In the example above, where the doctor performs the breast cancer-screening test, this was the point of having the doctor justify their diagnosis to the patients – to inform the patient about their breast cancer-risk level. When applied to technical systems, the goal is to transfer knowledge about the internal logic of how the system reached its conclusion to some individual (or class of individuals). In the case of our breast cancer-risk prediction, this would manifest itself as a way to justify why the algorithm predicted high risk as opposed to low risk. It is worth noting that for predictive algorithms, it is often difficult to truly achieve the social goal of explanations. Certain qualities of algorithms – such as their functional form (e.g., nonlinear, containing interaction terms), their input data, and other characteristics – make it particularly difficult to assess the internal logic of the algorithm itself, or for the system to even explain what it is doing. It is therefore difficult for these machine systems to transfer knowledge to individuals in the form of an explanation that is either causal or contrastive. To the extent that explanations are aimed at improving human understanding of the logic of algorithms, the qualities of some algorithms may be incompatible with this means of transferring knowledge. It may be that the knowledge transfer must come the other way around, from the human to the machine, which is then bound to particular way or ways of knowing.[29]

Thus, there are tensions between the paradigms of predictive algorithms and those characteristics laid out by Miller. As such, the discussion above suggests that our target is off. That is, to actually fully and critically engage with predictive algorithms, this suggests that we require something stronger than transparency and explainability. Enter *contestability* – the ability to challenge machine predictions.

TOWARD CONTESTABILITY AS A FEATURE OF EXPERT DECISION-SUPPORT SYSTEMS

Contestability fosters engagement rather than passivity, questioning rather than acquiescence. As such, contestability is a particularly important system quality where the goal is for predictive algorithms to enhance and support human reasoning, such as decision-support systems. Contestability is one way "to enable responsibility in knowing"[30] as the production of knowledge is spread across humans and machines. Contestability can support critical, generative, and responsible engagement between users and algorithms, users and system designers, and ideally between users and those subject to decisions (when they are not the users), as well as the public.

---

[29] Kroll, Joshua A., Joanna Huey, Solon Barocas, Edward W. Felten, Joel R. Reidenberg, David G. Robinson, and Harlan Yu. 2017. "Accountable Algorithms." *University of Pennsylvania Law Review* 165 (3): 633–705.

[30] Simon, Judith. 2015. "Distributed Epistemic Responsibility in a Hyperconnected Era." *The Onlife Manifesto*, pp. 145–59. Cham, CH: Springer International Publishing, at p. 146 (separating out two aspects of "epistemic responsibility": 1) the individualistic perspective, which asks, "what does it mean to be responsible in knowing?"; and 2) the governance perspective with asks, "what does it take to enable responsibility in knowing?").

Efforts to make algorithmic systems knowable respond to the individual need to understand the tools one uses, as well as the social need to ensure that new tools are fit for purpose. Contestability is a design intervention that can contribute to both.[31] However, our focus here is on its potential contribution to the creation of governance models that "support epistemically responsible behavior"[32] and support shared reasoning about the appropriateness of algorithmic systems behavior.[33]

Contestability, the ability to contest decisions, is at the heart of legal rights that afford individuals access to personal data and insight into the decision-making processes used to classify them,[34] and it is one of the interests that transparency

[31] For insights on how contestable systems advance individual understanding, see, e.g., Eslami, Motahhare, and Karrie Karahalios. 2017. "Understanding and Designing around Users' Interaction with Hidden Algorithms in Sociotechnical Systems." *CSCW Companion* (describing several studies finding that seamful designs, which expose algorithmic reasoning to users, facilitated understanding, improved user engagement, and in some instances altered user behavior); Eslami, Motahhare, et al. 2015. "I Always Assumed that I Wasn't Really That Close to [Her]: Reasoning about Invisible Algorithms in News Feeds." *Proceedings of the 33rd Annual ACM Conference on Human Factors in Computing Systems* (describing the lasting effects on how users engage with Facebook to influence the News Feed algorithm after an experimental design intervention that visualized its curatorial voice); Jung, Malte F., David Sirkin, and Martin Steinert. 2015. "Displayed Uncertainty Improves Driving Experience and Behavior: The Case of Range Anxiety in an Electric Car." *Proceedings of the 33rd Annual ACM Conference on Human Factors in Computing Systems* (CHI '15) (gradient plot that reveals uncertainty reduced anxiety over single point estimate of remaining range of electric vehicle); Joslyn, Susan, and Jared LeClerc. 2013. "Decisions with Uncertainty: The Glass Half Full." *Current Directions in Psychological Science* 22 (4): 308–15 (displaying uncertainty in weather predictions can lead to more optimal decision making and trust in a forecast: transparency about probabilistic nature of prediction engenders trust even when predictions are wrong); Stumpf, Simone, et al. 2007. "Toward Harnessing User Feedback for Machine Learning." *Proceedings of the 12th International Conference on Intelligent User Interfaces*; Stumpf, Simone, et al. 2009. "Interacting Meaningfully with Machine-Learning Systems: Three Experiments." *International Journal of Human-Computer Studies* 67 (8): 639–62 (explainable systems can improve user understanding and use of system and enable users to provide deep and useful feedback to improve algorithms); Moor, Travis, et al. 2009. "End-User Debugging of Machine-Learned Programs: Toward Principles for Baring the Logic" (salient explanations helped users adjust their mental models); Amershi, Saleema, et al. 2014. "Power to the People: The Role of Humans in Interactive Machine Learning." *AI Magazine* 35 (4): 105–20 (providing an overview of interactive machine learning research, with case studies, and discussing value of interactive machine learning approaches for machine learning community as well as users).

[32] Simon, Judith. 2015. "Distributed Epistemic Responsibility in a Hyperconnected Era." In *The Onlife Manifesto: Being Human in a Hyperconnected Era*, edited by Luciano Floridi, pp. 145–59. Cham, CH: Springer International Publishing, at p. 158.

[33] Reuben Binns argues that "*public reason* — roughly, the idea that rules, institutions and decisions need to be justifiable by common principles, rather than hinging on controversial propositions which citizens might reasonably reject — is an answer to the problem of reasonable pluralism in the context of algorithmic decision making," and requires transparency. Binns, Reuben. 2017. "Algorithmic Accountability and Public Reason." *Philosophy & Technology*, May.

[34] See, e.g., regulations under the notification provisions of the Equal Credit Opportunity Act 15 U.S.C. § 1691 et seq. that require those denied credit to be provided specific, principal reasons for the denial ECOA 12 C.F.R. § 1002.1, et seq. at §1002.9; Hildebrandt, M. 2016. "The New Imbroglio. Living with Machine Algorithms." In *The Art of Ethics in the Information Society*, edited by L. Janssens, 55–60. Amsterdam: Amsterdam University Press, p. 59 (arguing that the EU General Data Protection

Shaping Our Tools

serves. Contestability as a design goal, however, is more ambitious and far-reaching. A system designed for contestability would protect the ability to contest a specific outcome, consistent with privacy and consumer protection law. It would also facilitate generative engagement between humans and algorithms throughout the use of the machine-learning system and support the interests and rights of a broader range of stakeholders – users, designers, as well as decision subjects – in shaping its performance.

Hirsch et al. set out contestability as a design objective to address myriad ethical risks posed by the potential reworking of relationships and redistribution of power caused by the introduction of machine-learning systems.[35] Based on their experience designing a machine-learning system for psychotherapy, Hirsch et al. offer three lower-level design principles to support contestability: (1) improving accuracy through phased and iterative deployment with expert users in environments that encourage feedback; (2) heightening legibility through mechanisms that "unpack aggregate measures" and "trac[e] system predictions all the way down" so that "users can follow, and if necessary, contest the reasoning behind each prediction"; and relatedly, in an effort to identify and vigilantly prevent system misuse and implicit bias, (3) identifying "aggregate effects" that may imperil vulnerable users through mechanisms that allow "users to ask questions and record disagreements with system behavior" and engage the system in self-monitoring.[36] Together, these design principles can drive active, critical, real-time engagement with the reasoning of machine-learning system inputs, outputs, and models.

This sort of deep engagement and ongoing challenge and recalibration of the reasoning of algorithms is essential to yield the benefits of humans and machines reasoning together. Concerns that engineers will stealthily usurp or undermine the decision-making logics and processes of other domains have been an ongoing and legitimate complaint about decision support and other computer systems.[37]

Regulation requires "[Algorithmic] decisions that seriously affect individuals' capabilities must be constructed in ways that are comprehensible as well as contestable. If that is not possible, or, as long as this is not possible, such decisions are unlawful.") However, in reality, what the GDPR requires may be much more limited. *See also* Wachter, Sandra, Brent Mittelstadt, and Luciano Floridi. 2017. "Why a Right to Explanation of Automated Decision-Making Does Not Exist in the General Data Protection Regulation." *International Data Privacy Law* 7 (2): 76–99, p. 93 (arguing that a fairer reading of the GDPR provisions and recitals, and member states implementation of the EU Data Protection Directive it replaces, would require "limited disclosures of the 'logic involved' in automated decision making, primarily concerning system functionality rather than the rationale and circumstances of specific decisions").

35 Hirsch, Tad, Kritzia Merced, Shrikanth Narayanan, Zac E. Imel, and David C. Atkins. 2017. "Designing Contestability: Interaction Design, Machine Learning, and Mental Health." *DIS. Designing Interactive Systems (Conference)* 2017 (June): 95–99 (describing the way an automated assessment and training tool for psychotherapists could be used as a "blunt assessment tool" of management to the detriment of therapists and patients) at p. 98.

36 Id. at p. 98.

37 See Citron, Danielle Keats. 2008. "Technological Due Process." *Washington University Law Review* 85 (6): 1249–313 (identifying the slippage and displacement of case worker values by engineering rules embedded in an expert system); Moor, James H. 1985. "What Is Computer Ethics?" *Metaphilosophy*

Encouraging human users to engage and reflect on algorithmic processes can reduce the risk of stealthy displacement of professional and organizational logics by the logics of software developers and their employers. Where an approach based on explanations imagines questioning and challenging as out-of-band activities – exception handling, appeals processes, etc. – contestable systems are designed to foster critical engagement within the system. Such systems use that engagement to iteratively identify and embed domain knowledge and contextual values, as decision making becomes a collaborative effort within a sociotechnical system.

In the context of decision-support systems, increasing system explainability and interpretability is viewed as a strategy to address errors that stem from automation bias and to improve trust.[38] Researchers have examined the impact of various forms of explanatory material, including confidence scores, and comprehensive and selective lists of important inputs, on the accuracy of decisions, deviation from system recommendations, and trust.[39] The relationship between explanations and correct decision making is not conclusive.[40]

Policy debates, like the majority of research on interpretable systems, envision explanations as static.[41] Yet, the responsive and dynamic tailoring at which machine learning and AI systems excel could allow explanations to respond to the expertise and other context-specific needs of the user, yielding decisions that leverage, and iteratively learn from, the situated knowledge and professional expertise of users.

16 (4): 266–75 (identifying three ways invisible values manifest in technical systems – to hide immoral behavior, gap-filling during engineering that invisibly embeds coders' value choices, and through complex calculations that defy values analysis); Burrell, Jenna. 2016. "How the Machine 'Thinks': Understanding Opacity in Machine Learning Algorithms." *Big Data & Society* 3 (1): 1–13 (describing three forms of opacity in corporate or state secrecy, technical illiteracy, and complexity and scale of machine-learning algorithms).

[38] Nunes, Ingrid, and Dietmar Jannach. 2017. "A Systematic Review and Taxonomy of Explanations in Decision Support and Recommender Systems." *User Modeling and User-Adapted Interaction* 27 (3–5): 393–444 (reviewing approaches to explanations in "advice-giving systems"); Bussone, A., S. Stumpf, and D. O'Sullivan. 2015. "The Role of Explanations on Trust and Reliance in Clinical Decision Support Systems." In 2015 *International Conference on Healthcare Informatics*, 160–69.

[39] Bussone et al. 2015, supra note 38.

[40] Id. at 161 (describing different research finding explanations leading to better and worse decisions).

[41] Abdul, Ashraf, Jo Vermeulen, Danding Wang, Brian Y. Lim, and Mohan Kankanhalli. 2018. "Trends and Trajectories for Explainable, Accountable and Intelligible Systems: An HCI Research Agenda." In *Proceedings of the International Conference on Human Factors in Computing Systems*, 1–18 CHI '18 (research review concluding that the explainable AI research community generally produces static explanations focused on conveying a single message and recommending that research explore interactive explanations that allow users to more dynamically explore and interact with algorithmic decision-making systems); but see also Nunes, Ingrid, and Dietmar Jannach. 2017. "A Systematic Review and Taxonomy of Explanations in Decision Support and Recommender Systems." *User Modeling and User-Adapted Interaction* 27 (3–5): 393–444, p. 408 (describing research on interactive explanations that engage users by providing a starting point and allow them to probe systems through "(i) *what-if* (what the output would be if alternative input data were provided); (ii) *why* (why the system is asking for a particular input); and (iii) *why-not* (why the system has not provided a given output)" approaches).

The human engagement contestable systems invite would align well with regulatory and liability rules that seek to keep humans in the loop. For example, the Food and Drug Administration is directed to exclude from the definition of "device" those clinical decision support systems whose software function is intended for the purpose of:

> supporting or providing recommendations to a health care professional about prevention, diagnosis, or treatment of a disease or condition; and enabling [providers] to independently review the basis for such recommendations ... so that it is not the intent that such [provider] rely primarily on any of such recommendations to make a clinical diagnosis or treatment decision regarding an individual patient.[42]

By excluding systems that prioritize human discretion from onerous medical-device approval processes, Congress shows its preference for human expert reasoning. Similarly, where courts have found professionals exhibiting overreliance on tools, they have structured liability to foster professional engagement and responsibility.[43] Systems designed for contestability invite engagement rather than delegation of responsibility. They can do so through both the provision of different kinds of information and an interactive design that encourages exploration and querying.

Professionals appropriate technologies differently, employing them in everyday work practice, as informed by routines, habits, norms, values and ideas and obligations of professional identity. Drawing attention to the structures that shape the adoption of technological systems opens up new opportunities for intervention. Appropriate handoffs to, and collaborations with, decision-support systems demand that they reflect professional logics and provide users with the ability to understand, contest, and oversee decision making. Professionals are a potential source of governance for such systems, and policy should seek to exploit and empower them, as they are well-positioned to ensure ongoing attention to values in handoffs and collaborations with machine-learning systems.

Regulatory approaches should seek to put professionals and decision support systems in conversation, not position professionals as passive recipients of system wisdom who must rely on out-of-system mechanisms to challenge them. For these reasons, calls for explainability fall short and should be replaced by regulatory approaches that drive contestable design. This requires attention to both the *information* demands of professionals – what they need to know such as training data, inputs, decisional rules, etc. – and *processes* of interaction that elicit professional expertise and allow professionals to learn about and shape machine decision making.

---

[42] 21 U.S.C. § 360j(o)(1)(E)(ii)-(iii) (2016); the term "device" is defined in 21 U.S.C. § 321(h).

[43] *Aetna Cas. and Sur. Co. v. Jeppesen & Co.*, 642 F.2d 339, 343 (9th Cir. 1981) (rejecting district court finding that pilots who relied on map that was defectively designed (showing topographical and elevation in distinct scales) were not negligent, because it would endorse a standard of care that would consider "pilot reliance on the graphics of the chart and complete disregard of the words and figures accompanying them" "as reasonable attention to duty by a pilot of a passenger plane" and opting instead to apportion fault).

Contestable Design Directions

Contestable design is a research agenda, not a suite of settled techniques to deploy. The question of what information and interactions will prompt appropriate engagement and shaping of a predictive coding system by professionals is likely to be both domain- and context-specific. However, there are systems in use and under development that support real-time questioning, curiosity, and scrutiny of machine learning systems' reasoning. First, Google's People and AI Research (PAIR) Initiative's "What-if Tool" is an actual tool that allows users to explore a machine-learning model. For example, users can see how changes in aspects of a dataset influence the learned model, understand how different models perform on the same dataset, compare counterfactuals, and test particular operational constraints related to fairness.[44] Second, LIME (Local Interpretable Model-agnostic Explanations), which generates locally interpretable models to explain the outputs of predictive systems, and SP-LIME, which builds on LIME to provide insight into the model (rather than a given prediction) by identifying and explaining a set of representative instances of the model's performance, offer information that, if presented to users, could inform their interaction with the model.[45] While the tools themselves focus only on surfacing information about decisions and models, if integrated with an interactive user interface, they could promote the explorations of predictions and models necessary for sound use of predictive systems to inform professional judgement.

Other research is exploring the ways in which structured interaction between domain experts and predictive models can improve performance.[46] There are two distinct approaches. One approach enables interaction during the development process. Here, the machine-learning training process is reframed as an HCI task, allowing a set of users the ability to iteratively refine a model during its conception.[47] In contrast to interaction during the development process, the second approach has focused on ways in which subject matter experts, with domain-specific knowledge, can interact with predictive systems that have already been developed in real time to invoke collaboration, exploration of data, and introspection.[48] At the very least,

---

[44] Wexler, James. 2018. "The What-If Tool: Code-Free Probing of Machine Learning Models." *Google AI Blog* (blog). September 11, 2018. http://ai.googleblog.com/2018/09/the-what-if-tool-code-free-probing-of.html. For the tool's code repository, see https://pair-code.github.io/what-if-tool/.

[45] Ribeiro, Marco Tulio, Sameer Singh, and Carlos Guestrin. 2016. "'Why Should I Trust You?': Explaining the Predictions of Any Classifier." In *Proceedings of the 22nd ACM SIGKDD International Conference on Knowledge Discovery and Data Mining*, 1135–1144. KDD '16. New York: ACM.

[46] Micallef, Luana, Iiris Sundin, Pekka Marttinen, Muhammad Ammad-ud-din, Tomi Peltola, Marta Soare, Giulio Jacucci, and Samuel Kaski. 2017. "Interactive Elicitation of Knowledge on Feature Relevance Improves Predictions in Small Data Sets." In *Proceedings of the 22nd International Conference on Intelligent User Interfaces*, 547–52. IUI '17. New York: ACM.

[47] Dudley, John J. and Per Ola Kristensson. 2018. "A Review of User Interface Design for Interactive Machine Learning." *ACM Transactions on Interactive Intelligent Systems* 8 (2): 8:1–8, 37.

[48] Chander, Ajay, Ramya Srinivasan, Suhas Chelian, Jun Wang, and Kanji Uchino. "Working with Beliefs: AI Transparency in the Enterprise." In *Explainable Smart Systems Workshop, Intelligent User Interfaces*. 2018.

ensuring that decisions about things such as thresholds are decided by professionals in the context of use (and remain visible to those using the system), rather than set as defaults, can support greater engagement with predictive systems.

CONCLUSION

Contestability allows professionals, not just data, to train systems. In doing so, contestability transfers knowledge about how the machine is reasoning to the professional, and it allows the professional to collaborate, critique, and correct the predictive algorithm. While relevant professional norms, ethical obligations, and laws are necessary, design has a role to play in promoting responsible introduction of predictive ML/AI systems in professional, expert domains. Such systems must be designed with contestability in mind from the outset. Designing for contestability has some specific advantages compared to rules and laws. Opportunities to reflect on the inputs and assumptions that shape systems can avert disasters where they mis-align with the conditions or understandings of professional users. Reminders of professional responsibilities and potential risks of not complying with them can prompt engagement before undesirable outcomes occur. Contestable design can confer training benefits allowing users to learn through use. Finally, it can be used to signal the distribution of responsibility from the start rather than relying solely on litigation to retrospectively mete it out in light of failures. Contestability can foster professional engagement with tools rather than deferential reliance. To the extent the goal is to yield the best of human-machine knowledge production, designing for contestability can promote the responsible production of knowledge with machine learning tools within professional contexts.

PART III

Humanity

7

Why a Commitment to Pluralism Should Limit How Humanity Is Re-Engineered

Brett Frischmann and Evan Selinger[*]

What does it mean to be human? What matters about being human? Can uses of technology dehumanize, and if so, how? What moral values should guide normative evaluations of the networked digital world that we're building for ourselves, our children and future generations? These are the highly-contested questions we tackle in our recent book, *Re-Engineering Humanity*.

Our contribution here is to provide three conceptual tools to help people grapple with these difficult questions. First, we discuss *humanity*, distinguishing between what it means to be human and what matters about being human. We argue that humanity is a shared resource consisting of intergenerational ideals and commitments. Second, we discuss Robert Nozick's famous thought experiment: *the Experience Machine*. The scenario raises fundamental questions about the good life and does so from an individualistic perspective. Finally, we discuss our thought experiment: *the Experience Machine n.o.* This scenario also raises fundamental questions about the good life, but it does so from an interconnected social perspective that emphasizes how world building engineers humanity by shaping the possible lives of others, including future generations.

We present this analysis to help readers make better sense of their own lives and the supposedly smart techno-social systems that exert ever-greater influence on how we think, act, and relate to one another and our environment. The main position we defend is that (i) different views of the good life and their underlying conceptions of what it means to be human are justifiable and (ii) a commitment to pluralism requires building worlds that allow people to pursue diverse paths towards their conceptions of flourishing. Endorsing (ii) requires being committed ethically and politically to two related ideals for freedom: freedom to be off (in the "not always on" sense) and freedom from engineered determinism. Each ideal entails positive and negative liberties[1] that are

---

[*] This chapter is adapted from "To What End?," a chapter in our book, *Re-Engineering Humanity* (2018). For brevity, we include select references. For more, please consult the book.

[1] "Negative liberty is the absence of obstacles, barriers or constraints. One has negative liberty to the extent that actions are available to one in this negative sense. Positive liberty is the possibility of acting – or the fact of acting – in such a way as to take control of one's life and realize one's fundamental purposes." Carter

contingent on the dynamic relationships among individuals and between individuals and techno-social environments. We're asking for degrees of freedom engineered into our lived-in environments and thus our lives.

INTRODUCTION

Life can be understood as a role-playing game with the earth being our experience machine. For better or worse, humans haven't optimized the planet to give us all of the experiences we desire. But this situation can change. Our roles, desires, and capabilities are engineered and re-engineered, more than we typically appreciate.

Let's unpack the gaming metaphor. Popular role-playing games allow players to create their own characters. In Dungeons and Dragons, players roll dice and assign points to different *attributes*, such as Strength, Intelligence, Wisdom, Dexterity, Constitution, and Charisma. They also select their *race*. If players want to stick with what they know, they can remain Human. Or, if they're feeling more adventurous, they can try being an Elf or a Dwarf. That's not all. Players also get to choose their *alignment*, such as Good, Neutral, or Evil. And they decide on a *class*. Fighters, Clerics, Mages, and Thieves are all popular options.

Many video games follow similar procedures. Sometimes, players are given the option of using a pre-generated character that allocates a fixed number of points to a variety of attributes. Sometimes, they can create their own with a character generation screen. In this case, players choose how to spread points among the attributes. In both Dungeons and Dragons and similar video games, players can improve their attributes, usually by performing tasks and gaining experience in the game. The built environment – the rules, story lines, maps, algorithms, and so much more – constrains and thus shapes players' lives.

These fictional narratives tell us something important about how we see and, more importantly, how we imagine ourselves as human beings. Humanity is represented as a collection of basic characteristics that each person starts with. You might believe a divine spark pre-generates your "character." Or you might believe that evolutionary biology plays this role. You could believe both of these things, or something else altogether, since you are largely a product of social conditioning. Your cultural background, your religious affiliation (or lack thereof), your political orientation, and all of the other features that make you who you are, influence which characteristics you value. You might believe that some characteristics are more

---

(2016); Berlin (1969); Berlin (1978). "[I]n the first case liberty seems to be a mere absence of something (i.e. of obstacles, barriers, constraints or interference from others), whereas in the second case it seems to require the presence of something (i.e. of control, self-mastery, self-determination or self-realization)." Carter (2016). See, generally, Berlin (1969), pp. 121–22. (Negative liberty is relevant when one answers the following question: "What is the area within which the subject—a person or group of persons—is or should be left to do or be what he is able to do or be, without interference by other persons?" Positive liberty is relevant when one answers the following question: "What, or who, is the source of control or interference that can determine someone to do, or be, this rather than that?")

essential than others. If given the opportunity, perhaps you'd allocate more "points" to autonomy than sociality, or maybe it would be the other way around.

Regardless of your perspective on how human "characters" are generated and the relative weight of various characteristics that they can be constituted by, the gaming analogy usefully emphasizes the importance of identifying basic characteristics that constrain, define, and inspire us to be more, and recognizing how the built environment shapes them. Crucially, we have opportunities to shape ourselves, and these opportunities emerge in and through our built worlds.

In *Re-Engineering Humanity*, we closely examine these relationships. How do we engineer ourselves through the techno-social world we build? How does techno-social engineering impact important aspects of our humanity? We do not attempt to identify everything important about being human. Instead, we provide a framework for identifying and evaluating techno-social engineering of core capabilities that distinguish humans from an idealized construct that we call "simple machines." Other baselines are possible, for example, other species. We leave consideration of alternatives for future work. For now, keep in mind that simple machines are programmed and fully predictable. Humans generally are not. If humans consistently behave like simple machines, however, we might need to evaluate the techno-social environment.

We examine some core human capabilities in depth, including commonsensical thinking, sociality, and free will. We touch lightly on others, such as how our sensory capabilities mediate how we look at and relate to others as well as the physical environment. In an extended discussion of transformative tools, we highlight the power of imagination, language, and the collective construction of shared ideals, institutions, and reality. These core capabilities and ideals – and thus humanity – may be at risk as supposedly smart techno-social systems spread.

A world in which engineered determinism governs is a world in which fully predictable and programmable people *perform* rather than live their lives. Such a world would be tragic. People living in it could be described as human and still would qualify as *homo sapiens*. Nonetheless, they would have a thin normative status as human beings because much of what matters about being human would be lost.

BEING HUMAN AND WHAT MATTERS ABOUT BEING HUMAN

Many criticize the negative impact of technology for being dehumanizing, especially in recent decades with the widespread adoption of computers, the Internet, and, more recently, smartphones. It is difficult, however, to know when a line has been crossed, when the techno-social engineering has gone too far, when something meaningful has been lost. Do we know when technology replaces or diminishes our humanity? Can we detect when this happens? To begin to answer these questions, we would have to know what constitutes our humanity, what makes us human, and what matters about being human. We need to understand and appreciate our humanity if we are to preserve, protect, and sustain it for ourselves, our children and future generations.

Many have said that humanity can be taken away through slavery as well as its authoritarian political analogues, like totalitarianism. Psychologists label certain practices, such as confining people to pointless tasks and subjecting them to deindividuation, dehumanizing. On this view, humanity can be lost, fully or in increments, partial deprivations, or deteriorations.

Others, however, challenge the notion that one's humanity can ever be lost or taken away. They argue that one's humanity persists even when it is not acknowledged or respected. The slave is and always will be human, and thus, her humanity cannot be taken away. What those who support slavery do is fail to acknowledge and respect her humanity. While this is a reasonable perspective, we don't adopt it; the perspective doesn't adequately distinguish (i) being human from (ii) having access to, possessing, and sharing in humanity. We agree that the slave is and always will be human, but we don't think that means her humanity cannot be taken away. To elaborate, we'll say more about different conceptions of being human (descriptive) and what matters about being human (normative).

But first let us be clear: We are committed to what, over time, has come to be known as the Kantian rule on human dignity: "All human beings are worthy of respect and deserve to never be treated exclusively as a means to an end." Some might argue that our suggestion that slavery deprives the slave of her humanity means that the slave is no longer a human being and consequently no longer worthy of respect. Similarly, they might argue that since a newborn baby lacks various capabilities that we (elsewhere) identify as potentially essential components of humanity, the baby would not be a full-fledged human being worthy of respect. These arguments fundamentally misconstrue our approach. The slave and the newborn are and always will be human beings worthy of respect. The Kantian rule applies universally to all human beings, regardless of whether they have access to, possess, and/or share fully in the blessings of humanity.[2]

It's easy to believe that the meaning of "humanity" is simple, intuitive, and unproblematic. You know it when you see it. At least, it seems that way when we look in the mirror or talk to our children. We are human, and so humanity must be what we are and those who are like us are. Unfortunately, this commonsense view lulls us into believing that what matters about being human – what's special and

---

[2] The eighteenth-century philosopher Immanuel Kant insisted that this rule is a universal truth, a categorical imperative dictated by an inescapable moral logic. We maintain that the rule is the product of human imagination and collective recognition, just like Hammurabi's Code and the Declaration of Independence. The Universal Declaration of Human Rights enshrines the rule, recognizing "the inherent dignity and ... the equal and inalienable rights of all members of the human family is the foundation of freedom, justice and peace in the world." United Nations – *Universal Declaration of Human Rights.* According to Article 1, "All human beings are born free and equal in dignity and rights." As many have noted, the Declaration reflects an incredible crosscultural and intergenerational commitment to human dignity.

important and – worth protecting and cherishing—is whatever we happen to be in the present context. In short: What is = what ought to be. Our humanity is taken as a given, stable and safe, *as if* it's a persistent and seemingly inevitable and natural state of affairs. Proponents of this view risk being profoundly *ignorant* about history. It obscures what the present generation has inherited from past generations. It underplays incredible cultural variations in the present generation. It also turns a blind eye to how our actions in the present affect future generations. And, frankly, it allows a *lack of imagination* about possible futures for humanity and the worlds we're building.

Some would say that what it means to be human can and should be described biologically in terms of what differentiates us from other species. On this view, we identify the distinguishable, evolved characteristics and capabilities of *homo sapiens*, the species of humans that outlasted the rest.[3] For example, in contrast with all other known species, only *homo sapiens* evolved the complex cognitive and social capabilities needed for widely shared language, fiction (e.g., myth, imagined realities), and social institutions (e.g., trust and rules) that scale beyond small close-knit groups (~n = 150).[4] These basic capabilities and social infrastructure enabled humans to conquer the earth and reconstruct the environment within which we evolve.

The descriptive, biological approach has the advantage of being scientific and revealing a continuum and set of functions that relate humans with other species as well as our natural environment. This approach has its limits, however. Biology doesn't explain everything that's important about humanity. For example, biology can't account for the complex and nuanced ways we relate to and evolve within our reconstructed, built environment. Biology also doesn't fully explain the tools we choose to build and use, much less whether, how, why, or when we should engineer ourselves through our techno-social tools. To more fully understand what matters about being human, how we engineer ourselves and future generations, and how to conceptualize humanity as a shared resource, we need to move beyond evolutionary biology.

After all, we may have evolved certain capabilities that enable survival and our rise to the top of the food chain.[5] However, we don't necessarily value all of those capabilities as central expressions of who we are. Precisely because we have evolved to the point where we can shape ourselves and our society, several philosophical questions have arisen. *How should we exercise such power? What about us should we sustain and cultivate? What should we let go? Who should we aspire to be? How should we engineer ourselves? What type of society should we build and sustain?*

Crucially, human beings can contemplate and act on such questions only because of the various capabilities we've gained through evolution *and* practiced, honed, developed, and sustained collectively. Evolution is necessary but not

[3] Harari (2014), pp. 3–25.
[4] Harari (2014).
[5] Harari (2014), p. 11.

sufficient. What is also necessary, and this is both controversial and incredibly important, is our built world, engineered with our techno-social tools to sustain the basic capabilities that allow us to flourish individually and collectively within and across generations.[6]

According to our approach, (1) what meaningfully distinguishes *homo sapiens* from other species is our capability to imagine, conceptualize, and engineer ourselves and our environment; and, (2) *what matters about being human* is how we exercise such power over generations to collectively produce, cultivate, and sustain shared normative conceptions of humanity.

Humanity can thus be understood as a *set of ideals* about who we are and aspire to be. These ideals are valuable, intangible resources, particularly when shared, acted on, and reflected in our most sacred institutions as shared commitments. Ultimately, we might say that humanity as both a normative concept and as a collectively produced and shared resource (or set of resources) stems from the answers we give to the following fundamental questions:

- Who are we?
- What sort of people do we aspire to be?[7]
- What values and capabilities do we possess and commit ourselves to sustain?
- What sort of society do we want to build and sustain?
- What obligations do we owe to past, present, and future generations? And how should such obligations shape the technological and social institutions we build and sustain?

We – as societies, as communities, as generations, as families, as individuals – answer these constitutional questions directly and indirectly through our actions and the cultures, institutions, infrastructures, and environments we build and sustain.

Suppose we describe *states of human affairs* as the sum of who we currently are as a group, how we see ourselves, and who we want to be.[8] This description can include a set of characteristics and capabilities,[9] some of which we possess and some of which we aspire to possess. People with different normative conceptions (or value

---

[6] Several political questions accompany the philosophical ones. *Who decides? Who should exercise such power over humanity?*

[7] In this and the fourth bullet point, we use singular words (people, society) where we could use plural words (peoples, societies). We do so only for ease of reading. As we develop further in the text that follows, different groups of peoples and different societies can and do choose to possess and commit themselves to sustaining different values and capabilities. They can and do decide, in different ways, that they owe different obligations to past, present, and future generations.

[8] By focusing on the state of human affairs, we do not mean to overinflate the position of human beings. However, this chapter does have a particular focus: it is about the relationships between humans and the technologies we create and use. Of course, as Peter Singer has argued, the suffering of other species caused by humans and our technologies is important. Nevertheless, consideration of this issue would bring us beyond the scope of this chapter.

[9] The set could include more than characteristics and capabilities. One could focus on knowledge and moral virtues, for example.

Limiting How Humanity Is Re-Engineered 161

systems) might disagree about what characteristics and capabilities ought to be in the set, how to prioritize them, and how we sustain them through social institutions.[10] Such disagreement and diversity produce and are products of different cultures.

Despite such disagreement and diversity, there are some widely shared core ideals, for example, as reflected in the Universal Declaration on Human Rights.[11] These multinational, macro-level normative commitments answer some of the most fundamental constitutional questions about who we are and aspire to be collectively. International human rights laws and institutions create a global community committed to crosscultural standards and moral floors.[12] These and other political processes enable but do not guarantee moral progress over time and across generations and cultures.[13]

Ideals don't become permanent, true, or worth preserving just because lots of people endorse them. They may change and be supplemented with other ideals that vary by culture, as the history of slavery taught us.[14] But across cultures and generations, human beings have exercised our capabilities to conceptualize and engineer ourselves and our environment, to build and sustain a collective heritage, which we characterize as nothing less than humanity itself.

---

[10] While debates have raged for millennia over what matters about being human and what constitutes a good human life, there are persuasive philosophical accounts that identify several basic human capabilities. See Sen (2005), pp. 151–66; Sen (1985); Sen (2001); Nussbaum and Sen (2004); Nussbaum (2011), pp. 33–34 (2011); Rachels (2014), pp. 15–32 (making the case for universal values that exist across all societies).

[11] Some might criticize our approach because it allows for too much variation and cultural contingency. This objection presupposes too much for the reasons stated in the text. Others might criticize us for not being as sensitive to diversity as we aspire to be. After all, appeals to culture risk focusing on shared values at the expense of recognizing differences in race, class, and gender, as well as commonalities found in subcultures (of which there are many) and norms that only make sense in specific contexts (e.g., what's acceptable at work might not be at home). Our straightforward response to this charge is that we're using culture broadly to refer to any group that's constituted, even if only temporarily, by shared commitments, values, experiences, or yearnings.

[12] For an interesting take on moral floors, see Nussbaum (2007), p. 126 ("any minimally just society will make available to all citizens a threshold level of ten central capabilities, as core political entitlements."); Nussbaum (2011), pp. 33–34.

[13] For the same reasons that we reject technological determinism, we reject corresponding notions of moral determinism. Moral progress and regress are possible.

[14] Throughout history, cultures have built diverse worlds that allowed different values to become preeminent or techno-socially engineered into existence. In *The Order of Things*, philosopher Michel Foucault contends that fundamental values like what constitutes "humanity" have been constantly redefined throughout history to suit a variety of agendas and powerful actors (Foucault 1994). Indeed, it's hard to deny that the confluence of power and prejudice – racism, sexism, classicism, and ableism, among other pernicious "isms" – has had an oversized influence in determining who gets to count as being sufficiently similar to ingroups to qualify as human. Moreover, formulations of humanity and the imagined worlds that support these conceptions can lose their hold on us, just like perceptions of the gods do – a shift that's aptly illustrated by polytheism being displaced by monotheism in large parts of the world. We could create a laundry-list of the features that have differentiated worlds across human history.

Preserving the "fundamental blessings" of humanity is the most important constitutional commitment that unites cultures across generations.[15] In his Lyceum Address of 1838, Abraham Lincoln recognized that the "fundamental blessings" passed on from generation to generation extend beyond the blessings of the Earth to include the blessings of society – the communal heritage of law, political institutions, and fundamental rights of liberty and equality.[16] Lincoln reminded his generation, as his words ought to remind us today, that the fundamental resources on which any society depends include the blessings bestowed on any present generation by sacrifices of its ancestors. Lincoln's speech, like the Gettysburg Address,[17] offers a powerful vision of a transgenerational social contract firmly rooted in equity. Each generation inherits a wealth of natural and communal resources. In return for this boon, it's obligated to transmit these resources "to the latest generation that fate shall permit the world to know."[18] This duty to transmit a legacy to the future reverberates in many cultures. Lincoln's speech implicitly harkens back to the Athenian Ephebic Oath by which men of ancient Athens swore to "transmit my fatherland not diminished [b]ut greater and better than before."[19] The intergenerational moral obligation is rooted in a more traditional conception of equity, akin to the repudiation of unjust enrichment. The present generation is morally bound to perform its duty to transmit because its own welfare and humanity has been enriched by access to and use of the resources passed on to it. To accept the benefits without satisfying the attendant duty would constitute enrichment at the expense of future generations.[20]

Humanity, conceived of normatively as a shared set of ideals reflected in us and our built world of imagined realities, institutions, infrastructures, and environments, is at risk of deterioration by pervasive techno-social engineering. We focus on specific forms of techno-social engineering that affect the basic capabilities that enable us to ask and participate in answering fundamental questions about who we are and aspire to be, individually and collectively. Thus, we consider thinking

---

[15] This section draws from Frischmann's article *Some Thoughts on Shortsightedness and Intergenerational Equity*. See generally Frischmann (2005).

[16] Lincoln (1838).

[17] Jaffa (1959), p. 228 (citing Lincoln 1863). ("The 'people' is no longer conceived in the Gettysburg Address, as it is in the Declaration of Independence, as a contractual union of individuals in the present; it is as well a union with ancestors and with posterity; it is organic and sacramental.")

[18] Lincoln (1838). See also Akwesasne Notes (1977) (often referred to as "The Iroquois' Law of Seven Generations"); Morris (1995) (discussing the "centuries-old Haudenosaunee philosophy that all major decisions of a nation must be based on how those decisions will affect at least the next seven generations.")

[19] Swift (1947), p. 4 (describing the Athenian Ephebic Oath translation by Clarence A. Forbes).

[20] The analogy to unjust enrichment is imperfect. Unlike unjust enrichment in which the beneficiary to whom the benefit is conferred compensates the person who conferred the benefit and so involves only two parties looks to the past, the dynamic we describe involves three parties (past, present, and future generations) and looks to the future. We thank John Breen for pointing this out.

capacities, the ability to socialize and relate to each other, free will, autonomy, and agency.

Some may disagree with our choices of capabilities to examine. They may choose to examine others. The bottom line is that across cultures and generations, humans have engineered themselves and their built environments to sustain these and other core capabilities. In our view, they are part of our shared heritage, our humanity. And again, they are at risk of being whittled away through rampant techno-social engineering driven by many different forces and logics. Taylorism extended and fetishized computational power, and the allure of ever more powerful intelligent control systems promise tremendous gains in efficiency and productivity along with the convenience and happiness of optimized lives. But at what cost?

OPTIMIZED LIFE ON THE EXPERIENCE MACHINE

Over forty years ago, Robert Nozick wondered whether he or anyone else would choose to plug into a hypothetical "experience machine" that could convincingly simulate any desired experience. In the blink of an eye, the experience machine would let you take on the role of a renowned novelist, a caring father, an ascetic saint, or any one of myriad other possibilities, like rock star, brilliant scientist, or world-class athlete. Nozick's scenario offers a choice to plug into a virtual reality machine that guaranteed a "lifetime of bliss."[21]

If you were presented with the opportunity, would you choose to plug into the experience machine?

We don't claim to know the right answer for you. People have different intuitions. This classic thought experiment prompts imagination and deliberation about one's basic conception of a good life. Is there more to life – or better yet, the good life – than a person's subjective experience of happiness? Or, as Nozick put it, than how one's life feels from the inside?

For hardcore hedonists, the decision is straightforward: Plug in. It guarantees optimal happiness, the highest aggregation of moment-by-moment positive feelings. The movie *The Matrix* toyed with a more reflective version of the thought experiment when a character named Cipher announces that he understands he's living in a simulation but still prefers that world to alternatives where he'd be less happy. "I know this steak doesn't exist. I know when I put it in my mouth the Matrix is telling my brain that it is juicy and delicious. After nine years you know what I realize? Ignorance is bliss."[22]

---

[21] To make his objections vivid, Nozick introduced the experience machine thought experiment (1974 and revisited in 1989), a hypothetical scenario that bears a striking resemblance to Ray Bradbury's earlier short story, "The Happiness Machine" (1957). Weijers (2011).

[22] For an extended discussion of this issue, see Grau (2005).

Most people would not choose to plug in.[23] And that's because most people are not hardcore hedonists.[24] Of course, happiness matters for most people and is an important component of a life lived well. But many other things matter too, and they are not reducible to or commensurable with happiness. Pursuing pleasure exclusively, as the ultimate end, would lead to a rather shallow life.[25]

Nozick contended that it would be a mistake to plug into the experience machine.[26] His reservations revolved around a core conviction that many people share today: "[R]eality has intrinsic prudential value."[27] No matter how realistic a simulated world feels, it lacks the features of an independent reality conducive to human flourishing. It seems the epitome of a dehumanizing environment. It's a fully engineered reality wherein simulated people lack free will, simulated things bend to our will and desires, history has no weight, interdependence doesn't exist, and even the laws of physics can be broken. In such a programmed world, our actions wouldn't be meaningful. Our accomplishments, including caring for others, would be hollow. Our relationships would be fake. And at least some of our basic human capabilities would atrophy. Fortunately, we wouldn't realize any of this while living on the machine because we'd be programmed to be oblivious to such concerns. And we'd feel really good.

There's a related concern that plugging in would lead to an inauthentic life determined by others. A life lived on the experience machine would not be one's own. Too much of the life lived and happiness experienced would be determined by the machine, or, to be more precise, the engineers who created the machine. This concern has weight for those who insist that the means matter when evaluating the quality of one's life. On this view, a well-lived life requires some human agency and exercise of free will. By contrast, a fully programmed and determined life on the machine is not a well-lived life, regardless of how much pleasure the machine supplies.

It's important to appreciate that these considerations are perfectly legitimate products of the thought experiment. By forcing someone to choose upfront whether

---

[23] Weijers (2014); Kolber (1994). There is a debate among philosophers and experimentalists about whether thought experiments like Nozick's are amenable to empirical study. Smith (2011); De Brigard (2010).

[24] Bramble (2016). This may be an empirical claim worth exploring. We are unaware of a definitive study and are not certain that empirical testing would work well.

[25] Susan Wolf offers compelling examples that illustrate why thinkers like Nozick don't reduce meaningful experiences to instances where we strive for pleasure or even necessarily experience it. Wolf (2015), p. 51.

[26] Ben Bramble observes: "Hedonism has few contemporary advocates. This is mainly due to a single, highly influential objection to it, widely considered to be decisive: Robert Nozick's experience machine. Discussions of well-being—whether in scholarly journals, academic conferences, or university lecture halls—often begin with a quick dismissal of hedonism by reference to Nozick's objection before turning to 'more interesting matters' (usually the question of which desire-based or hybrid theory of well-being is true." Bramble (2016), p. 136.

[27] Weijers (2011).

Limiting How Humanity Is Re-Engineered

to plug in, the thought experiment prompts deliberation. Some argue that critical resistance to plugging in is rooted in the framing effects of the narrative. For example, status quo bias may lead people to prefer what they currently experience over the unknown life on a machine.[28] Or people can question whether the experience machine will actually work: *What happens when the power goes out? Will the unplugged be able to take advantage of those who are plugged in?* These arguments are valid, but too easily taken as the final word. Framing effects, cognitive biases, and other related concerns can and should be dealt with by engaging the thought experiment thoughtfully, rather than simply dismissing it. Behavioral psychology offers excellent grounds for criticizing and improving thought experiments but does not provide answers to the underlying normative questions.

Others, such as economist Richard Layard and philosopher Joseph Mendola, criticize the thought experiment for being "wildly unrealistic" and pumping unfair intuitions with "unfamiliar gadgetry which invokes our fear of the unfamiliar."[29] These criticisms might have had purchase a few decades ago. But they seem wildly exaggerated today. Modern technology and culture make the experience machine scenario reasonably familiar and sufficiently realistic for people to consider. Regardless, these objections to the thought experiment hardly provide a better explanation for people's preferences than the claim that reality has intrinsic prudential value.

In our view, a significant reason why many people would choose not to plug into the experience machine is that they believe in free will and value having it. To plug into the experience machine would be to accept engineered determinism and know, even if only at the moment of deliberation about whether to plug in, that any subsequent experience of free will would be illusory. Many people highly value free will. Arguably, it is one of the fundamental blessings of humanity, collectively cultivated and sustained across generations through the cultures, institutions, infrastructures, and environments we build and sustain.

But what if the promise of optimal happiness on the machine makes the thought experiment too outlandish? The utopian allure might exacerbate the framing effects, or it might trigger doubts, fears, or even guilt.

Suppose we adjust the thought experiment so that life on or off the machine would be the same in terms of aggregate happiness.[30] Suppose a person's life on the experience machine is assumed to be identical to the life they'd live off the machine.[31] If the

---

[28] Weijers (2014), p. 3.

[29] Mendola (2006), pp. 441–77; Layard (2005). See also Bronsteen, Buccafusco, and Masur (2014), pp. 172–75 (suggesting that the experience machine thought experiment pumps "inadmissible intuitions").

[30] Nozick tilted the scales in favor of hedonism by guaranteeing optimal happiness. He probably did this to show why hedonism, even in its most tempting form, is repugnant once you think carefully about it. By making the lives on and off the machine equivalent, we adjust the extreme framing of the tradeoffs. This might eliminate speculation about optimal happiness and elevate status quo bias as a factor.

[31] Crisp (2006), pp. 635–36. "According to hedonism, [the lives on and off the machine] have exactly the same level of well-being. And that is surely a claim from which most of us will recoil." Crisp goes on to argue that our beliefs about the value of accomplishment (and by extension free will) might be "an

life Jane experiences on and off the machine is identical from her subjective perspective, hedonists argue Jane would be equally well on and off the machine. Her well-being – the goodness of her life – is the same. And so, they argue, she should be indifferent to choosing one life over the other. She should be willing to flip a coin.

What about you? Would you be willing to flip a coin? Heads would mean you plug in. And tails would mean you do not plug in. Keep in mind that life on and off the machine is guaranteed to be identical.

If you are truly indifferent, you should be willing to flip a coin and accept the outcome either way. Perhaps some people would do so. We suspect most people would not actually be willing to flip a coin. Further, it's hard to imagine that anyone would choose to plug into the experience machine if it promised an identical life. Most people would choose not to plug in. Some might argue that unwillingness to flip a coin should be construed as an indication of irrational biases, whether the status quo bias or some irrational fear that fights the hypothetical. But we think a much better explanation is that they would not be indifferent to the two lives. They would choose to maintain the status quo and for good reason. They value free will, or, at least, the illusion of free will. In other words, they would take a pragmatic approach and wager in favor of free will rather than plug into the experience machine, which would eliminate free will, and, at best, offer an engineered illusion of it.[32] Thus, what people fear about the experience machine is precisely what Nozick highlighted: *The loss of authenticity in a world of engineered determinism.*

Let's flip the scenario around. Suppose you are informed that you're currently plugged into an experience machine and that you've been selected for a one-time opportunity to unplug and experience an authentic life. Unlike Cipher in *The Matrix*, your life unplugged is guaranteed to be identical to the plugged-in life you're currently living.

What would you choose if you were given the opportunity to (1) unplug, (2) stay plugged in, or (3) flip a coin such that heads would mean you unplug and tails would mean you stay plugged in?

It's a little more difficult to predict what people would do, although for somewhat surprising reasons. We don't think many people would choose to flip a coin. Most people are not hardcore hedonists; they wouldn't be indifferent to the two lives (worlds). Initially, one might think people would unplug and choose an authentic life. But most people would not do so.[33] Some have suggested that this demonstrates a cognitive bias infecting the thought experiment. A better explanation is that in the reality we know and experience, most people would take a pragmatic approach and wager in favor of free will, meaning their existing belief in free will. In a sense, this is a reaction that fights the hypothetical. But, importantly, it only fights the hypothetical

---

example of a kind of collective bad faith, with its roots in the spontaneous and largely unreflective social practices of our distant ancestors." Perhaps. But perhaps he has it backwards.

[32] See *Re-Engineering Humanity* for our Free Will Wager.

[33] De Brigard (2010), pp. 43–57.

claim about our reality being fully engineered and determined. Absent a high level of proof that our current reality is fully determined (naturally or by engineering), wagering in favor of free will remains the best strategy.

The experience machine thought experiment usefully highlights competing value systems and prompts deliberation about what matters to you about your life. Hardcore hedonists would choose to plug in; most other folks would not. There are many reasons people might choose not to plug in. But an important reason is that a programmed world governed by engineered determinism is not conducive to human flourishing. At the most basic level, life on the experience machine doesn't jibe with how most people answer any of the basic constitutional questions. We don't see ourselves, our lives, or our reality as fully programmed or determined, even though we understand that much of what we do and who we are is the product of various factors outside of our control. Neither do we aspire to such a fate.

Do we aspire to build such a world for our children and future generations? Notably, this is a moral question outside the scope of Nozick's thought experiment. To see why, consider the importance of the cord and plug. The decision about whether or not to plug into the experience machine served a few purposes:

- It kept the thought experiment focused on an individual decision about an individual life.
- It prompted deliberation by an individual about that individual's conception of a good life for that individual, which is often referred to as the individual's well-being or welfare.
- It eliminated concerns about paternalism, social engineering, or social welfare.
- It implied the existence of multiple worlds – at least, worlds on and off the machine.

The myopia of the thought experiment limits its relevance, however, when we turn our attention to social arrangements and world building. Yet that is where we must go if we are to answer the fundamental questions about the world we're building for posterity.

EXPERIENCE MACHINE N.O – LIFE IN THE MACHINE/WORLD

Let's eliminate the plug. Consider a different version of the experience machine, which we refer to as the Experience Machine n.o. Imagine a ubiquitous smart techno-social environment that spans the Earth and optimizes the planet to provide human inhabitants optimal happiness. Rather than ask you whether you'd plug yourself in, we'd like for you to consider whether such a machine/world should be built.

If you were given the ultimate decision-making authority, would you build such a machine/world?

Moving from a decision about whether (i) to plug yourself into the machine to (ii) building a machine/world for all humans complicates the analysis and shifts the focus from individual well-being to broader moral and social concerns. To make the situation less abstract, let's be clear about what we mean by optimal happiness. Assume that the Experience Machine n.o supplies all human beings on Earth with *maximum happiness*, measured moment-by-moment for each individual and aggregated over a lifetime, at *minimal social cost*. (Our arguments hold if we replace happiness with pleasure, positive affect, or other positive mental states.)

We must admit that this sounds pretty darn good. Optimal happiness appears to be an end worth pursuing. But *what about the means? Do they matter?*

What could the Experience Machine n.o look like and how might we build such a machine/world? Extrapolating from the present to the near future, we envision that the Experience Machine n.o would be comprised of interconnected sensor networks and data-driven automation of socio-technical systems around, about, on and in human beings. Imagine that within the next few decades, the following occurs. Large multinational companies[34] gradually build and connect smart techno-social environments that actually deliver on their promises. The scope of deployment expands to the point where there is seamless interconnection and integration across all environments within which humans live. The normative agenda executed throughout all this construction and deployment is optimal efficiency, productivity, and happiness.

Guided by the optimization criterion of maximum happiness at minimal social cost, the Experience Machine n.o necessarily would engineer human beings. After all, human beings are inefficient and costly to sustain. Optimization would entail minimization of various costs associated with humans being human. For example, our bodily and mental engagement with the physical world entails logistical, navigational, and various other transaction costs. Outsourcing to intelligent control systems would minimize these costs. Making decisions, experimenting, and learning (among other mental processes) are also costly endeavors. Again, the optimizing logic would press toward minimizing and potentially eliminating these costs. Interacting with one another, coordinating behaviors, developing relationships, and many other aspects of interdependent human relations entail transaction costs to be minimized.

Finally, there is a subtler type of techno-social engineering prevalent in the Experience Machine n.o. Since what makes us happy is in large part contingent on environmental conditions and experiences, and since those factors are fully determined within the machine/world, optimization also would entail engineered tastes, beliefs, preferences, and other factors that feed into our affective feelings of pleasure.

---

[34] We are not committed to identifying multinational companies as the architects. Governments, public–private partnerships, and others would also presumably be involved. As we explain elsewhere, the point is not to allocate blame to any master planner.

Bluntly, the cheapest way to make billions of human beings perfectly happy – particularly when using the sorts of technological means we're imagining – is to set the bar very low. In this case, the techno-social system need only meet or even barely surpass expectations. As hedonists know and often are prone to emphasize, people adapt their beliefs, preferences, and expectations to their conditions and, subsequently, their corresponding happiness levels typically adjust.[35] So, the goal might very well be to shape beliefs, preferences, and expectations in a manner that makes supplying happiness as cheap and easy as possible. At the end of the day, optimal happiness would boil down to satiation of engineered will.

There are many possibilities, however. Perhaps machine learning would settle on different equilibria. We can imagine extremely dystopian science fiction scenarios, such as Wall-E, where humans are dumb satiated fools. But we also can imagine scenarios where the machine/world manufactures higher happiness aggregates through different types of programs. John Stuart Mill famously argued that it is "better to be Socrates dissatisfied than a fool satisfied."[36] Perhaps the Experience Machine n.o would produce a world filled with happy sages. Cheap engineered bliss need not exclude higher pleasures of the sort Mill defended. Higher pleasures often are cultivated and learned, and cultivation and learning entail costs.[37] On one hand, minimizing these costs might lead to outsourcing or pushing toward engineering wills satiated with lower pleasures. On the other hand, cultivating certain sets of tastes that correspond to higher pleasures might be worth the cost if they produce even more net pleasure. *Who knows?* Frankly, it's impossible to know exactly how the optimization would work out. But that's really beside the point. One way or another, techno-social systems would determine whether and what to cultivate, who and what we are. What makes humans happy would be predetermined rather than produced through the exercise of free will, experimentation, and self-authorship.

Regardless of the scenario, our thought experiment raises a fundamental normative question: Would maximizing human happiness at minimal social cost through the Experience Machine n.o justify forcing everyone to live a fully determined life?

We strongly suspect few people would answer in the affirmative, at least on reflection.[38] Think about what it would mean. Building the Experience Machine n.o is functionally equivalent to forcing everyone to plug into Nozick's Experience

---

[35] As Amartya Sen argued long ago in his critique of welfarism, an incredibly poor person with very little opportunity in life might be subjectively happy because she has adapted to her conditions in life, but that cannot mean that society should not be committed to reducing poverty or investing in building the capabilities of her daughters and sons or of future generations of similarly situated people. Sen (1985); Sen (2001); Nussbaum and Sen (2004).

[36] Mill (1962), p. 9.

[37] Historically, not everyone has had the means to experience Mill's higher pleasures. Significant distributional and class-based concerns challenge appeals to higher pleasures. Further, strong commitment to individualism triggers concerns about paternalism – *who's to say what is higher?* We don't address these concerns, except to note that perhaps Experience Machine n.o could level the playing field. Of course, it is not clear how such leveling would affect humanity.

[38] Of course, if we're wrong, then that would tell us something about people's baseline normative values.

Machine. Even the most hardcore hedonist would hesitate before imposing a machine life on others. Such paternalism conflicts directly with longstanding ideals concerning free will, autonomy, and agency, which are shared by many cultures and widely regarded as fundamental blessings of humanity.

Yet hesitation does not mean rejection. We posed this thought experiment to Peter Singer, a renowned philosopher and incredibly thoughtful and generous person, and after some discussion and deliberation, he replied: "I'm a sufficiently hardcore hedonist to think that democracy is a means to an end rather than an end in itself. If we can really imagine achieving optimum happiness for all sentient beings, forever, that would be a greater value than democracy, which may be better than any other system of government, but so far hasn't got anywhere close to producing optimum happiness for all sentient beings." Optimal happiness for everyone on Earth is an end worth considering carefully, particularly in light of how much misery and suffering exists in our world.

The Experience Machine n.o poses a threat to the liberal democratic ideal that people should be generally free to choose their own ends with minimal interference. Commitments to forms of this ideal have proved to be the best way for diverse people to live together, have real opportunities to experiment with different ways of living, and determine, over time and with the accrual of experience, which ways to live well. A world that makes it very hard or impossible to opt out of Experience Machine n.o would violate this ideal by interfering too strongly with our capacity to freely set ends for ourselves. Such interference is morally wrong and should be politically resisted. Although different in some respects, the spread of hedonism through neo-Taylorism amped up by interconnected and ubiquitous smart devices functions much like an authoritarian government imposing a mandatory state religion.

But if longstanding ideals are socially constructed and thus contingent on techno-social engineering systems, would building the Experience Machine n.o be defensible so long as it was done gradually? Deployed and integrated incrementally over decades, people could be gradually prepared for and conditioned to accept this brave new world. Engineered beliefs could pave the slippery sloped path to the Experience Machine n.o. This is why we've emphasized the importance of asking these questions at a time when it's still possible to recognize and evaluate the path we're on.

Some would argue that any resistance people currently have toward building the machine/world is itself the product of techno-social engineering of beliefs, preferences, and values by past generations. This is true. The present generation has inherited the fundamental blessings of the past, including shared ideals about who we are and who we aspire to be. But this point doesn't undermine the inquiry or make it any easier to answer the difficult and pressing questions highlighted by our thought experiment and more thoroughly presented throughout our book.

Finally, some will argue that like Nozick's version, the Experience Machine n.o thought experiment is wildly unrealistic and nothing more than an unfair intuition pump. They also will argue that the scenario is scary and framed in a manner that unfairly triggers psychological biases that distort rational analysis. These are fair points. But they are easily overstated and taken too far. Again, we use the thought experiment to prompt deliberation, analysis, and discussion. It is not a theoretical proof or empirical experiment.

While we truly hope our imagined machine/world is wildly unrealistic, there are various reasons to believe the slippery sloped path we're on is headed in that direction. Regardless of whether we reach the end-state, we need to think more deeply about the world we're building, both because of what it means for our children and future generations and because of how it affects us as we proceed down the path.

Twenty-first century techno-social engineering deeply affects how we think, feel, and interact with one another. Outsourcing so many of these functions to techno-social systems can't and shouldn't be assumed to be in our interest, neutral, or mere natural extensions of ourselves. We need to be aware of atrophying capabilities, mind control, and the gradual loss of human dignity as more aspects of our lives are determined by smart techno-social systems.[39]

We are not fully predictable and programmable machines. In all likelihood, we never will be. But that is no reason to become complacent. Much of what matters about being human can be lost in partial deprivations as we march down the slippery sloped path we're on.

PLURALISM AS A CONSTRAINT ON TECHNO-SOCIAL ENGINEERING OF HUMANITY

The transition from Experience Machine to Experience Machine n.o marked a significant shift in focus, from evaluating individual well-being to evaluating humanity in a social world. We hope that on reflection, most people, including hardcore hedonists, would decline to build Experience Machine n.o because they recognize that there is more that matters about being human than subjective feelings of happiness.

We can build much better worlds that are conducive to human flourishing and a plurality of values.[40] Free will and agency matter, above and beyond how those

---

[39] The techno-social engineering test framework developed in *Re-Engineering Humanity* (2018) provides a set of conceptual tools for identifying and contextually evaluating these risks.

[40] This is an important caveat. Suppose the Experience Machine n.o thought experiment framed the choice in binary terms as follows: (1) Build the Experience Machine n.o; or (2) Retain our current world as it currently exists. This choice presents a more difficult decision. The first option might sacrifice actual free will, but it would provide the illusion of free will and tremendous welfare gains in terms of longer and happier lives for billions of people. The second choice might sustain free will, but it would sacrifice the opportunity for massive social welfare gains. If these are the only choices, the tradeoff might be very difficult. It is critical, in our view, to recognize that these are not the only choices. We can build much better worlds.

capabilities cash out in terms of subjectively experienced well-being. But worst case, even if most people say they would choose to build the Experience Machine n.o, that empirical attestation of their values does not provide sufficient justification. This is where liberalism and paternalism clash.[41] A confounding difficulty with liberalism and relying on individuals' existing preferences and beliefs is that such preferences and beliefs are contingent on the techno-social environment within which they've lived their lives. It's hard to fully credit preferences and beliefs that significantly discount the constitutional value of free will and agency. After all, deferring to individuals' choices only makes sense if the individuals themselves have free will and practical agency, and if they do, then it seems morally wrong to deny the same capabilities to future generations, to deny them access to the fundamental blessings of humanity passed on to the present generation.

In the end, a commitment to pluralism demands freedoms engineered into our built environments. Accordingly, one of the most important constitutional questions of the twenty-first century is how to sustain the freedom to be off, to be free from techno-social engineering, to live and develop within underdetermined techno-social environments. A precursor to implementing any potential responses is recognizing the threat that engineered determinism poses to humanity. The sirens call of data-driven, supposedly smart techno-social systems promises cheap bliss – a world of optimal happiness, but it ignores the carnage of humanity lost.

REFERENCES

Berlin, Isaiah (1969). Two Concepts of Liberty, in I. Berlin, *Four Essays on Liberty*, London: Oxford University Press. New ed. in Berlin 2002.

Berlin, Isaiah (1978). From Hope and Fear Set Free, in I. Berlin, *Concepts and Categories. Philosophical Essays*, ed. H. Hardy, London: Hogarth Press; Oxford: Oxford University Press, 1980. Reprinted in Berlin 2002.

Bramble, Ben (2016). The Experience Machine. *Philosophy Compass*, 11(3), 136–45.

Bronsteen, John; Buccafusco, Christopher; and Masur, Jonathon S. (2014). *Happiness and the Law*. Chicago, IL: Chicago University Press.

Carter, Ian (2016). Positive and Negative Liberty, *The Stanford Encyclopedia of Philosophy*, ed. Edward N. Zalta.

Crisp, Roger (2006). Hedonism Reconsidered. *Philosophy and Phenomenological Research*, 73(3), 619–45.

De Brigard, Felipe (2010). If You Like It, Does It Matter if It's Real. *Philosophical Psychology*, 23(1), 43–57.

Foucault, Michel (1994). *The Order of Things: An Archaeology of the Human Sciences*. New York: Vintage Books.

Frischmann, Brett M. (2005). Some Thoughts on Shortsightedness and Intergenerational Equity. *Loyola University Chicago Law Journal*, 36(2), 457–67.

---

[41] Paternalism kicks in where there is good reason to conclude that people don't know what's best for them; liberalism is skeptical of any such alleged state of affairs. The battle usually devolves into the core political question of "Who Decides?"

Grau, Christopher (ed.). (2005). *Philosophers Explore the Matrix*. New York: Oxford University Press.

Harari, Yuval Noah (2014). *Sapiens: A Brief History of Humankind*. New York: Vintage.

Jaffa, Harry V. (1959). *Crisis of the House Divided: An Interpretation of the Issues in the Lincoln-Douglas Debates*. Chicago, IL: University of Chicago Press.

Kolber, Adam J. (1994). Mental Statism and the Experience Machine. *Bard Journal of Social Sciences*, 3, 10–17.

Layard, Richard (2005). *Happiness: Lessons from a New Science*. New York: Penguin Group.

Lincoln, Abraham (1838, January 27). The Perpetuation of Our Political Institutions, Address Before the Young Men's Lyceum of Springfield, Illinois (January 27, 1838). Retrieved from http://Federalistpatriot.us/histdocs/Lincolnlyceum.html.

Mendola, Joseph (2006). Intuitive Hedonism. *Philosophical Studies: An International Journey for Philosophy in the Analytic Tradition*, 128(2), 441–77.

Mill, John S. (1962). *Utilitarianism: On Liberty*. London: Collins.

Morris, Glenn. For the Next Seven Generations: Indigenous Americans and Communalism. Fellowship for Intentional Community. Retrieved from www.ic.org/wiki/next-seven-generations-indigenous-americans-communalism/ (last visited January 6, 2005).

Nozick, Robert (2013). *Anarchy, State, and Utopia*. New York: Basic Books.

Nussbaum, Martha (2007). The Capabilities Approach and Ethical Cosmopolitanism: A Response to Noah Feldman. *Yale Law Journal Pocket Part*, 117, 123–29.

Nussbaum, Martha (2011). *Creating Capabilities: The Human Development Approach*. Cambridge, MA: Harvard University Press.

Nussbaum, Martha and Sen, Amartya K. (2004). *The Quality of Life*. Oxford: Oxford University Press.

Rachels, James (2014). The Challenge of Cultural Relativism. In Stuart Rachels (ed.), *Elements of Moral Philosophy* (pp. 15–32). New York: McGraw-Hill Education.

Sen, Amartya K. (1985). *Commodities and Capabilities*. Amsterdam: North-Holland.

Sen, Amartya K. (2001). *Development as Freedom*. Oxford: Oxford University Press.

Sen, Amartya K. (2004). *Rationality and Freedom*. Cambridge, MA: Harvard University Press.

Sen, Amartya K. (2005). Human Rights and Capabilities. *Journal of Human Development*, 6(2), 151–66.

Sen, Amartya, K. (2011). *Development as Freedom*. New York: Anchor Books.

Smith, Basil (2011). Can We Test the Experience Machine?, *Ethical Perspectives*, 18 (1), 29–51.

Swift, Fletcher H. (1947). *The Athenian Ephebic Oath of Allegiance in American Schools and Colleges*. Los Angeles, CA: University of California Press.

United Nations. *Universal Declaration of Human Rights*. Retrieved from www.un.org/en/universal-declaration-human-rights/.

Weijers, Dan (2011). A Review and Assessment of the Experience Machine Objection to Hedonism. Retrieved from www.danweijers.com/pdf/A%20Review%20 and%20Assessment %20of%20the%20Experience%20Machine%20Objection%20to%20Hedonism%20-% 20Dan%20Weijers.pdf.

Weijers, Dan (2014). Nozick's Experience Machine Is Dead, Long Live the Experience Machine. *Philosophical Psychology*, 27(4), 513–35.

Wolf, Susan R. (2015). *The Variety of Values: Essays on Morality, Meaning, and Love*. New York: Oxford University Press.

8

Caveat Usor: Surveillance Capitalism as Epistemic Inequality

Shoshana Zuboff

> Somebody take me home
> While I still believe
> While the pines are still the pines
> And there's something left of me
>
> Philip Roebuck
> "Somebody Take Me Home"

The world suffers under a dictatorship of no alternatives. Although ideas all by themselves are powerless to overthrow this dictatorship we cannot overthrow it without ideas.
Roberto Unger, The Dictatorship of No Alternatives

I. WHO KNOWS?

On August 9, 2011 the *New York Times* reported that the Spanish Data Protection Agency had chosen to champion the claims of ninety ordinary citizens who were determined to preserve inherited meaning for a world bent on change at the speed of light.[1] In the name of these citizens' "right to be forgotten," the Agency ordered Google to stop indexing contested links pertaining to their pasts.

Each had a unique complaint. One had been terrorized by her former husband and didn't want him to find her address. A middle-aged woman was embarrassed by an old arrest from her days as a university student. An attorney, Mario Costejo González, had suffered the foreclosure of his home years earlier. Although the matter had long been resolved, a Google search of his name continued to deliver links to the foreclosure notice, which, he argued, damaged his reputation.

The Agency concluded that citizens had the right to request the removal of links, and ordered Google to stop indexing the information and to remove existing links to its original sources. Google had unilaterally undertaken to change the rules of the information life cycle, when it decided to crawl, index, and make accessible personal

---

[1] Suzanne Daley, "On Its Own, Europe Backs Web Privacy Fights," *New York Times*, August 9, 2011, http://www.nytimes.com/2011/08/10/world/europe/10spain.html.

details across the World Wide Web without asking anyone's permission. As a result, information that would normally age had been transformed into a state of perpetual youth and highlighted in the foreground of each person's digital identity. After all, the Spanish Data Protection Agency reasoned, not all information is worthy of immortality. Some information should be forgotten, because that is only human.

Unsurprisingly, Google challenged the Agency's order before the Spanish High Court, which selected Mario Costeja González's case for referral to the Court of Justice of the European Union. On May 13, 2014, after lengthy and dramatic deliberations, the Court of Justice announced its decision to assert the "right to be forgotten" as a fundamental principle of European law.[2]

From the beginning, the case was framed in a peculiar way, pitting "privacy" against an indeterminate open-ended "right to know." As one expert told the *Times*: "Europe sees the need to balance freedom of speech and the right to know against a person's right to privacy or dignity."[3] Three years later when the Court of Justice ruled in favor of Costejo González and his right to be forgotten, Google's then CEO Eric Schmidt repeated that odd juxtaposition. Speaking to his company's shareholders, he characterized the Court's decision as a "balance that was struck wrong" in the "collision between a right to be forgotten and a right to know."[4]

In fact, there was no "balance" that was "struck wrong." The Court's decision was not one of "balancing" two conflicting goods, but rather one of redistributing a single good. The conceptual problem here is that the "right to be forgotten" does not stand in opposition to a "right to know." Rather, it *is* a "right to know." The distinction is critical, because it lifts the veil on a political contest over a new domain of fundamental rights: *epistemic rights*. Such rights confer inalienable entitlements to learning and to knowing. Epistemic rights are the cause of which privacy is the effect. This political contest has been obfuscated to the point of invisibility, despite the fact that its outcome will define the moral and political milieu of our information civilization.

The distribution of epistemic rights determines the degree of epistemic inequality, defined as unequal access to learning imposed by hidden mechanisms of information capture, production, analysis, and control. It is best exemplified in the fast growing abyss between what people can know and what can be known about them. The new axis of epistemic equality/inequality does not reflect what we can earn but rather what we can learn. It represents a focal shift from ownership of "the means of production" to ownership of "the production of meaning."

---

[2] "Google Spain SL v. Agencia Española de Protección de Datos – (Case C-131/12 (May 13, 2014))," *Harvard Law Review* 128, no. 2 (December 10, 2014): 735.

[3] Daley, "On Its Own, Europe Backs Web Privacy Fights."

[4] James Vincent, "Google Chief Eric Schmidt Says 'Right to Be Forgotten' Ruling Has Got the Balance 'Wrong,'" *Independent*, May 15, 2014, http://www.independent.co.uk/life-style/gadgets-and-tech/goo gle-chief-eric-schmidt-says-right-to-be-forgotten-ruling-has-got-the-balance-wrong-9377231.html.

Epistemic equality depends on epistemic justice, the scope of which is delineated by three essential questions that reflect the nested dilemmas of knowledge, authority, and power: What is the distribution of knowledge? What are the sources of authority that legitimate the distribution of knowledge? What is the power that sustains that authority? Put simply, "Who knows?" "Who decides who knows?" "Who decides who decides who knows?" The answers to these questions determine a society's progress toward epistemic equality.

From this vantage point, one may observe that the real decision faced by the Court of Justice was not one of balancing "privacy" against a "right to know," but rather about the just distribution of epistemic rights. It asked, "Who has the right to know about one's past and in what degree?" The Court judged whether an inalienable right to learn and to know about an individual's past adhered primarily to the individual or to Google. What dismayed Schmidt was that the Court rejected Google's self-authorized claim to a totality of epistemic rights and instead distributed this "right to know about one's past" in a new pattern.

The Court's decision answered the three essential questions. First, it privileged the individual with the right to learning and knowledge about one's own past. Second, it created a juridical "right to be forgotten" that stands as the source of legitimate authority. Third, it was to be Europe's democratic institutions and their power to govern through the rule of law that sustain this authority – not the private power of a corporation.

The primacy of epistemic rights as the cause of privacy was implied in Justice William O. Douglas's 1967 dissenting opinion in the Fourth Amendment case, *Warden v. Hayden*:

> Privacy involves the choice of the individual to disclose or to reveal what he believes, what he thinks, what he possesses .... the individual should have the freedom to select for himself the time and circumstances when he will share his secrets with others and decide the extent of that sharing.[5]

In Douglas's formulation, privacy is contingent on the individual's sovereign right to self/knowledge, a right that confers the ability to choose whether to disclose or withhold such knowledge, to what degree, and for what purpose. This choice has been an elemental right throughout most of human history. By "elemental," I mean to mark a distinction between, on the one hand, tacit rights that are given under the conditions of human existence, and, on the other, juridical rights codified in law.

Others have addressed this distinction, and linguistic philosopher John Searle's "pragmatic considerations of the formulation of rights" are useful here.[6] Searle argues that elemental conditions of existence are crystallized as formal human rights

---

[5] Justice William O. Douglas, Dissent, Warden v Hayden, 387 U.S. 294, 1967. https://www.law.cornell.edu/supremecourt/text/387/294#writing-USSC_CR_0387_0294_ZD

[6] John R. Searle, *Making the Social World: The Structure of Human Civilization* (New York: Oxford University Press, 2010), pp. 194–95.

only at that moment in history when they come under systematic threat. For example, the ability to speak is an elemental right born of an elemental condition. The right to "freedom of expression" is a juridical right, which only emerged when society evolved to a degree of political complexity that the freedom to express oneself came under threat. Searle observes that speech is not more central to human life than breathing or being able to move one's body. No one has declared a "right to breathe" or a "right to bodily movement" because these elemental rights have not come under attack and therefore do not require legal codification. What counts as a fundamental human right, Searle argues, is both "historically contingent" and "pragmatic."

As is the case with all elemental rights, many epistemic rights have not yet been codified into law for the simple reason that it has not been necessary to do so. The epistemic "right to be forgotten," for example, has always existed as an irreducible element of human experience. In a preliterate world no one needed a legal right to be forgotten when the primary record of the past was memory. One lives, one ages, and memories age too. The past is hazy, fragmented, dispersed, prismatic, and then drifts into some combination of oblivion, stories, and myth.

In traditional society, the past was preserved in ritual, and in the modern era it is technology. The printing press and widespread literacy, photography, voice recording – each made it easier to convey one's past to the next generation, chipping away at oblivion. With these inventions, elemental epistemic rights began their migration toward formal codification. For example, Justice Brandeis was moved to formalize the right to privacy, motivated in part by the invasiveness of the newspaperman's camera, as it bestowed an independent life on anyone's face, far from the elemental rights of the subject before she was framed in the camera's lens. As if in anticipation of Searle, Brandeis wrote:

> That the individual shall have full protection in person and in property is a principle as old as the common law; but it has been found necessary from time to time to define anew the exact nature and extent of such protection. Political, social, and economic changes entail the recognition of new rights, and the common law, in its eternal youth, grows to meet the demands of society.[7]

In retrospect, Brandeis's indignation aimed at the journalist's camera recalls the last stages of an infinitely long age of epistemic innocence that ended decisively over the last three decades, as the "digital tornado" abruptly transformed the conditions of existence for many twenty-first century humans. In 1986, just 1 percent of the world's capacity to store information was in digital format; 25 percent in 2000. The year 2002 was the tipping point, when more information was stored on digital than on analogue storage devices. By 2007 digitalization had exploded to 97 percent and

---

[7] Samuel D. Warren and Louis D. Brandeis, "The Right to Privacy," *Harvard Law Review* 4, No. 5. (December 15, 1890): 204.

by 2020 the shift was largely complete.[8] Information scholar Martin Hilbert and his colleagues observe that even the foundational elements of civilization, including "language, cultural assets, traditions, institutions, rules, and laws … are currently being digitized, and for the first time, explicitly put into visible code," then returned to society through the filter of "intelligent algorithms" deployed to govern a rapidly multiplying range of commercial, governmental, and social functions.[9]

Google Inc. was a product of, driving force in, and beneficiary of this sudden sweeping change. The digitalization of everything produced vast new information territories, planetary in scope, and once celebrated by Eric Schmidt as "the world's largest ungoverned space."[10] By 2002, Google was well on its way to elaborating a new economic logic that I have called *surveillance capitalism*, whose novel imperatives compelled it to hunt and capture ever more dimensions of once private experience as raw material for newly invented processes of datafication, production, and sales. Google was not alone. The vast lawless regions of the digital became the landscape in which companies and governments ruthlessly battle for information dominance, reenacting earlier epochs of invasion, conquest, and empire building in the physical world.

In order to achieve their objectives, the leading surveillance capitalists sought to establish unrivaled dominance over the totality of the world's information now rendered in digital format.[11] Their complex supply chains require hyperscale operations capable of storing and processing vast data flows. Surveillance capital has built most of the world's largest computer networks, data centers, populations of servers, undersea transmission cables, advanced microchips, and frontier machine intelligence, igniting an arms race for the 10,000 or so specialists on the planet who know how to coax knowledge from these vast new data continents.[12]

With Google in the lead, the top surveillance capitalists seek to control labor markets in critical expertise including data science and animal research, elbowing

---

[8] Martin Hilbert, "How Much Information Is There in the 'Information Society'?" *Significance* 9, no. 4 (August 1, 2012): 8–12, http://onlinelibrary.wiley.com/doi/10.1111/j.1740–9713.2012.00584.x/abstract; Michael R. Gillings, Martin Hilbert, and Darrell J. Kemp, "Information in the Biosphere: Biological and Digital Worlds," *Trends in Ecology & Evolution* 31, no. 3 (March 1, 2016): 180–89, http://www.sciencedirect.com/science/article/pii/S0169534715003249. Martin Hilbert, "Big Data for Development: From Information – to Knowledge Societies," *United Nations ECLAC Report*, 2013, https://doi.org/10.2139/ssrn.2205145.

[9] Gillings, Hilbert, and Kemp, "Information in the Biosphere."

[10] Eric Schmidt and Jared Cohen, *The New Digital Age: Transforming Nations, Businesses, and Our Lives* (New York: Vintage Books, A Division of Random House LLC, 2014).

[11] Hilbert, "How Much Information Is There in the 'Information Society'?"

[12] João Marques Lima, "Hyperscalers Taking over the World at an Unprecedented Scale," *Data Economy* (blog), April 11, 2017, https://data-economy.com/hyperscalers-taking-world-unprecedented-scale/; Cade Metz, "Building an AI Chip Saved Google from Building a Dozen New Data Centers," *Wired*, April 5, 2017, https://www.wired.com/2017/04/building-ai-chip-saved-google-building-dozen-new-data-centers/; Cade Metz, "Tech Giants Are Paying Huge Salaries for Scarce A.I. Talent," *New York Times*, October 22, 2017, sec. Technology, https://www.nytimes.com/2017/10/22/technology/artificial-intelligence-experts-salaries.html.

out competitors such as start-ups, universities, high schools, municipalities, state and federal government agencies, established corporations in other industries and less wealthy countries. In 2016, 57 percent of American computer science Ph.D. graduates took jobs in industry, while only 11 percent became tenure-track faculty. With so few teaching faculty, colleges and universities have had to ration computer science enrollments, which has significantly disrupted the knowledge transfer between generations. It's not just an American problem. In Britain, university administrators contemplate a "missing generation" of data scientists. A Canadian scientist laments, "the power, the expertise, the data are all concentrated in the hands of a few companies."[13]

Under these unprecedented conditions, elemental epistemic rights can no longer be taken for granted. It's not that such rights are eliminated. Rather, they fall to hidden powers – commandeered, stolen, redistributed, cornered, and hoarded.

More than 600 years ago the printing press put the written word into the hands of ordinary people, bypassing the priesthood, rescuing the prayers, and delivering spiritual communion directly into the hands of the prayerful. It was perhaps the first great event in the annals of technological disintermediation, removing the "middleman" in favor of a direct line to the end consumer.

The Internet was welcomed as an equally fearsome force of empowerment: the ultimate disintermediator, amplifying Gutenberg's revolution as it liberates information from the old institutions and distributes it directly to the people. Thanks to the mighty powers of the digital, corporations would no longer decide the music people buy, the news they read, the knowledge they access, or the goods and services they enjoy.

Celebration distracted from a parallel development that moved in stealth just beyond the sightlines as the Internet became a Trojan horse for a novel economics that would eventually infiltrate every aspect of peoples' lives. The shooting star of disintermediation quickly faded, leaving in its wake the secretive new middleman, that is, surveillance capitalism, which quietly remediated the relationship to all things digital. The result has been that the Internet is not ungoverned. Rather, it is owned and operated by this dark economic logic and wholly subject to its iron laws.

The digital century was to have been democracy's Golden Age. Instead, many societies enter the third decade of the twenty-first century marked by an extremely

[13] Madhumita Murgia, "AI Academics under Pressure to Do Commercial Research," *Financial Times*, March 13, 2019, https://www.ft.com/content/94e86cd0-44b6-11e9-a965-23d669740bfb; Sarah McBride and Ashlee Vance, "Apple, Google, and Facebook Are Raiding Animal Research Labs," *Bloomberg.com*, June 18, 2019, https://www.bloomberg.com/news/features/2019-06-18/apple-google-and-facebook-are-raiding-animal-research-labs; Committee on the Growth of Computer Science Undergraduate Enrollments et al., *Assessing and Responding to the Growth of Computer Science Undergraduate Enrollments* (Washington, DC: National Academies Press, 2018), https://doi.org/10.17226/24926; Michael Gofman and Zhao Jin, "Artificial Intelligence, Human Capital, and Innovation," August 20, 2019, 55; Ian Sample, "Big Tech Firms' AI Hiring Frenzy Leads to Brain Drain at UK Universities," *Guardian*, November 2, 2017, sec. Science, http://www.theguardian.com/science/2017/nov/02/big-tech-firms-google-ai-hiring-frenzy-brain-drain-uk-universities.

new form of social inequality that threatens to remake the social order as it unmakes democracy. A new age of epistemic inequality has dawned in which individuals' inalienable rights to learning and knowing about one's own life must be codified in law if they are to exist at all.

Unequal knowledge about us produces unequal power over us, turning epistemic inequality into a critical zone of social contest in our time. Twentieth-century industrial society was based on a division of labor, and it followed that the struggle for economic equality would shape the politics of that age. Our digital century shifts society's coordinates from a division of labor to a division of learning, and it follows that the struggle for epistemic equality will shape the politics of this age.

In redistributing the "right to be forgotten" to individuals, the European Court of Justice declared that Google's was not to be the last word on the human or the digital future. It asserted that decisive authority must rest with the people, their laws, and their democratic institutions, even in the face of a great private power. It was to be the beginning, not the end, of a bitter struggle over the fundamental rights that will define the digital future.

The remainder of this chapter explores the iron laws of this private power, their consequences for people and the democratic polis, the historical significance of this struggle, and its remedies.

II. WHAT IS SURVEILLANCE CAPITALISM?

It has long been understood that capitalism evolves by claiming things that exist outside of the market dynamic and turning them into market commodities for sale and purchase. In historian Karl Polanyi's 1944 grand narrative of the "great transformation" to a self-regulating market economy, he described the origins of this translation process in three astonishing and crucial mental inventions that he called "commodity fictions." The first was that human life could be subordinated to market dynamics and reborn as "labor" to be bought and sold. The second was that nature could be translated into the market and reborn as "land" or "real estate." The third was that exchange could be reborn as "money."[14]

Surveillance capitalism originates in an even more startling mental invention, declaring private human experience as free raw material for translation into production and sales. Once private human experience is claimed for the market, it is translated into behavioral data for computational production.

Early on, it was discovered that, unknown to users, even data freely given harbor rich predictive signals, a surplus that is more than what is required for service improvement. It isn't only what you post online, but whether you use exclamation points or the color saturation of your photos; not just where you walk but the stoop of

---

[14] Karl Polanyi, *The Great Transformation: The Political and Economic Origins of Our Time* (Boston, MA: Beacon Press, 2001), pp. 75–76.

your shoulders; not just the identity of your face but the emotional states conveyed by your "micro-expressions"; not just what you like but the pattern of likes across engagements. Soon this behavioral surplus was covertly hunted and captured across virtual and real worlds, accessible to the always-on ubiquitous digital architecture that I call "Big Other" and claimed as proprietary data.

Behavioral surplus is ultimately conveyed through complex supply chains of devices, tracking and monitoring software, and ecosystems of apps and companies that specialize in niche data flows captured in secret.[15] Data flows empty into surveillance capitalists' computational factories, called "artificial intelligence," where they are manufactured into behavioral predictions. A leaked 2018 Facebook document provides some insight into factory operations.[16] Facebook's "prediction engine" is built on a machine intelligence platform called "FB Learner Flow," which the company describes as its "AI backbone" and the key to "personalized experiences" that deliver "the most relevant content." The machine learning system "ingests trillions of data points every day, trains thousands of models – either offline or in real time – and then deploys them to the server fleet for live predictions." The company explains that, "since its inception, more than a million models have been trained, and our prediction service has grown to make more than 6 million predictions per second."[17]

Finally, these prediction products are rapidly swept up into the life of the market, traded in newly constituted marketplaces for behavioral predictions: human futures markets. These markets link surveillance capitalists to business customers with a keen interest in the future behavior of current and potential "users" or consumers. Certainty in human affairs is the lifeblood of these markets, where surveillance capitalists compete on the quality of their predictions, which are about individuals but are not for individuals. Surveillance capitalists have grown immensely wealthy from these trading operations, as many companies are eager to lay bets on future human behavior.

Surveillance capitalism was invented as the solution to financial emergency in the teeth of the dot.com bust when the fledgling company called Google faced the loss of investor confidence. As pressure mounted, Google's leaders decided to boost ad revenue by using their exclusive access to user data logs, in combination with their

[15] Sam Schechner and Mark Secada, "You Give Apps Sensitive Personal Information. Then They Tell Facebook.," *Wall Street Journal*, February 22, 2019, sec. Tech, https://www.wsj.com/articles/you-give-apps-sensitive-personal-information-then-they-tell-facebook-11550851636; "Out of Control: How Consumers Are Exploited by the Online Advertising Industry" (Forbruker Rådet, January 14, 2020), https://fil.forbrukerradet.no/wp-content/uploads/2020/01/2020–01-14-out-of-control-final-version.pdf.

[16] Sam Biddle, "Facebook Uses Artificial Intelligence to Predict Your Future Actions for Advertisers, Says Confidential Document," *Intercept* (blog), April 13, 2018, https://theintercept.com/2018/04/13/facebook-advertising-data-artificial-intelligence-ai/.

[17] "Introducing FBLearner Flow: Facebook's AI Backbone," Facebook Code, May 9, 2016, https://code.facebook.com/posts/1072626246134461/introducing-fblearner-flow-facebook-s-ai-backbone/.

already substantial analytical capabilities and computational power, to fabricate predictions of user click-through rates, regarded as a signal of an ad's relevance.

Operationally, this meant that Google would both repurpose its growing cache of behavioral data, now put to work as a behavioral surplus, and develop methods to aggressively seek new sources of behavioral surplus. According to its own scientists' accounts, the company developed new methods of surplus hunt and capture that were prized for their ability to find data that users intentionally opted to keep private and to infer extensive personal information that users did not or would not provide. This surplus would be analyzed for predictive patterns that could match a specific ad with a specific user. These new operations institutionalized a new logic of accumulation derived from the social relations of the one-way mirror: surveillance. Its mechanisms and methods are carefully engineered to produce user ignorance through obfuscation, undetectability, indecipherability, and misdirection. Success relies on bypassing individual awareness and thus overriding the individual's rights to decide the privacy of one's experience and one's future course of action. Surveillance is essential to the DNA of this market form.

The elements of this economic logic were discovered, invented, elaborated, and deployed at Google from 2000 to 2004, while held in the strictest secrecy. Only when Google went public in 2004 did the world learn that during that period its revenues increased by 3,590%.[18] This increase represents the "surveillance dividend," which raised the bar for attracting investors to the new Internet domain. The shift in the use of behavioral surplus was an historic turning point: the game-changing zero-cost asset that could be diverted from service improvement toward a genuine market exchange. This was not an exchange with "users" but rather with other companies that learned how to profit from low risk bets on users' future behavior.

Surveillance capitalism migrated to Facebook with Google-turned-Facebook executive Sheryl Sandberg and quickly become the default model of information capitalism, attached to nearly every Internet company, start-up, and app. Like an invasive species with no natural predators, its financial prowess quickly overwhelmed the networked sphere, grossly disfiguring the earlier dream of digital technology as an empowering and emancipatory force.

While online advertisers were the dominant players in the early history of the new futures markets, surveillance capitalism is no more restricted to online ad targeting than mass production was restricted to the fabrication of the Model T. Today any actor with an interest in monetizing probabilistic information about behavior can pay to play in a range of human futures markets where behavioral predictions are told and sold.

In a world of highly commoditized products and services, companies now turn to the surveillance dividend as the source of higher margins. The result is whole new

---

[18] Securities and Exchange Commission, "Amendment No. 9 to Form S-1 Registration Statement under The Securities Act of 1933 for Google Inc.," Securities and Exchange Commission, August 18, 2004, https://www.sec.gov/Archives/edgar/data/1288776/000119312512025336/d260164d10k.htm.

ecosystems of behavioral surplus suppliers, as companies from every sector seek ways to participate in the unilateral dispossession of private experience. Surveillance capitalism now spreads across the "normal" economy in traditionally information intensive sectors such as insurance and finance, but also in healthcare, retail, education, real estate development, and automobiles, to name but a few.

One poignant illustration of these new facts is found in the birthplace of mass production, the Ford Motor Company. One hundred years ago, pioneer capitalists like Ford bent to the revolutionary task of making things at a price that people could afford and shaping a new century of mass consumption. Henry Ford was proud to author the definition of "mass production" for the Encyclopedia Britannica, the Google of his day, describing it as "a productive organization that delivers in quantities a useful commodity of standard material, workmanship, and design, at minimum cost."[19] Ford understood that the mass production revolution was the result, not the cause, of new era of demand in US society – farmers and shopkeepers who wanted automobiles too, but at a price they could afford. "The necessary, precedent condition of mass production is a capacity, latent or developed, of mass consumption," he wrote. "The two go together and in the latter may be traced the reasons for the former."[20] In Ford's cosmos, demand and supply were twinborn, with customers and workers forever linked in a cycle of production and sales that combined low cost goods with consumption-worthy wages immortalized by the five-dollar day.

Had Henry Ford been listening to the Freakonomics Radio podcast in November 2018, he would have learned that his authoritative rendition of supply and demand had been relegated to the dustbin of history by his own distant successor, Jim Hackett. In response to the sustained slump in global auto sales, the company is already cutting thousands of jobs and eliminating models in pursuit of a price-earnings ratio befitting a high tech data company: Hackett wants Ford to become more like Facebook and Google. In this vision, the work of making and selling cars gives way to proprietary monetizable data flows – a "transportation operating system."[21] Hackett wants Henry's company to collect data from the "100 million people … that are sitting in Ford blue-oval vehicles …. We have as much data in the future coming from vehicles, or from users in those vehicles, or from cities talking to those vehicles, as the other competitors that you and I would be talking about [like Facebook and Google] that have monetizable attraction."

---

[19] Henry Ford, "Mass Production," in *Encyclopedia Brittannica* (New York, NY: Encyclopedia Britannica, Inc., 1926), http://memory.loc.gov/cgi-bin/query/h?ammem/coolbib:@field(NUMBER +@band(amrlg+lg48)).

[20] Ford.

[21] William Boston, "Ford to Slash Jobs, Shut Plants in Major European Revamp," *Wall Street Journal*, January 10, 2019, sec. Business, https://www.wsj.com/articles/ford-announces-major-european-restructuring-11547117814; Greg Rosalsky, "Can an Industrial Giant Become a Tech Darling? (Ep. 357)," *Freakonomics* (blog), http://freakonomics.com/podcast/ford/.

Once customers are reinvented as data sources, it's easy for Hackett to imagine the next step in which the data that stream from vehicles in real time are combined with Ford's financing data, where, he says, "we already know ... what people make ... we know where they work; we know if they're married. We know how long they've lived in their house." Hackett concludes, "And that's the leverage we've got here with the data ... I think our higher purpose is that the smart vehicle and the smart world have an interaction in the future that's much bigger than it was in the past."[22] As one industry analyst put it, Ford "could make a fortune monetizing data. They won't need engineers, factories, or dealers to do it. It's almost pure profit."[23]

This is where we live now: a world in which nearly every product or service that begins with the word "smart," "personalized," or "connected," from cars to "digital assistants," to devices, appliances, and more, is a supply-chain interface for the unobstructed flow of behavioral surplus. The growth of these connections continuously increases what military strategists call the digital "attack surface," where behavioral surplus is relentlessly tracked, hunted, coaxed, and captured. What began as a solution to financial emergency is now a burgeoning surveillance-based economic order: a surveillance economy. The dominant market form shifts under our gaze: once profits from products, then services, then profits from speculation, and now profits from surveillance.

Surveillance capitalism can no longer be defined as a specific group of corporations, neither can it be conflated with the digital technologies on which it depends. While it is impossible to imagine surveillance capitalism without the digital, it is easy to imagine the digital without surveillance capitalism. The point cannot be emphasized enough: Surveillance capitalism is not technology. Digital technologies can take many forms and have many effects, depending on the social and economic logics that bring them to life. Surveillance capitalism relies on data-gathering devices like computers, phones, sensors, microphones, and cameras. It deploys machine intelligence and platforms. It expresses itself in algorithms. But it is not the same as any of those. Just as an X-ray reveals bone and muscle, but not the soft tissue that binds them, technology is the bone and muscle here, while surveillance capitalism is the soft tissue that binds the elements and directs them into action. It is the shadow that falls over the digital, the hidden pattern that explains how this once emancipatory project transformed people and society into raw material for others' economic gain, as the Internet itself falls to the ownership and operations of surveillance capital.

The phrase "surveillance capitalism" is not arbitrary. Surveillance capitalism's operations are designed for the social relations of the one-way mirror. They know everything about users, but users know nothing about them. Surveillance is baked

---

[22] Rosalsky, "Can an Industrial Giant Become a Tech Darling?"

[23] Phoebe Wall Howard, "Data Could Be What Ford Sells Next as It Looks for New Revenue," *Detroit Free Press*, November 13, 2018, https://www.freep.com/story/money/cars/2018/11/13/ford-motor-credit-data-new-revenue/1967077002/.

into the DNA of this logic of accumulation, because without it the surveillance dividend as expressed in the revenues, profits, and market capitalization that mark the first two decades of the twenty-first century would have been impossible to achieve.

III. SURVEILLANCE CAPITALISM'S ECONOMIC IMPERATIVES

Surveillance capitalists sell certainty. They compete in human futures markets on the quality of their prediction products, which aim to guarantee outcomes or at least the ever-improving approximation to such guarantees. These guarantees have value, but in the novel logic of surveillance capitalism, their value is a function of markets that bear no organic reciprocities with their populations, now repurposed as the source of unlimited raw material supplies. The competitive dynamics thus set into motion reveal key economic imperatives, and it is these imperatives that compel epistemic inequality, setting surveillance capitalism on a collision course with democracy itself.

First, because predictions must improve in the direction of something like certainty, surplus extraction must move in the direction of something like totality. Machine learning for behavioral prediction wants data in volume and thus economies of scale in data production lay the foundation for all operations.

Once competition for prediction products intensifies, volume is not enough. Surveillance capitalists are compelled to search out ever more predictive sources of behavioral surplus. Machine learning needs volume but also variety, economies of scale but also economies of scope. This realization helped drive the "mobile revolution" sending users into the real world armed with cameras, gyroscopes, and microphones packed inside their smart new pocket-size computers, the ubiquitous interface that conveys surplus supplies to the AI hub. In the competition for scope, surveillance capitalists want your home and what you say and do within its walls.[24] They want your car, your medical conditions, and the shows you stream; your location as well as all the streets and buildings in your path and all the behavior of all the people in your city.[25] They want your voice and what you eat and what you

---

[24] Jingjing Ren et al., "Information Exposure From Consumer IoT Devices: A Multidimensional, Network-Informed Measurement Approach," in *Proceedings of the Internet Measurement Conference* (IMC '19: ACM Internet Measurement Conference, Amsterdam Netherlands: ACM, 2019), pp. 267–79, https://doi.org/10.1145/3355369.3355577.

[25] Geoffrey A. Fowler, "What Does Your Car Know about You? We Hacked a Chevy to Find Out," *Washington Post*, December 17, 2019, https://www.washingtonpost.com/technology/2019/12/17/what-does-your-car-know-about-you-we-hacked-chevy-find-out/; Natasha Singer and Daisuke Wakabayashi, "Google to Store and Analyze Millions of Health Records," *New York Times*, November 11, 2019, sec. Business, https://www.nytimes.com/2019/11/11/business/google-ascension-health-data.html; Hooman Mohajeri Moghaddam et al., "Watching You Watch: The Tracking Ecosystem of Over-the-Top TV Streaming Devices," in *Proceedings of the 2019 ACM SIGSAC Conference on Computer and Communications Security* (CCS '19: 2019 ACM SIGSAC

buy; your children's play time and their schooling; your brainwaves and your bloodstream.[26] Nothing is exempt.[27]

With continued competitive intensification, surveillance capitalists discovered that the most predictive data come from intervening in behavior to tune, herd, and modify action in the direction of commercial objectives. Data scientists describe this as the shift from monitoring to actuation, in which a critical mass of knowledge about a machine system enables the remote control of that system. Now people become targets for remote control, as a third imperative, *economies of action* emerges as an arena of intense experimentation. Here are the practical grounds on which unequal knowledge morphs into unequal power. Epistemic inequality widens to include the distance between what people can do and what can be done to them. "We are learning how to write the music," one data scientist explained, "and then we let the music make them dance."[28]

How shall we understand this new power "to make them dance?" Unlike twentieth-century totalitarianism, it does not employ soldiers and henchmen to threaten terror and murder. It arrives with a cappuccino, not a gun. It is a new *instrumentarian power* that works its will through Big Other's medium of ubiquitous digital instrumentation to manipulate subliminal cues, psychologically target communications, impose choice architectures, trigger social comparison dynamics, and levy rewards and punishments – all of it aimed at remotely tuning, herding, and modifying human

Conference on Computer and Communications Security, London United Kingdom: ACM, 2019), pp. 131–47, https://doi.org/10.1145/3319535.3354198; Stuart A. Thompson and Charlie Warzel, "Twelve Million Phones, One Dataset, Zero Privacy," *New York Times*, December 19, 2019, sec. Opinion, https://www.nytimes.com/interactive/2019/12/19/opinion/location-tracking-cell-phone.html; Ellen P. Goodman and Julia Powles, "Urbanism Under Google: Lessons from Sidewalk Toronto," *Fordham Law Review* 457, no. 88 (December 19, 2019): 42.

[26] Ron Amadeo, "Users Alarmed by Undisclosed Microphone in Nest Security System," *Ars Technica*, February 20, 2019, https://arstechnica.com/gadgets/2019/02/googles-nest-security-system-shipped-with-a-secret-microphone/; Gary Hawkins, "Real-Time Insights on Amazon Prime and Whole Foods Integration," *Winsight Grocery Business*, August 15, 2018, https://www.winsightgrocerybusiness.com/retailers/real-time-insights-amazon-prime-whole-foods-integration; Joel Winston, "Google Keeps an Eye on What You Buy, and It's Not Alone," *Fast Company*, August 6, 2019, https://www.fastcompany.com/90349518/google-keeps-an-eye-on-what-you-buy-and-its-not-alone; Katie Collins, "My Friend Cayla Doll Banned in Germany as 'Espionage Device,'" *CNET*, February 17, 2017, https://www.cnet.com/news/parents-told-to-destroy-connected-dolls-over-hacking-fears/; Betsy Morris, "Schools Wrestle with Privacy of Digital Data Collected on Students," *Wall Street Journal*, July 10, 2019, sec. Tech, https://www.wsj.com/articles/one-parent-is-on-a-mission-to-protect-children-from-digital-mistakes-11562762000; Sigal Samuel, "Brain-Reading Tech Is Coming. The Law Is Not Ready to Protect Us," *Vox*, August 30, 2019, https://www.vox.com/2019/8/30/20835137/facebook-zuckerberg-elon-musk-brain-mind-reading-neuroethics; Kirsten Ostherr, "You Don't Want Facebook Involved with Your Health Care," *Slate*, September 19, 2019, https://slate.com/technology/2019/09/social-determinants-health-facebook-google.html.

[27] Benjamin Romano, "Amazon Rolls Out New Devices amid Swirl of Privacy Questions," *Seattle Times*, September 25, 2019, https://www.seattletimes.com/business/amazon/amazon-rolls-out-new-devices-amid-swirl-of-privacy-questions/.

[28] Shoshana Zuboff, *The Age of Surveillance Capitalism: The Fight for a Human Future at the New Frontier of Power* (New York: Public Affairs, 2019), p. 295.

behavior in the direction of profitable outcomes and always engineered to preserve users' ignorance.

Although he did not name it, the visionary of ubiquitous computing, Mark Weiser, foresaw the immensity of instrumentarian power as a totalizing social project. He did so in a way that suggests both its utter lack of precedent and the danger of confounding it with what has gone before: "[H]undreds of computers in every room, all capable of sensing people near them and linked by high-speed networks, have the potential to make totalitarianism up to now seem like sheerest anarchy."[29] In fact, all those computers are not the means to a digital totalitarianism. They are, as I think Weiser sensed, the foundation of an unprecedented power that can reshape society in unprecedented ways. If instrumentarian power can make totalitarianism look like anarchy, then what might it have in store for this century?

While all power yearns toward totality, instrumentarian power's specific purposes and methods are not only distinct from totalitarianism but they are in many ways its precise opposite. Instrumentarian power has no principle to instruct, no interest the reformation of the soul. There is no aim toward spiritual salvation, no ideology against which to judge human action. Totalitarianism was a political project that converged with economics to overwhelm society. Instrumentarianism is a market project that converges with the digital to achieve its own unique brand of social domination. Totalitarianism operated through the means of violence, but instrumentarian power operates through the means of behavioral modification.

Instrumentarianism's specific "viewpoint of observation" was forged in the controversial intellectual domain of "radical behaviorism." Thanks to Big Other's capabilities, instrumentarian power reduces human experience to measurable, observable behavior, while remaining profoundly, infinitely, and radically indifferent to the meanings and motives of its targets. Radical indifference produces observation without witness. Instead of an intimate violent political religion, Big Other's way of knowing yields the remote but inescapable presence of impenetrably complex machine systems and the interests that author them, carrying individuals on a fast-moving current to the fulfilment of others' ends. Trained on measurable action, Big Other cares only about observing behavior and ensuring that it is continuously accessible to its ever-evolving operations of monitoring, datafication, calculation, actuation, and monetization.

Instrumentarianism's radical indifference is operationalized in Big Other's dehumanized methods of evaluation that produce equivalence without equality by reducing individuals to the lowest common denominator of sameness – organisms among organisms. There is no need for mass submission to social norms, no loss of self to the collective induced by terror and compulsion, no inducements of acceptance and belonging as a reward for bending to the group. All of that is superseded by a market-based digital order that thrives within things and bodies, transforming

---

[29]   Mark Weiser, "The Computer for the 21st Century," *Scientific American*, July 1999: 104.

volition into reinforcement and action into conditioned response. Thanks to Big Other's capabilities to know and to do, instrumentarian power aims for a condition of certainty without terror in the form of guaranteed outcomes. In the execution of economies of action, Big Other transforms "natural selection" into the "unnatural selection" of variation and reinforcement authored by market players and the competition for surveillance revenues.

The paradox is that because instrumentarianism does not claim bodies for some grotesque regime of pain and murder, many are prone to undervalue its effects and lower their guard. Under the regime of instrumentarian power, the mental agency and self-possession of autonomous human action are gradually submerged beneath a new kind of automaticity: a lived routine of stimulus-response-reinforcement that operates outside of awareness and is aggregated as statistical phenomena: the comings and goings of mere organisms.

The challenges associated with successful economies of action have become a critical experimental zone for the elaboration of instrumentarian power. It is likely that much of this experimentation is invisible to the public, but at least some hides in plain sight, where one can observe how knowledge tips into power, epistemic inequality into epistemic injustice.

For example, Facebook conducted "massive-scale contagion experiments," the results of which were published in 2012 and 2014. The first aimed to subliminally induce voting in the lead-up to the 2010 US mid-term elections. The second aimed to influence users to feel "happy" or "sad." As a result of these experiments researchers concluded that, (1) it is possible to deploy subliminal cues on Facebook pages to alter real-world behaviour and emotions and (2), it is possible to accomplish such remote behavioral and affective modification with undetectable methods designed to bypass human awareness. Indeed, the very first paragraph of the 2014 research article on emotional contagion celebrates these findings: "Emotional states can be transferred to others via emotional contagion, leading people to experience the same emotions without their awareness."[30]

Facebook provides yet another observation point for the development of economies of action. In May 2017, three years after the publication of the contagion studies, The Australian broke the story on a confidential twenty-three-page Facebook document written by two Facebook executives and aimed at the company's Australian and New Zealand advertisers. The report depicted the corporation's systems for gathering "psychological insights" on 6.4 million high school and tertiary students as well as young Australians and New Zealanders already in the workforce. The Facebook document detailed the many ways in which the corporation uses its stores of behavioral surplus to

[30] Robert M. Bond et al., "A 61-Million-Person Experiment in Social Influence and Political Mobilization," *Nature* 489, no. 7415 (September 12, 2012): 295–98, https://doi.org/10.1038/nature11421; Adam D. I. Kramer, Jamie E. Guillory, and Jeffrey T. Hancock, "Experimental Evidence of Massive-Scale Emotional Contagion through Social Networks," *Proceedings of the National Academy of Sciences* 111, no. 24 (June 17, 2014): 8788–90, https://doi.org/10.1073/pnas.1320040111.

simulate and predict individual and group affective patterns in order to pinpoint the exact moment at which a young person needs a "confidence boost" and is therefore most vulnerable to a specific configuration of advertising cues and nudges: "By monitoring posts, pictures, interactions, and Internet activity, Facebook can work out when young people feel 'stressed,' 'defeated,' 'overwhelmed,' 'anxious,' 'nervous,' 'stupid,' 'silly,' 'useless,' and a 'failure.'"[31]

The report reveals Facebook's interest in leveraging this affective surplus for the pivot from monitoring to actuation. It boasts detailed information on "mood shifts" among young people based on "internal Facebook data," and it claims that not only can Facebook's prediction products "detect sentiment," they can also predict how emotions are communicated at different points during the week. These data are then used to match each emotional phase with appropriate ad messaging for the maximum probability of guaranteed sales. "Anticipatory emotions are more likely to be expressed early in the week," the analysis counsels, "while reflective emotions increase on the weekend. Monday–Thursday is about building confidence; the weekend is for broadcasting achievements." The young adults of Australia's and New Zealand's cities and towns had no reason to suspect that their fears and fantasies were being routinely exploited for commercial result at the precise moment of their greatest vulnerability. ("NEED A CONFIDENCE BOOST? CLICK HERE! BUY THIS BLACK LEATHER JACKET NOW! FREE OVERNIGHT DELIVERY!")

Facebook publicly denied these practices, but former Facebook product manager Antonio Garcia-Martinez, the author of *Chaos Monkeys*, a useful account of Silicon Valley, described in the *Guardian* the routine application of such practices and accused the corporation of "lying through their teeth." He concluded: "The hard reality is that Facebook will never try to limit such use of their data unless the public uproar reaches such a crescendo as to be un-mutable."[32] It is Facebook that knows. It decides who knows. It decides who decides.

The public's intolerable knowledge disadvantage is deepened by surveillance capitalists' perfection of mass communications as gaslighting. Indeed, these firms have long mastered the tactical arts of disinformation and fake news, paving the way for social complacency toward the crisis of truthfulness and social trust that has engulfed public communications. A few examples are illustrative. On April 30, 2019 Mark Zuckerberg made a dramatic announcement at the company's annual developer conference, declaring: "The future is private."[33] A few weeks later, a Facebook

---

[31] Darren Davidson, "Facebook Targets 'Insecure' to Sell Ads," *Australian*, May 1, 2017, https://www.theaustralian.com.au/business/media/facebook-targets-insecure-young-people-to-sell-ads/news-story/a89949ado16eee7d7a61c3c30c909fa6.

[32] Antonio Garcia-Martinez, "I'm an Ex-Facebook Exec: Don't Believe What They Tell You about Ads," *Guardian*, May 2, 2017, sec. Technology, https://www.theguardian.com/technology/2017/may/02/facebook-executive-advertising-data-comment.

[33] Nick Statt, "Facebook CEO Mark Zuckerberg Says the 'Future Is Private,'" *The Verge*, April 30, 2019, https://www.theverge.com/2019/4/30/18524188/facebook-f8-keynote-mark-zuckerberg-privacy-future-2019.

litigator appeared before a federal district judge in California to thwart a user lawsuit over privacy invasion, arguing that the very act of using Facebook negates any reasonable expectation of privacy "as a matter of law."[34] While leaked internal documents describe the firm's sophisticated methods for accruing granular psychological insights for targeting and triggering individuals, in early 2020 its Vice President of Public Policy told a public forum: "We don't do surveillance capitalism, that by definition is surreptitious; we work hard to be transparent."[35] In May 2019, Google CEO Sundar Pichai wrote in the *New York Times* of his corporation's commitment to the principle that "privacy cannot be a luxury good."[36] Five months later Google contractors were observed offering $5 gift cards to homeless people of color in an Atlanta park in return for a facial scan.[37] While Amazon cracked down on employees for violating the company's privacy by publicly discussing its policies and practices, the corporation aggressively strengthens the one-way mirror, marketing its collection of surveillance-as-a-service connected devices and appliances based on the Alexa voice recognition system. Its latest suite of Internet-enabled devices was characterized by the *Seattle Times* as "a sweeping vision of automation, entertainment, ubiquitous surveillance and commerce permeating nearly every aspect of life."[38]

Facebook's denial of psychological targeting practices invites even more scrutiny in light of the leaked 2018 company document, which described its "AI Hub."[39] That report also indicated that the company's extraordinary data flows and computational production are dedicated to meeting its corporate customers' "core business challenges" with procedures that link prediction, microtargeting, intervention, and behavior modification. For example, a Facebook service called "loyalty prediction" was touted for its ability to plumb proprietary behavioral surplus in order to predict which individuals are "at risk" of shifting their brand allegiance. This knowledge

[34] Sam Biddle, "In Court, Facebook Blames Users for Destroying Their Own Right to Privacy," *The Intercept* (blog), June 14, 2019, https://theintercept.com/2019/06/14/facebook-privacy-policy-court/.

[35] Tekla S. Perry, "CES 2020 News: Tech Executives Answer Tough Questions about Privacy," *IEEE Spectrum*, January 8, 2020, https://spectrum.ieee.org/view-from-the-valley/telecom/internet/ces-2020-news-tech-executives-answer-tough-questions-about-privacy; Biddle, "Facebook Uses Artificial Intelligence to Predict Your Future Actions for Advertisers, Says Confidential Document"; Darren Davidson, "Facebook Targets 'Insecure' to Sell Ads."

[36] Sundar Pichai, "Google's Sundar Pichai: Privacy Should Not Be a Luxury Good | Opinion," *New York Times*, May 22, 2019, sec. Opinion, https://www.nytimes.com/2019/05/07/opinion/google-sundar-pichai-privacy.html.

[37] Ginger Adams Otis and Nancy Dillon, "City Worker Saw Homeless People Lined Up to Get $5 Gift Card for Face Scan Uploaded to Google," *Nydailynews.com*, October 3, 2019, https://www.nydailynews.com/news/national/ny-witness-saw-homeless-people-selling-face-scans-google-five-dollars-20191004-j6z2vonllnerpiuakt6wrp6l44-story.html.

[38] Shirin Ghaffary, "Amazon Threatened to Fire Employees Who Spoke Out against Its Environmental Policies," *Vox*, January 2, 2020, https://www.vox.com/recode/2020/1/2/21046886/amazon-climate-change-fired-activists-sustainability-walkout-pledge-carbon-emissions-activism; Benjamin Romano, "Amazon Rolls out New Devices amid Swirl of Privacy Questions."

[39] Biddle, "Facebook Uses Artificial Intelligence to Predict Your Future Actions for Advertisers, Says Confidential Document."

alerts advertisers to intervene promptly with targeted messages designed to stabilize loyalty just in time to alter the course of the future.

Google's experimentation with economies of action moved boldly into the real world with the augmented reality game Pokémon Go. The project had been incubated at Google for many years, led by John Hanke, an early inventor of satellite mapping and leader of Google's mapping operations including Google Earth and Street View, both critical sources of surplus data supplies. Later Hanke headed up his own augmented reality shop inside Google, Niantic Labs, where Pokémon Go was developed and spun off from the company just in time to go to market with Hanke as its head and Goggle its principal investor.[40]

Pokémon Go brought the emerging science of remote population tuning and herding to the real world: real streets, real towns, real cities. It added the rewards and punishments of gamification to the methods of subliminal cueing and the manipulation of social comparison dynamics in order to bypass users' awareness of the situational facts: families and friends were engaged in a search game without knowing that it was they who were being searched and gamed. Players were, in fact, unwitting pawns in a hidden higher-order game that aimed to provide "footfall" to fee-paying establishments as they vied for real-world consumer visits in exactly the same way that online advertisers pay for the virtual visits of clicks and engagement. Niantic used immense caches of data collected from game players' devices in order to apply the incentives and reinforcements of gamification for the sake of herding players to the real-world business customers in its futures markets, from McDonald's and Starbucks to Joe's Pizza.[41]

These escalating zones of experimentation and their practical success suggest a disturbing conclusion: the competitive necessity of economies of action means that surveillance capitalists must use all means available to supplant autonomous action with heteronomous behavior. Human awareness is a threat to surveillance revenues because the mobilization of awareness endangers the larger project of behavior modification. Philosophers recognize "self-regulation," "self-determination," and "autonomy" as expressions of "freedom of will," and a flourishing research literature illuminates the antecedents, conditions, consequences, and challenges of human self-regulation as a universal need. The capacity for self-determination is understood as an essential foundation for behaviors associated with critical human capabilities such as empathy, volition, reflection, personal development, authenticity, integrity, learning, goal accomplishment, impulse control, creativity, and the sustenance of intimate relationships. "Implicit in this process is a self that sets goals and standards, is aware of its own thoughts and behaviors, and has the capacity to change them. Indeed, some theorists have

---

[40] Dyani Sabin, "The Secret History of 'Pokemon GO' as Told by the Game's Creator," *Inverse*, February 28, 2017, https://www.inverse.com/article/28485-pokemon-go-secret-history-google-maps-ingress-john-hanke-updates.

[41] For a full discussion of John Hanke, Pokémon Go and Niantic Labs, see Zuboff, *The Age of Surveillance Capitalism*, pp. 309–19.

suggested that the primary purpose of self-awareness is to enable self-regulation." Every threat to human autonomy begins with an assault on awareness, "tearing down our capacity to regulate our thoughts, emotions, and desires."[42]

The salience of self-awareness as a bulwark against self-regulatory failure is also highlighted in recent research on "susceptibility to persuasion," which concludes that "the ability to premeditate" is the single-most-important determinant of one's ability to resist persuasion.[43] People who harness self-awareness to think through the consequences of their actions are more disposed to chart their own course and are thus significantly less vulnerable to persuasion techniques. Self-awareness also figures in the second highest-ranking protection from susceptibility to persuasion: commitment. Those who consciously commit to a course of action or set of principles are less likely to be persuaded to do something that violates their commitment.

In one sense, there is nothing remarkable in observing that capitalists would prefer individuals who submit to arrangements that advantage capital. It would be incorrect, however, to conclude that today's surveillance capitalists simply represent more of the same. The structural requirements of economies of action turn the means of behavioral modification into an engine of growth. At no other time in history have the wealthiest private corporations had at their disposal a pervasive global architecture of ubiquitous computation able unilaterally to amass unparalleled concentrations of information about individuals, groups, and populations sufficient to mobilize the pivot from knowledge about behavior to the actuation of commercially desirable behavior. In other words, when we climb the mountain of the division of learning and peek into the fortress, we see a frontier operation run by geniuses and funded by vast capital outlays that is furiously dedicated to knowing everything about us and pivoting that knowledge to the remote control of people. These are unprecedented conditions that bestow an unprecedented instrumentarian power on private capital.

IV. INFORMATION WARFARE

While democracy slept, epistemic inequality was produced, institutionalized, and protected by an unequal power that annuls the possibility of conflict by denying the

---

[42] Dylan D. Wagner and Todd F. Heatherton, "Self-Regulation and Its Failure: The Seven Deadly Threats to Self-Regulation," in *APA Handbook of Personality and Social Psychology* (Washington, DC: American Psychological Association,2015), pp. 805–42, https://pdfs.semanticscholar.org/2e62/15047e3a296184c3698f3553255ffabd46c7.pdf; William M. Kelley, Dylan D. Wagner, and Todd F. Heatherton, "In Search of a Human Self-Regulation System," *Annual Review of Neuroscience* 38, no. 1 (2015): 389–411, https://doi.org/10.1146/annurev-neuro-071013–014243.

[43] David Modic and Ross J. Anderson, "We Will Make You Like Our Research: The Development of a Susceptibility-to-Persuasion Scale," *SSRN* (Rochester, NY: Social Science Research Network, April 28, 2014), https://papers.ssrn.com/abstract=2446971; Mahesh Gopinath and Prashanth U. Nyer, "The Influence of Public Commitment on the Attitude Change Process: The Effects of Attitude Certainty, PFC and SNI," *SSRN*, 2007, https://doi.org/10.2139/ssrn.1010562.

right of combat. In this case, denial is achieved through Big Other's hidden techno-economic systems that steal, know, and shape human behavior for the sake of others' gain. These capabilities depend on the evasion of human awareness. This entails the denial of the epistemic rights that confer individual sovereignty over self/knowledge. Instrumentarian power is the guarantor of epistemic inequality, the hammer of epistemic injustice, and the usurper of epistemic rights.

Because one's self and all the selves are meant to sleepwalk peacefully through this known unknown, sudden news from behind the veil can have an electrifying effect, if only for a while. This helps to explain the force with which the story of Cambridge Analytica broke on the world in March 2018, when Chris Wylie, the young mastermind-turned-whistleblower, unleashed a torrent of information on that company's secret efforts to predict and influence individual voting behavior, quickly riveting the world on the small political analytics firm and the giant source of its data: Facebook. There are many unanswered questions about the legality of Cambridge Analytica's complex subterfuge, its actual political impact, and its relationship with Facebook. My interest here is restricted to how it replicated surveillance capitalism's ordinary practices, and the implications of that fact.[44]

Academic researchers had already demonstrated the predictive power of behavioral surplus culled from Facebook pages, the insights into human personality that it can yield, the resulting opportunities for behavioral manipulation and modification, and the commercial value of such methods. Wylie recounted his fascination with these studies, especially as they might be pivoted from commercial to political outcomes.[45] Through a complicated chain of events, it was Wylie who persuaded Cambridge Analytica's owner, the secretive software billionaire and active enemy of democracy Robert Mercer, and his operatives, including anti-democracy's dark theorist Steve Bannon, to use Facebook data to advance Mercer's political aims.

Cambridge Analytica's operations followed the surveillance capitalist playbook. They were designed to produce ignorance through secrecy and the careful evasion of individual awareness: "We exploited Facebook to harvest millions of people's profiles," Wylie admitted, "and built models to exploit what we knew about them and target their inner demons."[46] The objective was "behavioral micro-targeting . . . influencing voters based not on their demographics but on their personalities."[47] "I think it's worse than bullying, because people don't necessarily know it's being done to them," Wylie reflects. "At least bullying respects the agency of people because they know . . . if you do not respect the agency of people, anything that you're doing

---

[44] For a full account of the Cambridge Analytica story, see Zuboff, *The Age of Surveillance Capitalism.*, pp. 278–82, 482–3.

[45] Zuboff, *The Age of Surveillance Capitalism*, pp. 272–78.

[46] Andy Kroll, "Cloak and Data: The Real Story behind Cambridge Analytica's Rise and Fall," *Mother Jones* (blog), March 2018, https://www.motherjones.com/politics/2018/03/cloak-and-data-cambridge-analytica-robert-mercer/.

[47] Kroll.

after that point is not conducive to a democracy. And fundamentally, information warfare is not conducive to democracy."[48]

Wylie describes Cambridge Analytica's operations as "information warfare," correctly acknowledging that this form of shadow warfare originates in significant asymmetries of knowledge and the power produced by such knowledge. In other words, information warfare exploits epistemic inequality, while its effects intensify epistemic injustice.

However, the Cambridge Analytica narrative suggests an even more disturbing conclusion. The political firm was only able to operate as an information warrior because the conditions for successful warfare and its weapons had already been developed by surveillance capital. Surveillance capitalist operations like Facebook, Google, Amazon, Microsoft, and countless others are best understood as examples of information-warfare-for-profit. These firms are information mercenaries that leverage unprecedented asymmetries of knowledge/power for the sake of revenues, which, in turn, fund their continued dominance and the intensification of epistemic inequality.

Consider how a small firm such as Cambridge Analytica was able to enter the fray of information war. The so-called political consultancy functioned as a parasite buried into the host of Facebook's vast behavioral data supply chains, while adapting its host's foundational mechanisms and methods: secret data capture, extraction of behavioral surplus, predictive computational analysis, behavioral microtargeting in the service of economies of action.

Cambridge Analytica channeled these methods and mechanisms, merely pivoting the surveillance capitalist machinery from commercial markets in human futures toward guaranteed outcomes in the political sphere. Its strategies of secret invasion and hidden conquest were the same standard operating procedures to which billions of innocent "users" are subjected each day. What better description of the unsavory treatment of 6.6 million young people in Australia and New Zealand whose social anxieties were extracted and manipulated for profit than to say that we "built models to exploit what we knew about them and target their inner demons"? What more apt reflection on "loyalty prediction" interventions based on trillions of data points, or Pokémon Go's manipulative game within the game than, "I think it's worse than bullying, because people don't necessarily know it's being done to them"?

It is worthwhile noting that it was Google's Eric Schmidt who first pried open this Pandora's box, transferring surveillance capitalism's core mechanisms of behavioral microtargeting to the Obama presidential campaigns, where Wylie enjoyed some of his early training under Obama's Director of Targeting.[49] In little over a decade,

---

[48] Carole Cadwalladr, "'I Made Steve Bannon's Psychological Warfare Tool': Meet the Data War Whistleblower," *Guardian*, March 18, 2018, sec. News, http://www.theguardian.com/news/2018/mar/17/data-war-whistleblower-christopher-wylie-faceook-nix-bannon-trump.

[49] Kroll, "Cloak and Data."

Schmidt's innovations have become the envy of every enemy of democracy, well within reach of the plutocrat's wallet or the more modest budgets of other non-state actors. Indeed, information warfare is widely assumed to originate in the State for the purposes of political, cultural, and, or, military destabilization, just as we once considered behavioral modification or surveillance as projects of the State. But recent theories of information warfare have begun to recognize the growing ease with which non-state actors, such as Robert Mercer or ISIS, can undertake information warfare.[50]

What has not yet been adequately recognized is that surveillance capitalism has already institutionalized information warfare as a market project. It is only on the strength of this construction that states and non-state actors alike can succeed as information warriors. Such operations exist as parasites on the host of the larger surveillance capitalist body. A simple set of distinctions framed by US Naval Academy professor and cyber-security expert Martin Libicki are useful here as they help to describe the contributions of the surveillance capitalist host that deliver triple nourishment by providing what Libicki identifies as (1) the conditions, (2) the weapons, and (3) the opportunity to wage information war.[51]

Conditions

Surveillance capitalism's economic imperatives increase the range of societal vulnerabilities for parasitic exploitation. Libicki observes that US companies lead the world in the collection and processing of personal information. Pervasive datafication and connectivity, largely driven by surveillance capital, substantially increases society's "attack surface" leaving it more vulnerable to a range of assault capabilities. Libicki asks: "[W]hy collect what can be stolen?"[52]

Weapons

The surveillance capitalism host also provides the "weapons" (data, methods, and mechanisms) necessary to exploit the vulnerabilities that it creates. "Ultimately it has been the evolution of the information economy that has provided the means by which hostile others can run a pervasive harassment campaign," Libicki

---

[50] Frederik Zuiderveen Borgesius et al., "Online Political Microtargeting: Promises and Threats for Democracy," *SSRN* (Rochester, NY: Social Science Research Network, February 9, 2018), https://papers.ssrn.com/abstract=3128787.

[51] Martin C. Libicki, "The Convergence of Information Warfare," *Strategic Studies Quarterly*, 2017: 49–65; For other relevant discussions, see Gary P. Corn and Robert Taylor, "Sovereignty in the Age of Cyber," *AJIL Unbound* 111 (2017): 207–12, https://doi.org/10.1017/aju.2017.57; Duncan Hollis, "The Influence of War; The War for Influence," *Temple International & Comparative Law Journal* 32, no. 1 (2018): 31–46; Herbert Lin, "The Existential Threat from Cyber-Enabled Information Warfare," *Bulletin of the Atomic Scientists* 75, no. 4 (July 4, 2019): 187–96, https://doi.org/10.1080/00963402.2019.1629574.

[52] Martin C. Libicki, "The Convergence of Information Warfare," 51.

acknowledges.[53] He cites "data-mining techniques" that construct "realistic simulations of individuals, indeed perhaps of most of a population ... integrating data streams with enormous cloud-based storage, powerful processing, and a dash of artificial intelligence." Such simulations, he notes, "may be used to test every individual's reaction to events," including "advertising, political campaigns, and psychological operations, and even to guess what might go viral through person-to-person interactions," just as we saw in the case of Facebook's contagion experiments.[54]

Libicki catalogues some of these weapons, which are already essential methods in surveillance capitalism's arsenal: "exquisite psychological operations," "messages tailored to one person at a time," and data-mining able to characterize individuals precisely enough for "crafting the message most likely to resonate with them." These achievements permit the "optimization" of "psychological operations," "new conduits for persuasion," and "the manipulation of fear," all of which are amply on display in surveillance capital's expanding zones of experimentation as it learns to translate knowledge into power.[55]

Opportunity

Libicki notes that information warfare unfolds in an atmosphere of "deep secrets" protected by "a dense fog of ambiguity."[56] These conditions are structurally enabled. First, they reproduce and extend the asymmetries of knowledge and power already compelled by economic imperatives. Second, as long as the surveillance capitalist host operates from the perspective of radical indifference, it is like a Cyclops whose single line of sight leaves it blind to everything but its prey. Parasitic operations succeed because they fall on the blind sides of radical indifference. This means that parasites can persist unchallenged for long periods. It is difficult to find them, disable them, and to confirm their destruction. Such was the case with Cambridge Analytica, which fed off illegitimately collected Facebook data that were illegitimately sold for nefarious purpose – all of it secreted in the shadow of Facebook's single eye. Radical indifference creates a void where social reciprocities once thrived. Surveillance capitalists cannot fill this void because doing so would violate the logic of accumulation on which everything depends. The rogue forces of disinformation grasp this fact more crisply than anyone else, as they cleverly exploit the Cyclops of radical indifference and escalate the perversion of information in an open society.[57]

---

[53] Libicki, 63.
[54] Libicki, 51–52.
[55] Libicki, 53–54.
[56] Libicki, 55–56.
[57] For a detailed discussion, see Zuboff, *The Age of Surveillance Capitalism*, pp. 504–12.

Surveillance capitalism's antidemocratic and antiegalitarian consequences are best described as a market-driven coup from above. It is not a coup d'état in the classic sense but rather a coup de gens: an overthrow of the people concealed in the technological Trojan horse that is Big Other. On the strength of its audacious annexation of human experience, this coup achieves exclusive concentrations of knowledge and power that undermine democracy at root and crown. It poisons democracy at its roots by usurping the epistemic rights that confer individual sovereignty over self/knowledge, thus weakening self-determination and undermining human autonomy without which democratic society is unimaginable. It poisons democracy from above by imposing a new axis of epistemic inequality that now threatens to remake society while unmaking the structure and function of democratic institutions. Surveillance capital wages a quiet information war for epistemic hegemony and the power over human behavior that it promises, thus channeling capitalism's adversarial bloodline not toward groups like workers or consumers who are defined by their economic function, but rather toward the widest possible category of people: "users." This broad target of all people engaged in all forms of life is as all-encompassing as the economic imperatives that compel surveillance capitalism toward societal domination. It bears a single message: CAVEAT USOR.

V. THE POISONED CROWN: THE DIVISION OF LEARNING IN SOCIETY

When the young Emile Durkheim wrote *The Division of Labor in Society*, a treatise that would become a foundational text of modern sociology, the title itself was controversial. Why this was the case is relevant to our predicament today. Because the transformation that we witness in our time echoes many of the century-old observations in Durkheim's seminal work, a few key points are reviewed here.

The division of labor had been understood as a critical means of achieving labor productivity through the specialization of tasks. Adam Smith memorably wrote about this new principle of industrial organization in his description of a pin factory, and the division of labor remained a topic of economic discourse and controversy throughout the nineteenth century. Durkheim recognized labor productivity as an economic imperative of industrial capitalism that would drive the division of labor to its most extreme application, but that was not what held his fascination.

Instead, Durkheim trained his sights on the social transformation already gathering around him, observing that "specialization" was gaining "influence" in politics, administration, the judiciary, science, and the arts. He concluded that the division of labor was no longer quarantined in the industrial workplace. Instead it had burst through those factory walls to becoming the central organizing principle of industrial society: "Whatever opinion one has about the division of labor," Durkheim wrote, "everyone knows that it exists, and is more and more becoming one of the fundamental bases of the social order."[58]

Economic imperatives predictably mandated the division of labor in production, but what was the purpose of the division of labor in society? This was the question that motivated Durkheim's analysis, and his century-old conclusions are relevant for us now. He argued that the division of labor accounts for the interdependencies and reciprocities that link the many diverse members of a modern industrial society in a larger prospect of solidarity. This new principle of social order was an essential response to the breakdown of traditional communities as the old sources of meaning that had reliably bonded people across space and time melted away. What would hold society together in the absence of the rules and rituals of place, clan, and kin? Durkheim's answer was "the division of labor." Society's need for a coherent new source of meaning and structure was the cause, and the effect was an ordering principle that enabled and sustained a healthy modern community. The reciprocities of the division of labor would breed mutual need, interdependence, and respect, all of which imbue this new ordering principle with moral force. As the young social theorist explained:

> The most remarkable effect of the division of labor is not that it increases output of functions divided, but that it renders them solidary. Its role ... is not simply to embellish or ameliorate existing societies, but to render societies possible which, without it, would not exist .... It passes far beyond purely economic interests, for it consists in the establishment of a social and moral order sui generis.[59]

Durkheim's vision was neither sterile nor naive. He recognized that things can take a dark turn and often do, resulting in what he called an "abnormal division of labor" (sometimes translated as "pathological") that produces social distance, injustice, and discord in place of reciprocity and interdependence. In this context, Durkheim singled out the destructive effects of inequality on the division of labor in society, especially what he viewed as the most dangerous source of inequality: extreme asymmetries of power that make "conflict itself impossible" by "refusing to admit the right of combat." Such pathologies can only be cured by a politics that asserts the people's right to contest, confront, and prevail in the face of unequal and illegitimate power over society. In the late nineteenth and most of the twentieth centuries, that contest was defined by economic inequality and led by labor and other social movements that asserted rights to economic justice through new institutional constructions: unions, collective bargaining, public education.

But now it is a division of learning that follows the same migratory path from the economic to the social domain once traveled by the division of labor. The progress of digitalization and information intensification began in the offices and factories of the 1980s, when workplaces mobilized around the new questions concerning

---

[58] Emile Durkheim, *The Division of Labor in Society* (New York, NY: Free Press, 1964), p. 41.
[59] Durkheim, pp. 60–61.

knowledge, authority, and power, thus drawing labor and capital into a novel and poorly understood crisis of epistemic equality.[60]

Forty years later it is possible to see that the labor crisis of the late twentieth century was an early phase of a longer struggle over the division of learning in society that would engulf twenty-first century societies as the dilemmas of knowledge, authority, and power broke through the boundaries of the economic sphere to overwhelm and finally saturate everyday life. Now the division of learning "passes far beyond purely economic interests," as it establishes the basis for a new social order and its moral content. But scientists warn that the world's capacity to produce information has substantially exceeded its ability to process and store information.[61] Information is digital, but its volume exceeds our ability to discern its meaning.

As the solution to this problem, Martin Hilbert counsels, "The only option we have left to make sense of all the data is to fight fire with fire," using "artificially intelligent computers" to "sift through the vast amounts of information … Facebook, Amazon, and Google have promised to … create value out of vast amounts of data through intelligent computational analysis."[62] The rise of surveillance capitalism, however, necessarily turns Hilbert's advice into a damning vision of social pathology. Although he does not mean to, Hilbert's suggestion merely confirms the self-authorized epistemic dominance of the surveillance capitalists and the institutionalization of epistemic inequality as the division of learning in society is bent to the commercial interests of private surveillance capital.

Surveillance capitalism's command of the division of learning in society begins with the problem of what may be called "the two texts." The first is the public-facing text, familiar and celebrated for the universe of information and connection that it brings to our fingertips. We are its authors and its readers. Google Search codifies the informational content of the World Wide Web. Facebook's News Feed binds the social network. Much of this public-facing text is composed of what we inscribe on its pages: posts, blogs, videos, photos, conversations, music, stories, observations, "likes," tweets, and all the great massing hubbub of lives captured and communicated.

Under the regime of surveillance capitalism, however, the first text does not stand alone; it trails a shadow close behind. The first text, full of promise, actually functions as the supply operation for this second shadow text. Everything that is contributed to the first text, no matter how trivial or fleeting, becomes a target for surplus extraction. That surplus fills the pages of the shadow text, hidden from view and "read only" for surveillance capitalists.[63] In this text, private experience is

---

[60] Zuboff, *In the Age of the Smart Machine.*

[61] Hilbert (2012).

[62] Viktor Mayer-Schönberger and Kenneth Cukier, *Big Data: A Revolution That Will Transform How We Live, Work, and Think* (Boston, MA: Houghton Mifflin Harcourt, 2013), p. 9.

[63] Harvard legal scholar John Palfrey observed the "read only" nature of electronic surveillance in his wonderful 2008 essay, John Palfrey, "The Public and the Private at the United States Border with Cyberspace," *Mississippi Law Journal* 78 (2008): 241–94, see especially p. 249.

dragooned as raw material to be accumulated and analyzed as means to others' market ends. The shadow text conceals more about us than we can know about ourselves, exemplified in Facebook's ingestion and calculation of trillions of behavioral data points each day. Worse still, it is nearly impossible to refrain from contributing to this vast concentration of shadow knowledge, as Big Other feeds on the normal and necessary routines of daily life.

Finally, shadow knowledge ricochets back into lives, morphing into the instrumentarian power to shape what is seen, learned, and done. As Frank Pasquale describes Google: "The decisions at the Googleplex are made behind closed doors ... the power to include, exclude, and rank is the power to ensure which public impressions become permanent and which remain fleeting ... Despite their claims of objectivity and neutrality, they are constantly making value-laden, controversial decisions. They help create the world they claim to merely 'show' us."[64] When it comes to the shadow text, we are the objects of its narratives from whose lessons we are excluded. As the source from which all the treasure flows, the shadow text is about us, but it is not for us. Instead it is created, maintained, and exploited outside our awareness for others' profit.

Just as Durkheim warned his society a century ago of an abnormal division of labor, we now enter the third decade of the twenty-first century with our societies already disfigured by a division of learning that drifts into pathology marked by epistemic inequality and injustice at the hands of the unprecedented asymmetries of knowledge institutionalized in the shadow text. The pathology does not stop here. Asymmetries of knowledge feed the progress of instrumentarian power as exclusive knowledge is translated through the networked layer of digital instrumentation to produce new capabilities of actuation at scale – influencing, tuning, herding, and modifying human behavior toward others' commercial ends. The division of learning is thus both the ascendant principle of social order in the twenty-first century and already hostage to surveillance capital's privileged position, empowered by its ownership of the texts and its exclusive command of analysis and prediction capabilities.

More than thirty years ago, the legal scholar Spiros Simitis published a remarkable essay on the theme of privacy in an information society. Simitis grasped early on that the already visible trends in public and private "information processing" harbored threats to society that transcended narrow conceptions of privacy and data ownership. "[P]ersonal information is increasingly used to enforce standards of behavior," he wrote. "Information processing is developing, therefore, into an essential element of long-term strategies of manipulation intended to mold and adjust individual conduct."[65] Simitis argued that these trends were incompatible not only with privacy but with the very possibility of democracy, which depends

---

[64] Frank Pasquale, *The Black Box Society* (Cambridge, MA: Harvard University Press, 2015), pp. 60–61.
[65] Spiros Simitis, "Reviewing Privacy in an Information Society," *University of Pennsylvania Law Review* 135, no. 3 (1987): 710, https://doi.org/10.2307/3312079.

on a reservoir of individual proficiencies associated with autonomous moral judgment and self-determination.

Building on Simitis's work, Paul Schwartz warned in 1989 that computerization would transform the delicate balance of rights and obligations upon which privacy law depends: "Today the enormous amounts of personal data available in computers threaten the individual in a way that renders obsolete much of the previous legal protection." Most important, Schwartz foresaw that the scale of the still emerging epistemic crisis would impose risks that exceed the scope of privacy law. "The danger that the computer poses is to human autonomy," he warned. "The more that is known about a person, the easier it is to control him. Insuring the liberty that nourishes democracy requires a structuring of societal use of information and even permitting some concealment of information."[66]

Both Simitis and Schwartz sensed the ascent of the division of learning as the axial principle of a new computational societal milieu, but they could not have anticipated the rise of surveillance capitalism and its consequences. While the explosive growth of information territories shifts a crucial axis of the social order from a twentieth-century division of labor to a twenty-first century division of learning, it is surveillance capitalists who command the field and unilaterally lay claim to a disproportionate share of the epistemic rights that shape the division of learning in society.

Instead of the long anticipated explosion of democratization, the competitive struggle over surveillance revenues has dragged our societies into a regressive "pre-Gutenberg" pattern, in which a pathological division of learning is captured by private capital, presided over by a narrow priesthood of privately employed computational specialists, their privately owned machines, and the economic interests for whose sake they learn. This epistemic violence runs free of law, of market restraints, and of organic reciprocities with its communities, which are no longer required as sources of customers or employees but rather as a passive unwitting cornucopia of raw material for production and sales.

The result is best understood as *the unauthorized privatization of the division of learning in society*. Just as Durkheim warned of the subversion of the division of labor by the powerful forces of industrial capital a century ago, today's successful prosecution of information warfare aimed at citizen-users by surveillance capital now exerts private power over the definitive principle of social order in our time. Epistemic inequality is enshrined as the signature deformation of this epoch as the pathologies of the division of learning infect the societal superstructure.

Here is democracy's poisoned crown: As things currently stand, it is the surveillance capitalist corporations that know. It is the market form that decides. It is surveillance capital that decides who decides. Experts in the disciplines associated

---

[66] Paul M. Schwartz, "The Computer in German and American Constitutional Law: Towards an American Right of Informational Self-Determination," *American Journal of Comparative Law* 37 (1989): 676.

with machine intelligence know this, although they have little grasp of its implications as the signal of the defining axis of social inequality in our time. One data scientist writes: "Whoever has the best algorithms and the most data wins . . .. Google with its head start and larger market share, knows better what you want . . . whoever learns fastest wins."[67] In 2018, the *New York Times* reported that Google CEO Sundar Pichai had located his office on the same floor as the company's AI research lab, noting it as a trend among many CEOs – a literal take on the concentration of knowledge and power.[68]

Here is the paradox in which citizens are caught: *Democracy is the target of this epistemic poison, and its only antidote.*

VI. REMEDIES

Despite the variation of motives among the ninety Spanish citizens, their collective assertion of a "right to be forgotten" announced a new twenty-first-century contest over once elemental epistemic rights now under global assault from private surveillance capital. The European Court of Justice's decision on the "right to be forgotten" so often reduced to the legal and technical considerations related to the deletion or delinking of personal data, was in fact a key inflection point at which elemental epistemic rights successfully sought the protection of democratic institutions as they undertook the long migration toward law. It was the Court of Justice that wrote an early chapter in what is now an epoch-defining struggle to claw back epistemic rights from the powerful forces of surveillance capital and its determination to assert authority over what can be learned and known. There is evidence that citizens and lawmakers around the world are finally picking up the pen, as a new wave of public "techlash," legislative initiatives, and regulatory actions begins to take shape.

The past offers good counsel at this key juncture. In his Pulitzer prize-winning history, *Prophets of Regulation*, Thomas McCraw recounts the phases and distinct purposes of regulatory regimes in the US: the 1870s and the initial period of industrialization; the early twentieth century, especially 1900–1916; the 1930s and the New Deal; and the onset of deindustrialization during the 1970s and 1980s. The challenges of each era brought distinct forms of law and regulatory leadership. At the dawn of the twentieth century it was the muckrakers and progressives who defined the regulatory paradigm. Later, the lawyers dominated. It was only the past few decades that saw the economists as framers of the regulatory vision.

McCraw observes that this "economists' hour" will certainly end and wonders what will follow. In considering the arc of this history, he finds clues, noting that

[67] Pedro Domingos, *The Master Algorithm: How the Quest for the Ultimate Learning Machine Will Remake Our World* (New York, NY: Basic Books, 2015), pp. 12–13.

[68] Cade Metz, "Why A.I. Researchers at Google Got Desks Next to the Boss," *New York Times*, February 19, 2018, sec. Technology, https://www.nytimes.com/2018/02/19/technology/ai-researchers-desks-boss.html.

concerns for justice and fairness have generally overshadowed the more narrow aims of economic growth in the construction of regulatory regimes. "Regulation," he writes, "is best understood as a political settlement."[69]

This perspective suggests that the chartering frameworks of a digital future compatible with the principles of a democratic society are most likely to be defined and led by champions of democracy. The key principles here must be: (1) the redistribution of epistemic rights to the sovereign individual, (2) under the authority of the rule of law, and (3) sustained by the power of democratic institutions and their governance. Elected officials, citizens, and specialists can seize this opportunity, allied in the knowledge that despite its failures and shortcomings, democracy is the one idea to emerge from the long human story that enshrines the peoples' right to govern themselves and asserts the ideal of the sovereign individual as the single most powerful bulwark against tyranny.

McCraw delivers a warning with his observations, however, and it is significant for us now. The historical record shows that regulators failed when they were unable "to frame strategies appropriate to the particular industries they were regulating."[70] The lesson is that today's new legislative and regulatory challenges will not be met effectively without a clear grasp of surveillance capitalism as a novel economic logic defined by distinct economic imperatives and the specific practices and consequences that they compel. Twenty-first century solutions to our twenty-first century challenges may build on existing paradigms of privacy and antitrust but will also have to move beyond and even transform those paradigms, as we learn how to interrupt and outlaw surveillance capitalism's key mechanisms, methods, and markets. As the European Commissioner for Competition Margrethe Vestager recently put it: "One of the things I have learned from surveillance capitalism . . . is [that] it's not you searching Google, it is Google searching you. And that gives a very good idea about not only what you want to buy but also what you think. So we have indeed a lot to do."[71]

The prospects of a new regulatory paradigm are improved with a clear grasp of the forces that have impeded its emergence during the first two decades of the twenty-first century. Lawmakers have been reluctant to challenge surveillance capitalism for many reasons.[72] Among these was an unwritten policy of "surveillance exceptionalism" forged in the aftermath of the September 11 terrorist attacks, when the government's concerns shifted from online privacy protections to a new zeal for "total information awareness." In that political environment, the fledgling surveillance

---

[69] Thomas K. McCraw, *Prophets of Regulation: Charles Francis Adams; Louis D. Brandeis; James M. Landis; Alfred E. Kahn* (Cambridge, MA: Belknap Press: An Imprint of Harvard University Press, 1986), l. 3990.

[70] McCraw, l. 4037.

[71] Natasha Lomas, "Europe's Recharged Antitrust Chief Makes Her Five-Year Pitch to Be Digital EVP," *TechCrunch* (blog), October 8, 2019, http://social.techcrunch.com/2019/10/08/europes-recharged-antitrust-chief-makes-her-five-year-pitch-to-be-digital-evp/.

[72] Zuboff, *The Age of Surveillance Capitalism*, chapter 4.

capabilities emerging from Silicon Valley appeared to hold great promise. Another reason has been the unparalleled lobbying infrastructure pioneered by Google and later joined by Facebook and others. A third is the value of behavioral microtargeting to political campaigns.[73]

As a new wave of public mobilization and lawmaking gathers force, doing "a lot" will require overcoming these old impediments. It also means confronting surveillance capitalism's strategic propaganda campaigns and its mass communications tactics based on gaslighting and mendacity. Strategies and tactics have been designed as defensive fortifications intended to undermine and intimidate lawmakers and citizens alike, confounding judgment and freezing action. What follows are three examples of strategic propaganda that have received relatively little scrutiny compared to the damage they do.

The Innovation Defense

Surveillance capitalist leaders vigorously portray democracy as the enemy of innovation. Facebook's Head of Global Policy and Communications, Sir Nick Clegg, warned in 2019 that any restrictions resulting from "tech-lash" risked making it "almost impossible for tech to innovate properly," invoking the threat of Chinese ascendance as the price the West would pay for law. "I can predict that … we will have tech domination from a country with wholly different sets of values," he insisted.[74]

Clegg was only repeating what surveillance capitalist leaders had been proselytizing for years. In 2010, Mark Zuckerberg announced that privacy was no longer a "social norm," celebrating Facebook's explosive new "privacy policies" that publicly displayed personal information by default as evidence of his determination to innovate rather than "be trapped" by conventions or law. "We decided that these would be the social norms now and we just went for it."[75] In 2011, former Google CEO Eric Schmidt warned that government overreach would foolishly constrain innovation: "We'll move much faster than any government."[76] That year Google founder Larry Page complained that "old institutions like the law" impede the firm's freedom to "build really great things."[77] All of this rhetoric is actually a hand-me-down from another era when Gilded Age barons, whom we now call "robbers,"

---

[73] See, ibid., pp. 112–27.

[74] Natasha Lomas, "Facebook Makes Another Push to Shape and Define Its Own Oversight," *TechCrunch* (blog), June 24, 2019, http://social.techcrunch.com/2019/06/24/facebook-makes-another-push-to-shape-and-define-its-own-oversight/.

[75] Bobbie Johnson, "Privacy No Longer a Social Norm, Says Facebook Founder," *Guardian*, January 10, 2010, sec. Technology, https://www.theguardian.com/technology/2010/jan/11/facebook-privacy.

[76] Pascal-Emmanuel Gobry, "Eric Schmidt to World Leaders at EG8: Don't Regulate Us, or Else," *Business Insider*, May 24, 2011, http://www.businessinsider.com/eric-schmidt-google-eg8-2011-5.

[77] Jay Yarow, "Google CEO Larry Page Wants a Totally Separate World Where Tech Companies Can Conduct Experiments on People," *Business Insider*, May 16, 2013, http://www.businessinsider.com/google-ceo-larry-page-wants-a-place-for-experiments-2013-5.

insisted that there was no need for law when one had the "law of evolution," the "laws of capital," and the "laws of industrial society." As historian David Nasaw put it, the millionaires preached "democracy had its limits, beyond which voters and their elected representatives dared not trespass lest economic calamity befall the nation."[78]

George Orwell observed that the rhetorical silences and blatant contradictions of power are designed so that "to see what is in front of one's nose needs a constant struggle."[79] The tech companies' innovation rhetoric helped to suppress criticism from users and their lawmakers for many years, despite what was in front of their noses. Facebook and Google were regarded as innovative companies that sometimes make dreadful mistakes at the expense of privacy. Since then the picture has sharpened and we are getting better at seeing what's in front of our collective nose. It is now possible to recognize that what were once regarded as mistakes – Google Glass, Gmail scanning, Street View's theft of private data, Facebook's Beacon program, its sale of private information to developers, and more – were, in fact, the innovations.

The Freedom Defense

Lawmakers also have been held back in their work by confusion about the relationship between knowledge and freedom. Surveillance capitalists are no different from other capitalists in demanding freedom from any sort of constraint. They insist on the "freedom to" launch every novel practice while aggressively asserting the necessity of their "freedom from" law and regulation. This classic pattern reflects two bedrock assumptions about capitalism made by its own theorists: The first is that markets are intrinsically unknowable. The second is that the ignorance produced by this lack of knowledge requires wide-ranging freedom of action for market actors.

The notion that ignorance and freedom are twinborn characteristics of capitalism is rooted in the conditions of life before the advent of modern systems of communication and transportation, let alone global digital networks, the Internet, or the ubiquitous architectures of Big Other. Until the last few moments of the human story, life was necessarily local, and the "whole" was necessarily invisible to the "part."

Adam Smith's famous metaphor of the "invisible hand" drew on these enduring realities of human life. Each individual, Smith reasoned, employs his capital locally in pursuit of immediate comforts and necessities. Each one attends to "his own security ... his own gain ... led by an invisible hand to promote an end which was

---

[78] David Nasaw, "Gilded Age Gospels," in *Ruling America: A History of Wealth and Power in a Democracy*, eds. Steve Fraser and Gary Gerstle (Cambridge, MA: Harvard University Press, 2005), pp. 124–5, 148.

[79] Sonia Orwell and Ian Angus, *In Front of Your Nose 1945–1940: The Collected Essays, Journalism, and Letters of George Orwell*, vol. 4 (New York, NY: Harcourt, Brace & World, Inc., 1968), p. 125.

no part of his intention." That end is the efficient employ of capital in the broader market: the wealth of nations. The individual actions that produce efficient markets add up to a staggeringly complex pattern, a mystery that no one person or entity could hope to know or understand, let alone to direct: "The statesman, who should attempt to direct private people in what manner they ought to employ their capitals, would ... assume an authority which could safely be trusted, not only to no single person, but to no council or senate whatever."[80]

The neoliberal economist Friedrich Hayek, whose work laid the foundation for the market-privileging economic policies of the past half century, drew the most basic tenets of his arguments from Smith's assumptions about the whole and the part. "Adam Smith," Hayek wrote, "was the first to perceive that we have stumbled upon methods of ordering human economic cooperation that exceed the limits of our knowledge and perception. His 'invisible hand' had perhaps better have been described as an invisible or unsurveyable pattern."[81]

In Hayek's framing, the mystery of the market is that a great many people can behave effectively while remaining ignorant of the whole. Individuals not only can choose freely, but they must freely choose their own pursuits because there is no alternative, no source of total knowledge or conscious control to guide them. "Human design" is impossible, Hayek says, because the relevant information flows are "beyond the span of the control of any one mind." The market dynamic makes it possible for people to operate in ignorance without "anyone having to tell them what to do."[82]

When it comes to surveillance capitalist operations, the classic quid pro quo of freedom for ignorance is shattered. The "market" is no longer invisible, certainly not in the way that Smith or Hayek imagined. The competitive struggle among surveillance capitalists produces the compulsion toward totality. Total information tends toward certainty and the promise of guaranteed outcomes. These operations mean that the supply and demand of human futures markets are rendered in infinite detail. Surveillance capitalism aims to replace mystery with certainty as it substitutes datafication, behavioral modification, and prediction for the old "unsurveyable pattern."

The result is a fundamental reversal of the classic ideal of the "market" as intrinsically unknowable. Now the market is visible. As the head of Facebook's data science team once reflected: "This is the first time the world has seen this scale and quality of data about human communication. For the first time, we have a microscope that ... lets us examine social behavior at a very fine level that we've never been able to see before."[83] A top Facebook engineer put it more succinctly:

[80] Adam Smith, *The Wealth of Nations*, ed. Edwin Cannan (New York, NY: Modern Library, 1994), p. 485.

[81] Friedrich August von Hayek, *The Collected Works of Friedrich August Hayek*, ed. William Warren Bartley (Chicago, IL: University of Chicago Press, 1988), p. 14.

[82] Friedrich Hayek, "The Use of Knowledge in Society," in *Individualism and Economic Order* (Chicago, IL: University of Chicago Press, 1980). See the discussion on pp. 85–89.

[83] Tom Simonite, "What Facebook Knows," *MIT Technology Review*, June 13, 2012, https://www .technologyreview.com/s/428150/what-facebook-knows/.

"We are trying to map out the graph of everything in the world and how it relates to each other."[84] The same objectives are echoed in the other leading surveillance capitalist firms. As Google's Eric Schmidt observed in 2010: "You give us more information about you, about your friends, and we can improve the quality of our searches. We don't need you to type at all. We know where you are. We know where you've been. We can more or less know what you're thinking about."[85] Microsoft's Satya Nadella understands all physical and institutional spaces, people, and social relationships as indexable and searchable: all of it subject to machine reasoning, pattern recognition, prediction, preemption, interruption, and modification.[86]

Although there is nothing unusual about the prospect of capitalist enterprises seeking every kind of knowledge advantage in a competitive marketplace, the surveillance capitalist capabilities that translate ignorance into knowledge are unprecedented because they rely on the one resource that distinguishes the surveillance capitalists from traditional utopianists: the financial and intellectual capital that permits the actual transformation of the world, materialized in the continuously expanding architectures of Big Other. More astonishing still is that surveillance capital derives from the dispossession of human experience, operationalized in its unilateral and pervasive programs of rendering private experience as computational data.

This new condition unravels the economic justification for the triumph of raw capitalism: its free markets, free-market actors, and self-regulating enterprises. It suggests that surveillance capitalists mastered the rhetoric and political genius of the neoliberal ideological defense while pursuing a novel logic of accumulation that belies the most fundamental postulates of the capitalist worldview. It's not just that the cards have been reshuffled; the rules of the game have been transformed into something that is both unprecedented and unimaginable outside the digital milieu and the vast resources of wealth and scientific prowess that the surveillance capitalists bring to the table. Surveillance capitalism's command and control of the division of learning in society is the signature feature that breaks with the old justifications of the invisible hand and its entitlements. The combination of knowledge and freedom works to accelerate the asymmetry of power between surveillance capitalists and the societies in which they operate. This cycle will be broken only when we acknowledge as citizens, as lawmakers, as societies, and indeed as a civilization that surveillance capitalists know too much to qualify for freedom.

---

[84] Ashlee Vance, "Facebook: The Making of 1 Billion Users," *Bloomberg.com*, October 4, 2012, http://www.bloomberg.com/news/articles/2012–10-04/facebook-the-making-of-1-billion-users.

[85] Derek Thompson, "Google's CEO: 'The Laws Are Written by Lobbyists,'" *Atlantic*, October 1, 2010, https://www.theatlantic.com/technology/archive/2010/10/googles-ceo-the-laws-are-written-by-lobbyists/63908/.

[86] Shoshana Zuboff, "The Road to Digital Serfdom? The Visible Hand of Surveillance Capitalism," *Promarket*, February 22, 2019, https://promarket.org/road-to-digital-serfdom-surveillance-capitalism-visible-hand/.

The Success Defense

A third propaganda strategy is the argument that the financial success of the leading surveillance capitalist firms reflects the real value they bring to people. In this view, financial success is prima facie evidence that no laws are required. But data from the demand side evident in a range of research conducted over the last decade and a half suggest a more disturbing picture. In forty-six of the most prominent forty-eight opinion surveys on the subject of privacy administered in the US and Europe between 2008 and 2016, substantial majorities support measures for enhanced privacy and user control over personal data. (Only two early surveys were somewhat less conclusive, because so many participants said they did not understand how or what personal information was being gathered.)

By 2008 it was well established that the more information people have about "Internet privacy practices," the more they are "very concerned" about privacy.[87] A major 2009 survey found that when people were informed of the ways that companies gather data for targeted online ads, more than 73 percent rejected such advertising.[88] A substantial 2015 survey found 91 percent of respondents disagreed that the collection of personal information "without my knowing" was a fair trade-off for a price discount.[89] Fifty-five percent disagreed that it was even a fair exchange for improved services. By late 2019 the disjuncture was even more pronounced: An important survey from PEW Research reported that 81 percent of Americans believe the potential risks of companies' data collection outweigh the benefits, compared to 66 percent who felt that way about government data collection.[90] A similar Swedish study in 2020 found that 55 percent of Swedes were most concerned about data collection by private companies, compared to 11 percent concerned about government data collection.[91]

The surveillance capitalist firms typically dismiss these results, pointing instead to users' actual behavior and the spectacular revenues it produces as justification for

---

[87] Chris Jay Hoofnagle and Jennifer King, "Research Report: What Californians Understand About Privacy Offline," *SSRN*, May 15, 2008 (Rochester, NY: Social Science Research Network), http://papers.ssrn.com/abstract=1133075.

[88] Joseph Turow et al., "Americans Reject Tailored Advertising and Three Activities That Enable It" (Annenberg School for Communication, September 29, 2009), http://papers.ssrn.com/abstract=1478214.

[89] Joseph Turow, Michael Hennessy, and Nora Draper, "The Tradeoff Fallacy: How Marketers Are Misrepresenting American Consumers and Opening Them Up to Exploitation," Survey Results (Pennsylvania, PA: Annenberg School for Communication, June 2015), https://www.asc.upenn.edu/news-events/publications/tradeoff-fallacy-how-marketers-are-misrepresenting-american-consumers-and.

[90] Brooke Auxier et al., "Americans and Privacy: Concerned, Confused and Feeling Lack of Control Over Their Personal Information," *Pew Research Center: Internet, Science & Tech* (blog), November 15, 2019, https://www.pewresearch.org/internet/2019/11/15/americans-and-privacy-concerned-confused-and-feeling-lack-of-control-over-their-personal-information/.

[91] Markus Lahtinen, "Big Tech Greater Threat to Privacy than Big Brother," Lund University School of Economics and Management, January 23, 2020, https://lusem.lu.se/news/big-tech-greater-threat-to-privacy-than-big-brother.

the status quo. Recall former Google CEO Eric Schmidt's infamous 2009 privacy brushoff: "If you have something that you don't want anyone to know, maybe you shouldn't be doing it in the first place."[92] Scholars have called the gap between attitudes and behavior "the privacy paradox," but there really is no paradox here, only the predictable consequence of the pitched battle between supply and demand expressed in the difference between what surveillance capitalism imposes on people and what they really want.[93]

The data suggest that surveillance capitalism is best understood as a market failure that would not survive a genuinely competitive commercial environment. Few people who get a glimpse of surveillance capitalism's hidden operations actually want to be their target. Most want an alternative path to the digital future, one that will fulfill their needs without compromising privacy and usurping epistemic rights. This is one of those disjunctures in economic history, when nearly everyone wants something that they cannot have, just as early twentieth-century farmers and shop-keepers wanted automobiles too, but at a price they could afford. Instead of a close alignment of supply and demand, people use surveillance capitalism's services because they have no comparable alternatives and because they are ignorant of its shadow operations and their consequences. Corporate success is best understood as the result of coercion and obfuscation, practices that are only sustainable when they are conducted in secret.

Surveillance capitalism has thrived in the absence of law and regulation. Rather than mourning this state of affairs, the lack of prior action may be regarded as a positive. Democracy has not failed to reign in this rogue capitalism, it has simply not yet tried. And further, democratic societies have successfully confronted destructive forms of raw capitalism in the past, asserting new laws that tethered capitalism to the needs of people and democratic values. Democracy moderated some of the excesses of early industrialization. It ended the Gilded Age. It mitigated the destruction of the Great Depression. It built a strong post-War society. It protected earth, creatures, water, air, consumers, and workers.

According to Lawrence Friedman's history of American law in the twentieth century, the appetite for new law and regulation in the 1930s came from decades of anger, frustration, outrage, and helplessness at the growing scale and complexity of the industrial behemoths.[94] Only law was up to the task of tethering the giant industrial corporations to the needs of a democratic society. The swell of survey data,

---

[92] Richard Esguerra, "Google CEO Eric Schmidt Dismisses the Importance of Privacy," *Electronic Frontier Foundation*, 10 December 2009, https://www.eff.org/deeplinks/2009/12/google-ceo-eric-schmidt-dismisses-privacy.

[93] Susanne Barth and Menno D. T. de Jong, "The Privacy Paradox—Investigating Discrepancies between Expressed Privacy Concerns and Actual Online Behavior: A Systematic Literature Review," *Telematics and Informatics* 34, no. 7 (November 2017): 1038–58, https://doi.org/10.1016/j.tele.2017.04.013.

[94] Lawrence M. Friedman, *American Law in the 20th Century* (New Haven, CT: Yale University Press, 2004).

the gradual awakening to surveillance capitalism's mass communication tactics, and the drumbeat of novel legislative and regulatory discussions and initiatives appears to point in a similar direction. The question remains: What is to be done? What kinds of new law and regulation are likely to be effective? Will it be comprehensive privacy legislation? Will it be an antitrust approach, as many counsel? McCraw's warning suggests that we need new economic, legal, and collective action paradigms born of a close understanding of surveillance capitalism's economic imperatives and foundational mechanisms.

Privacy and antitrust law are vital, but there is reason to believe that neither will be wholly adequate to this new challenge. An example is privacy law's call for "data ownership" and related data rights. Such formulations legitimate the original sin that is the theft of human experience for rendition into data in the first instance. All discussions that begin with existing data flows serve to institutionalize that theft. Negotiating data ownership is like negotiating how many hours a day a seven-year-old should be allowed to work in a factory, rather than contesting the fundamental legitimacy of child labor. Data rights also fail to reckon with the realities of behavioral surplus. Even if "users" achieve "ownership" of the data that they provided to a company, they will not achieve "ownership" of the behavioral surplus that floods the shadow text, the predictions gleaned from it, or the fate of those predictions in markets that trade in human futures. Finally, data ownership is a recipe for a new epistemic underclass, in which economically disadvantaged individuals, families, and groups sell their data in the same way that one might sell one's organs in an illicit market. The Google contractors who induced homeless people of color to "sell" their faces for $5 offered a portent of that bleak future.

The prospect of "breaking up" the largest surveillance capitalist firms also fails to reckon with the actual mechanisms of this economic logic. Surveillance capitalists achieve scale by cornering behavioral surplus supplies and driving up the value chain for more predictive forms of surplus. If there are monopolies here, they are monopolies of behavioral surplus supplies, of scientific labor, and of material infrastructures for predictive analytics. These features do not correspond neatly to conventional monopoly criteria, neither do they reflect the conventional categories of "consumer harms" that most antitrust laws are designed to combat.

It is necessary to rethink the meaning of "size" and "monopoly" when a company with relatively few employees but huge capital reserves can corner data flows from large domains of human experience (e.g., "search" or "social networking") while simultaneously cornering the capabilities to compute those data flows. Assistant Attorney General Makan Delrahim offered an initial analysis of such distinctions in 2019 noting: "Broadly speaking, in some digital markets, the competition is for user attention or clicks. If we see the commercial dynamics of Internet search, for example, in terms of the Yellow Pages that were delivered to our doors a generation ago, we cannot properly assess practices and transactions that create, enhance, or entrench market power – and in some cases monopoly power."[95] Breaking up the largest surveillance capitalists – Google, Facebook, Microsoft, and Amazon – can address important anti-competitive problems, but without measures tailored to the actual mechanisms of surveillance capitalism, it will not prevent the emergence of smaller and more efficient surveillance capitalist firms, while opening the field for new surveillance capitalist competitors.

The most efficient legislative and regulatory strategies would be aimed at disrupting the surveillance dividend by disrupting the raw material supplies and financial incentives that sustain it. In other words, it means legislative and regulatory strategies that interrupt and in some cases outlaw surveillance capitalism's mechanisms of supply and demand. Such measures would create space for alternative citizen-based and commercial action, building ecosystems that realign with individual needs and democratic practice.

Supply: The relentless expansion of extractive supply chain operations is only likely to be constrained when the legal and regulatory focus shifts from data ownership and management to the originating processes of datafication: the secret theft of private human experience as free raw material for rendition into data. The boundary in dispute must move upstream, from contest over data as property to the codification of epistemic rights that link individual sovereignty to inalienable rights of self/knowledge and establish a rights-based moat around private experience.

This codification of epistemic rights to self/knowledge would interrupt data supply chains by safeguarding the boundaries of human experience before they come under assault from the forces of datafication. It assigns the choice to turn any aspect of one's life into data as a right that adheres to individuals and communities by virtue of law sustained by democratic governance and as an extension of elemental rights now explicated and translated into juridical rights. This means, for example, that companies cannot claim the right to your face as you walk down the street, or use your face as free raw material for analysis, or fabricate, own, or sell any computational products that derive from your face and its depths of personal information. Such epistemic rights can be understood as the cornerstone of individual freedom under twenty-first-century conditions of existence.

The conversation on epistemic rights has already begun. In the absence of a comprehensive epistemic right to self/knowledge, for example, legal scholars, practitioners, and neural scientists have begun to frame epistemic rights claims to "freedom of thought." They cite the sanctity of the "forum internum," the interior space of human awareness and thought, and the need for codified individual rights that protect this domain of human experience from unwanted intrusion, theft, and

---

[95] Makan Delrahim, "Assistant Attorney General Makan Delrahim Delivers Remarks for the Antitrust New Frontiers Conference," United States Department of Justice, June 11, 2019, https://www.justice .gov/opa/speech/assistant-attorney-general-makan-delrahim-delivers-remarks-antitrust-new-frontiers.

manipulation.[96] Some of this work is a direct response to surveillance capitalism's unrelenting drive to eliminate every barrier to the datafication of human experience, including recent breakthroughs in translating brain signals into speech.[97] Columbia University is home to a "neurorights initiative,"[98] the OECD issued formal recommendations for "responsible innovation in neurotechnology,[99] and Amnesty International issued a path-breaking report on the human rights implications of the "surveillance business model."[100] As contests over epistemic rights multiply, there is a strong likelihood that surveillance assets will be reinterpreted as toxic "fruit of the poisonous tree" that can only be acquired at the price of fundamental epistemic rights.

Demand: The opportunity on the demand side is to disrupt or eliminate the financial incentives that sustain the surveillance dividend. This can be accomplished with sanctions that outlaw the trade in human futures. This is not a radical prospect. For example, societies outlaw markets that trade in human

[96] Examples include, Susie Alegre, "Using Freedom of Thought to Limit 'Surveillance Capitalism'?" Doughty Street Chambers (blog), July 3, 2019, https://insights.doughtystreet.co.uk/post/102fn86/using-freedom-of-thought-to-limit-surveillance-capitalism; Susie Alegre, "Time to Think about Freedom of Thought," *International Law Bulletin*, November 2017, https://doughty-street-chambers.newsweaver.com/International/rn8wy1p800g?a=1&p=2047237&t=174031; Marcello Ienca and Roberto Andorno, "Towards New Human Rights in the Age of Neuroscience and Neurotechnology," *Life Sciences, Society and Policy* 13 (April 26, 2017), https://doi.org/10.1186/s40504-017-0050-1.

[97] Antonio Regalado, "Facebook Is Funding Brain Experiments to Create a Device That Reads Your Mind," *MIT TechnologyReview*, July 30, 2019, https://www.technologyreview.com/s/614034/facebook-is-funding-brain-experiments-to-create-a-device-that-reads-your-mind/; Sigal Samuel, "Facebook Is Building Tech to Read Your Mind. The Ethical Implications Are Staggering.," *Vox*, August 5, 2019, https://www.vox.com/future-perfect/2019/8/5/20750259/facebook-ai-mind-reading-brain-computer-interface; David A. Moses et al., "Real-Time Decoding of Question-and-Answer Speech Dialogue Using Human Cortical Activity," *Nature Communications* 10, no. 1 (July 30, 2019): 1–14, https://doi.org/10.1038/s41467-019-10994-4; Sigal Samuel, "Brain-Reading Tech Is Coming. The Law Is Not Ready to Protect Us," *Vox*, August 30, 2019, https://www.vox.com/2019/8/30/20835137/facebook-zuckerberg-elon-musk-brain-mind-reading-neuroethics; "Surge in US 'Brain-Reading' Patents," *BBC News*, May 7, 2015, sec. Technology, http://www.bbc.com/news/technology-32623063; Anderson Cooper, "What Is 'Brain Hacking'? Tech Insiders on Why You Should Care," *CBS News*, April 9, 2017, https://www.cbsnews.com/news/brain-hacking-tech-insiders-60-minutes/; Christopher N. Cascio, Christin Scholz, and Emily B. Falk, "Social Influence and the Brain: Persuasion, Susceptibility to Influence and Retransmission," *Current Opinion in Behavioral Sciences* 3 (June 2015): 51–57, https://doi.org/10.1016/j.cobeha.2015.01.007; Kiyoto Kasai et al., "The Future of Real-World Neuroscience: Imaging Techniques to Assess Active Brains in Social Environments," *Neuroscience Research* 90 (January 2015): 65–71, https://doi.org/10.1016/j.neures.2014.11.007; "Brain-Connected Computers," *Week*, July 28, 2017.

[98] "NeuroRights Initiative," accessed February 23, 2020, https://nri.ntc.columbia.edu/.

[99] "New Frontiers of the Mind: Enabling Responsible Innovation in Neurotechnology," The OECD Forum Network, December 19, 2019, http://www.oecd-forum.org/users/338762-david-winickoff/posts/57641-new-frontiers-of-the-mind-enabling-responsible-innovation-in-neurotechnology.

[100] Amnesty International, "Surveillance Giants: How the Business Model of Google and Facebook Threatens Human Rights" (2019), https://amnestyusa.org/wp-content/uploads/2019/11/Surveillance-Giants-Embargo-21-Nov-0001-GMT-FINAL-report.pdf.

organs, babies, and slaves. In each case, such markets are recognized as morally repugnant operations that produce predictably violent consequences and violate democratic principles. Human futures markets can be shown to produce equally predictable outcomes that challenge human freedoms, violate epistemic rights, and undermine democracy.

✳✳✳✳✳✳✳✳✳✳✳✳✳✳✳✳

Consider the Aware Home, a collaboration between computer scientists and engineers in the year 2000, intended as a "living laboratory" for the study of "ubiquitous computing."[101] The project envisioned a "human-home symbiosis" in which animate and inanimate processes would be captured by an elaborate network of "context aware sensors" embedded in the house and by wearable computers worn by the home's occupants. The Aware Home information system was designed as a simple closed-loop controlled entirely by the home's occupants. Because the house would be "constantly monitoring the occupants' whereabouts and activities . . . even tracing its inhabitants' medical conditions," the engineers concluded, "there is a clear need to give the occupants knowledge and control of the distribution of this information." All the information was to be stored on the occupants' wearable computers "to insure the privacy of an individual's information."

In 2017 University of London scholars published a detailed analysis of a single "smart home" device, the Google-owned Nest thermostat.[102] They determined that the purchase of a single Nest thermostat entails the need to review nearly 1,000 so-called "contracts," each with its own burdensome and audacious terms of service for third-party data sharing.[103] Should the customer refuse to agree to Nest's stipulations, the Terms of Service indicate that the functionality and security of the thermostat may be deeply compromised, no longer supported by the necessary updates meant to ensure its reliability and safety. The consequences can range from frozen pipes to failed smoke alarms to an easily hacked internal home system.[104]

Today we might mourn the innocence of the Aware Home but, like a message in a bottle from a bygone age, it tells us something important. Once we were the

---

[101] Cory D. Kidd et al., "The Aware Home: A Living Laboratory for Ubiquitous Computing Research," in *Proceedings of the Second International Workshop on Cooperative Buildings, Integrating Information, Organization, and Architecture*, CoBuild '99 (London: Springer-Verlag, 1999), pp. 191–98, http://dl.acm.org/citation.cfm?id=645969.674887.

[102] Ron Amadeo, "Nest Is Done as a Standalone Alphabet Company, Merges with Google," *Ars Technica*, February 7, 2018, https://arstechnica.com/gadgets/2018/02/nest-is-done-as-a-standalone-alphabet-company-merges-with-google/; Leo Kelion, "Google-Nest Merger Raises Privacy Issues," *BBC News*, February 8, 2018, sec. Technology, http://www.bbc.com/news/technology-42989073.

[103] Guido Noto La Diega, "Contracting for the 'Internet of Things': Looking into the Nest," Research Paper (London: Queen Mary University of London, School of Law, 2016); Robin Kar and Margaret Radin, "Pseudo-Contract & Shared Meaning Analysis," *SSRN* (November 16, 2017), https://papers.ssrn.com/abstract=3083129.

[104] Grant Hernandez, Orlando Arias, Daniel Buentello, and Yier Jin, "Smart Nest Thermostat: A Smart Spy in Your Home," *Black Hat USA* (2014), https://www.blackhat.com/docs/us-14/materials/us-14-Jin-Smart-Nest-Thermostat-A-Smart-Spy-In-Your-Home-WP.pdf.

subjects of our lives, now we are its objects. We once looked to the digital future as a human future – a place we could call home. The Aware Home is testimony to what we have lost and what we can find again: the rights to know and decide who knows and decide who decides who knows about our lives: Individual epistemic sovereignty, law, and democracy. Such rights and principles have been and remain the only possible grounds for human freedom, a functional democratic society, and an information civilization founded on equality and justice.

9

The Siren Song: Algorithmic Governance by Blockchain

Kevin Werbach

A mysterious new technology emerges ... its effects become profound; and later, many people wonder why its powerful promise wasn't more obvious from the start. What technology am I talking about? Personal computers in 1975, the Internet in 1993, and – I believe – Bitcoin in 2014.[1]

[L]et them bind thee in the swift ship, hand and foot, upright in the mast-stead, and from the mast let rope-ends be tied, that with delight thou mayest hear the voice of the Sirens. And if thou shalt beseech thy company and bid them to loose thee, then let them bind thee with yet more bonds.[2]

A central theme in internet history since the 1990s is the rise of algorithmic power, enabled through the self-restraint of human governments.[3] Digital platforms were born weak and clumsy. Governments could have stamped them out to enforce traditional territorial boundaries and regulatory categories. They chose not to.[4] Once the digital tornado was unleashed, however, its path was not easily directed. Fledgling innovators in need of protection developed into dominant platforms that transformed many aspects of the world for the better, but also created serious harms through pervasive data collection and automated decision-making. The threats arose from the very attributes that made these digital systems so appealing.

The cycle is repeating itself. Another broad-based technological shift promises huge gains in both efficiency and freedom by replacing established points of control with open decentralized mechanisms. Startups spin visions of overwhelming established industries and surmounting government-established controls. And once again, a great challenge is how to restrain their own penchant for algorithmic overreach.

---

[1] Marc Andreessen, Why Bitcoin Matters, N.Y. *Times DealBook* (Jan. 21, 2014, 11:54 AM), https://deal book.nytimes.com/2014/01/21/why-bitcoin-matters/.

[2] Homer, The Odyssey, Book XII (Trans. S.H. Butcher and L. Lang, 1937).

[3] See, e.g., John Danaher, The Threat of Algocracy: Reality, Resistance and Accommodation, 29 *Phil. & Tech.* 245 (2016). Most of the contributions to this volume concern the challenge of algorithmic power in one form or another.

[4] See Kevin Werbach, The Federal Computer Commission, 84 *N.C. L. Rev.* 1 (2005).

This time, the candidate technology is blockchain, and the broader phenomenon of "distributed ledger" systems.[5] Blockchain technology is still relatively immature. There is significant uncertainty about how it will develop in the future, and whether it will achieve anything like its promised level of impact. Already, however, blockchain and its related phenomenon, cryptocurrencies, have captured the imagination of technologists, entrepreneurs, business executives, and governments around the world. The driver for this activity is the belief that blockchain can foster an "internet of value"[6] – a new internet that overcomes the intermediation and centralized control that are increasingly prominent in the current digital environment.[7]

THE NEXT WAVE?

Like the internet, blockchain and cryptocurrencies are stimulating dramatic levels of investment, startup activity, and media attention, as well as creating massive disruption of industries and passionate visions of societal transformation.[8] As with the internet, this excitement often gets ahead of reality. The internet economy recovered from the dotcom crash of the early 2000s to realize its potential through the growth of social media, cloud computing, and mobile connectivity. The crypto economy seems likely to experience a similar trajectory over time. To succeed at scale, however, blockchain-based networks and services will need to address the problem of governance. Immutability, the mechanism that allows these systems to generate trust without central authorities, also creates inherent weaknesses that sometimes turn into catastrophic failures.

The Blockchain Phenomenon

For centuries, ledgers have been the foundation for the accounting and record-keeping around which societies are organized.[9] However, they have always been centralized: controlled by one or more entities with power over the recording and

---

[5] See Kevin Werbach, *The Blockchain and the New Architecture of Trust* 14 (2018) [hereinafter Werbach, New Architecture]. I use blockchain here as a generic term for the collection of cryptocurrency, blockchain, and distributed ledger technologies. Not all blockchain networks have an integral cryptocurrency, and not all cryptocurrencies use a data structure involving chains of transaction blocks. What they share are common properties such as decentralization (no one entity can control the status of the ledger) and immutability (transactions once made are, ideally, impossible to alter).

[6] Although now widely used, the "internet of value" phrase is most widely associated with the blockchain payments firm Ripple. See, e.g., Shanna Leonard, The Internet of Value: What It Means and How It Benefits Everyone, *Ripple Insights*, June 21, 2017, https://ripple.com/insights/the-internet-of-value-what-it-means-and-how-it-benefits-everyone/.

[7] See Steven Johnson, Beyond the Bitcoin Bubble, N.Y. *Times Mag.*, Jan. 16, 2018, *available at* https://www.nytimes.com/2018/01/16/magazine/beyond-the-bitcoin-bubble.html.

[8] See, e.g., Don Tapscott and Alex Tapscott, *Blockchain Revolution* (2016).

[9] See Quinn DuPont and Bill Maurer, *Ledgers and Law in the Blockchain*, King's Rev., June 23, 2016; Douglas Allen, *The Institutional Revolution: Measurement and the Economic Emergence of the Modern World* (2011).

approval of transactions. Even when there are multiple copies of information, one must either be designated as the master or there must a reconciliation process to redress any inconsistencies. Blockchain offers a decentralized alternative. Each party to a transaction can control its own information, while still trusting the information it sees from others.

Someone, or a group of people, using the pseudonym Satoshi Nakamoto kicked off the blockchain phenomenon on October 31, 2008 with the distribution on an internet mailing list of a short whitepaper titled *Bitcoin: A Peer-to-Peer Electronic Cash System*.[10] As extraordinary a breakthrough as it represented, there were virtually no technical advances in the paper. Instead, Nakamoto cleverly combined concepts from several streams of academic research and hobbyist tinkering, and then applied them to create the first workable form of private digital cash.[11] The Bitcoin network, based on voluntary participation and open-source software, launched in January 2009. Other cryptocurrencies followed. Many added additional functionality and expanded the technology beyond financial applications. A blockchain ledger can reliably record anything. Even more exciting, the ledger can function as a global distributed computer, which operates reliably without anyone in charge. Blockchain technology thus promises to eliminate inefficient intermediaries and overcome interorganizational trust gaps in an extraordinary range of contexts, from supply chain management to digital collectibles to the internet of things to property transfers.[12]

Although designed for functions such as payments and decentralized software applications, cryptocurrencies have so far found their most active use in speculative trading as a financial asset class. The price of bitcoin fluctuated for several years and then skyrocketed during 2017. At its peak in December 2017, the aggregate value of bitcoin in circulation exceeded $200 billion, and the overall cryptocurrency market was more than triple that.[13] Thousands of startups around the world began developing blockchain-based technologies, many of them issuing digital "tokens" to fund their networks. Most of the world's major financial services and industrial firms began to explore potential applications, and virtually all of the leading enterprise information technology services vendors developed substantial blockchain practices.[14]

---

[10]   Satoshi Nakamoto, *Bitcoin: A Peer-to-Peer Electronic Cash System*, https://bitcoin.org/bitcoin.pdf.
[11]   See Arvind Narayanan and Jeremy Clark, Bitcoin's Academic Pedigree, 60 *Comms.* ACM 36 (2017).
[12]   See Werbach, New Architecture, supra note 5, at 82–3.
[13]   See Stan Higgins, *$600 Billion: Cryptocurrency Market Cap Sets New Record*, *Coindesk* (Dec. 18, 2017, 6:50 PM UTC), https://www.coindesk.com/600-billion-cryptocurrency-market-cap-sets-new-record/; Historical Snapshot- December 31, 2017, *CoinMarketCap* (2017) (valuing the market cap of Bitcoin at approximately $221 Billion). These numbers somewhat overstate the actual value of available bitcoin, as it ignores the substantial amount of the cryptocurrency that has been stolen or for which the cryptographic keys have been lost.
[14]   See Werbach, New Architecture, supra note 5, at 84.

For those who lived through the dotcom bubble of the late 1990s, the parallels are striking. Projects with little more than a whitepaper raised tens of millions of dollars from investors around the world. Companies saw their value skyrocket overnight, without any real customer adoption. Experts talked of a new economy in which old metrics were no longer useful, and established industry leaders were soon swept away. And, as with the dotcom bubble of 1998–99, the 2017 cryptocurrency bubble was quickly followed by a brutal "crypto winter," in which prices plummeted and many projects were abandoned.[15]

Despite overexuberant claims and widespread illicit activity, however, blockchain technology itself, like the internet, is no fraud. It represents an immature but foundational development whose impacts will unfold over time. Where the internet lowered costs of transferring information, blockchain lowers costs of transferring value.[16] The impacts of this shift will be broad. Secure value exchange is not just a property of banking and payments; it is a basic building block of markets and society. Standing behind the money and security is a deeper property of trust.[17]

Blockchain as a Trust-Based Technology

Blockchain is fundamentally a trust-based technology.[18] Although Bitcoin relies on blockchain architecture as its foundation for digital currency, blockchain technology itself has been applied to a broad range of other applications. The unifying attribute of these applications is that they require a network of participants to preserve the integrity of shared information. If digital assets on the network cannot be trusted, for example, they are of little value. The distinctive attribute of the blockchain approach is that it expands trust in the system as a whole by minimizing trust in specific authorities or intermediaries that may prove fallible.[19] Investor and LinkedIn co-founder Reid Hoffman cleverly calls this, "trustless trust."[20] The key technical arrangement is known as consensus: All participants must converge on, and receive verifiable assurances of, the exact state of the network, without any enforceable formal agreements.

---

[15] See Paul Vigna, Bitcoin Is in the Dumps, Spreading Gloom Over Crypto World, *Wall St. J.*, March 19, 2019, https://www.wsj.com/articles/bitcoin-is-in-the-dumps-spreading-gloom-over-crypto-world-11552927208.

[16] See Christian Catalini and Joshua Gans, *Some Simple Economics of the Blockchain*, Rotman School of Mgmt. Working Paper No. 2874598 (2017), https://papers.ssrn.com/sol3/papers.cfm?abstract_id=2874598; Marco Iansiti and Karim R. Lakhani, *The Truth about Blockchain*, 95 *Harv. Bus. Rev.* 118 (Jan./Feb. 2017).

[17] See Werbach, New Architecture, supra note 5, at 84–6.

[18] See id.; Sinclair Davidson et al., Blockchains and the Economic Institutions of Capitalism, 14 *J. Institutional Econ.* 639 (2018).

[19] See Kevin Werbach, Trust, but Verify: Why the Blockchain Needs the Law, 32 *Berkeley Tech. L.J.* 489 (2018) [hereinafter Werbach, Trust but Verify]; Werbach, New Architecture, supra note 5, at 28–30.

[20] Werbach, Trust but Verify, supra note 19, at 79–81.

Bitcoin, for example, uses a system called proof of work to avoid the need to trust a bank or intermediary to verify payments. It establishes a competition every ten minutes to validate chunks of transactions (referred to as blocks) and earn a reward (in bitcoin). The winner is effectively selected at random, however the amount of computer processing power each Bitcoin validator, known as "miner," brings to bear will increase their likelihood of winning. Bitcoin miners will therefore spend tens of millions of dollars per day in hardware and electricity to increase the likelihood of winning. The purpose of the proof of work system is twofold: To incentivize participation (on the part of the miners) and to constrain behavior (on the part of anyone who might undermine the integrity of the system). It also enhances the security of the system as a whole: An attacker must compete against the computational power as the rest of the network combined.

Thus, even if any participant in Bitcoin's proof of work system is selfishly motivated to steal from the network, none has the power to do so. Moreover, the network is "censorship-resistant," meaning any transaction cannot easily be altered or removed. There is no master control point that everything depends on. Anyone around the world can become a Bitcoin node by running some open-source software, and the network functions as long as there is enough mining activity to guarantee security.

Bitcoin's proof of work system is the most well-established blockchain consensus mechanism. Since the network launched in 2009, no one has successfully undermined it to alter the transaction ledger or spend the same coin twice.[21] However, it is not the only possible approach. Bitcoin's success sparked an explosion of research and experimentation with approaches making different fundamental tradeoffs among scalability, security, and decentralization. Other prominent blockchain networks include Ethereum, Ripple, EOS, Dash, Monero, and ZCash. There is also ongoing work to address the inherent scalability and functionality limitations in Bitcoin's design. And in recent years, enterprises and governments have begun to implement permissioned blockchain networks that, unlike Bitcoin, are limited to authorized participants.[22]

---

[21] This does not mean no bitcoin has been stolen. Cryptocurrencies are bearer instruments. Whoever controls a private cryptographic key effectively owns the currency associated with it. The wallets and exchanges where most users store their cryptocurrency are separate from the decentralized consensus ledger itself. Those centralized systems can be hacked, or keys can be stolen through other means. An estimated $1.2 billion of cryptocurrency was stolen between the beginning of 2017 and May 2018. See Gertrude Chavez-Dreyfuss, About $1.2 Billion in Cryptocurrency Stolen Since 2017: Cybercrime Group, *Reuters* (May 24, 2018, 10:59 AM), https://www.reuters.com/article/us-crypto-currency-crime /about-1-2-billion-in-cryptocurrency-stolen-since-2017-cybercrime-group-idUSKCN1IP2LU.

[22] See UK Government Chief Scientific Advisor, Distributed Ledger Technology: Beyond Block Chain (2015), https://www.gov.uk/government/uploads/system/uploads/attachment_data/file/492972/gs-16-1-distributed-ledger-technology.pdf; Tim Swanson, Consensus-as-a-Service: A Brief Report on the Emergence of Permissioned, Distributed Ledger Systems (Apr. 6, 2015), http://www.ofnumbers.com /wp-content/uploads/2015/04/Permissioned-distributed-ledgers.pdf.

The other important innovation of blockchain systems is the smart contract.[23] Smart contracts are securely self-executing software code that run on a blockchain network. Essentially, smart contracts allow a blockchain application to function as a parallel distributed computer, in which every machine running the application provably does so in exactly the same way. Smart contracts are the foundation of the functionality of blockchain technology. Smart contracts are broader than legal contracts, in that they can – within limits of performance scalability – encode anything that can be written into a computer program. From a conceptual and doctrinal perspective, however, they are simply contracts.[24] They allocate rights and responsibilities among parties who voluntarily bind themselves into enforceable commitments. Contracts are a powerful means of generating trust because they backstop voluntary human commitments with formalized legal enforcement embodying the power of the state. Smart contracts are designed to offer a similar kind of confidence backed by the integrity of the blockchain ledger. Which is to say, blockchain is a legal or regulatory technology.[25] It is a method of governance.[26]

However, to the extent blockchain is a governance technology, it is immature, without the flexibility or capacity to correct for errors or unforeseen situations. In order to garner broader trust and move past its current limited applications, blockchain governance must become more robust.

LASHED TO THE MAST: THE TWO SIDES OF IMMUTABILITY

In Homer's *The Odyssey*, the hero Odysseus encounters sirens, mermaids who lure sailors to their deaths with their enchanting song.[27] Odysseus is curious about the content of their songs, but he knows that if he hears them, he will not be able to resist plunging into the ocean. So he orders his men to lash him to the mast of his ship. He further orders them to fill their ears with wax, so that if he later urges them to untie him, they will not hear his pleas. Odysseus thus empowers himself to hear the music

---

[23]   See Kevin Werbach and Nicolas Cornell, Contracts Ex Machina, 67 *Duke L.J.* 314 (2017); Nick Szabo, Formalizing and Securing Relationships on Public Networks, 2 *First Monday* (1997), http://ojphi.org/ojs/index.php/fm/article/view/548.

[24]   See Werbach and Cornell, supra note 23.

[25]   See Lawrence Lessig, *Code and Other Laws of Cyberspace* (2nd revised ed. 2006); Werbach, New Architecture, supra note 5, at 189; Primavera de Filippi and Aaron Wright, *Blockchain and Law: The Rule of Code* (2018).

[26]   See Rachel O'Dwyer, Code != Law: Explorations of the Blockchain as a Mode of Algorithmic Governance (2018), https://www.academia.edu/34734732/Code_Law_Explorations_of_the_Blockchain_as_a_Mode_of_Algorithmic_Governance; Sinclair Davidson, Primavera De Filippi, and Jason Potts, Economics of Blockchain (March 8, 2016), http://dx.doi.org/10.2139/ssrn.2744751; Marcella Atzori, Blockchain Technology and Decentralized Governance: Is the State Still Necessary? (2015), http://nzz-files-prod.s3-website-eu-west-1.amazonaws.com/files/9/3/1/blockchain+Is+the+State+Still+Necessary_1.18689931.pdf.

[27]   See The Odyssey, supra note 2.

The same strategy lies at the heart of the blockchain's capability to decentralize trust. In the blockchain context, this strategy is known as immutability. Immutability is a great strength of blockchain-based governance systems, but also potentially a catastrophic weakness.

that no mortal man can survive. He does so, ironically, by radically disempowering himself and his sailors at the critical moment.

Blockchain Immutability

Immutability on a blockchain means that once a transaction has been incorporated into a validated block and added to the ledger, it cannot be altered.[28] This kind of guarantee is quite difficult to achieve in digital systems, whose records are naturally ephemeral and encoded in the universal language of binary ones and zeros. In the words of computer scientist and smart contracts pioneer Nick Szabo: "Typical computers are computational etch-a-sketch, while blockchains are computational amber."[29] Blockchain systems enforce immutability by making every piece of information reflect the consensus agreement of a network of computers. Changing even the smallest fact means convincing a large percentage of the network to reconsider its settled transaction history. The algorithms and cryptography of the consensus system are designed to make that exceedingly difficult.

From an internet policy perspective, immutability seems to put things backwards. The internet regulation debate is fundamentally about freedom. Decentralized global networks make it easier for people to engage in conduct that some would like to prevent, whether that involves dissidents challenging authoritarian regimes or consumers accessing media they didn't pay for. As only became clear over time, those networks also concentrate power in digital platforms whose freedom of action is difficult to shackle under conventional mechanisms of antitrust, contract, or privacy protection. Governments responded to the first concern through a variety of mechanisms; their ability to put the platform power and surveillance capitalism genies back in the bottle is yet to be seen.

Like the internet, blockchain systems are often described as technologies of freedom, but in their core functioning they are just the opposite. What makes a blockchain trustworthy is precisely that it restricts freedom to diverge from the consensus state of the ledger. This characteristic is important for security. Transactions involving scarce or valuable assets would not be trustworthy if someone could easily alter the ledger. Beyond

---

[28] See Nick Szabo, *Money, Blockchains, and Social Scalability, Unenumerated* (Feb. 9, 2017), http://unenumerated.blogspot.com/2017/02/money-blockchains-and-social-scalability.html ("To say that data is post-unforgeable or immutable means that it can't be undetectably altered after being committed to the blockchain."); Angela Walch, The Path of the Blockchain Lexicon (and the Law), 36 *Rev. Banking & Fin. L.* 713 (2016–2017); Marc Pilkington, Blockchain Technology: Principles & Applications, in *Research Handbook on Digital Transformations* 15 (F. Xavier Olleros & Majlinda Zhegu eds., 2016).

[29] Szabo, supra note 28.

that, however, immutability is blockchain's most significant contribution to governance. It is also the property that creates the most significant risks of catastrophic failure.[30]

Immutability poses a novel set of legal and regulatory challenges. For the most part, cyberlaw is concerned with the plasticity of digital systems. Software can be coded to arbitrage around legal rules. Information can be combined and analyzed to create challenges not present at the outset, such as data aggregation to undermine privacy protections. The challenge has been to tie down actors and systems to particular jurisdictions or classifications. Immutability creates a different problem. The illegitimacy or harm of certain actions may be well-established, but no one may have the ability to do anything about it.

Immutability as a Means of Trust

Immutability is essential to blockchain technology in several ways. It is a proxy for the basic security of the network. If you know that information you see on a blockchain is immutable, you can rely on it. Even more significant, immutability is implicit in blockchain's approach to trust. If any actor had the power to change the ledger retrospectively, everyone else would need to trust that actor not to do so in secret or illegitimate ways. This is true whether the empowered entity is a thief, a validator, an intermediary, or a government. A blockchain network must be immutable to be censorship-resistant, because a censor is a government agent that demands changes to the information recorded. Thus, the decentralized model of blockchain trust depends on immutability.

Satoshi Nakamoto emphasized this point in the original Bitcoin whitepaper. In the centralized financial system, he or she or they pointed out: "[C]ompletely non-reversible transactions are not really possible, since financial institutions cannot avoid mediating disputes."[31] This need for dispute resolution puts power in the hands of governments and intermediaries. And thus, as Nakamoto continued: "With the possibility of reversal, the need for trust [in particular entities] spreads."[32] In order to separate generalized trust in transactions from trust in specific fallible actors, Bitcoin had to ensure that records on the ledger could not be reversed.

Immutability is not a precise concept.[33] In particular, it does not mean changing the ledger is categorically precluded.[34] For Bitcoin and similar blockchain networks,

---

[30] There are also plenty of ill-intentioned parties that use blockchain technology to facilitate illegal or unethical activity. See, e.g., Kevin Werbach, What the Russia Hack Indictments Reveal about Bitcoin, N.Y. Times, July 22, 2018, https://www.nytimes.com/2018/07/22/opinion/russia-hacking-indictments-bitcoin.html. These issues lie beyond the scope of this paper.

[31] Nakamoto, supra note 10.

[32] Id.

[33] See Walch, supra note 28.

[34] See id. at 738–41; Werbach, Trust but Verify, supra note 19; Gideon Greenspan, The Blockchain Immutability Myth, Coindesk (May 9, 2017), http://www.coindesk.com/blockchain-immutability-myth/.

immutability is a statistical property. The more time that has passed since a block was validated, the less likely it has been altered.[35] However, the integrity of the network can never be established absolutely; there is always some miniscule possibility that an attacker has successfully altered the chain.[36] Some other blockchain systems provide for "finality," which after a certain time prohibits changes to a validated block.[37] Even then, however, the ledger is not truly immutable.[38] And public blockchains are always potentially vulnerable to "51% attacks" if someone can obtain a majority of the total power in the network.[39] There has never been a successful 51 percent attack against Bitcoin, but there have been several against less-valuable cryptocurrencies.[40]

There are also situations in which changing the status of validated blocks may be desirable. Because blockchain networks are decentralized, every node can independently propose a new block to add to the existing chain. The consensus process is designed to ensure that the network continually converges to a single valid chain. When some percentage of nodes on a blockchain network choose to follow a different path than the rest of the network, it is called a fork.[41] This may occur for mundane reasons. For example, developers may upgrade a network's software with new features that are not backward-compatible with the earlier version. Those nodes running the non-upgraded software will remain on a different blockchain from everyone else, although if all goes well, that chain will quickly die out. Sometimes a fork is necessary to fix problems with the network, as when denial-of-service attacks were grinding the Ethereum network to a halt in late 2016.[42] A successful fork, however, can effectively reverse or alter prior transactions, thus undermining immutability.

The imperfection of blockchain immutability corresponds to the imperfection of trust. Trust is not the same as certainty. No one would say they trusted that 2 + 2 = 4, or that a heavy object dropped from a height will fall toward the ground. Neither

---

[35] See Tim Ferriss, *The Quiet Master of Cryptocurrency — Nick Szabo*, Tim Ferriss Show (June 4, 2017), https://tim.blog/2017/06/04/nick-szabo/.

[36] Of course, this is true of centralized financial networks as well.

[37] See Vitalik Buterin, *On Settlement Finality*, Ethereum Blog (May 9, 2016), https://blog.ethereum.org/2016/05/09/on-settlement-finality/.

[38] The consensus algorithms that provide for finality also generally trade off some other property, such as security or decentralization, for the guarantee that prior blocks may not be changed.

[39] For proof of work systems like Bitcoin, this means a majority of computation devoted to mining.

[40] See Daniel Oberhaus, *Cryptocurrency Miners Are Sabotaging Blockchains for Their Personal Gain*, Motherboard (May 25, 2018, 11:00 AM), https://motherboard.vice.com/en_us/article/a3a38e/what-is-a-51-percent-attack-silicon-valley-bitcoin-gold-verge-monacoin-cryptocurrency. The lower the total value of a cryptocurrency, the less resources it makes economic sense to spend on mining, which means the costs of a successful 51 percent attack are also lower.

[41] A soft fork means both paths are compatible. There is still one consensus chain of blocks, but some network nodes have access to different features than the others. A hard fork means there are two incompatible chains after a certain point.

[42] See Thomas Jay Rush, *Defeating the Ethereum DDOS Attacks*, Medium (Feb. 12, 2017), https://medium.com/@tjayrush/defeating-the-ethereum-ddos-attacks-d3d773a9a063.

unshakable confidence in an outcome nor a rational calculus that drives reliance is equivalent to trust. Trust is a human quality, and as such, it requires some modicum of vulnerability.[43] It is the willingness to commit even though there is some residual risk in doing so. What makes trust valuable is that it goes beyond certainty. A trustworthy counterparty allows one to dispense with cumbersome verification or self-help enforcement, greatly enhancing the scope and efficiency of transactions.[44]

Trustworthy systems must therefore balance the necessary confidence to inspire action with the acknowledgement of imperfection. A thick bank vault may nonetheless be cracked, just as blockchain immutability may in some circumstances be undermined. Moreover, trust expands with experience or relationships. A system that is foolproof on paper may not be in practice. The design of Bitcoin published in 2008 convinced a small number of early adopters, but it was only after years of secure operation that more mainstream users were willing to trust their money to the seemingly strange decentralized system. Just as validated blocks on a public blockchain become more trustworthy over time, the entire blockchain becomes more trustworthy with successful experience.

Immutability as Commitment Device

Another way to think of blockchain immutability is as a kind of commitment device. Economists define a commitment device as "an arrangement entered into by an agent who restricts his or her future choice set by making certain choices more expensive, perhaps infinitely expensive."[45] Commitment devices bridge between our present and future selves. Odysseus rationally knew ahead of time that he should not heed the call of the sirens. However, he also realized that, in that nonrational moment, he would be powerless to resist. So he prospectively deprived himself not only of the capability to act, but of the capability to belay his earlier order to his crew.

The need for commitment devices is not limited to mythical mermaids. It comes up virtually any time we envision our future selves. Many of us have an easier time resisting the prospect of ice cream tomorrow than the Ben & Jerrys in front of us right now. In addition, behavioral economists have identified several cognitive biases that make actual behavior in the future diverge from rational expectations in the present.[46] Most notably, people tend to discount benefits hyperbolically. According to textbooks, the net present value of a future benefit declines linearly

---

[43] See Werbach, New Architecture, supra note 5, at 77.

[44] See Francis Fukuyama, *Trust: The Social Virtues and the Creation of Prosperity* (1995); Niklas Luhmann, *Trust and Power* (1979).

[45] Gharad Bryan et al., Commitment Devices, 2 Ann. Rev. Econ. 671–98 (2010). The authors include two additional conditions for precision. The agent must value the commitment effect itself, as opposed to, for example, merely paying now for a benefit later. And the commitment must not be for some strategic purpose, such as deterring action that might invoke it or influencing someone else.

[46] See id.

The Siren Song

over time based on the relevant discount rate. In practice, most people overvalue near-term benefits and strongly undervalue those arriving far in the future.[47] Just as they have a hard time imagining the beneficial results of compound interest, they fail to properly appreciate even large far-off gains.

A commitment device allows us to bind our future selves to our present rational calculus. Yale University economists Gharad Bryan, Dean Karlan, and Scott Nelson give a simple example of a runner about to embark on a ten-mile training session.[48] She wants to run the whole way, but she knows that at some point she will become tired and likely slow to a walk. So she signs a contract agreeing to pay a friend $1,000 if she fails to run the whole way. The committed payment makes the walking option considerably less desirable.

Those who commit transactions to a blockchain do so with the knowledge that they are not easily reversible. As Satoshi Nakamoto explained in the Bitcoin whitepaper, they are choosing nonreversibility ahead of time to avoid the trust-inducing processes of mediation and dispute resolution that will seem appealing in the future. Their commitment is necessary if the blockchain itself is to be trusted.

Credible commitments are essential to any bargaining relationship.[49] If I tell you I won't pay more than $100, your willingness to agree to my terms depends on your assessment of my credibility. In particular, contractual arrangements depend on the ability of the parties to convince one another that their commitments are credible. If you do not believe I will deliver the products you are paying for, you will not enter into such a contract with me. As elaborated by economist Oliver Williamson, the game theorist Thomas Schelling analogized credible commitments to hostage-taking in primitive societies.[50] The hostages were part of the agreement process. Each side would be confident in the performance of the other, because otherwise it would kill its hostages. Such gruesome mechanisms seemed necessary in the absence of legal dispute resolution mechanisms. As Williamson explains, we no longer require human hostages because we assume "efficacious rules of law regarding contract disputes are in place and that these are applied by the courts in an informed, sophisticated, and low-cost way."[51]

The philosopher John Elster, in his essay *Ulysses and the Sirens*, points out that commitment devices turn the rational actor model of neoclassical economics against itself.[52] Credible commitments are necessary for the contractual process of market exchange; otherwise, counterparties would breach agreements at will. However, carrying out those threats often requires behaving in a way that would

---

[47] See Richard Thaler, Some Empirical Evidence on Dynamic Inconsistency, 8 *Econ. Lett.* 201 (1981).

[48] See id. at 674.

[49] See Thomas Schelling, An Essay on Bargaining, 46 *Am. Econ. Rev.* 281–306 (1956).

[50] See Oliver Williamson, Credible Commitments: Using Hostages to Support Exchange, 73 *Am. Econ. Rev.* 519, 519 (1983).

[51] Id. at 520.

[52] See John Elster, Ulysses and the Sirens: A Theory of Imperfect Rationality, 16 *Soc. Sci. Info.* 469 (1977). Elster uses the Roman name of Ulysses instead of the Greek Odysseus.

otherwise be irrational. At the later moment when parties have already made relationship-specific investments in a contract, for example, consenting to an unjustified reduction in price would be preferable to walking away entirely. In an extreme case, Thomas Schelling famously applied game theory to the doctrine of mutually assured destruction in the Cold War. The United States and the Soviet Union avoided nuclear war by committing themselves to retaliation that would end life on Earth in the event of an attack. Humans, Elster concludes, are "imperfectly rational creatures able to deal strategically with their own myopia."[53]

THINGS GO WRONG

Serious problems emerge when the imperfect rationality implicit in credible commitments is implemented through the perfectly rational vehicle of computers executing smart contracts on a blockchain. The dark side to immutability is that even invalid or illegitimate transactions cannot easily be reversed. Immutability creates the potential for catastrophic failures with no clear means of remediation.

Three examples illustrate the problems with blockchain immutability: The DAO hack, the Parity wallet bug, and the abortive Segwit2x fork.

The DAO Hack (2016)

In June 2016, approximately \$50 million in Ether cryptocurrency was extracted from the DAO, a decentralized crowdfunding application.[54] The DAO was a set of smart contracts on the Ethereum network that allowed individuals who purchased tokens to vote "yes" or "no" on financing a given project.[55] The more money a user put into the DAO, the more votes the user would receive, and subsequently the greater share the user would receive of income from successful projects. The fund raised 11.5 million Ether through its initial crowd sale, worth approximately \$150 million at the time and representing nearly 15 percent of Ether in circulation.[56] Before it ever began funding projects, however, the DAO was undermined by a catastrophic hack.

---

[53] Id. at 502.

[54] See Klint Finley, A \$50 Million Hack Just Showed that the DAO Was All Too Human, *Wired* (June 18, 2016), https://www.wired.com/2016/06/50-million-hack-just-showed-dao-human/.

[55] DAO is an abbreviation for decentralized autonomous organization, a concept of a corporation governed through self-executing smart contracts. See Vitalik Buterin, DAOs, DACs, DAs and More: An Incomplete Terminology Guide, *Ethereum Blog* (May 6, 2014), https://blog.ethereum.org /2014/05/06/daos-dacs-das-and-more-an-incomplete-terminology-guide/. The DAO was styled as the first real-world implementation of the concept, which cryptocurrency advocates such as Ethereum founder Vitalik Buterin had developed a few years earlier.

[56] See Toshendra Kumar Sharma, *Details of the DAO Hacking in Ethereum in 2016*, *Blockchain Council* (Aug. 20, 2017), https://www.blockchain-council.org/blockchain/details-of-the-dao-hacking-in-ethereum-in-2016/.

Someone took advantage of a vulnerability in the smart contract code that governed a narrow component of the fund's payment structure.[57] By repeatedly executing the same request function, the hacker was able to drain roughly one-third of the pool of committed investment currency into a private "child DAO." Thankfully, the system included a failsafe that prohibited fund withdrawals from the system for thirty days. During that period, the Ethereum Foundation produced a software upgrade that forked the entire blockchain to a new state in which the stolen funds were returned to their rightful owners.[58] However, the fork was controversial. It essentially broke the immutability of the blockchain in order to reverse the theft. Most members of the community considered this a worthwhile tradeoff. The price of Ether recovered from the uncertainty the DAO hack generated, and then climbed dramatically the following year. Many viewed the Ethereum Foundation's willingness to act a comforting example of effective governance.[59]

Others were not convinced. Immutability, they argued, was the essence of block-chain decentralization. If the Ethereum Foundation could convince most network nodes to roll back $50 million of transactions once, it could do so again. Perhaps the next time would be less clearly a case of theft. Perhaps it would be a controversial move that advantaged the Foundation's leadership over the rest of the community. And given the disruption involved in implementing a hard fork, it made no sense to take this tack every time someone exploited a smart contract bug. Where was the line to determine when immutability should be broken? While these opponents were a minority and couldn't prevent the hard fork, they could do something else. They started mining the other side of the fork, the chain in which the DAO funds were still in possession of the hacker.[60] This fork, labeled Ethereum Classic (ETC), continues today to exist in parallel to the main Ethereum (ETH) blockchain.[61]

The ETC objection to the DAO fork centered around credible commitments. Why trust the blockchain if it can be forked whenever something goes wrong? A noncredible commitment is worth nothing, or worse. When financial institutions in the 2000s realized they were "too big to fail" and would be bailed out for the government if their bets failed to pay off, their appetite for risk grew to the unsustainable levels that precipitated the global financial crisis of 2008. When several Central and Eastern European governments experienced hyperinflation in the years after World War I, in spite of increasingly vigorous monetary policy initiatives, they

---

[57] See id.

[58] See E. J. Spode, The Great Cryptocurrency Heist, *Aeon* (Feb. 14, 2017), https://aeon.co/essays/trust-the-inside-story-of-the-rise-and-fall-of-ethereum.

[59] See Nathaniel Popper, Move Over, Bitcoin. Ether Is the Digital Currency of the Moment, *N.Y. Times DealBook*, June 19, 2017, https://www.nytimes.com/2017/06/19/business/dealbook/ethereum-bitcoin-digital-currency.html.

[60] See David Morris, The Bizarre Fallout of Ethereum's Epic Fail, *Fortune* (Sept. 4, 2016), http://fortune.com/2016/09/04/ethereum-fall-out.

[61] The two chains are identical up to the moment of the fork, then diverge. All holders of Ether at the time saw their holdings double, although Ethereum Classic coins are worth substantially less than those of the more popular Ethereum.

mandated convertibility of their currencies into gold.[62] The gold standard made it impossible to debase the currency too far. By the 1970s, when countries were more stable and central banks more sophisticated, the gold standard and its limiting tether to physical assets were no longer needed.

The ideal credible commitment is strong enough to promote the desired behavior, but weak enough to be overcome through appropriate mechanisms when absolutely necessary. The ad hoc nature of the response to the DAO hack, and the fact that most of those connected with the DAO were also associated with the Ethereum Foundation, created skepticism about the need to break immutability.

The Parity Wallet Bug (2017)

In November 2017, Parity Technologies, an Ethereum-based blockchain developer, suffered a critical security vulnerability that affected certain users of the company's wallet software for storing cryptocurrency.[63] An update caused a bug that could have allowed a malicious user to control a large number of Parity's "multsignature" wallets. A user found the flaw and, allegedly to prevent theft, deleted the smart contract involved.[64] Unfortunately, this made it impossible for anyone to access the relevant wallets. As a result of this hack more than $280 million of Ether was frozen.[65] While the Ether was still immutably recorded on the Ethereum blockchain, it was simply inaccessible. Like the DAO, Parity had close ties to the Ethereum Foundation. Gavin Wood, its CEO, was the co-founder and chief technologist of Ethereum, and a large component of the frozen Ether was associated with Parity's own token offering for a blockchain interoperability project called Polkadot. A hard fork to restore the trapped Ether would seem like a bailout for insiders. Other solutions met with similar skepticism.[66] As of summer 2018, the funds remained trapped.

Unlike the DAO hack, the Parity wallet bug had no villain.[67] The cryptocurrency was apparently rendered inaccessible by accident. Yet the impact was similar.

---

[62] See Thomas J. Sargent, The Ends of Four Big Inflations, in *Inflation: Causes and Effects* (R.E. Hall, ed., 1982).

[63] See Parity Technologies, Security Alert (November 8, 2017), https://paritytech.io/security-alert-2/.

[64] See Jordan Pearson, Ethereum Wallet Company Knew about Critical Flaw That Let a User Lock Up Millions, *Motherboard* (Nov. 15, 2017, 2:21pm), https://motherboard.vice.com/en_us/article/d3djwj/ethereum-wallet-parity-knew-about-critical-flaw-that-let-user-devops199-lock-up-millions.

[65] See Ryan Browne, "Accidental" Bug May Have Frozen $280 Million Worth of Digital Coin Ether in a Cryptocurrency Wallet, *CNBC* (Nov. 8, 2017, 6:42 AM), https://www.cnbc.com/2017/11/08/accidental-bug-may-have-frozen-280-worth-of-ether-on-parity-wallet.html.

[66] See Rachel Rose O'Leary, The New Last-Ditch Effort to Unfreeze a $260 Million Ethereum Fortune, *Coindesk* (Apr. 18, 2018, 4:00 UTC), https://www.coindesk.com/new-last-ditch-effort-unfreeze-260-million-ethereum-fortune/.

[67] There is some question whether the user, Devops199, offered a truthful account, or was actually behaving maliciously. Even if deletion of the smart contract was malicious, however, it was not theft, because no one obtained access to the trapped funds.

Legitimate users who relied on the immutability of the blockchain lost their money as a consequence of that very immutability function. There was no mechanism to alter undesirable transactions after the fact, even when a transaction – locking every user permanently out of their wallets – produced benefits for no one.

Parity wallet users had good reason to trust the firm's software with their cryptocurrency. Parity's leaders were highly respected technologists who were intimately involved in the creation of Ethereum. Gavin Wood, in fact, was the primary creator of the Solidity programming language used for Ethereum smart contracts. One would not expect his company to make a relatively elementary Solidity coding flaw. And one would certainly not expect it to leave the flaw in place for months after being told about it.[68] Yet the reality is that individual and companies are fallible. Trusting Parity was as reasonable as trusting the banks that imploded during the 2008 financial crisis. The difference was that, thanks to a combination of government-mandated insurance and operational mechanisms, no one would ever find their money "permanently stuck" in a bank's savings account with no recourse.

Trust is a double-edged sword. Users trust Parity because its software operates on an immutable blockchain. However, they don't necessarily trust Parity enough to implement a hard fork to restore its frozen Ether. The second requires trust in specific human organizations, which is exactly what the blockchain's immutability was designed to overcome.

The SegWit 2x Battle (2017)

For a number of years, there has been a contentious technical debate among leading Bitcoin developers about how to scale the network. Bitcoin can process a theoretical maximum of seven transactions per second, which is thousands of times fewer than centralized payment-processing systems. As the price of Bitcoin rose and transaction activity increased, the network began to slow down even further. Some developers believed the solution was to change the protocol to increase the amount of data processed in each block. However, that would require a hard fork. It would represent the first substantial step away from the basic architecture that Satoshi Nakamoto outlined in 2008, which is the basis for the Bitcoin network's remarkable run of secure, uninterrupted operation. Other developers felt that different mechanisms could address the scalability challenge without changing the core protocol, or that rock-solid security was simply more important than handling more transactions.

In spring 2017, a compromise was brokered among major Bitcoin-related companies to implement two competing scalability proposals.[69] The first, SegWit, could go

---

[68] See O'Leary, supra note 64.

[69] See Laura Shin, Will This Battle for the Soul of Bitcoin Destroy It?, *Forbes* (Oct. 23, 2017, 1:35 pm), https://www.forbes.com/sites/laurashin/2017/10/23/will-this-battle-for-the-soul-of-bitcoin-destroy-it /#42adb77f3d3c.

into effect prior to a hard fork.[70] It provided foundation for scaling Bitcoin without disturbing the core protocol. The second component was a doubling of the block size referred to as 2x, which was to be implemented in a hard fork later in the year. The SegWit implementation proceeded smoothly. As the date for the 2x hard fork approached, however, controversy reemerged. Critics labeled the compromise, known as the New York Agreement, an illegitimate back-room deal and a corporate takeover of Bitcoin.[71] And it began to seem likely that, as with Ethereum Classic, some network nodes would continue mining the original, small block-size chain even after the fork. That led to speculation about which chain deserved to carry forward the "Bitcoin" name and its BTC ticker symbol on exchanges.[72] The hard fork was ultimately abandoned.[73]

The Segwit 2x battle, unlike the prior two examples, didn't deprive anyone of their cryptocurrency. It involved neither theft nor buggy code. Yet it provoked a similar sense of existential crisis over the essence of Bitcoin. Does immutability mean it must be next to impossible to change the basic properties of a blockchain network, in addition to the transaction records it stores? Removing human intervention from every commitment by means of a software-implemented commitment device seems well and good, but software is created by humans too. They can't ever fully anticipate the needs of the future. At some point, there will be a need to evolve the system if it is to remain trustworthy. Yet the upgrade process itself opens the Pandora's Box that immutability was supposed to seal shut.

BE CAREFUL ABOUT YOUR COMMITMENTS

Political theorist Kenneth Shepsle distinguishes two forms of commitment device: Motivational and imperative.[74] The first involves commitments that are incentive compatible. That is to say, at the time the device operates, the person involved rationally desires to comply. The second form of commitment device requires coercion, because otherwise the person involved would not follow through on the commitment. Blockchain systems employ both. Consensus systems like proof of

---

[70] The term is short for "segregated witness," an allusion to the famous prisoners' dilemma scenario in game theory. Two alleged witnesses to a crime must be put in separate rooms in a prison, unable to communicate, in order to produce the classic result that both will confess.

[71] See Shin, supra note 69.

[72] See id.

[73] See Paul Vigna, Bitcoin Dodges Split that Threatened Tts Surging Price, *Wall St. J.* (Nov. 8, 2017, 3:25 pm), https://www.wsj.com/articles/bitcoin-dodges-split-that-threatened-its-surging-price -1510172701/. The price of Bitcoin spiked to new highs when the hard fork was called off, indicating that uncertainty about its outcome was a substantial overhang for investors. See Evelyn Cheng, Bitcoin Hits Record High after Developers Call Off Plans to Split Digital Currency, *CNBC* (Nov. 8, 2017, 12:40 pm), https://www.cnbc.com/2017/11/08/bitcoin-surges-11-percent-to-record-above-7800- after-developers-call-off-plans-to-split-digital-currency.html.

[74] See Kenneth A. Shepsle, Institutions and the Problem of Government Commitment, in *Social Theory for a Changing Society*, pp. 245, 247 (Pierre Bordieu and James S. Coleman, eds., 1991).

work create economic incentives for accurate validation of the ledger. In cryptocurrency circles, this approach is known as cryptoeconomics.[75] The blockchain is immutable because the costs of breaking it exceed the returns. By the same token, the immutability of smart contracts is imperative. The victims of the DAO hack or the Parity wallet bug were strongly incentivized to overturn the outputs of the smart contracts. They lacked the power to do so.

If, instead of approaching the beautiful sirens, Odysseus saw his boat heading directly for dangerous rocks, his cries to his men to turn the rudder would be futile. His commitment device would be operating beyond the intended scope, leading to disaster. As the three examples described earlier illustrate, the same issue appears in the blockchain context. Smart contracts cannot necessarily distinguish the scenarios for which immutability was designed from those where it causes harm. There are two fundamental reasons. Contracts of any consequence are generally incomplete; that is to say, they do not precisely specify outcomes for every possible scenario.[76] Smart contracts magnify this incompleteness. They can only express their terms in sharp-edged software code, eliminating the interpretive discretion of human judges and juries.[77]

The strong immutability of blockchain systems therefore creates significant opportunities for dramatic failures that undermine trust rather than cementing it. As Shepsle concludes: "[W]e should ... not be too precipitous in our admiration of commitment and our condemnation of discretion."[78] To avoid causing significant harm, blockchain-based solutions must do more than enforce immutability; they must incorporate regimes of governance to temper its excesses.[79]

Blockchain Governance by Design

Blockchain is a governance technology. Consensus algorithms shape how users of networks behave. Through affirmative incentives and cryptographically enforced limits on certain actions, these systems combat hostile conduct and promote cooperative behavior. They establish and enforce rules for "good order and workable arrangements," which is how the Nobel Prize-winning economist Oliver Williamson defines governance.[80] Governance provides a framework for establishing accountability, roles, and decision-making authority in an organization.

---

[75] See Werbach, New Architecture, supra note 5, at 47–8.
[76] See Werbach and Cornell, supra note 23; Oliver D. Hart, Incomplete Contracts and the Theory of the Firm, 4 J. L. Econ. & Org. 119–39 (1998).
[77] See Werbach and Cornell, supra note 23.
[78] Shepsle, supra note 74, at 249.
[79] Permissioned blockchain and distributed ledger networks do not face quite the same challenges. Because participants are identified and authorized, traditional mechanisms of consortium governance can be applied. While not always effective, such arrangements only require the agreement of a relatively small group of organizations to make governance decisions for the network.
[80] Oliver Williamson, The Economics of Governance, 95 Amer. Econ. Rev. 1, 1 (2005).

Digital governance is not a new phenomenon.[81] Software code, as Lawrence Lessig famously declared and many others have elaborated since, can function as a kind of law, with its own affordances and limitations.[82] Software-based systems can serve as alternatives to the state, markets, firms, and relational contracting as means of governing relationships. Facebook's newsfeed algorithms, YouTube's ContentID system for digital right management, and Uber's mobile application are examples of digital systems that constitute and shape communities. However, these communities are centralized. The operators of the network control the algorithms and adapt them to ultimately serve their interests. Blockchain instead maintains the possibility of decentralized digital governance. By disempowering intermediaries and network operators, it promises both greater efficiency and greater fairness. Nick Szabo, one of the original developers of the idea of smart contracts, describes this property as social scalability.[83] A blockchain-based system can, it is claimed, avoid the human biases, imperfections, and inefficiencies that make it difficult for communities to scale without rigid hierarchy.[84]

FROM COMMITMENTS TO INSTITUTIONS

Blockchain governance epitomizes a broader challenge in our increasingly connected and digitized world. There is a growing gap between rule definition and rule execution. The terms of a smart contract must be specified entirely ex ante. A conventional legal contract, by contrast, is subject to relational development, the potential for mutual modification, and ex post judicial dispute resolution.[85] The case for smart contract modification can be analogized to human intervention in artificial intelligence technology. Machine learning systems produce outputs based on statistical analysis that cannot easily be traced back to their inputs, opening the door for hidden biases to creep in.[86] To avoid this issue, there is a growing consensus that humans must remain in the loop to ensure the machines avoid bias and unforeseen outputs.[87] Blockchain-based systems need something similar. The hard problem is how to reincorporate humans without forfeiting the benefits of decentralization and automation that blockchain systems promote.

---

[81] See, e.g., Lisa Welchman, *Managing Chaos: Digital Governance by Design* (2015).
[82] See Lessig, supra note 25.
[83] See Szabo, supra note 28.
[84] See id.
[85] See Werbach and Cornell, supra note 23.
[86] See Andrew Selbst and Solon Barocas, The Intuitive Appeal of Explainable Machines, 87 *Fordham L. Rev.* 1085 (2018).
[87] See Rachel Courtland, Bias Detectives: The Researchers Striving to Make Algorithms Fair, *Nature* (June 20, 2018), https://www.nature.com/articles/d41586-018-05469-3; Frank Pasquale, toward a Fourth Law of Robotics: Preserving Attribution, Responsibility, and Explainability in an Algorithmic Society, 78 *Ohio St. L.J.* 1243 (2017).

The Siren Song   233

In the wake of the controversies of 2016–17, prominent new blockchain networks such as Tezos, Decred, and Dfinity touted their "on-chain" governance mechanisms.[88] With these systems, proposals, such as an increase in a block size, can be decided by voting of token holders, with one coin in the relevant cryptocurrency equal to one vote. The will of the majority is automatically implemented on the blockchain network.

On-chain governance is a promising area of experimentation, although it raises a host of questions.[89] For example, are those holding a majority of the cryptocurrency always the ones who should decide the fate of the network? Or what happens when, as in real-world elections, a substantial percentage of voters do not participate or lack full understanding of the issues? How might those with a vested interest manipulate the vote? Even if effective, however, on-chain governance systems are at best only one piece of the solution. Just as every possible scenario cannot be coded into smart contracts, every desirable governance action cannot be coded into a self-executing election. On-chain mechanisms cannot completely solve the problem of blockchain governance because they rely on the same immutability that generates it.

To address the governance gap, blockchain systems need credible commitments that are not absolute. This is a well-established concept. Structures that marry the security of credible commitments with the flexibility of human governance are known as institutions. The economic historian Douglass North, the great theorist of institutionalism, defined institutions as "humanly devised constraints that structure political, economic, and social interaction."[90] Institutions are voluntarily adopted constraints; that is to say, they are commitment devices.[91] As North described, the development of both public and private institutions was the defining factor in the establishment of the complex global economy. Effective institutions fused the trustworthiness of family and community ties with the social scalability needed for modern society.

Most institutions, however, are centralized. A court system or a stock market can facilitate trustworthy transactions between strangers, but those strangers must accept their authority. Is this level of trust attainable within a decentralized network? The communities around blockchain networks can effectively govern, as when the Ethereum Foundation shepherded support for the hard fork that reverted the theft of funds from the DAO. The process was somewhat chaotic, but many different interests in the community had the opportunity to be heard, several alternatives were thoroughly vetted, and in

---

[88] See Werbach, New Architecture, supra note 5, at 217.
[89] See Vitalik Buterin, Notes on Blockchain Governance, Vitalik Buterin's Website (Dec. 17, 2017), https://vitalik.ca/general/2017/12/17/voting.html.
[90] Douglass North, Institutions, 5 J. Econ. Persp. 97, 97 (1991).
[91] See Douglass North, Institutions and Credible Commitment, 149 J. Instit. & Theoretical Econ. 11 (1993).

the end, network nodes voted with their software whether to adopt the proposed hard fork.

However, this leads to a conundrum identified by Oxford economic sociologist Vili Lehdonvirta.[92] The theoretical problem with the blockchain practical success story is that it was a triumph of conventional governance. Respected leaders in the community debated solutions, took input, and converged on a response. As Lehdonvirta points out, this human-centric process contrasted with the vision of a decentralized, machine-centric blockchain. If trusted parties are going to make the rules anyway, who needs a blockchain, he argues. Lehdonvirta effectively rebuts the overheated claims that blockchain represents a "paradigm shift in the very idea of economic organization."[93] As incidents such as the DAO hack, the Parity wallet bug, and the Segwit2x battle illustrate, effective consensus on immutable distributed ledgers does not resolve the hard problems of governance. In some ways, it accentuates them.

Blockchain decentralization enthusiasts strike strikingly similar notes to the cyberlibertarians of the 1990s. As their poet laureate, Electronic Frontier Foundation co-founder John Perry Barlow declared: "We are creating a world where anyone, anywhere may express his or her beliefs, no matter how singular, without fear of being coerced into silence or conformity."[94] In this new world of cyberspace, he continued, governments "have no moral right to rule us nor do [they] possess any methods of enforcement we have true reason to fear."[95] We know how that story turned out. The internet has indeed been a radically empowering force. Yet many are still "coerced into silence or conformity" by governments that have found ways to overcome the internet's decentralization (such as China's Great Firewall) and, surprisingly, by the privately operated platforms such as Facebook and Google that now dominate cyberspace and its communities.

If the blockchain economy is to replicate the successes of the internet while avoiding some of its failings, governance is critical. In fact, the scope of governance must be expanded beyond its traditional domains. Here again, a comparison with internet law and policy proves enlightening.

---

[92] See Vili Lehdonvirta, The Blockchain Paradox: Why Distributed Ledger Technologies May Do Little to Transform the Economy, Oxford Internet Institute (Nov. 21, 2016), https://www.oii.ox.ac.uk/blog/the-blockchain-paradox-why-distributed-ledger-technologies-may-do-little-to-transform-the-economy/.

[93] Id. The quote, which appears in the introduction to the online transcript of Lehdonvirta's talk, is from Seth Bannon, The Tao of "The DAO" or: How the Autonomous Corporation Is Already Here, Techcrunch (May 16, 2016), https://techcrunch.com/2016/05/16/the-tao-of-the-dao-or-how-the-autonomous-corporation-is-already-here/.

[94] John Perry Barlow, A Declaration of the Independence of Cyberspace, Electronic Frontier Foundation (Feb. 8, 1996), https://www.eff.org/cyberspace-independence.

[95] Id.

PERVASIVE GOVERNANCE

The internet gave birth to what Shoshana Zuboff calls surveillance capitalism:[96] A global economy built increasingly on the collection, aggregation, analysis, and utilization of data related to the behaviors and intentions of individuals. "Privacy protection" online became an increasingly quaint response to the totalizing nature of information platforms. In response privacy advocates turned increasingly to an approach of totalized privacy, known as privacy by design.[97]

Privacy by design takes the position that privacy protections cannot simply be added on to technical systems. They must be built in from their inception.[98] In other words, privacy by design means more than just raising the bar for protection of personal information. As former Ontario, Canada, Information and Privacy Commissioner Ann Cavoukian explains: "Privacy must be incorporated into networked data systems and technologies, by default. Privacy must become integral to organizational priorities, project objectives, design processes, and planning operations. Privacy must be embedded into every standard, protocol and process that touches our lives."[99] The implementation of this vision in legislation and business practice has left something to be desired, but the premise is sound.

Something similar, call it governance by design, should be incorporated into the development and oversight of blockchain-based systems.[100] Given the structure of blockchains, governance cannot be an afterthought. Neither can it be limited to

---

[96] See Shoshana Zuboff, Big Other: Surveillance Capitalism and the Prospects of an Information Civilization, 30 J. Info. Tech. 75–89 (2015); Shoshana Zuboff, *The Age of Surveillance Capitalism: The Fight for a Human Future at the New Frontier of Power* (2019).

[97] It is now widely accepted by policymakers in a variety of contexts, most notably the European General Data Protection Regulation that went into force in 2018. See Lee Bygrave, Data Protection by Design and by Default: Deciphering the EU's Legislative Requirements, 4 *Oslo L. Rev.* 105 (2017).

[98] See *Privacy-Enhancing Technologies: The Path to Anonymity, Vol.* 1 (Aug. 1995), http://www.ontla.on .ca/library/repository/mon/10000/184530.pdf; Peter Schaar, Privacy by Design, 3 *Identity in Info. Soc.* 267 (2010).

[99] Ann Cavoukian, Privacy by Design: The 7 Foundational Principles, *IAB.org* (2009), https://www .iab.org/wp-content/IAB-uploads/2011/03/fred_carter.pdf. Cavoukian was the first to develop the concept of privacy by design.

[100] A few other authors employ the same term, but generally in different ways than I do here. Deirdre Mulligan and Kenneth Bamberger use "governance-by-design" to refer to efforts to promote value or implement regulatory mandates through manipulation of technological systems. Deirdre K. Mulligan and Kenneth Bamberger, Saving Governance-by-Design, 106 *Calif. L. Rev.* 697 (2018); Primavera de Filippi uses "governance by the design" for self-governance models in which "rules are embedded directly into the underlying technology of the platforms they use to operate." Rachel O'Dwyer, Commons Governance and Law with Primavera De Filippi, *Commons Transition* (July 31, 2015, 10:55 AM), http:// commonstransition.org/commons-centric-law-and-governance-with-primavera-de-filippi/. Embedding governance structures into code, such as through the on-chain governance technology of systems such as Tezos, is a subset of what I propose here. Governance by *design* means systematically embedding governance into all relevant processes, whether implemented in software, in regularized procedures for human discussion, or in decisional structures.

formalized voting on changes to network algorithms. Voting structures insufficiently address the diversity of governance challenges that can arise, as highlighted by the three examples provided earlier.

In the blockchain context, governance by design means recognizing that perfect immutability creates systems with unacceptable fragility. They work well until they don't, and then they have no good means to recover. Advocates of strong immutability see an inherent tradeoff in which flexibility to human decision-making undermines decentralization.[101] However, if we want solutions that can resolve unexpected problems smoothly, we must trust someone to resolve them.

Incorporating governance by design principles, rather than bolt-on governance functionalities, counters this tradeoff. As Cavoukian argues in the analogous context of privacy by design: "Privacy is often positioned in a zero-sum manner as having to compete with other legitimate interests, design objectives, and technical capabilities, in a given domain. Privacy by Design rejects taking such an approach – it embraces legitimate non-privacy objectives and accommodates them, in an innovative positive-sum manner."[102] Governance by design can have a similar effect by incorporating governance as a baseline function at every level, not a "get out of jail free" override.

In her work on common-pool resource systems, Nobel Prize-winner Elinor Ostrom emphasizes that governance is polycentric and hierarchical.[103] Multiple governments, as well as private mechanisms, may shape the management of a resource or community. Ostrom describes three levels of rule: Operational, collective-choice, and constitutional-choice.[104] Operational governance addresses the day-to-day issues that directly affect a given system. Collective-choice governance determines two things: Who can take certain operational actions and who can change operational rules. Constitutional-choice governance determines who has the authority to change collective-choice rules. A system that works for mundane problems will not necessarily address unusual situations that require extraordinary override. And a system for addressing particular crises will fail to resolve fundamental disagreements about the direction of the community.

A starting point for thinking about governance by design in a blockchain context would be to recognize four hierarchical domains:

1) *Consensus.* Analogous to Ostrom's operational rules, the consensus algorithms of a blockchain network promote honest verification and agreement on status

---

[101] See Jordan Pearson, The Ethereum Hard Fork Spawned a Shaky Rebellion, *Motherboard* (July 27, 2016, 5:55pm), https://www.vice.com/en_us/article/z43qb4/the-ethereum-hard-fork-spawned-a-shaky-rebellion-ethereum-classic-etc-eth.

[102] Cavoukian, supra note 99.

[103] See Elinor Ostrom, *Governing the Commons: The Evolution of Institutions for Collective Action* (1990).

[104] See id. at 52.

of the ledger. In the normal mode of day-to-day operation, the dynamics of the consensus mechanism determine the attributes of the blockchain network. Discussions of blockchain technology as "governance by code" or a new "Lex Cryptographica"[105] generally focus on the consensus layer, which is where transactions are designed to be immutable.

2) *Override.* When immutability produces problematic results, as in the case of the DAO hack, override governance offers a means to reverse immutability by establishing decision-making power at the outset. This is analogous to the first sense of Ostrom's collective-choice rules, in that they define who has decision-making power in such situations. The Ethereum community struggled in responding to the hack because it was not clear who should be part of the decision-making process, and how a consensus of decision-makers should be implemented.[106]

3) *Rule Change.* Bitcoin's Segwit2x fight concerned a general property of the network: The size of blocks. As in Ostrom's constitutional-choice layer, governance here requires a means of determining who sets policy for the network. In the Segwit2x case, groups in the community such as exchanges, miners, users, and core developers had differing views. There was no good mechanism to resolve these views given insufficient structures and norms of governance.

4) *Community Governance.* Ostrom's constitutional-choice layer is about who judges the judges: How the entities empowered to participate in governance and change the rules are constituted. This is often a blind spot in blockchain networks. For example, the launch of Tezos was delayed when the organization developing the software had a conflict with the foundation designed to oversee the network after the project raised over $200 million in a token offering.[107] The irony that a system designed to automate rule-change governance struggled at community governance was not lost.

This high-level framework is just a starting point for blockchain governance by design.[108] There will be many practical decisions to make in any network. While

---

[105] De Fillippi and Wright, supra note 25.

[106] On-chain governance systems are one approach to this challenge. See supra notes 88–9 and associated text. Another is to structure decentralized arbitration mechanisms that leverage the incentive mechanisms of cryptocurrencies themselves. See Werbach, New Architecture, supra note 5, at 215–16 (describing Augur's "computational juries" as an example).

[107] See Paul Vigna, Tezos Raised $232 Million in a Hot Coin Offering, Then a Fight Broke Out, *Wall St. J.* (Oct. 18, 2017, 12:07 AM), https://www.wsj.com/articles/tezos-raised-232-million-in-a-hot-coin-offering-then-a-fight-broke-out-1508354704.

[108] As Mulligan and Bamberger point out, embedding policy prescriptions directly into technological systems can create new problems. Governance by design may fail to address specific cases in a nuanced way, deprecate important human rights values, or reduce transparency of the regulatory process. These considerations should be taken into account in designing blockchain governance mechanisms. They offer a series of recommendations to ameliorate the dangers of governance by design, which are consistent with the layered, polycentric approach proposed here. See Mulligan and Bamberger, supra note 100.

governance and decentralization are not fundamentally in conflict, there is room for different workable tradeoffs dependent on either the goals of the network or the culture of its community. The different ways the Bitcoin and Ethereum communities addressed the Segwit2x hard fork and the DAO hack, respectively, illustrate that both processes and norms play a role in solving for decentralized issues.

The final important factor that Ostrom's polycentric framing emphasizes is that private self-governance and public oversight through sovereign governments are not necessarily in conflict. Her classic study of common-pool resources, *Governing the Commons*, identifies several cases in which the state facilitated private ordering and the creation of community-based institutions.[109] The developers of blockchain networks often begin with a strong resistance to government involvement, just like the pioneers of the internet economy. However, as became clear in the development of the internet, governments can do much more than ban or allow technological innovation.[110] As just one example, the need for strong government-issued network neutrality rules became a rallying cry for advocates of the open internet, as a check on the power of broadband access providers.[111] There are similar calls today for the state to intervene in order to break the stranglehold of large digital platforms such as Google, Amazon, and Facebook.[112] We should not ignore the ways in which government might contribute to the health of the blockchain economy.

CONCLUSION

At this early stage in blockchain development, the adoption path of the technology is quite uncertain. Despite the spike in the price of cryptocurrencies, usage for payments, Bitcoin's original purpose remains limited.[113] Many enterprise blockchain pilots built on specialized cryptocurrency models have failed to see the rapid adoption their boosters predicted.[114] However, blockchain technology itself will continue to see investment and development because it addresses fundamental challenges in organizational recordkeeping and the need for interorganizational trust.[115] Further, there are major applications of the approach such as trading

---

[109]   See Ostrom, supra note 96, at 212.

[110]   See Kevin Werbach, The Song Remains the Same: What Cyberlaw Might Teach the Next Internet Economy, 69 *Fla. L. Rev.* 887 (2017).

[111]   See id. at 915–16.

[112]   See, e.g., Jonathan T. Taplin, *Move Fast and Break Things: How Facebook, Google, and Amazon Cornered Culture and Undermined Democracy* (2017); Lina M. Khan, Amazon's Antitrust Paradox, 126 *Yale L.J.* 710 (2017).

[113]   See Paul Vigna, People Love Talking about Bitcoin More Than Using It, *Wall St. J.* (Apr. 12, 2017, 5:30 AM), https://www.wsj.com/articles/people-love-talking-about-bitcoin-more-than-using-it -1491989403.

[114]   See Olga Kharif, Blockchain, Once Seen as a Corporate Cure-All, Suffers Slowdown, *Bloomberg* (July 31, 2018), https://www.bloomberg.com/news/articles/2018-07-31/blockchain-once-seen-as-a-cor porate-cure-all-suffers-slowdown.

[115]   See Werbach, New Architecture, supra note 5, at 226, 236–7.

The Siren Song of the blockchain, however, does not depend on any

markets in cryptoassets that seem poised for continued growth even if they do not disrupt traditional markets.[116] Nonetheless, it is far from certain that any blockchain network will achieve the scope and influence of Google, Facebook, Amazon, Tencent, and Alibaba, let alone realize the grand visions of societal disruption that boosters promulgate.

The importance of blockchain governance, however, does not depend on any particular story of blockchain adoption. Blockchain has proved to be a governance technology that seeks to balance on the knife edge of freedom and constraints. That challenge is as old as civilization. In working to overcome this challenge, we can learn from the ways that blockchain networks try – or don't try – to resolve the implicit tensions of immutability. Both theory and practice must play a role. There is no shortcut to designing governance mechanisms, watching how they operate in practice, and iterating based on their shortcomings.

Appropriately, that is also the lesson of Odysseus' encounter. Odysseus has himself tied to the mast so that he, alone, can hear the song of the sirens in safety. What do they sing that is so tempting? The sirens offer a shortcut to knowledge: "For lo, we know all things, all the travail that in wide Troy-land the Argives and Trojans bare by the gods' designs, yea, and we know all that shall hereafter be upon the fruitful earth."[117] The seductive appeal of the sirens is the promise of wisdom without experience, just as the seductive appeal of the blockchain is trust through cryptography and economic incentives without human governance. Believing too strongly in either leads to disaster. Finding the proper balance is the road to valuable insight.

---

[116]   See Kevin Werbach, Blockchain Isn't a Revolution, *Medium* (June 18, 2018),https://medium.com/ s/story/blockchain-isnt-a-revolution-it-s-two-big-innovations-and-one-promising-idea-988fca6bofca; Shawn Tully, The NYSE's Owner Wants to Bring Bitcoin to Your 401(k). Are Crypto Credit Cards Next?, *Fortune* (Aug. 14, 2018), http://fortune.com/longform/nyse-owner-bitcoin-exchange-startup/.

[117]   The Odyssey, supra note 2 (Book XII).

For EU product safety concerns, contact us at Calle de José Abascal, 56–1°, 28003 Madrid, Spain or eugpsr@cambridge.org.

www.ingramcontent.com/pod-product-compliance
Ingram Content Group UK Ltd.
Pitfield, Milton Keynes, MK11 3LW, UK
UKHW020208060825
461487UK00018B/1621